The Merovingian Kingdoms and the Mediterranean World

Studies in Early Medieval History

Series editor: Ian Wood

Concise books on current areas of debate in late antiquity/early medieval studies, covering history, archaeology, cultural and social studies, and the interfaces between them.

Dark Age Liguria: Regional Identity and Local Power, c 400–1020, Ross Balzaretti
Inventing Byzantine Iconoclasm, Leslie Brubaker
The Irish Scholarly Presence at St. Gall: Networks of Knowledge in the Early Middle Ages, Sven Meeder
Pagan Goddesses in the Early Germanic World: Eostra, Hreda and the Cult of Matrons, Philip A. Shaw
Reading the Bible in the Middle Ages, edited by Jinty Nelson and Damien Kempf
Vikings in the South, Ann Christys
Saxon Identities, AD 150-900, Robert Flierman

The Merovingian Kingdoms and the Mediterranean World

Revisiting the Sources

Edited by
Stefan Esders, Yitzhak Hen, Pia Lucas
and Tamar Rotman

BLOOMSBURY ACADEMIC
LONDON • NEW YORK • OXFORD • NEW DELHI • SYDNEY

BLOOMSBURY ACADEMIC
Bloomsbury Publishing Plc
50 Bedford Square, London, WC1B 3DP, UK
1385 Broadway, New York, NY 10018, USA
29 Earlsfort Terrace, DUblin 2, Ireland

BLOOMSBURY, BLOOMSBURY ACADEMIC and the Diana logo are trademarks of
Bloomsbury Publishing Plc

First published in Great Britain 2019
This paperback edition published 2022

Copyright © Stefan Esders, Yitzhak Hen, Pia Lucas and Tamar Rotman, 2019

Stefan Esders, Yitzhak Hen, Pia Lucas and Tamar Rotman have asserted their right under
the Copyright, Designs and Patents Act, 1988, to be identified as Editors of this work.

For legal purposes the Acknowledgments on p. vii constitute an extension of this
copyright page.

Cover design: Terry Woodley
Cover image © Ivory belt buckle of Caesarius of Arles, depicting the Holy Sepulchre in
Jerusalem. Photo courtesy of Xavier de Jauréguiberry.

All rights reserved. No part of this publication may be reproduced or transmitted
in any form or by any means, electronic or mechanical, including photocopying,
recording, or any information storage or retrieval system, without prior permission
in writing from the publishers.

Bloomsbury Publishing Plc does not have any control over, or responsibility for, any
third-party websites referred to or in this book. All internet addresses given in this
book were correct at the time of going to press. The author and publisher regret
any inconvenience caused if addresses have changed or sites have ceased
to exist, but can accept no responsibility for any such changes.

A catalogue record for this book is available from the British Library.

Library of Congress Cataloging-in-Publication Data
Names: Esders, Stefan, editor. | Hen, Yitzhak, editor. | Lucas, Pia, editor. |
Rotman, Tamar, editor.
Title: The Merovingian kingdoms and the Mediterranean world : revisiting the sources /
edited by Stefan Esders, Yitzhak Hen, Pia Lucas and Tamar Rotman.
Description: London, UK ; New York, NY : Bloomsbury Academic, 2019.
Series: Studies in early medieval history | Includes bibliographical references and index.
Identifiers: LCCN 2018048913 (print) | LCCN 2018055683 (ebook) |
ISBN 9781350048409 (epub) | ISBN 9781350048393 (epdf) |
ISBN 9781350048386(hb)
Subjects: LCSH: Merovingians—France—History. | France—Relations—Mediterranean
Region. | Mediterranean | Region—Relations—France.
Classification: LCC DC65 (ebook) | LCC DC65 .M47 2019 (print) | DDC 944/.013—dc23
LC record available at https://lccn.loc.gov/2018048913

ISBN:	HB:	978-1-3500-4838-6
	PB:	978-1-5266-2968-5
	ePDF:	978-1-3500-4839-3
	eBook:	978-1-3500-4840-9

Series: Studies in Early Medieval History

Typeset by RefineCatch Limited, Bungay, Suffolk

To find out more about our authors and books visit www.bloomsbury.com
and sign up for our newsletters.

Contents

Acknowledgments — vii
List of Contributors — ix
List of Abbreviations — x
Maps — xii

Introduction *Pia Lucas and Tamar Rotman* — 1

Part One The Wider World: Setting the Context of the Post-Roman World

1 History, Geography, and the Notion of *Mare Nostrum* in the Early Medieval West *Yitzhak Hen* — 11

2 True Differences: Gregory of Tours' Account of the Council of Mâcon (585) *Helmut Reimitz* — 19

Part Two Mediterranean Ties and Merovingian Diplomacy

3 East and West from a Visigothic Perspective: How and Why Were Frankish Brides Negotiated in the Late Sixth Century? *Anna Gehler-Rachůnek* — 31

4 Friendship and Diplomacy in the *Histories* of Gregory of Tours *Hope Williard* — 41

5 Private Records of Official Diplomacy: The Franco-Byzantine Letters in the Austrasian Epistolar Collection *Bruno Dumézil* — 55

6 The Language of Sixth-century Frankish Diplomacy *Yaniv Fox* — 63

Part Three Bridging the Seas: Law and Religion

7 Mediterranean Homesick Blues: Human Trafficking in the Merovingian *Leges* *Lukas Bothe* — 79

8   The Fifth Council of Orléans and the Reception of the "Three
    Chapters Controversy" in Merovingian Gaul   *Till Stüber*   93

9   Reconciling Disturbed Sacred Space: The Ordo for "Reconciling
    an Altar Where a Murder Has Been Committed" in the *Sacramentary
    of Gellone* in Its Cultural Context   *Rob Meens*   103

10 Imitation and Rejection of Eastern Practices in Merovingian Gaul:
    Gregory of Tours and Vulfilaic the Stylite of Trier   *Tamar Rotman*   113

Part Four   Shifting Perspectives: Emperors, Tributes and Propaganda

11 *Magnus et Verus Christianus*: The Portrayal of Emperor Tiberius II
    in Gregory of Tours   *Pia Lucas*   127

12 When Contemporary History Is Caught Up by the
    Immediate Present: Fredegar's Proleptic Depiction of
    Emperor Constans II   *Stefan Esders*   141

13 Byzantium, the Merovingians, and the Hog: A Passage of
    Theophanes' *Chronicle* Revisited   *Federico Montinaro*   151

Conclusion   *Stefan Esders and Yitzhak Hen*   159

Notes   163
Bibliography 223
Index   253

Acknowledgments

The present volume is the product of a joint German-Israeli project—*East and West in the Early Middle Ages: The Merovingian Kingdoms in Mediterranean Perspective*—that was funded by the German-Israeli Foundation for Scientific Research and Development (GIF). The core of this project was a series of four small workshops that took place at the Freie Universität Berlin and Ben-Gurion University of the Negev. These workshops were attended by PhD and Master students from Israel and Germany, and in each of these meetings, participants presented their own research and discussed some of the major issues concerning the Merovingian period with outstanding scholars in the field. In fact, the entire project was designed as a series of workshops for the benefit of research students. Writing a thesis in history is a very solitary experience and can be very frustrating. By shaping these workshops as a platform for students to meet, present their research, get criticism in a friendly environment, and exchange ideas, we attempted to create a collaborative community that would remain in touch long after the project was finished. The experience of these workshops also shaped the structure of this volume. The close reading of the sources that guided our meetings welcomed students and scholars alike to join the discussion, hence each of the chapters in this volume opens with a relevant text on which the discussion is based. Following our project's objective to bring together established scholars and junior researchers, this publication combines contributions by "veterans" alongside more fresh authors.

This volume could not have been published without the help and advice of many friends and colleagues. We would first wish to express our deepest gratitude to the German-Israeli Foundation for their generous support, as well as to our host institutions—Freie Universität Berlin and Ben-Gurion University of the Negev—for providing the friendliest and welcoming atmosphere. We should also like to thank our contributors, and all scholars and students who joined our meetings in Berlin, Be'er Sheva, and Leeds, for their valuable input—Heiko Behrmann, Omer Glickman, Kai Grundmann, André Fischer, Gerda Heydemann, Alexander O'Hara, Mayke de Jong, Conrad Leyser, Yonatan Livneh, Jamie Kreiner, Rob Meens, Stephan Ridder, Laury Sarti, Lia Sternizki, Dimitri Tarat, and Phillip Wynn.

Finally, warm thanks should also go to Ian Wood, the editor of Bloomsbury's series *Studies in Early Medieval History* for his support and encouragement throughout. Likewise, we would like to express our gratitude to our reviewers for their insightful suggestions, to Ellora Bennett for her helpful language advice, to Philipp Franck for drafting the maps, and our editors at Bloomsbury providing us with copyediting, for their patience and for making this volume possible.

Contributors

Lukas Bothe	PhD candidate and research associate, Friedrich-Meinecke-Institut, Freie Universität Berlin
Bruno Dumézil	Professor of Medieval History, Sorbonne Université
Stefan Esders	Professor of Late Antique and Early Medieval History, Friedrich-Meinecke-Institut, Freie Universität Berlin
Yaniv Fox	Senior Lecturer of Late Antique and Medieval History, Department of General History, Bar-Ilan University
Anna Gehler-Rachůnek	PhD candidate at the Berlin Graduate School of Ancient Studies (BerGSAS), Freie Universität Berlin
Yitzhak Hen	Professor of Late Antique and Early Medieval History, Department of History, The Hebrew University of Jerusalem and Director of the Israel Institute for Advanced Studies
Pia Lucas	PhD candidate and research associate, Friedrich-Meinecke-Institut, Freie Universität Berlin
Rob Meens	Senior Lecturer, Department of History and Art History, Utrecht University
Federico Montinaro	Postdoctoral research associate, Eberhard Karls Universität Tübingen
Helmut Reimitz	Professor of History, Department of History, Princeton University
Tamar Rotman	Postdoctoral fellow, Department of General History, Bar Ilan University
Till Stüber	Postdoctoral research associate, Friedrich-Meinecke-Institut, Freie Universität Berlin
Hope Williard	Academic Subject Librarian, University of Lincoln

Abbreviations

AASS	Acta Sanctorum
BHG	Bibliotheca Hagiographica Graeca (Brussels, 1907)
BHL	Bibliotheca Hagiographica Latina
CCSL	Corpus Christianorum, series Latina
CSCO	Corpus Scriptorum Christianorum Orientalium
CSEL	Corpus Scriptorum Ecclesiasticorum Latinorum
EA	*Il Liber epistolarum della cancelleria Austrasica (sec. V-VI)*, edited by E. Malaspina (Rome, 2001)
Fredegar *Chron.*	*Chronicarum quae dicuntur Fredegarii scholastici libri IV cum continuationibus*, edited by Bruno Krusch, MGH SS rer. Merov. II (Hannover: Hahn, 1888), 1–193
Joh. Eph. *Eccl.*	*Iohannis Ephesini Historiae ecclesiasticae pars tertia*, edited by E. W. Brooks, CSCO 106 (1936)
Evagrius *HE*	*The Ecclesiastical works of Evagrius*, edited by J. Bidez and L. Parmentier, London: Methuen & Co., 1898
GC	Gregorius Turonensis, *Liber in Gloria Confessorum*, edited by Bruno Krusch, MGH SS rer. Merov. 1.2 (Hannover, 1885), 284–370
GM	Gregorius Turonensis, *Liber in Gloria Martyrum*, edited by Bruno Krusch, MGH SS rer. Merov. 1.2 (Hannover, 1885), 34–111
Hist.	Gregorius Turonensis, *Decem Libri Historiarum*, edited by Bruno Krusch and Wilhelm Levison, MGH SS rer. Merov. 1.1 (Hannover, 1937)
MGH	Monumenta Germaniae Historica
Capit.	Capitularia regum Francorum
Conc.	Concilia
DD	Diplomata
Epp.	Epistolae
LL	Leges
LL nat. Germ.	Leges nationum Germanicarum

	Poetae	Poetae Latini medii aevi
	SS	Scriptores

Subsections of SS:

	Auct. ant.	Auctores antiquissimi
	rer. Merov.	Scriptores rerum Merovingicarum
	rer. Lang.	Scriptores rerum Langobardicarum et Italicarum saec. VI–IX

PG	Patrologia Graeca
PL	Patrologia Latina
Procopius *Bell. Goth.*	Procopius, *De bello Gothorum*, in *Procopii Caesariensis opera omnia. Vol. 2: De bellis libri V–VIII*, edited by Jakob Haury (Leipzig: Teubner, 1963)
PO	Patrologia Orientalis
RE	Realencyklopädie der classischen Altertumswissenschaft
SC	Sources Chrétiennes
VP	Gregorius Turonensis, *Liber Vitae Patrum*, edited by Bruno Krusch, MGH SS rer. Merov. 1.2 (Hannover, 1885), 211–83
VSJ	Gregorius Turonensis, *Liber de Passione et Virtutibus Sancti Iluiani martyris*, edited by Bruno Krusch, MGH SS rer. Merov. 1.2, (Hannover, 1885), 112–33
VSM	Gregorius Turonensis, *Libri I-IV de Virtutibus Sancti Martini Episcopi*, edited by Bruno Krusch, MGH SS rer. Merov. 1.2 (Hannover, 1885), 134–211

Maps

Map 1   The Mediterranean World
        Map tiles by Ancient World Mapping Center. "À-la-carte."
        http://awmc.unc.edu/awmc/applications/alacarte/
        (Accessed: April 4, 2018)   xiii

Map 2   Merovingian Gaul
        Map tiles by Ancient World Mapping Center. "À-la-carte"
        http://awmc.unc.edu/awmc/applications/alacarte/
        (Accessed: April 4, 2018)   xiv

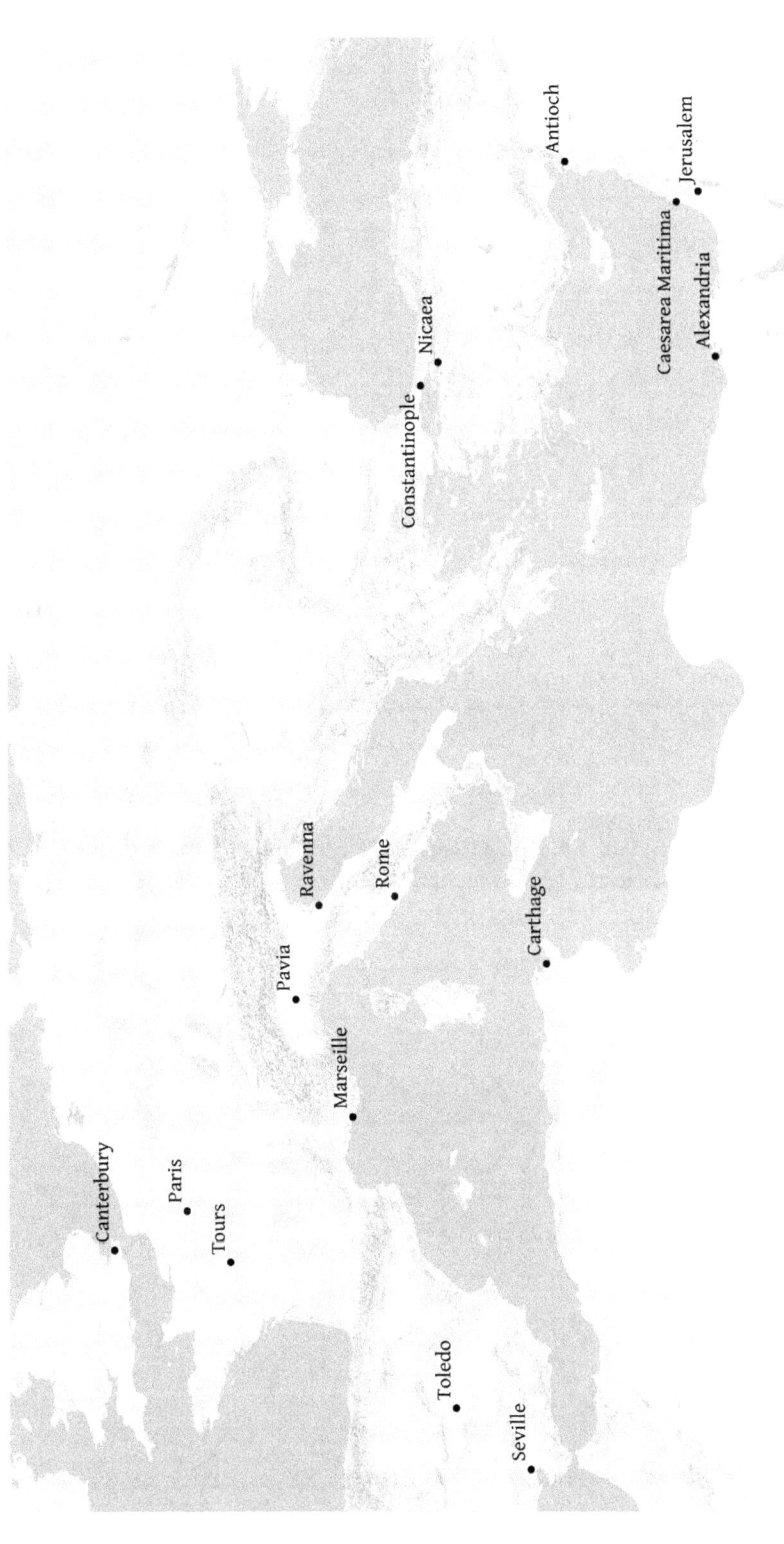

Map 1. The Mediterranean World
Map tiles by Ancient World Mapping Center. "À-la-carte." http://awmc.unc.edu/awmc/applications/alacarte/ (Accessed: April 4, 2018).

Tiles © AWMC, CC-BY-4.0

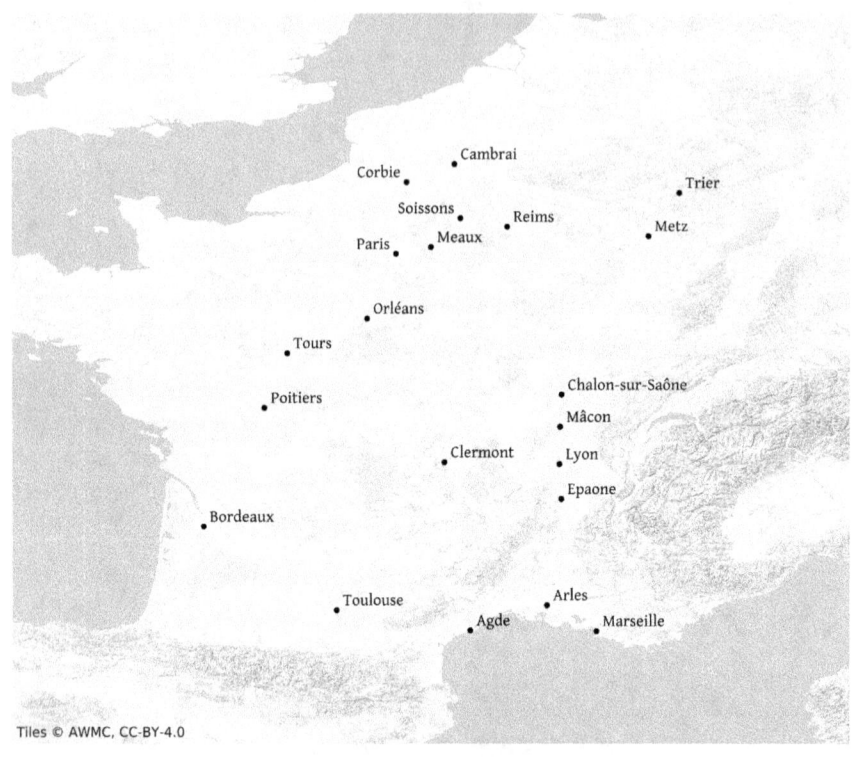

Map 2. Merovingian Gaul
Map tiles by Ancient World Mapping Center. "À-la-carte." http://awmc.unc.edu/awmc/applications/alacarte/ (Accessed: April 4, 2018).

Introduction

Pia Lucas and Tamar Rotman

Gregory of Tours, *Histories* VI.6

> At this time, close to Nice there lived a recluse called Hospicius, a man of great abstinence, who had iron chains wound round his body, next to the skin, and wore a hair-shirt on top. He ate nothing but dry bread and a few dates. During Lent, he fed on the roots of Egyptian herbs like the hermits use, which merchants brought home for him. First, he would drink the water in which they were cooked, and then he would eat the herbs themselves. [...] Once, the Holy Ghost revealed to him the coming of the Lombards into Gaul.

This inconspicuous hagiographic passage from Gregory of Tours' *Histories* contains plenty of information on how we should envisage the horizon of the Merovingian world. At first glance, this episode seems like a standard piece on ascetic life, reiterating established conventions; but a closer look reveals that these ascetic practices, as described by Gregory of Tours, were not inspired by Gallic traditions alone. The saint in question was very well connected, both spiritually and practically. Not only did God reveal to him the future incursion of the Lombards, he also knew merchants who traveled back and forth throughout the Mediterranean world. The recluse from Gaul ate the very same herbs the hermits of Egypt did, which some merchants imported for him. We can only guess which ports these merchants visited, and it is possible that they were the ones who informed the saint about the roving Lombards. Alternatively, he could have heard about it from pilgrims going to or coming back from Rome. It seems that such pilgrims were a common sight in the early medieval West, and Hospicius himself had spoken to a deacon and a pilgrim setting out to the city of the Apostles.[1] Hospicius, despite being a recluse, was very much rooted in a society oriented around the Mediterranean. This brief episode, one of many in Gregory's works, does not only illustrate long-distance mobility, economic and cultural exchange, but also gives us an idea of the geographical scope that determined people's imagination in the Merovingian period. In revisiting even well-known sources, like the *Histories* of Gregory of Tours, we are able to assess the extent to which cross-regional ties were perceived by contemporaries.

The world of the Merovingian kingdoms, which were the most long-lasting polity of the post-Roman "successor states," has received a renewed historical interest in recent years. The Merovingian era is increasingly recognized as a unique period in its own right, rather than a stage between empires (the Roman on the one hand, and the Carolingian on the other). This increased attention is reflected in numerous recent publications on a plethora of related topics, such as the Merovingian female elite, bishops and hagiography, monasticism, or historiography.[2] Noteworthy in this burgeoning literature on the Merovingian kingdoms are the indispensable *Companion to Gregory of Tours*,[3] and the upcoming *Oxford Handbook of the Merovingian World*,[4] which offer up-to-date research on various aspects of Merovingian history.

Their genesis as barbarian "successor states," established in the wake of the Western Roman Empire, and their debt to Roman traditions and practices notwithstanding, the Merovingian kingdoms maintained manifold and multilayered ties across the Mediterranean. Despite these links, the politics and culture of the Merovingian kingdoms in Gaul were interpreted by scholars in terms of local phenomena. This has been largely due to the lingering effects of nationalist historiographic traditions and a predominantly Western point of view, which generated a misleading notion of the Early Middle Ages as period detached from "Roman" (antique) or "Byzantine" history. This notion has been challenged in recent decades, and scholars such as Peter Brown, Michael McCormick, Chris Wickham, Ian Wood and Andreas Fischer, to name only a few, have contributed immensely to the study of late antique and early medieval history in a more comprehensive perspective.[5] A similar point of view has been adopted by the "Byzantinist" Averil Cameron, who has also argued against this historiographic separation.[6] By looking at issues of economic or cultural exchange across the Mediterranean, these scholars have submitted the relationships between the different political entities across the region to a new evaluation. The current volume continues this trend in scholarship[7] by looking at the Merovingian kingdoms from a wider cross-Mediterranean perspective.

The Mediterranean world did not cease to exist when the Western Roman Empire gave way to barbarian kingdoms. The Merovingians were aware of the politics and culture of Byzantium, they even had a fair amount of knowledge of the Muslim East from the seventh century onwards, and more so of their Spanish and Italian neighbors, the Visigoths and the Lombards. Merovingian Gaul did not operate in a vacuum. It was deeply rooted in Mediterranean politics, society and culture: understanding the inner workings of the Merovingian kingdoms means that we cannot sever them from these links. With this objective in mind, the chapters in this volume examine subjects ranging from the construction of identities, through the formation of international diplomacy, up to social, legal and religious issues that reflect cultural transfer. Further chapters deal with perspectives on the "other," and can add significant insights to contextualizing political entities in their Mediterranean world.

Consequently, this volume covers a wide range of sources, including historiography, hagiography, law codes, church council acts, liturgical texts, geographic treatises and letters. By revisiting these sources, the authors of the various papers examine texts that have either been neglected entirely thus far or have only been analyzed from a more restricted perspective. The scarce evidence that has come down to us from the early medieval period often makes it necessary to work with fragmentary or one-sided information. Developing a method out of this necessity, each of the papers in this volume aims at showing how a close reading of a short section from a larger written source can be used as point of departure to the study of wide-ranging issues from a broader perspective. Hence, excerpts from the selected sources will precede each chapter as a springboard for the subsequent deliberations and arguments. The authors have provided new translations of these texts, some of which have never been translated into English before.

The articles are grouped into four thematic sections. The first section approaches the subject from a wider angle, asking how people of the Early Middle Ages positioned themselves in a post-Roman, but still Mediterranean, context. The first chapter shows how post-Roman identity continued to rely on Roman geographic and historiographic traditions for integrating current events into a coherent worldview. It examines the renewed interest in the fifth and sixth century in the *Expositio totius mundi et gentium*, a fourth-century geographical treatise which has been largely overlooked in modern scholarship (Hen). The manner in which this text was translated, adapted and used illustrates the processes of identity formation after the Western Roman Empire had ceased to exist.

In the context of the formation of identities after Rome, actors within the Merovingian kingdoms opted for different routes, with some choosing to draw authority from Roman models, while others deliberately tried to find other ways. One example at hand is the account of the Council of Mâcon (585) as represented in Gregory of Tours' *Histories* (Reimitz). A comparison between this account and the actual text of the canons shows that Gregory's emphasis on the issues dealt with at Mâcon differed greatly from the bishops' agenda. The bishops assembled at Mâcon resorted to precedents from Roman legislation and canon law in order to establish their authority. Gregory of Tours, on the other hand, adapted the presentation of the council to fit into the construction of his historiographical narrative—instead of underlining Roman traditions, he sought to base the relationships between kings and bishops on a *lex Dei*.

The chapters in the second section of the book delve into the political contacts of the Merovingian kingdoms, with special attention to their diplomatic ties across the Mediterranean. Chapter 3 offers a closer look into alliances and dependencies between the Franks, the Visigoths and the Byzantines in the turbulent later sixth century. These decades were characterized by an usurpation and civil war in the Merovingian kingdoms, a princely rebellion in Visigothic Spain, and Byzantine efforts to build up resistance against the Lombards in Italy, in face of their inability to withdraw troops from their Eastern flanks and deploy them in the West. Understanding how strongly these polities were interconnected, not least by marriage ties, leads to a deeper understanding of these events that should no longer be regarded as mere simultaneous incidents (Gehler-Rachůnek). Chapter 4 focuses on an important concept that was crucial to diplomatic exchange and contacts, that is, *amicitia*. The use of *amicitia* is traced through the *Histories* of Gregory of Tours, where it occurs as a political tool fraught with ambiguity in the context of personal as well as diplomatic relations (Williard). Exploring the meanings associated with the concept of *amicitia* sheds new light on the social relations within the Merovingian kingdoms, and it helps us to better understand diplomatic conventions and politics.

Chapter 5 introduces the Austrasian letter collection, an indispensable source for the study of the diplomatic ties in the Merovingian period (Dumézil). The *Epistolae Austrasicae* are currently the subject of a growing body of research, and this paper provides an important contribution to this discourse. It offers an intriguing new perspective on the genesis of this collection, which contains letters from the fifth to the late sixth century, and which survives in a single manuscript from the ninth century. Although it has been suggested that the collection was compiled in Carolingian times, the article advances a Merovingian date for this collection of letters, and points at a powerful later sixth-century figure as its compiler. The next chapter goes deeper into the contents of the *Epistolae Austrasicae* by focusing on two particular diplomatic issues addressed in several of the letters, the recent invasion of the Lombards into Byzantine Italy, because of which the Byzantines tried to obtain Frankish support, and the fate of the young prince Athanagild, nephew of the Frankish king Childebert II, who ended up in Byzantine hands in the course of the rebellion in Visigothic Spain. From a careful scrutiny of the language used by both sides in their letters, it appears that both the Franks and the Byzantines skillfully employed a similar religious rhetoric to convey their opposing views (Fox).

The third section of this volume looks into the effects of cross-Mediterranean connections on different aspects of the social and religious life. Instead of using traditional historiographical accounts, this section attempts to reconstruct the social, cultural and religious history of the Merovingians as part of the Mediterranean orbit by using sources such as legal documents, papal correspondence, hagiographical anecdotes and liturgical tracts.

The legal provisions against kidnapping, human trafficking, and slave trade in law codes, such as the *Lex Salica* and the *Lex Ribuaria*, are the focus of the first chapter in this section (Bothe). These provisions, when read against a broader Mediterranean context of networks of commerce, reveal that the Franks were aware of the moral and social complexities of slave trade in the seventh and the eighth century, and therefore attempted to regulate it through legal procedures. Tracing the origins of the terminology of the laws and their social, economic and legal implications, which go back to Roman legislation and conventions, gives us a better understanding of the social and legal practices used by the Franks. It also serves as an indicator of the continuity of legal and social conventions in times of dramatic change, such as the one caused by the disintegration of the Roman Empire in Late Antiquity.

A different way to study the effects of exchange on the social and political life in Merovingian Gaul is through an examination of religious controversies and the response to them. A letter sent by Pope Vigilius, who was detained in Constantinople at the time, to Aurelianus, the bishop of Arles, illustrates the effect that quarrels about orthodox belief had on the political dynamics throughout the Mediterranean (Stüber). Pope Vigilius' epistle and the Three Chapters controversy serve as a gateway to a discussion about the diplomatic and religious relationship between the Merovingians and their counterparts in Italy and Constantinople.

The last two chapters of this section demonstrate different ways to understand social and cultural developments by exploring religious practices and traditions in liturgical and hagiographical texts. Chapter 9 looks into a late Merovingian *ordo* in the *Sacramentary of Gellone* that included a prayer for restoring the purity of an altar where a murder has been committed (Meens). This paper allows us to follow the manner in which Frankish devotional practices and concepts of purity and impurity developed in Gaul during Late Antiquity and the Early Middle Ages. Tracing the origins of these practices reveals that they were rooted in Roman regulations of asylum and asylum seekers. Thus, the paper points at a continuation from Roman to Merovingian times and situates late-Merovingian religious practices within the broader context of Mediterranean religious developments. Chapter 10 examines a hagiographical record from the *Histories*, in which Gregory of Tours relates the story of Vulfilaic's failed attempt to imitate the Syrian holy man, Simeon Stylites (Rotman). The story of Vulfilaic and his role in the *Histories* is best understood when examined against the background of the rising types of authoritative systems and norms that marked the aftermath of the disintegration of the Roman world. Whereas in the East holy men, such as Simeon Stylites, gained authoritative power similar to those of the traditional Roman patrons, in the West, the clergy, and most significantly the bishops, held this power tightly and refused to let it go. A comparison between these developments explains the resistance of the Merovingian clergy to Vulfilaic's attempt to become Gaul's first stylite. Moreover, this episode exhibits the depth of Merovingian familiarity with Byzantium and the dynamics between the two major post-Roman entities.

The volume closes with a section that examines the perception of the Merovingians and the Byzantines of their respective "other." The first two papers delve into the Merovingian perspective on Byzantium and show the different literary devices authors used in their accounts of Byzantine emperors. Gregory of Tours, for instance, barely mentions Roman or Byzantine emperors, with the exception of Tiberius II and Justin II. The first chapter in this section examines these occurrences and, by comparing them with Gregory's depictions of Merovingian kings, explains their role in his narrative (Lucas). These episodes are not merely reports on global historical events and leaders, they serve as a comment on the Merovingian rulers of his time, and on qualities of Christian rulership. Moreover, these passages offer an opportunity to trace Gregory's eastern sources and reach a better understanding of his knowledge of Byzantine matters. The *Chronicle of Fredegar*, written about 70 years later, also mentions several Byzantine emperors. A close reading of Fredegar's description of the Arab expansion in the East and the different ways in which he relates the role played by the Byzantine emperors Heraclius and Constans II, reveals the depth of Fredegar's acquaintance with events outside the Frankish kingdoms (Esders). But, no less important, these episodes helped Fredegar to situate Frankish history within a broader Mediterranean context by equating similar events that took place in the East and in the Frankish kingdoms.

The Byzantines were also interested in Frankish history, as exemplified by two excerpts from the ninth-century chronicle of the Byzantine author Theophanes the Confessor (Montinaro). The passages, which describe the end of Merovingian rule and Charlemagne's coronation, contain some dubious chronology. By focusing on these inaccuracies, whether accidental or not, and by trying to ascertain their origin and meaning, it appears that Theophanes was well aware of historical developments in the West and that he altered his chronicle in accordance to them. Furthermore, tracing the sources Theophanes used when writing on the Merovingians reveals that his descriptions were also influenced by Frankish depictions of the same events.

It seems, then, that the process of exchange between the Franks and their Mediterranean counterparts, which is, at the core of all chapters in this volume, was not one-sided. It was mutual in many respects, and it involved the exchange of traditions, practices, oral and written records, social norms and cultural and religious practices. The post-Roman Mediterranean world was inhabited by various peoples who shared a common past, culture, religion and legal traditions. They continued to communicate with each other; they exchanged letters, stories, relics, commodities and envoys; and the result of this exchange is attested in a variety of written sources and material evidence. The papers in this volume focus on the written evidence. We are all aware of the fact that the material evidence has a lot to offer, and can enrich our discussion. But unfortunately, spatial limits and the original nature of this project prevented us from incorporating this illuminating aspect into our discussions. Analyzing the written sources through a wider Mediterranean prism, as done by the authors of this volume, clearly reveals the strong ties and interactions that connected the various political entities of the Mediterranean world. Examining these ties and considering their effect on the lives of all of these peoples unveils the complexity of this exchange. It also emphasizes our need, as historians, to explore these cross-Mediterranean connections in order to reach a better understanding of the past.

Part One

The Wider World: Setting the Context of the Post-Roman World

1

History, Geography, and the Notion of *Mare Nostrum* in the Early Medieval West

Yitzhak Hen

A survey of the entire world and its peoples

55. Beyond the [province of Campania] lies Italy, which is renowned by this word alone [i.e. Italy], and reveals its glory by its name. It has many different towns and, full of all good things, it is governed by providence. You can find in that Italy many types of wine: [from the regions] of Picenum, Sabinum, Tibur and Tuscany, which borders the above-mentioned province [i.e. Italy], and whose beauty we shall recount shortly. Italy, abounding in everything, also possesses this ultimate good – the largest, most eminent and royal city, which reveals her virtue by its name, and which is called Rome; it was founded, we are told, by the child Romulus. It is much decorated with divine buildings, since each of the emperors, past and present, wanted to build something there, and every single one of them established something under his name. If you just think of the Antonine [dynasty], you can find innumerable monuments [sponsored by them], such as the so-called forum of Trajan, which has an outstanding and famous basilica. It also has a well-situated circus, decorated with numerous bronze statues. Also, in that same Rome, there are seven virgins of free and noble birth, who, consecrated to the gods for the benefit of the city, perform [their religious duties] according to the ancient customs; they are called the Vestal virgins. Similarly, it [i.e. Rome] also has a river, known to many as the Tiber, which is useful for the above-mentioned city, because it crosses it before reaching the sea, so that anyone who comes from abroad has to climb eighteen miles. And so, the city abounds in all goods. It also has the greatest senate of rich men; and if you want to check each of them, you will find that they were all governors, or will be [governors] or have the potential [to become governors], but they do not want to, because they rather enjoy their wealth with no obligations. They worship the gods, among them Jupiter and Sol; it is also said that they perform the sacred [ceremonies] of the Mother of gods, and it is certain that they also have *haruspices* [i.e. priests who interpret omens by inspecting the entrails of sacrificial animals]. [...]

58. After Pannonia lies the province of Gaul. Since it is large and always in need of an emperor, it has one for itself. Because of the ruler's presence, it abounds with everything in huge quantities, but at a very high price. It has, we are told, a large town which is called Trier, where the master [i.e. the emperor] resides, and [that town] is located in the middle of the country. Similarly, it has another town, which helps [Trier] in every respect; it is located on the sea-shore, and its name, so they say, is Arles. Receiving merchandise from all over the world, it dispatches them to the above-mentioned town [i.e. Trier]. The entire region is inhabited by strong and noble men; and this is why the army of the Gauls is large and strong. Everything in this province is admirable. It has the barbarian people of the Goths as neighbours.[1]

Inserting a short geographical description into an otherwise pure historical treatise was a common historiographical exercise in the Roman world. It would suffice to mention here the detailed description of Numidia given by Sallust in his *De bello Iugurthino*,[2] the grand opening of *De bello Gallico* by Julius Caesar,[3] Appian's description of the Roman Empire in his *Ρωμαϊκά*,[4] or even Tacitus' opening sentences of his *Germania*,[5] to demonstrate that such a historiographical practice was quite widespread among Roman historians of the later Republic and early Principate. It has been assumed that such a practice was nothing but a mere historiographical device, used by Roman historians to mark the geographical boundaries of their work, to demonstrate their rhetorical and literary skills, and probably to establish their place among a long list of well-known and well-read historians.[6] Tacitus' opening of the *Germania*, for example, clearly echoes Caesar's description of Gaul and Sallust's description of Numidia, and thus makes him their par.

From the second century onwards, and because of unknown reasons, the historiographical tradition that incorporated geographical passages into historiographical narratives slowly died out. It is impossible to gauge whether that was a calculated move made by historians, or simply an impression created by the paucity of the sources that survive. Whatever may have been the case, it appears that the vast majority of historical compositions that came down to us from the fourth century, such as Aurelius Victor's *Liber de caesaribus*, Eutropius' *Breviarium ab urbe condita*, and many others, did not incorporate any geographical description into their historical narrative.[7] The same holds true for the Christian historiographical tradition, as reflected in Eusebius' *Ecclesiastical History*, Jerome's *Chronicle*, or Rufinus' translation and adaptation of Eusebius' work.⁸ It was only in the fifth century, as part of a new wave of creativity that swept the western provinces of the Roman Empire, that geographical descriptions found their way back into the writing of history. Such a geographical digression can be found in the opening chapters of Orosius' *Historiarum libri adversus paganos*, that gives a full description of the entire world from an utterly Christian point of view,⁹ in Jordanes' *De origine actibusque Getarum*,¹⁰ or in Isidore of Seville's *Historia Gothorum, Vandalorum et Sueborum*.¹¹ There is little place to doubt that this geographical revival was partly nourished by the intensive events that changed completely the geo-political balance of the West during the later fourth and throughout the fifth century, events which traditionally and rather anachronistically are called "the Barbarian Invasions."¹²

In his excellent book, *History and Geography in Late Antiquity*, Andy Merrills studied four late-antique and early medieval historians—Orosius, Jordanes, Isidore, and Bede—in whose historical writings one can find substantial geographical descriptions as part of the grand narrative.¹³ Like many historians before him, Merrills noted that during the fifth century there had been a resurgence of interest in geography that resulted in a growing number of geographical digressions incorporated into historical compositions. But, according to Merrills, unlike the historiographical tradition known to us from the late Republic and the early Principate, the geographical digressions were incorporated into fifth-century narratives because of their authors' new understanding of the past. "It is assumed," writes Merrills, "that when a society experiences a dramatic shift in the understanding of its own past, as reflected in its modes of historical expression, its attitudes to the physical world will undergo comparable change."¹⁴ In other words, in the changing world of Late Antiquity and the Early Middle Ages, in which Christianity and the Barbarian peoples gave the tone, geographical digressions became a way to challenge the Romano-centric (and I would add, Pagano-centric) historiography, or *Weltbild*. Hence, the return of geographical accounts was part of a conscientious search for a rhetorical device that would enable fifth- and sixth-century authors to disengage their writing from the Romano-centrism that characterized their predecessors. It would be impossible and rather pointless to disprove Merrills' observations. Indeed, the chaotic geo-political reality of the fifth and the sixth centuries was confused and constantly shifting, and must have left an impact on people's perception of their past and understanding of their place in the newly emerging world order. Nevertheless, I would submit that the rising number of geographical digressions in early medieval sources had more to do with an attempt to integrate current events into a Romano-centric worldview.

In order to validate my point, I should like to focus for a moment on an extremely important (but alas, largely overlooked) geographical treatise, that stood at the heart of most early medieval geographical digressions. This treatise, commonly known as the *Expositio totius mundi et gentium* ("A survey of the entire world and its peoples"),[15] is a detailed geographical and economic description of the Roman Empire and beyond. It surveys the territory of the *mare nostrum* (that is, the Mediterranean) and its periphery, with a special interest in the *megalopoleis* of the Roman Empire—Alexandria, Antioch, Carthage and Rome. The *Expositio*'s first part (chapter 1–21) surveys the countries beyond the eastern borders of the Roman Empire, and it consists mainly of recycled mythical stories taken from Menander of Ephesus, Herodotus and Thucydides, as the author himself points out.[16] The second part (chapter 22–68) surveys the provinces of the Roman Empire from east to west,[17] and although it does not change dramatically our image of the Roman Empire in the fourth century, it does illuminate some aspects of the geo-political, economic, and cultural perceptions at the time.

The history of the *Expositio* itself is intriguing and far from being straightforward. No manuscript of the *Expositio* survives, but luckily it was transcribed by the French historian François Juret (1553–1626) at the very beginning of the seventeenth century.[18] Unfortunately, though, Juret's transcription is now lost, and we have to rely on the *editio princeps* of the work, which was published by Jacques Godefroy (1587–1652) in 1628.[19] Godefroy was honest enough to tell us what he had changed and added to Juret's transcription, so we can reconstruct Juret's version quite accurately. Since neither Juret, nor Godefroy, tell us in which codex the *Expositio* was found, and with which other compositions it was coupled, all the information on its author and the circumstances of its composition has to be gleaned from the *Expositio* itself.

The *Expositio*, so it seems, was composed during the reign of Emperor Constantius II (337–361), whom the author calls "master of the world" (*dominus orbis terrarum*).[20] A more accurate date, probably between 357–362, can be postulated, since the *haruspices*, who are mentioned in chapter 56, were banned by Constantius II in 357/8,[21] and Nisibis, which is mentioned in chapter 22 as part of the Roman Empire, was surrendered to the Persians in 363.[22] It was composed, most probably, in *koinē* Greek by an educated man (who possibly could also read Latin),[23] in the eastern parts of the Roman Empire, possibly in Syria or Palestine.[24] The author's reasonable acquaintance with the eastern provinces, and the fact that he calls Mesopotamia "my country" (*nostra terra*),[25] strengthen this assertion. Moreover, as pointed out by Tibor Grüll, the farther a place is from the author's eastern Mediterranean hub, the more inaccuracies and blunt errors can be found in the text.[26] Hence, the *Expositio* projects an utterly Romano-centric and eastern-Mediterranean perception of the world.[27]

The author's conspicuous interest in emporia led some scholars to conclude that he himself was a merchant, and some went even further in arguing that he traded in textiles.[28] Others suggested he was a rhetor, a sophist, an entrepreneur, a bureaucrat, or simply a *vir rusticus*, whatever that means.[29] His religious affiliation is also an intriguing question. The bubbling pagan atmosphere of the late third and early fourth century is well attested in some passages of the *Expositio*, in which the author demonstrates a fair knowledge of some pagan cults of the eastern Mediterranean.[30] Moreover, he does not refer to Christianity even once, which is extremely odd, given the fact that Christianity at the time was a crucial component in the social, political and religious structure of the Roman world, not to mention its impact on the urban landscape.[31] This led some historians to argue that the author of the *Expositio* was pagan, and to attribute the work to the time of Julian the Apostate, disregarding the fact that Constantius II is mentioned explicitly.[32] Alternatively, the author's acquaintance with the work of Josephus, whom he calls "a wise man, teacher of the Jews" (*vir sapiens, Iudaeorum praeceptor*),[33] may actually point at a Judeo-Christian intellectual circle.[34]

Towards the end of the fifth century, the *Expositio* was translated into Latin, a fact which confirms its immense popularity. Jean Rougé, the modern editor of the text for the *Sources chrétiennes*, suggests (and I tend to agree with him) that the Latin translation of the *Expositio* was part of the lively cultural activity that swept Ostrogothic Italy under Theoderic the Great (493–526).[35] There is no direct and unequivocal proof for that assertion in the text itself, but the Latin of the *Expositio* is very close to the Latin used in Ostrogothic Italy,[36] and we know that Theoderic himself was very much interested in geography. The so-called anonymous Cosmographer of Ravenna tells us that three Goths at the court of Theoderic—Athanaric, Heldebald and Marcomir—composed an exhaustive survey of the entire world, relying on classical sources.[37] Did they also use the *Expositio*? Or translate it into Latin? It seems we will never know, before some more evidence is unearthed. Nevertheless, the circulation and use of the *Expositio* fit extremely well the cultural atmosphere and preoccupations of the Ostrogothic intellectual court of Ravenna. An abridged version of the Latin *Expositio*, the so-called *Descriptio totius mundi*, was prepared around the same time, and three manuscripts of it survive from the Middle Ages (*saec.* xi, xii, xiv), all of which are of Italian provenance.[38]

On the vast circulation and popularity of the *Expositio* one can also learn from the ways it was used and abundantly cited by later authors. Orosius, for example, who was the first historian to bring back the geographical digressions into his historical account, probably knew the Greek version of the *Expositio*, and relied on it when describing the geography of the Roman Empire.[39] Moreover, there is plenty of evidence that demonstrates its immense impact on early medieval authors. The first, and most obvious one, is Cassiodorus, whose writings are imbued with direct and nearly direct quotations from the *Expositio*,[40] and it may well be that his *Gothic History* also included a geographical digression, that was later adopted by Jordanes in his revision of Cassiodorus' Work.[41] Whether taken from Cassiodorus, or composed out of scratch, Jordanes' geographical excursus owes much to the *Expositio* as well.[42] Cassiodorus', and subsequently Jordanes', use of the *Expositio* strengthen the Ostrogothic connection of the Latin version of both the *Expositio* and the *Descriptio*, and hence raise a whole set of questions regarding the role of geography in the writing of history throughout the post-Roman barbarian world.

Let us, then, dwell a little longer on the case of Cassiodorus, as it may clarify some points in the use of geography in the writing of history. Cassiodorus joined the Ostrogothic royal court in Ravenna at the beginning of the sixth century, and by 523/4 he had already replaced Boethius as the *magister officiorum*, that is, the most important figure in the Ostrogothic royal administration. Unlike Boethius, who was a conservative Roman, aloof and reserved (a kind of senatorial sense of superiority and contempt, that is also familiar from other sources), Cassiodorus was quick to adapt to the changing reality of the Ostrogothic kingdom, and willingly cooperated with the Ostrogothic kings and their administration. No wonder, then, that shortly after joining the court at Ravenna, he was completely engrossed in Ostrogothic propaganda, and became one of its most eloquent speakers and engineers.[43]

In his *Chronicle*, which was published in 519, Cassiodorus' pro-Ostrogothic stance is already clearly visible. Gothic mischiefs, such as the capture of Rome by Alaric in 410, were unashamedly gilded; Gothic failures, such as Claudius II's celebrated victory in 271, were elegantly masked or simply ignored; and Gothic successes were blown out of proportions.[44] By distorting some facts and omitting others, Cassiodorus produced a brief summary of Roman history as the Ostrogothic rulers of Italy would have liked to see it. The Gothic past was carefully integrated into the Roman past, so as to present the Ostrogothic kingdom and its king as the worthy successors of Rome and its rulers.[45] Hence, Cassiodorus' *Chronicle*, it appears, was deliberately designed to mobilize public opinion, especially that of the senatorial aristocracy.[46]

The publication of Cassiodorus' *Chronicle* was carefully scheduled. Not only did it mark Eutharic's joint consulate with Justin I, it also coincided with the end of the so-called Acacian Schism, and the subsequent reconciliation of the eastern and the western churches.[47] It was a moment not to be taken lightly, and it undoubtedly served the Ostrogothic craving for legitimacy and recognition. No wonder, then, that Cassiodorus himself was chosen to deliver the panegyric in honor of Eutharic, which betrays a similar message of integration by calling Eutharic "an indefatigable *triumphator*, who, through his fightings, restored the exhausted members of the *res publica* and brought back the old happiness to our own time."[48]

Cassiodorus' other historical composition, the so-called *Gothic History*, probably had similar propagandistic aims. Unfortunately, this composition did not survive, but in his short autobiography, Cassiodorus states that "at the command of king Theoderic, he wrote a history of the Goths, setting out their origins, habitations, and character in twelve books";[49] and in one of the letters, in which he gives a short account of his historiographical method, he writes that "from Gothic origins he made a Roman history, gathering, as it were, into one garland, flower-buds that had previously been scattered throughout the fields of literature." Hence, the *Gothic History* was meant to integrate the Goths into Roman history, and to anchor their origins and rise to power in the Roman past, or, in Cassiodorus' own words, "to make Gothic history Roman."[50]

Cassiodorus, like many early medieval historians after him, did not attempt to challenge the Romano-centric perception of history, or to introduce an alternative historiographical framework. On the contrary! He looked at the past through a Romano-centric prism, and made an effort to integrate the Barbarian present into that worldview. Similarly, Romano-centrism dominates each and every historiographical composition that came down to us from the post-Roman Barbarian West, including the *Histories* of Gregory of Tours, Marius of Avenches' *Chronicle*, the *Liber historiae Francorum*, or the so-called *Chronicle of Fredegar*, all from Merovingian Gaul and Burgundy;[51] Isidore of Seville's *History of the Goths, Vandals and Sueves* and his *Chronicle*, as well as John of Biclaro's *Chronicle* from Visigothic Spain; Victor of Tununna's *Chronicle* from Byzantine North Africa; or Bede's *Ecclesiastical History of the British People* from Anglo-Saxon England.

Against this background, it appears that geographical digressions in the sources from the late fifth century onwards did not challenge the common Romano-centric point of view, but rather adopted it as a means to integrate the barbarians into the Roman world. If we go back to the compositions mentioned by Merrills in his book, then Orosius gives a description of the Roman world in order to integrate Christianity into that world;[52] Jordanes, like Cassiodorus and probably following him, turned the Gothic history into Roman history by narrating the events up to Justinian's reconquest, that is, up to the full absorption of the Goths into the Roman Empire; and Isidore's *Laus Spaniae* focuses on the Goths, their new homeland, and their new religion within a Roman framework. All these authors made ample use of the *Expositio* and, in fact, duplicated its geographical understanding of the Roman world, or as they would have put it "The World." The Roman Empire, or more precisely the Mediterranean—the Roman *mare nostrum*—was at the heart of this geographical understanding of the world, and it remained the most important component in the early medieval perception of the newly formed geo-political and cultural divisions of the Roman West.

2

True Differences: Gregory of Tours' Account of the Council of Mâcon (585)

Helmut Reimitz

Gregory of Tours, *Histories* VIII.20[1]

Meanwhile the day of the assembly came, and the bishops gathered in the city of Mâcon on the orders of king Guntram. Faustian, who had been appointed by Gundovald, was removed from office, on condition that Bertram, Orestes and Palladius, who had ordained him, would support him in turn with hundred pieces of gold every year. Nicetius, a former layman, who had earlier procured his appointment from king Chilperic, took over the episcopal office at Dax. Ursicinus, bishop of Cahors, was excommunicated because he openly confessed that he had supported Gundovald. The council imposed a penance on him for three years; during this time he was to abstain from cutting his hair or beard, enjoying meat and wine, celebrating Mass, ordaining clergy, blessing churches, and the holy chrism, or offering blessed bread. The business of the diocese, however, was to be conducted entirely under his direction as usual.

At this synod there was a certain bishop who came forward with a proposition that women should not be included in the term "man" (*homo*). He accepted, however, the reasoning of the other bishops and did not press his case; for the holy book of the Old Testament teaches us clearly: right at the beginning in its account of the creation of mankind, it says: "God created male and female and gave them the name Adam which means men of the earth, thus referring to woman as well as to the man, calling them both man (*homo*). [...]" The bishops supported their arguments with many other references and he said no more.

Praetextatus, bishop of Rouen, read out before the bishops prayers he had written while he had been in exile. Some bishops found them pleasing, and others reproached them for their neglect of literary forms. The style, however, was in all places suitable for the church and decent.

A great discord broke out between the servants of bishop Priscus (of Lyon) and Duke Leudegisel and bishop Priscus dug deep in his pockets to establish peace.

> In those days King Guntram fell so seriously ill, that some believed he would not survive. I believe that this was God's providence, for the king was planning to send many bishops into exile.

This is the report of Gregory of Tours on the episcopal synod that took place in 585 at the city of Mâcon in central France.[2] Presided over by Archbishop Priscus of Lyon, the council was attended by fifty-four bishops and twelve episcopal delegates from the episcopal cities of the territories of the Merovingian king Guntram, who at that time ruled over Burgundy and over parts of Neustria on behalf of his recently born nephew Chlothar II.[3] This was the second synod held in Mâcon within a few years. Either in 581 or 583, the bishops had also convened there on the orders of King Guntram.[4] Guntram's position, however, had changed considerably between the two synods. After the death of his half-brother Chilperic in 584, he was the only living son of the four heirs of Chlothar I, who had divided their father's kingdom among themselves in 561.[5] By the spring of 585, Guntram had also ended the so-called Gundovald affair.[6] Gundovald had claimed to be a son of Chlothar I, like Guntram, and he had found some support from various Merovingian elites, particularly in Aquitaine. Gundovald, however, was not just a would-be Merovingian, but had some considerable support from Byzantium and was most likely invited to Gaul by the Austrasian court, probably by the widow of Sigibert I, Queen Brunhild.[7] The Austrasian queen had been looking for a new Merovingian spouse since the death of her husband Sigibert in 575 to secure the position of the Austrasian kingdom. Just a year after Sigibert's death, she had married Merovech, the son of Chilperic I. This alliance ended poorly for her new husband and archbishop Praetextatus of Rouen, who had married the couple. Chilperic separated the couple by dismissing their alliance as an incestuous marriage between a nephew and his aunt.[8] Merowech was captured, tonsured and, after he managed to escape the monastery where he was initially confined, killed. Praetextatus was brought before a synod in 577, where he was deposed and sent into exile.[9]

Gundovald might have provided Brunhild with another opportunity to marry a Merovingian. Such a marriage, however, would have presented its opponents with a difficult dilemma.[10] The alliance could only be dismissed as an incestuous relationship (like the one with Merowech) if Gundovald's claim to be a son of Chlothar I was accepted. Once married to Brunhild, Gundovald would have been a Merovingian king. While such accession to power never occurred, even without his marriage, Gundovald was a major political threat to Guntram, since his claims to power revealed how tenuous Guntram's support was among the secular and the ecclesiastical elites, particularly in southern Gaul.

Guntram confronted Gundovald's challenge with military force in the late winter of 585. His army crossed the Garonne river and trapped Gundovald in the city of Comminges. Gundovald lost most of his followers during the siege and was brutally killed by Guntram's soldiers. With Gundovald dead, Guntram was the uncontested *senior* of the Merovingian family. The young heir of Sigibert I, Childebert II, was his adopted son, while the son of Chilperic I—Chlothar II—who had only recently been born, was supposed to become his godchild. In this situation, Guntram felt strong enough to hold his opponents and their supporters accountable for the Gundovald affair. The episcopal assembly at the Second Council of Mâcon in the fall of 585 was, then, an opportunity to settle scores with the bishops who had sided with the "pretender" Gundovald.

Our most comprehensive narrative account of these events comes, as often for sixth century Merovingian history, from the *Histories* of Gregory of Tours.[11] Gregory also provides the above mentioned account of the synod, which is unusual for the *Histories*, which rarely offers detailed accounts of synods. In this case, Gregory even relates the assembly's prehistory. As he wrote at the start of the eighth book, already by early July of 585, Guntram had met and confronted several bishops who had supported Gundovald while he visited Orléans.[12] Gregory singles out four bishops by name: Bertram of Bordeaux, Palladius of Saintes, Nicasius of Angoulême and Antidius of Agen.[13] Moreover, Gregory discussed the ongoing investigation against the bishops of Bordeaux and Saintes, since they had ordained Faustianus as bishop of Dax on Gundovald's orders. Gregory also reports about Palladius of Saintes, who was celebrating the mass on the Sunday the king was visiting Orléans. When Guntram realized that Palladius was holding the mass, the king wanted to leave the church immediately. He had no intention of listening to the sacred words of a bishop who had betrayed him and treacherously broken his oath.[14] The other bishops only resolved the embarrassing situation by promising that they would deal with Palladius at a synod. If he was found guilty, the full force of canon law—*censura canonicae sanctionis*—would be brought down upon him.

Guntram, however, was concerned not only with Palladius but with other supporters of Gundovald as well. Before leaving Orléans he asked both Bertram of Bordeaux and Palladius to give *cautiones et fideiussores* to ensure their appearance at a council to be held on October 23. Another prominent bishop on the top of Guntram's punishment list was Theodore of Marseille, whom Guntram even imprisoned before the synod.[15] Theodore of Marseille had already been charged with high treason and imprisoned once before, since he appears to have played an important role in the Gundovald affair. In 581 he had received

Gundovald in Marseille and given his support. When he was charged with high treason, however, he was able to present a letter Austrasian nobles had written as proof he had only acted on the order of his Austrasian lords.[16] Moreover, other bishops had been imprisoned for this very reason.[17] It is very likely there were other similar cases, and it is not surprising that the arrest of bishops became an important issue at Mâcon. In Gregory's report of the synod, however, the question of episcopal imprisonment seems to have been of secondary importance.

The first item on the agenda was the unlawful ordination of Faustianus, the bishop of Dax, whom Gregory had discussed in the previous chapter. Gregory reports that Faustianus was deposed at the Synod of Mâcon, and the three bishops who had consecrated him, Bertram of Bordeaux, Palladius of Saintes and Orestes of Bazas, were required to pay him a yearly support of 100 *aurei*.[18] As the new bishop of Dax, the bishops appointed a certain Nicetius who had already been nominated by King Chilperic.[19] Another bishop at the synod, Ursicinus of Cahors, publicly confessed his earlier support for Gundovald, but he was not deposed. The bishops instead decreed he should do penance for three years, during which time he was not allowed to cut his hair or beard, eat meat, drink wine, celebrate mass or ordain priests.

After a bizarre intervention of a bishop who maintained that woman could not be included in the term "man" which was quickly dismissed by the other bishops,[20] bishop Praetextatus of Rouen advanced the next agenda item in Gregory's account. Praetextatus recited in front of his fellow bishops some poetical prayers he had composed. The bishop of Rouen had written these poems in exile, after he was sentenced by the episcopal synod of 577. Guntram had allowed him to return to his bishopric after Chilperic's death in the fall of 584.[21] This was not the first time that Praetextatus appeared in Gregory's *Histories*. A trial against Praetextatus is the subject of a long chapter in Book V, in which Gregory makes his own first appearance as a protagonist in the events. Gregory portrayed himself as one of the few clerics who dared to stand up against the king and defend Praetextatus after Chilperic accused him of high treason and perjury. The speech Gregory puts in Praetextatus' mouth when summoned by Chilperic attests to the Gallic episcopate's self-consciousness in the sixth century and their idea of *iustitia*.[22] Gregory used the trial as an opportunity to discuss fundamental questions regarding the limits and legitimation of secular and ecclesiastical jurisdiction, and to assert the responsibility of the ruler and the bishops to orient themselves to divine laws.

Praetextatus' reappearance at the Synod of Mâcon might as well have helped to remind his readers of Gregory's important role in the previous trial. At Mâcon, the bishop of Tours had to be content with the role of a reporter. Gregory's diocese belonged to the Austrasian kingdom of Guntram's nephew Childebert II, and the Austrasian bishops had been invited to the synod, but other than Gregory they did not attend (or perhaps Childebert had not allowed them to attend). According to Gregory's portrayal of the synod, the bishops in attendance did not need his help anyway. God himself stepped in at Mâcon. As Gregory reports at the conclusion to his report of the council:

> In those days King Guntram fell so seriously ill, that some believed he would not survive. I believe that this was God's providence, for the king was planning to send a great number of bishops into exile.[23]

It has long been observed that Gregory of Tours was not merely an historian. As the bishop of the prestigious shrine of St Martin, he was deeply involved in the political and social undertakings of the Merovingian kingdoms.[24] But in most instances Gregory is the only source we have for the events, and his text must be closely scrutinized to decipher his agenda. The Second Synod of Mâcon, however, is an exception, since the canons of the synod have come down to us as well.[25]

It is interesting to note that the two reports on the Synod of Mâcon provide us with two different accounts. There is some overlap, such as the names of the bishops Gregory mentions as participants. The bishops who were involved in the "unlawful" ordination of Faustianus of Dax (Bertram of Bordeaux, Palladius of Saintes and Orestes of Bazas) are among the signatories of the synodal acts of Mâcon. The deposition of Faustianus is not mentioned in the canons, although he seems to have been one of the episcopal signatories that were listed as bishops without a see.[26] Praetextatus of Rouen appears in the canons as well, not for reciting prayers, but for bringing forward a motion regarding the protection of ecclesiastical freedmen. Any legal disputes involving a bishop should be tried by an episcopal court (*iudicium episcopi*) and not by a secular judge (*magistratus*).[27]

Altogether the canons give a different impression of the bishops' agenda than Gregory's account. The bishops had significantly less trust in God's providence than the bishop of Tours—at least as far as Guntram's plan to confront some of them about their role during the Gundovald revolt is concerned. The sixty-six bishops and delegates, who took part in the council, were much more concerned with secular interventions in ecclesiastical affairs and/or protection from secular jurisdiction than Gregory's account suggests. As Stefan Esders and I have shown at a greater length elsewhere, the bishops were prepared in advance to make their case.[28] Building upon precedents from canon and Roman laws as well as their own interpretations of these precedents, they published canons that sought to secure an exclusive social role of the clergy and to protect them from persecution by secular authorities. Written in an elegant style, the synodal acts highlight the education and intellectual background of the bishops at Mâcon. No less impressive is the radical programmatic style with which the bishops handled a great number of issues. A drastic tone emerges on several occasions, for instance when the bishops imposed severe ecclesiastical sanctions on incestuous persons and denounced them as "the most detestable pigs wallowing in the mud of their own excrement."[29] Another canon sought to make the payment of the ecclesiastical tithe obligatory for the first time.[30] The overarching agenda, however, was to define the clergy as a separated social order with the bishops at the top of this new hierarchy. Regulations on episcopal dress suggest this goal,[31] while prohibiting clerics from dog-hunting sought to create a clerical ethos.[32] Tellingly, the bishops threatened lay people with excommunication if they did not greet clerics by bowing their heads and dismounting their horses if the cleric was on foot.[33] Most of the canons show the bishops' intimate acquaintance with both canon law and Roman law,[34] which they skillfully reconfigured to support the claims in the canons of Mâcon to respond to the most pressing problem—king Guntram's persecution of their members.

One might wonder why Gregory's report does not convey anything of the ambitious and programmatic claims of the episcopal proceedings. As many recent studies on the *Histories* have shown, one of Gregory's main goals was to promote a Christian vision of community for the post-Roman Merovingian kingdom.[35] The history and presence of the church of Gaul played a crucial role in providing infrastructure and guidance towards this vision in the *Histories*. As has also been noted, Gregory was quite selective in regard to the history and persons who were qualified to guide people towards his Christian vision.[36] The bishop who presided the Second Council of Mâcon, Priscus of Lyon, was certainly not among them.[37] Priscus became bishop after Gregory's uncle, Nicetius of Lyon, died in 573. Nicetius' holiness was soon confirmed by miracles at his tomb.[38] In Gregory's account in the *Histories*, however, Priscus did not appreciate the *sanctitas* of his predecessor and showed himself to be an unworthy successor.[39] Not only did his wife continue to live together with her husband, but also both of them harassed, persecuted and even killed many members of Nicetius' clergy and staff and replaced them with people who shared their distaste of Nicetius. One of them, a deacon who had been accused of adultery and was excommunicated by Nicetius, went so far as to climb on top of the church that Nicetius had renovated and started to dismantle the roof. Saint

Nicetius reacted promptly. Right after the deacon insulted the saint by throwing pieces of the roof down to earth, he fell from the roof and died. Moreover, Priscus' wife went insane and ran through the city with hair flying around her. Priscus likewise suffered a severe fever and never fully recovered. He continued to tremble and was dull-witted. Even the whole *familia* became pale and feeble-minded and no one doubted that Nicetius' miraculous power had struck them.[40]

Gregory's negative portrayal of Priscus was undoubtedly a caricature of the bishop. Priscus not only played an important role at Mâcon, where he presided and signed as *patriarcha*. He was also an energetic church politician presiding over a number of minor councils throughout his episcopate.[41] When Priscus died in 586, he was buried in the church of the Apostles in Lyon, next to his predecessor Nicetius. The extant epitaph provides a much more positive portrayal of the bishop.[42] The epitaph also mentions that his secular office, *domesticus,* had prepared him as a highly qualified man for the episcopate—not least for his jurisdictional duties of his episcopal office. His experience and expertise allowed him to settle the disputes with ease and good judgment: *iurgia componens more sereniferi.*[43] As Peter Brown suggested, however, the line might also contain a tacit dig at Priscus' predecessor lying next to him in the church of the Apostles.[44] On Nicetius' epitaph, which was likely composed during the time of Priscus' episcopate,[45] Gregory's uncle was presented as avoiding involvement in disputes, but rather relying on God's providence.[46]

Gregory's account of the Council of Mâcon, showing how the providence of God solved all the problems, might well be an echo of this passage in the epitaph. The parallels hint at fundamental disagreements between Priscus and Nicetius and between Gregory and Priscus about the resources for legitimation for the church in this post-Roman kingdom. As noted earlier, Priscus and the bishops of Mâcon constructed their argument based on *leges* and *canones* precedents, Roman and church law, along with their reinterpretation of them. In the aftermath of the Gundovald affair and with some of them threatened with accusations of high treason, the bishops used the new circumstances to move beyond of what these laws had stipulated. They articulated a maximal position for these precedents as a way to solidify the foundations for their independent and sacrosanct ecclesiastical jurisdiction.[47]

Gregory, however, had his own position on these issues as we can see from his report on another synod at which accusation of high treason against a bishop was discussed: the trial against bishop Praetextatus of Rouen. At this synod Gregory was—in contrast to his role as an onlooker at Mâcon—a highly active participant.[48] The assembly took place in 577, but Gregory's report dates from later. It is likely that Gregory either started or continued to work on his *Ten Books of Histories* after the death of his bête noir king Chilperic in 584.⁴⁹ As Guy Halsall suggested, it was after the death of Chilperic that Gregory could more easily style him as a model of a bad king which might also have been a strategy to advise the man who actually controlled politics in the Merovingian kingdom after 584, Chilperic's half-brother Guntram.⁵⁰ It is thus likely that Gregory had the events of 585, the Gundovald revolt and its aftermath as well as the Council of Mâcon in mind, when he wrote his account of the Praetextatus trial.

However, in his *Histories* Gregory suggested dealing with the issue quite differently than the bishops of Mâcon. At the beginning of the trial he appealed to his fellow bishops to take on their responsibility in this case and to find their own solution as a corporate body of the church of Gaul. He particularly warned against building upon Roman imperial resources and models and suggested to develop instead the foundations of the church of Gaul. After Chilperic was informed about the contents of Gregory's sermon, he summoned Gregory to talk to him in private.⁵¹

The ensuing altercation was not only about Praetextatus, but reveals a fundamental debate about the nature and the politics of justice. Chilperic even challenged Gregory's own sense of *iustitia*. If even the king cannot agree with his bishop on what is just, what chance do the common people have of finding justice? Gregory does not agree with Chilperic's secular approach to law and justice based on consent between humans. The arbiter of such consensus, Gregory argues, is ultimately the king. But who judges the king? In the end, only God's justice would decide what was right or wrong. For the here and now, the only guide was the *lex* and *canones*, which Chilperic ought to know. If he does not heed their command, he will be judged by the *iudicium Dei*. In Gregory's report Chilperic accepts this view and promises to follow the *lex* and *canones*. This might have saved Praetextatus' life and also allowed him to reappear as a bishop at Mâcon in 585. At this council, Praetextatus himself seemed to have tried to save other bishops from royal persecution, although with a different strategy. The bishops at Mâcon built their argument based on ecclesiastical laws (*reverentissimae canones*) and Roman imperial law (*sacratissimae leges*) to make their case. Gregory, however, regarded such an employment of the legal legacy of the Christian Roman Empire as a step back. It was too strongly shaped by a political theology that "could not envisage a situation in which it would be impossible to separate what belonged to Caesar from what belonged to Christ."⁵² For Gregory that was the difference between his time and the Roman imperial past. While the bishops of Mâcon built on *reverentissimae canones* and *sacratissimae leges* and provided their own re-interpretation of these laws in a post-Roman world, Gregory urged Chilperic to follow the *lex et canones*. In using the singular *lex* instead of the plural *leges* (which was common in references to Roman imperial laws) Gregory shifts the attention of Chilperic (and his readers) away from Roman imperial *leges* to the *lex Dei* as the actual foundation of the kingdom. There is, however, one point where Gregory and the bishops at Mâcon would certainly have some sort of consensus: that a bishop, once in office, should be treated as inviolable (which becomes particularly clear from the last words of Praetextatus in Gregory's account of his death[53]) and that only a synod would be allowed to depose him.

This is not the place to go into further detail about the use and reconfiguration of Roman law in sixth-century Gaul,[54] nor about Gregory's approach to the Roman imperial past.[55] The discussion of Gregory's report of the Council of Mâcon in this volume offers an example that helps reflect on the opportunities and limits of the interpretation of his *Histories*. It has often been observed that Gregory's works are the only comprehensive source for the events he recounts. That does not mean, however, that they transmit just the voice of the author. In his double role as an author and an actor he has a strong presence in the narrative and in this double role Gregory does not only reveal his own view of his world and its history. He had to build on a horizon of expectations and experiences that he hoped to share with these imagined or real readers.[56] As Peter Brown has elegantly put it in his introduction to the *World of Gregory of Tours*, "there is always a middle ground between the shaping author and the author as a member of his society."[57] Approaches from textual and literary criticism, as they have been developed and applied in the last decades, built upon such notions of a shared discourse that defines expectations and conventions along with memories and ways of remembering. However, many recent works on Gregory focusing on the literary strategies and rhetorical finesse of Gregory seem to have rather the effect of distancing the author from the society in which he wrote. Gregory's agenda, his literary strategies, his employment of rhetorical traditions and devices were rather used to argue for the singularity of his approach cutting Gregory the rhetor off from a society that was imagined as being much less educated and sophisticated. As I tried to illustrate with the brief discussion of sources, texts and events of 585, a careful study of Gregory's literary strategies suggests the opposite. As I hope to have shown, there is indeed ample evidence to study the literary trickery of Gregory as window into the social and political maneuvering and debates of his time. The differences between Gregory and the bishops at Mâcon show how open these debates could be. This becomes even more obvious in contexts when we see the rulers and elites of the Merovingian kingdoms confronted with serious challenges such as those connected to the claims of Gundovald which were supported by Merovingian dynastic traditions on the one hand and by Byzantine political and financial support on the other. The challenge of fundamental legal traditions and claims demanded programmatic answers. In the quickly and constantly changing world of sixth-century Gaul the programs behind these responses could be quite different, but it is precisely these differences that allow us to reconstruct the social, religious and political horizons they helped to define.

Part Two

Mediterranean Ties and Merovingian Diplomacy

3

East and West from a Visigothic Perspective: How and Why Were Frankish Brides Negotiated in the Late Sixth Century?[1]

Anna Gehler-Rachůnek

Gregory of Tours, *Histories* IX.15–16[2]

IX.15

[...] [Having summoned the Arian and Catholic bishops of Spain] Reccared questioned them and realized that the one God should be worshipped under the distinction of three faces (*personae*), namely the Father, the Son and the Holy Ghost, and that the Son is not inferior to the Father or to the Holy Ghost, nor the Holy Ghost inferior to the Father or the Son, but this equal and omnipotent trinity should be acknowledged as the true God. Perceiving the truth, Reccared ended the dispute and submitted to the Catholic faith, and having received the sign of the blessed cross through the anointment with chrism, he [confessed] his belief in Jesus Christ, the Son of God, equal to the Father with the Holy Ghost, who reigns unto ages of ages. Amen.

Hereupon he sent messengers to the province of Narbonne to tell them what he had done, so that the people there would be connected [to him] through the same belief. [...]

IX.16

Afterwards, Reccared sent an embassy to Guntram and Childebert for the sake of peace, since, as he asserted, he was one with them in the faith, he could also show himself united with them in friendship. But they were rejected by King Guntram, who said: "What sort of trust can they promise me and how can I believe them, after they delivered my niece Ingund into captivity, her husband was murdered through their deceitfulness, and she herself died on her journey? I will not receive Reccared's embassy, until God grants me vengeance on these enemies." [...]

At the Third Council of Toledo in 589 the Visigoths discarded their Arian creed and officially converted to the Catholic faith.[3] In his *Histories*, Bishop Gregory of Tours (573–594) describes how the Visigothic king Reccared (586–601) converted a few years earlier in 586/587.[4] As Gregory puts it, Reccared, "moved by the divine mercy,"[5] finally recognized the truth of the Catholic faith. In Gregory's narrative, this is linked with Reccared's embassy to Septimania, the Gallic territories under Visigothic rule which bordered the Frankish kingdoms, and with his embassies to the Frankish kings Guntram (562–592) and Childebert II (575–595). By arranging the events in this order, Gregory links the conversion with the embassies, implying that Reccared had used his conversion as a ploy in order to form political alliances. This aspect of Reccared's conversion has often been underestimated in the analysis of the diplomatic relations in the Mediterranean world of the late sixth century. Such a religious rhetoric of shared faith has also been used by the Byzantines in order to convince Childebert to invade Lombard Italy on their behalf. Although the success of the Byzantine moves was rather limited,[6] Reccared was more successful when approaching the Austrasian court in an attempt to establish an alliance. As this paper hopes to demonstrate, Reccared actually used the very same strategies and channels as his father, King Leovigild (569–586) did when handling the diplomatic challenges of an interweaved Mediterranean world. Yet, Reccared could add a new axis for the foundation of new diplomatic alliances.

To understand the developments that led Reccared to use the Visigothic conversion as a political justification it is necessary to be aware of the strong bonds with which the actors of the Mediterranean world were interconnected. In 1957 and again in 2012, Walter Goffart referred to this diplomatic network as the "Frankish-Visigothic-Byzantine Triangle."[7] This notion of a diplomatic network remains useful to describe the strong bonds between the Frankish kingdoms, the Visigoths, and Byzantium, without which the outcome of political decision-making at the end of the sixth century cannot be fully understood.

The first example which is pertinent to such an analysis is that of the Visigothic prince Hermenegild (573–585), who rebelled against his father, Leovigild, in 580 or shortly before. It is important to understand how and why alliances were formed and which strategies were used in order to form them. Furthermore, it is important to note how the Frankish-Visigothic-Byzantine network of alliances was changed after the defeat of Hermenegild and after Leovigild's most important ally, Chilperic, had been murdered in 584. When Leovigild died in 586, Reccared inherited his father's conflicts and alliances and therefore had to deal with Guntram's attacks. Much of the Frankish-Visigothic alliances under both

Leovigild and Reccared had to do with marriage negotiations, which should be understood against the broader background of the Frankish-Visigothic-Byzantine triangular nexus.

By the late sixth century, networking by negotiating marriages was a well-established political strategy in the West. Both the Austrasian and the Neustrian kingdoms had linked themselves with the Visigothic king Athanagild I (551–567).[8] The Austrasian king Sigibert I (561–575) married Athanagild's daughter, Brunhild (d. 613); and Chilperic I (561–584), the king of Neustria, followed his example. Instead of marrying a non-royal woman, as was common among Merovingian kings, he married a princess, Athanagild's older daughter, Galsuinth (d. 567/568).[9] Lacking male heirs, Athanagild benefited from giving his two daughters to the Frankish kings as he gained some extended family and could hope for grandsons.[10] Whereas the Visigothic-Austrasian connection was extremely significant in future maneuvers, the Visigothic-Neustrian link was cut off with the murder of Galsuinth. Ian Wood has pointed out that this murder must have taken place shortly after her father's death (567) and the appointment of new rulers, who were not related to Athanagild.[11] If we assume that Chilperic had Galsuinth killed in order to marry his mistress Fredegund, this also means that at that point Chilperic did not regard the Visigothic-Neustrian alliance as useful anymore.

In 579, in an attempt to establish his authority in the Iberian Peninsula, the Visigothic king Leovigild had married his elder son from an unknown wife, Hermenegild, to the daughter of the Austrasian king Sigibert and his Visigothic queen Brunhild, Ingund (d. 585). This marital alliance established an interesting connection. When Ingund moved to Spain, she actually lived with her own grandmother, since Leovigild had married his predecessor's widow, Goisuinth (d. 589), in order to attract Athanagild's and Goisuinth's followers. Gregory of Tours describes how badly Goisuinth treated her pious Catholic granddaughter, forcing her to convert to Arianism and "dipping her in a fishpond."[12]

These Visigothic-Austrasian family ties became important when Hermenegild, ruling his sub-kingdom from Seville, rebelled against his father in 580,[13] *factione Goswinthae reginae* (with a faction loyal to Queen Goisuinth).[14] As if to illustrate this Hermenegild-Goisuinth-Brunhild axis,[15] Goisuinth's daughter, Brunhild, sent an envoy to Spain in 580.[16] Even though this envoy died on the way, most likely without fulfilling his mission, the fact that he was sent in the first place attests to the Visigothic-Austrasian alliance.

According to our sources, the Visigothic-Austrasian axis was not Hermenegild's only connection. It appears that he had tried to ensure the success of the rebellion against his father by spinning a wide net of alliances. He probably had some connections with Septimania, namely with the Frankish bishop Frominius of Agde, who, as Gregory tells us, urged Ingund to keep her Catholic faith.[17] Following the map further north, we may assume that Hermenegild had some connections with Guntram, or at least had tried to establish such connections.[18] Gregory reports on an embassy, which had been sent to Guntram by another ally of Hermenegild, the Suevic king Miro (570–583).[19]

Leovigild responded immediately to the potential threat imposed on him by the Hermenegild-Goisuinth-Brunhild axis, in an attempt to counterbalance his son's widely spun network. In the early 580s, Leovigild started negotiating with the Neustrian king Chilperic, who had cut off the Visigothic-Neustrian ties when he had Galsuinth, the daughter of Leovigild's predecessor, killed.[20] By starting these negotiations the connection was renewed, and resulted in an agreement to wed Leovigild's younger son, Reccared, to Chilperic's and Fredegund's daughter, Rigunth. Interestingly, it took some time before this agreement was finalized in 584,[21] and throughout that period Leovigild and Chilperic frequently exchanged envoys on various matters.[22]

Leovigild did not only resort to "diplomatic" measures. Shortly after his son had started his rebellion, Hermenegild converted to the Catholic faith, most likely under the influence of his Frankish wife. Thereafter, the conflict between father and son surely obtained a religious dimension. Concurrently with Hermenegild's conversion, in 580, Leovigild convened a synod in Toledo proclaiming a "compromising" dogma, to the effect that no second baptism was required from those willing to convert. Furthermore, Christological questions were revisited.[23] Consequently, some influential Catholics, such as Bishop Vincentius of Saragossa, confessed to the new dogma.[24] For Leovigild this meant that he had won more supporters. It is worth noting that in the same year (580) Chilperic had presented his own interpretation of the Trinity to Gregory of Tours, who vigorously rejected those ideas as being of heretical nature.[25] One is tempted to suggest a connection between the Visigothic synod of 580 and Chilperic's Christological position. It is intriguing that Gregory's reports on both matters directly follow one another in his *Histories* (chapters V.43 and V.44). Keeping in mind Gregory's rhetorical finesse, this seems no mere coincidence and it clearly points at the enormous significance of Leovigild's synod. The question is whether the similar Christological positions were also something that connected Leovigild and Chilperic, and whether Leovigild exploited these common religious beliefs for his diplomatic needs.

Brunhild and Childebert, the Suevic kingdom, and, presumably, Guntram were not the only strong allies of Hermenegild that Leovigild had to deal with. Hermenegild was also supported by an old "friend," that is, Byzantium. The Byzantines had regained some territories in Spain after Athanagild had called Emperor Justinian I (527–565) for help when trying to overcome Agila I (549–554).[26] Since then, Byzantium had been both a political and a military challenge to the Visigoths.

The fact that Hermenegild obtained Byzantine support is part of a diplomatic ballet, rooted in Justinian's *Reconquista*.[27] When the Lombards invaded Italy in 568, Byzantium desired to drive them out,[28] but could not afford sending more troops to this arena due to its engagement at its eastern borders. Therefore, they were seeking other strategies to intervene in the Western Mediterranean.[29] In the case of Hermenegild, Emperor Tiberius II (574/78–582) certainly hoped that supporting him in his fight against his father Leovigild would allow Byzantium to extend imperial influence on the Iberian Peninsula, and at the same time strengthening the East Roman position in southern Gaul would also enable Byzantium to pursue a more active policy in Italy.

If indeed Tiberius had such hopes, they were soon dashed, when Leovigild successfully offered a bribe of 30,000 *solidi* to the Byzantine governor of Spain for withdrawing their support from Hermenegild.[30] Being robbed of his Byzantine support, Hermenegild had no military and political backing to oppose his father.[31] The rebellious son managed to flee to Cordoba, but Leovigild eventually arrested him and exiled him to Valencia. One year later, in 585, Hermenegild was executed in captivity.[32]

We do not know whether, by accepting Leovigild's bribe, the Spanish governor acted independently,[33] or whether the abandonment of Hermenegild in Seville—thereby practically turning him over to his father—was an initiative ordered by Constantinople. When Leovigild was besieging his son in Seville in 584,[34] Childebert's campaign against the Lombards in Italy did not generate the desired outcome.[35] Hence, Emperor Maurice (582–602), who had succeeded Tiberius in 582, might have decided to establish the Exarchate of Ravenna and to accept Leovigild's generous bribe. It is also plausible that Maurice had used this money, or parts of it, to support Gundovald's second attempt to establish himself in Gaul, after the death of Chilperic in the fall of 584, leaving only a newborn baby son, Chlothar II. Tiberius II had already provided Gundovald with financial aid in 582, when he went from Constantinople to Gaul in order to usurp Aquitaine and proclaim himself as the legitimate heir of Chlothar I.[36] After Gundovald's first attempt had failed and he had lost his financial resources, he withdrew to an island—supposedly in Byzantine territory—where he received new financial resources.[37] This scenario, although plausible, cannot be ascertained before some more new evidence is unearthed. Nevertheless, there is no doubt that by accepting Leovigild's bribe, the Byzantines crafted a turning point in Hermenegild's rebellion.

After Leovigild had defeated his son, the Visigothic king found himself in a new situation. Ingund and her son, Athanagild II, were still in Byzantine hands, where Hermenegild had left them before setting out to battle his father.[38] Leovigild was well aware of the potential threat from what was left of the Hermenegild-Goisuinth-Brunhild axis. As Gregory of Tours clearly points out, the Visigothic king feared an Austrasian retaliation that would avenge the imprisonment of Hermenegild, Ingund and their son.[39] In reality, a retaliation by Childebert was rather unlikely. However, in order to solidify his alliance with King Chilperic, Leovigild sent embassies to Neustria in order to finalize the marriage of the Neustrian princess Rigunth.[40] In September 584, Rigunth finally started her journey to Spain. While she was stopping over in Toulouse, in October 584, Chilperic was killed. Thereupon, *dux* Desiderius came to capture her to confiscate her bridal treasure, using it later on to support Gundovald.[41] Rigunth remained in Toulouse until her mother, Fredegund, set out to bring her back one year later.[42]

After her father had died, Rigunth was of no use to Leovigild and Reccared, and Neustria was no longer a viable ally. Therefore, the Visigothic prince and the Neustrian princess did not conclude their marriage. In need of an alternative ally, Leovigild was supposedly interested in a liaison with Gundovald, who might have contacted the Visigothic king.[43] We do know that Gundovald had sent his two sons to Spain, but there is no indication whatsoever as to where exactly in Spain they were sent to.[44] Goffart rules out a sojourn in Byzantine Spain.[45] If Gundovald's sons were sent to the Visigothic court, then we may assume that Leovigild had hoped that Gundovald would establish himself in Chilperic's realm and be of assistance to the Visigoths not only against Childebert, but also against Guntram.[46]

However, in 584 Guntram had defeated Gundovald. Having overcome the Frankish pretender, Guntram could focus on another strategic target. The king of Burgundy invaded Septimania, which, at the time, was still under Visigothic rule. For the Burgundians, Septimania was pivotal, because it guaranteed permanent access to the Mediterranean Sea and hence expanded their sphere of control. In Provence, which also had access to the sea, the Burgundian king had only a limited influence—Arles, which is connected to the Mediterranean via the river Rhône, was under Burgundian rule, and so was Marseille, which gave direct access to the sea. However, the situation in Marseille was very difficult. Since the death of Sigibert in 575, Guntram and Childebert had an agreement that granted Guntram parts of Marseille, including the port revenue.[47] Guntram's refusal to return his share to the young Childebert is perceived as one of the reasons for their estrangement in the years 581–583.[48] Eventually, Guntram gave Marseille back.[49] In 585, after he had learned of Hermenegild's and Ingund's death,[50] Guntram promised to avenge his niece and her husband. Consequently, he invaded Septimania. The excuse of taking revenge for the brother-in-law, Hermenegild, turned out to be extremely useful. Reccared was the one who drove the Franks out of Septimania, and subsequently devastated some Frankish territories. This was only the beginning of a bitter conflict between Guntram and the Visigothic kings.[51]

Dealing with Guntram's threat was one of Reccared's first priorities when, in 586, he succeeded his father, *cum tranquillitate*.[52] Repeatedly, Reccared tried to make peace with Guntram, who, not forsaking his revenge and interests in Septimania, consistently refused the peace offerings from the Visigothic side.[53] For the Visigoths Septimania was also extremely important, not the least because of the cities of Carcassonne and Narbonne. *Gallia Narbonensis* had already been part of their kingdom for a long time. When, in 568, Liuva appointed his brother Leovigild as co-regent and successor, he gave up the rule over Spain, but he reserved the right to decide on Septimania. Keeping in mind that large parts of the Iberian Peninsula were only recently taken by Athanagild and Leovigild, defending the old heartland was vital.

As we have already noted, soon after Leovigild's death, Reccared converted to the Catholic faith (as described in the text from Gregory's *Histories* cited at the beginning of this paper).[54] Immediately after his conversion, Reccared sent an embassy to Septimania and another one to Guntram, who rejected the peace offerings once again. Then, the embassy proceeded to the Austrasian court in order to secure the hand of Childebert's other sister, Chlodosuintha. Although, just like his father, Reccared resorted to the well-known diplomatic measures of negotiating marriages, this time was different because Reccared explicitly mentioned the Visigoths' recent conversion in an attempt to convince Childebert.[55] This was, in fact, Reccared's first use of his conversion in order to secure political alliances.

Childebert was slow to respond, since he had to consult his uncle, Guntram. They had always had a problematic relationship,[56] and it was only after Guntram and Childebert had concluded the Treaty of Andelot in 587 that they both agreed to the marriage of Chlodosuintha and Reccared.[57] This, however, must not be taken to imply that Guntram gave up his desire to conquer Septimania. With the support of Goisuinth[58] and her daughter, Brunhild, Reccared had successfully reactivated the old axis that once benefited his brother, Hermenegild. An inevitable precondition for this marriage was Reccared's oath that he had nothing to do with the death of Hermenegild, and the capture of Ingund, and Athanagild II.[59]

As Gregory indicates, Childebert must have considered marrying his sister Chlodosuintha to the Lombard king Authari (584–590).[60] Such a plan, if ever existed, was never materialized, first and foremost because the new␣Lombard king was still trying to win general recognition among the Lombards, and marrying a Frankish princess might have interfered with these efforts. But it was also the fact that Childebert had some expedient relations with Byzantium. Maurice, who had succeeded the Byzantine emperor Tiberius II in 582, had asked Childebert II to invade Italy (and reconquer it on his behalf) several times. He claimed that he had already paid for this campaign, possibly referring to the financial support Emperor Tiberius had granted Gundovald, a considerable amount of which found its way to Childebert's court thanks to Guntram Boso.[61]

After Leovigild had defeated Hermenegild, Austrasia was not interested in opposing the East Roman emperor, because, as already mentioned, Ingund, Brunhild's daughter and Childebert's sister, and her son Athanagild II had fallen into Byzantine hands. Ingund died on the way to Constantinople.[62] This is why Childebert repeatedly waged war against the Lombards, albeit lackadaisically. Eventually, Childebert made peace with the Lombards. Notwithstanding this peace, Brunhild tried unsuccessfully to get her grandson back, and she could not arrange the marriage of Chlodosuintha to the Lombard king.[63] As Gregory notes, it was Reccared's change of heart and adherence to a common creed that tipped the scales towards Chlodosuintha's betrothal to the Visigothic king.[64] Hence, if we choose to follow Gregory's interpretation, Reccared's strategy to use his conversion for political purposes finally paid off and he received permission to marry Chlodosuintha.

Yet, in the records of the Third Council of Toledo, which took place in 589 and which reflects the official Visigothic stance of the matter, we do not find Chlodosuintha's signature, but the signature of Queen Baddo.[65] Apparently, the bachelor Reccared had rejected his second fiancée, as well. By negotiating with Chilperic and Childebert over Rigunth and Chlodosuintha, Leovigild and later Reccared had hoped for their protection against Guntram. But evidently, Reccared also had to take into account some domestic political issues, in face of some revolts that broke out in Spain immediately after his conversion.[66] It is also possible that by the time of the Third Council of Toledo, Reccared had no need of an Austrasian alliance. After all, he had just defeated Guntram, who had supported some factional uprisings in Septimania.[67] Guntram's defeat marked a turning point in Frankish foreign policy. The Franks would not return to Septimania again until 631, and Reccared's success might have encouraged him to disregard his second Frankish fiancée.

In general, the conversion to Catholicism was part of an ongoing effort to Romanize the Visigothic realm and the result of a favorable "Catholic climate."[68] In many respects, Reccared continued his father's policy.[69] Both encountered similar challenges, many of which involved Frankish and Byzantine foreign policy. Both deployed similar strategies in meeting some international challenges, namely negotiating marriages. For Leovigild we cannot be sure whether he used his new dogma as an argument when negotiating with Chilperic. But we do know, or at least Gregory tells us, that Reccared exploited his new creed. Reccared, who has been called "Reccared the Catholic,"[70] was the first Visigothic king to use a "Catholic argument." Hence, the conversion, so it seems, was to a considerable extent motivated by political expediency and influenced by external (f)actors.

To conclude, both, Leovigild and Reccared had to dance on the diplomatic floor of the Mediterranean. For both, negotiating marriages was a pivotal instrument of creating political alliances. Leovigild had to deal with a rebellious son, who was supported by the family of his wife (that is, the Hermenegild-Goisuinth-Brunhild axis), Byzantium, the Suevic king Miro and possibly even the Frankish king Guntram. Consequently, he had to negotiate with the potent King Chilperic, with whom he agreed upon wedding their children. After defeating Hermenegild, whose wife and son remained in Byzantine hands, Leovigild feared Childebert's revenge, especially after the death of Chilperic. Reccared inherited this potential Austrasian threat, but he was also under a constant threat from Burgundy, especially after King Guntram had defeated Gundovald. Therefore, Reccared tried to win over Childebert by asking for Chlodosuintha's hand, stressing his recent conversion. Reccared's conversion, then, was, for a large part, political and it was leveraged by the Visigothic king in the intricate and interlocking political situation of the Mediterranean world around the end of the sixth century.

4

Friendship and Diplomacy in the *Histories* of Gregory of Tours

Hope Williard

Gregory of Tours, *Histories* IX.20[1]

[...] After reading the provisions of the treaty, the king said, "May I be struck by the judgement of God, if I should go against any of the provisions which this treaty preserves." And turning to Felix, who had—that time—come with me as a legate, he said: "Tell me, Felix, really? have you now completely fixed up friendship between my sister Brunhild and the enemy of God and man, Fredegund?" After Felix denied it, I said, "Do not doubt, my king, that those 'friendships' they cherish among themselves are passed down for lo these many years. For without a doubt, as you may know, that hatred, which was established between them long ago, still grows, not withers. If only you, most glorious king, would have less goodwill towards her! For, as we have often noted, you receive her embassy more fittingly than ours." And he said: "Know, bishop of God, that I receive her embassy in such a way as not to lose the goodwill of my nephew King Childebert. For I cannot make friendships with a woman who has often sent her men to take my life." When he had said these things, Felix said, "I believe it has reached Your Glory that Reccared has sent an embassy to your nephew to ask for your niece Chlodosuintha, the daughter of your brother, in marriage. But he did not wish to promise anything there and then without your advice." The king said, "Indeed, it is not for the best that my niece should go there, where her sister was killed. And rationally, it is not acceptable that the death of my niece Ingund is not avenged." Felix replied, "They very much want to absolve themselves from that, either by oaths or by whatever terms you may order. Only give your assent that Chlodosuintha, just as he asks, may be given to Reccared in marriage." The king said, "If indeed my nephew fulfils what he was willing to commit to in the agreements, I will do his will concerning these things." Promising that we would fulfill it in all respects, Felix added, "He entreats Your Goodness that you support him against the Lombards. Should you help in this way they would be driven from Italy and he would retake the former region, which his father conquered in living memory—yes, the rest of Italy could be restored to imperial authority by your support and his." The king replied: "No." He said, "I cannot order my army into Italy since I would wantonly deliver them to their deaths. For a very great pestilence now lays waste to Italy." [...] He said these and other things. Favoring us with sweet affection and honoring us with gifts, he ordered us to depart, commanding that King Childebert always be taught things which would stand him in good stead.

Introduction: *amicitia* in the world of Gregory of Tours

For the period of transition between late Roman and medieval worlds, diplomacy remains inadequately understood. Previous studies have stopped at the deposition of the last western emperor in 476 or the attempt by the surviving Eastern Roman Empire to retake the West beginning in 533. In failing to pursue the language of diplomacy into the sixth and seventh centuries, scholars disconnect early medieval diplomacy from its late antique precedents, leaving a gap in our understanding of how medieval writers responded to these precedents. This chapter aims to examine the response of one writer in particular: Gregory of Tours. Bishop, biographer of saints, and prolific author, Gregory was also directly involved in some of the most significant diplomatic events of sixth-century Merovingian Gaul. His use of the word *amicitia* (friendship) in relation to diplomatic alliances is illuminating: Gregory rarely thought diplomatic *amicitia* was a good thing, which has broader implications for how he understood and valued friendship. First, this chapter examines the classical roots and definitions of *amicitia*, before considering Gregory's views on personal friendships. Then it turns to a set of diplomatic incidents in the *Histories* and concludes by examining the language and framing of Gregory's account of the Treaty of Andelot.

Sixth-century ideas of *amicitia* had their roots in classical thought, which viewed *amicitia* with ambivalence. Friendship implied a relationship involving mutual affection and benefit and the exchange of services and favors; the tension between the pragmatic and personal was mitigated by ideals of friendly behavior which encompassed both.[2] Classical friendship idealized the equality and parity of friends, an idea that continued to be important to early medieval writers, such as Venantius Fortunatus and Alcuin.[3] As Verena Epp argued in her study of friendship between the fifth and seventh centuries, *amicitia* can be characterized as "a reciprocal, values-based, and morally binding obligation," with affective and contractual elements, binding two or more individual or collective partners.[4]

Personal friendships, relationships of clientage, alliances between political communities, and the connection between God and the saints, were all different kinds of friendships.[5] The flexibility and variety of relationships that fell within the bounds of *amicitia* meant that each late antique aristocrat was a member of multiple friendship networks. Furthermore, the growing influence of Christianity shaped the language in which these networks were made and maintained; shared faith provided a means for friendships to be made. So too did the schools of the late antique world and—particularly relevant for the sixth century—the courts of the barbarian kings.[6] Late antique Christian writers re-conceptualized classical friendships as being founded in God, rather than solely in human affection, and in expressions of personal friendship they used a more affective and emotional vocabulary than their classical predecessors.[7] Whatever its relationship to genuine feelings of affection, such emotional language also stood to indicate connections and the language of *amicitia* was invoked in the creation of peace agreements, alliances, and treaties.[8]

The *Histories* of Bishop Gregory of Tours allow us to examine different types of friendship over a broad span of Merovingian history. Gregory's ten books cover the period from the creation of the world to the year 591. The *Histories* do not cover this period evenly but concentrate on the recent past. Whereas book two covers 114 years, approximately from the death of St Martin to the death of Clovis, the entirety of books five through ten covers the events of only sixteen years.[9] Scholarly work of the past several decades has established that Gregory was not, as had previously been thought, the credulous narrator of contemporary affairs scribbling away as events occurred. Instead, his episodic storytelling was carefully structured to fit a moral and theological vision that contrasted and juxtaposed the actions of the wicked and the righteous.[10] For the study of *amicitia*, this suggests that we should be aware of the placement and purpose of accounts of friendship within the wider context of the events Gregory describes.

Personal friendships in the *Histories*

Gregory uses the word *amicitia* eight times to refer to personal friendships.[11] In some of these stories the creation of a friendship is a tool of wicked men, such as the tale of the rise and fall of the former slave Andarchius, who befriended a man named Ursus, in order to take advantage of him and his family.[12] The most well-studied episode in which Gregory uses the word *amicitia* to evoke ties anything but friendly is in his recounting of the feud between the families of Sichar and Chramnesind. In part, a friendship, between Sichar and the village priest of Manthelan, lay at the start of the feud: the violence began after the priest's servant was killed.[13] Althoff argues that the subsequent friendship between Sichar and Chramnesind was part of a further effort to make peace.[14] This *magna amicitia* ended with Sichar's murder by Chramnesind.[15] One gets the sense that Gregory was using *amicitia* to mean anything but.

Gregory speaks of *amicitia* in a positive light as well, but less often—of those eight personal friendships, in only two does something good come out of it. The rescue of the nephew of Bishop of Gregory of Langres by the bishop's slave, Leo, was accomplished because the two men fled to a priest of Reims with whom the bishop had an old friendship.[16] According to the *Histories*, *amicitia* also played a role in the advancement of Gregory the Great to the pontificate. At the beginning of book ten, the Bishop of Tours records how Gregory the Great was unanimously elected pope, despite having sent a letter to the late sixth-century Byzantine emperor Maurice pleading that the emperor stand in the way of his election. Gregory of Tours adds the dramatic detail that the letter was seized and destroyed before the messenger could deliver it and the results of the election were presented as unanimous. There is a political element to this story: the future pope was descended from an important family and had spent six years in Constantinople as *apocrisiarius*, the representative of the bishop of Rome at the court of Constantinople, a position which had been held by previous popes.[17] Gregory frames the emperor's *amicitia* in terms of personal affection but was undoubtedly aware of the role the new pope's previous diplomatic experience had played in the election.

How to create a bond of *amicitia*

Gregory's use of the word *amicitia* pertaining to individuals tended to describe connections which were either between unsavory characters or which came to a bad end. When Gregory describes the trajectory of a particular relationship, as with Sichar and Chramnesind, his account of *amicitia* and its aftermath also serves to structure his narrative. It seems to be a strategy in the creation of a "tragic" narrative, as in Gregory's use of the interplay between oath-taking and oath-breaking in his *Histories* and hagiography.[18] Actions beget their consequences and the start of a friendship contains the seeds of its unfortunate end.

This holds true for his accounts of the *amicitiae* between political communities and their leaders as well. Diplomatic activity is a frequent feature of Gregory's work: he mentions over sixty diplomatic events for the period following the death of Clovis, over half of which are concerned with warfare or peacemaking.[19] There are more embassies between the Merovingian kingdoms than there are embassies to areas outside the Merovingian realms. Andrew Gillett argues that Gregory treats internal and external legations the same, and does not vary his language and description according to the destination of the embassy. Furthermore, Gregory uses embassies as a narrative device, frequently beginning and ending chapters with the arrival or departure of an embassy.[20] One might expect that the frequency of diplomatic activity would correspond with frequent mention of *amicitia*, but this is not the case. When we look at how often Gregory uses *amicitia* in the context of diplomatic alliances, we find that the word is used infrequently but consistently across the *Histories*.[21] That is to say, Gregory refers to embassies and the mechanisms of diplomacy far more often than he refers to bonds of *amicitia* in the context of diplomacy and political communication.

Gregory's stories illuminate how and why bonds of *amicitia* were created. A particularly illustrative series of narratives are found in book two of the *Histories*, where Gregory refers to *amicitia* three times, all in the context of the career of the first Merovingian king, Clovis. As Ian Wood had shown, Gregory constructs his account of Clovis' career to create a picture that the king's conversion to Catholicism was responsible for his success. This makes the chronology of the bishop of Tours' account, and indeed some of his information, unreliable; in some cases, there is enough evidence to show that Gregory deliberately falsified "what really happened."[22] However, this deliberate shaping of the narrative makes Gregory's accounts of *amicitia* even more interesting. Gregory the interpreter of history, not Gregory the historian, gives us an idea of how he and his contemporaries viewed such bonds.

There are two principles which seem to be borne out by Gregory's description of the vicissitudes of diplomatic *amicitia*. The first is that the group or leader in the weaker position tended to take the initiative in making the initial overture of *amicitia*. The Visigothic king Alaric II, the Huns during the time of Sigibert I, and the Lombards in the time of Childebert II, all sought to make friendship in the face of possible defeat by the Franks.[23] Secondly, an overture of *amicitia* needed to be handled delicately since an incorrect response could be turned into the reason for an attack, as it was when Clovis turned on an erstwhile ally.[24]

The first of Gregory's references to an alliance of *amicitia* occurs in the context of a meeting between the Visigothic king Alaric II and Clovis. According to

Gregory, Alaric sent envoys to request the meeting from Clovis after observing Frankish military successes with trepidation.[25] Gregory strongly implies that the meeting took place as a defensive move on Alaric's part: observing the military defeats inflicted by the Franks, he tried to prevent the kingdom of Toulouse from becoming Clovis' next target. Later historians have distrusted this picture: Wolfram argues that the purpose of the meeting "was merely to furnish proof that the kings were equal in rank and power."[26] It is worth underscoring the idea that personal relationships of *amicitia* were concluded between equals but here Gregory seems to put the initiative for creating a relationship of diplomatic *amicitia* on the party he perceived to be in the weaker position.

Gregory recorded that the two kings met on an island in the Loire, on land which belonged to the diocese of Tours. In its location on a river island, this resembles earlier diplomatic meetings. In 369, the emperor Valens and the Gothic king Athanaric met on an island in the Danube and agreed on an *amicitia*.[27] The meeting between Clovis and Alaric was similar. The two kings conferred, ate together, promised friendship to each other, and went away having made peace. There is no way to date the meeting precisely, other than by its place in Gregory's narrative: the meeting is between the end of the Burgundian civil war in 500/2 and the Battle of Vouillé in 507.[28] It temporarily ended Frankish-Visigothic warfare.

From Alaric and Clovis' meeting, a conclusion follows that a bond of *amicitia* was more than just a diplomatic agreement but involved a series of actions designed to create a relationship between the two parties, such as an in-person meeting, a discussion of terms, and breaking of bread together. Building up and ruthlessly manipulating relationships of *amicitia* was part of Clovis' consolidation of his position during the early sixth century. In two consecutive chapters, Gregory describes how Clovis secured his position through the elimination of other Frankish kings. In the first of these narratives, Clovis secretly contacted the son of one of his rivals to suggest that he might gain Clovis' friendship if he acted in the king's interests.[29] Chloderic, the son of king of the Ripuarian Franks, was told that if his father, who was old and lame, were to die, Chloderic would inherit his kingdom and Clovis' *amicitia*. Whether or not Chloderic had already contemplated hastening his inheritance, Gregory presents Clovis' suggestion that the kingdom was not the only thing to be gained as the catalyst for Chloderic's actions.

Chloderic had his father murdered and sent envoys to Clovis to announce that his father was dead, offering Clovis free choice of whatever he wanted from the treasury he had just inherited. This did not cement the alliance in the way he intended: Clovis declined the gift but asked that his envoys be shown all of the treasure. While he was doing so, Clovis' men tricked and murdered him. Gregory reports that Clovis came to Cologne, assembled all the people, disclaimed all responsibility for what had happened (including rumors that he had encouraged Chloderic's patricide), and urged the people to accept him as their ruler. Clovis gained both kingdom and treasury. The promise of *amicitia* started a chain of events which led to the death of two kings and the elimination of their family's rule.

In Clovis' machinations, *amicitia* was both bait and switch: a means to encourage potential allies to do what he wanted, and a reason to attack them for failing to do so. The king's next target after destroying the royal family of the Ripuarian Franks was the family of Chararic, king of the Salian Franks. Clovis summoned him to help defeat the Roman ruler Syagrius in 486 but Chararic preferred to wait and see who won, then ally himself in friendship with the victor.[30] This is the second of two instances in which Gregory discusses the defeat of Syagrius. In the first, where Chararic is not mentioned, the attack on Syagrius is the first major event of Clovis' reign, and he was aided by his royal relative Ragnachar, who he would later eliminate.[31]

Interestingly, in this instance Clovis himself seems to be the one seeking *amicitia* from a position of relative weakness and attempting to build alliances in the face of uncertain victory. Gregory's chronology, which places Clovis' attack after the defeat of Alaric II and Chloderic, suggests a date post-507, at least twenty years after the defeat of Syagrius. Clovis captured and tonsured Chararic and his son, and then had both murdered when they threatened to grow out their hair and avenge their humiliation. The story is situated within Gregory's wider point about the ruthless, divinely-favored success with which Clovis expanded his rule, but what it suggests about Gregory's beliefs about *amicitia* is also striking. Handling it incorrectly could be a convincing provocation for attack.

The patterns that *amicitia* was sought from a position of weakness rather than from one of strength, and that responding appropriately to a request for an alliance could matter for future stability, are borne out by other instances of diplomacy in Gregory's *Histories*. Gregory records that the Huns attacked Gaul in around 562, perhaps taking opportunistic advantage of the death of Chlothar. Chlothar's brother Sigibert led an army against them and sent them packing. "But afterwards their king earned friendship with him [Sigibert] through legates," is Gregory's laconic narrative of what happened in the aftermath of the Hunnic defeat.[32] The Huns, being in the weaker position as defeated aggressors, were the ones who sought *amicitia*.

This pattern recurs again when Gregory describes an incident in Merovingian-Lombard relations during the reign of Childebert II. Late sixth-century Merovingian-Lombard diplomacy was complicated, involving as it did the three-way negotiations of the Lombards, the Franks, and the Byzantines. The *Epistolae Austrasicae* discuss the Byzantine-Frankish side of these maneuverings in terms of *amicitia* but Gregory does so only once, in the context of one of Childebert's abortive attacks on Italy. The king had raised an army and made ready to attack Italy, only to be forestalled by the messengers and gifts of the Lombards. "Let there be friendship between us," Gregory records their envoys saying, "and let us not perish, and we shall pay tribute to your sovereignty, and whenever it is necessary to get help against your enemies, it will not come reluctantly."[33] Further exchanges and messengers followed, as Childebert gave his uncle Guntram the news, received Guntram's advice to make peace, and sent legates back to the Lombards saying he would disband his army if they would confirm their promises.[34] In the end, Childebert's troops did not go home and the promise of *amicitia* was not realized.

Letters of diplomacy

Where there were messengers, there were more than likely letters of diplomacy as well. Letter exchange was an essential part of diplomatic practice, since ambassadors used letters as preludes to speeches and as credentials.[35] A number of late sixth-century diplomatic letters survive, preserved in a ninth-century collection of Merovingian epistolary material known as the *Epistolae Austrasicae*.[36] The last twenty-four letters of the collection are addressed by the Merovingian rulers Childebert II and Brunhild to the Byzantine emperor, empress, and various imperial officials; they also include letters from Emperor Maurice. They can be subdivided into packets, reflecting the missions of three embassies.[37]

The set of diplomatic letters contained in the *Epistolae Austrasicae* make reference to *amicitia*—indeed, this is the purpose some of them state for their writing.[38] The reason for sending a letter to create *amicitia* is explained by a letter addressed to one Megas the Curator: "To Your Highness acknowledging the famous worth of your merits, we think it suitable to send the conversation of letters, because the long distance prohibits our presence."[39] Most of the Austrasian diplomatic letters are full of seemingly empty statements of this sort. The letter itself served to authorize the envoy to speak in the name of those who sent him. The carrier of a letter might be entrusted with supplementary written or verbal messages relating to the purpose for which he had been sent.

A story Gregory tells to illustrate the paranoia of King Guntram suggests that even the formulaic letters of introduction carried by envoys could be significant.

In her efforts to arrange the marriage of her daughter Chlodosuintha to the Visigothic king Reccared, the Austrasian queen Brunhild sent an envoy, Ebregisel, with diplomatic gifts. Ebregisel had been chosen because of his previous experience of missions to Spain but it was reported to Guntram that he had set out to deliver presents from Brunhild for the sons of the pretender Gundovald. After hearing this, Guntram had all the roads of his kingdom guarded and all travelers on them searched. "Even the clothes and shoes of travelers were examined," says Gregory, "and all their possessions too, to see if a letter were hidden there."[40] When Ebregisel came to Paris, he and his gifts were seized and brought before Guntram, who assumed that the gifts were part of an attempt to support the family of Gundovald in another bid for Merovingian kingship and threatened to have the envoy executed for plotting against him. Ebregisel managed to convince the king that the gifts were for Reccared and was allowed to continue on his way with them.

When he mentions diplomatic *amicitia*, Gregory usually refers only to the names of the rulers involved and their agents, who are sometimes anonymous and sometimes named. This story gives us a sense of why these agents might be trusted and valued by those who sent them—as an experienced envoy, Ebregisel was relied upon by the queen who sent him, and seen as a potential threat by the king who apprehended him and sought to obtain the message he carried.

Amicitia and treaties

Envoys such as Ebregisel carried the messages by which diplomatic relationships were made and maintained.[41] Some *amicitiae* resulted in the writing of treaties: Gregory's description of the Treaty of Andelot and its aftermath, translated at the beginning of this chapter, provide us with a detailed look at the language of such agreements and how they were perceived by contemporaries. Treaties might, as was the case with Andelot, be made in the presence of those agreeing to them, but they might also be made by envoys working on behalf of one or both parties.

It is in the context of the work of envoys that Gregory discusses the negotiations of *amicitiae* made by the inhabitants of Greater Armenia with the Persians and Byzantines. In book four of the *Histories*, Gregory describes the death of Justinian, the reign and madness of Justin II, and the succession of Tiberius.[42] He knew the names of the two envoys Sigibert sent to seek peace from the new emperor, and wrote in some detail about other activities of one of them, Firminus, the Count of Clermont.[43] They returned after a year and Gregory describes a series of embassies and events which occurred after their return. Within this relatively short passage, Gregory uses the word *amicitia* three times in quick succession. After the capture of Antioch and Apamea by the Persians, the inhabitants of Greater Armenia visited Tiberius seeking *amicitia*. They brought along gifts of a great quantity of unwoven silk and declared themselves to be enemies of the Persian emperor. This was in response to an earlier, Persian embassy, the activities of which Gregory reports in direct speech: the envoys asked the Persarmenians they intended to keep their treaty (*foedus*) with the Persian emperor. When the if Persarmenians confirmed their intention to uphold the agreement (*amicitia*) they had made, the Persian envoys demanded that they prove their intentions to keep their friendship by worshipping fire. Gregory reports with approval that they refused and their bishop mocked the envoys for worshipping something which was not divine. The envoys, greatly offended, began to beat him with their staffs, and the people rushed to his defense and killed them.

Gregory's repeated use of the word *amicitia* is a unique feature of this passage: in no other description of diplomatic activity is it used so often. It breaks with his usual pattern of using *amicitia* to describe morally ambiguous alliances, as in the case of the diplomatic bonds between Clovis and other contemporary kings. Gregory normally uses *amicitia* to evoke its opposite but that is not what he does here. The *amicitia* of the Persians is a longstanding connection, simply being reaffirmed in changed circumstances, as Gregory's initial description of the Persian embassy's account of itself and the Persarmenians' response shows. This rapidly gains a negative cast as it becomes clear that *amicitia* is to be had only at the price of religious conversion. Gregory frames this story by beginning and ending with the far more acceptable *amicitia* with the good Christian emperor Tiberius.

There are several possible reasons that Gregory uses the word *amicitia* in a different manner than he normally does. Firstly, the story features personages and actions of which Gregory approved: Gregory had written glowingly of the ascension and virtues of Tiberius, the Byzantine emperor whose alliance was sought, earlier in the chapter. This echoed contemporary sentiment. As Averil Cameron notes, Gregory's comments on Byzantine rulers are strikingly similar to those made by Byzantine sources, particularly the ecclesiastical histories written by Evagrius and John of Ephesus, and his knowledge of Byzantine matters ought to be seen as neither inaccurate nor trivial.[44] Indeed, Gregory's narrative corresponds in its broad outlines to other contemporary accounts of the events leading up the Armenian revolt of 571–572.[45] The Persarmenians are the most distant of the foreign peoples Gregory mentions in his *Histories*, so it is striking that he reports the entire diplomatic episode in direct speech.[46] It is also noteworthy that a diplomatic episode between non-Romans (a rarity in Gregory's accounts of diplomacy), is described as though it were a standard late Roman alliance. The unusual repeated use of the word *amicitia*, the broad similarities with other contemporary narratives, and the description of the narrative within a standard classical framework all suggest that Gregory may have had or even copied a chronicle entry or other external source into his account. Elsewhere in the *Histories*, Gregory evidently got information from merchants passing through Tours, travelers returning from Rome, as well as returning Merovingian envoys.[47] It is possible that one of these may have been his source for this story.

As a witness to and participant in the diplomatic events of his own day, Gregory wrote about treaties in which he had played a part. One of the biggest diplomatic moments in Gregory's *Histories* is the Treaty of Andelot, a pact made in 587 between Guntram, Brunhild, and Childebert II. The text of the treaty is introduced within the frame story of another diplomatic meeting in 588, between a legation from Childebert, which included Gregory, Bishop Felix of Châlons-en-Champagne and Guntram. This frame story involves a particularly interesting use of the word *amicitia* and the passage is translated at the beginning of this chapter. Before discussing this, it is worth examining the language of the treaty itself in more detail.

Anna-Maria Drabek, and Wolfgang Fritze point to the influence of late Roman legal language on the text of the treaty.[48] The text of the treaty itself never uses the word *amicitia*, but as Gerd Althoff argues, Gregory was nevertheless still describing an alliance of *amicitia*. The text of the treaty refers to promises of mutual loyalty (*fides*) and repeatedly uses the word *caritas* (affection) to describe the purpose of the treaty and the nature of the bond between its signers.[49] The meeting between Childebert II, Brunhild, and Guntram took place in the aftermath of Gundovald's failed coup and settled territorial disputes between the rulers, as well as providing for succession, inheritance, and post-mortem protection of their families.[50] Gregory was present as Childebert's envoy and presumably had some input on the text of the treaty.

Gregory was present during further negotiations relating to the treaty. Sent on an embassy by Childebert II, Gregory met with Guntram at Chalon-sur-Saône to discuss the appropriate observance of the terms of the treaty. In the course of these negotiations, the full text of the treaty was read out. Gregory uses the word *amicitia* three times, in recounting the conversation between Guntram, himself, and his fellow bishop and envoy Felix. Two uses of *amicitia* are in jest:

Guntram, Felix, and Gregory banter about the state of *amicitia* between Fredegund and Brunhild. Guntram jokingly accused Felix of having fostered a friendship between Fredegund and her archenemy Brunhild. After Felix denied it, Gregory spoke up and claimed that the friendship—i.e. implacable hostility— between the two queens continued to grow ever stronger. Once again, Gregory uses the word *amicitia* to evoke its opposite. Then on behalf of King Childebert Gregory complains about the *caritas* (translated here as "goodwill") with which Fredegund's envoys are received, relative to those of Childebert, an interesting echo of the language of the treaty.

Guntram responds to this in terms of both *caritas* and *amicitia*. He claims that he receives Fredegund's embassies appropriately only in deference to principles of diplomacy such as *caritas*, not for their own sake. His reception of Fredegund's envoys is not intended to demonstrate neglect of the diplomatic relationship between himself and Childebert. It may in fact be a gesture of courtesy to his nephew since it serves to maintain the balance between competing branches of the Merovingian family. Guntram implies that his true diplomatic alliance lies with Childebert. Because Fredegund's emissaries have sometimes come with murderous intent, he cannot trust them. A true *amicitia* with Fredegund is therefore impossible, and their connection can only be of a superficial and expedient sort. Althoff interprets this conversation as a negotiation over the nature of the ties each party should have with Fredegund: neither should maintain a connection with her which goes against the spirit of their agreement.[51] This interpretation seems to be borne out by the objection of envoys of Childebert II to Guntram's standing as godfather to Fredegund's son Chlothar.[52]

The negotiations continued with specific attempts to define what the mutual fidelity and *caritas* promised by the treaty would mean in practice. This included asking for Guntram's approval of the marriage of Childebert's sister Chlodosuintha to the Visigothic king Reccared, a marriage of which Guntram expressed disapprobation given the fate of her elder sister Ingund. Felix urged Guntram to accept the Visigothic envoys' efforts to clear their king and country of blame for Ingund's death, whereupon Guntram cannily bound his approval of the marriage to Childebert's keeping of the conditions of the treaty. Taking a different tack, Felix added a plea for Guntram's support of an Austrasian military expedition against the Lombards. Felix reminded Guntram that parts of Italy had been under Merovingian control and could be so again with his help, but Guntram refused to expose his army to the risk of disease. The meeting ended on a note of goodwill: the envoys departed with Guntram's affection, good wishes, and command that they always provide Childebert with good guidance.

Conclusion

This chapter examined the place of *amicitia* in the *Histories* of Gregory of Tours. It discussed a series of instances where this word is used to describe a diplomatic relationship, in order to highlight the ambiguity with which Gregory viewed friendship. Gregory used the beginning, development, and end of particular relationships as a device for structuring parts of his work, such as the dramatic scenes of the friendship and feud of Sichar and Chramnesind or the rise of Gregory the Great to the papacy. Accounts of diplomatic *amicitia* also give the work structure. The movement of embassies served as a device to mark the beginning or end of chapters on diplomacy in the *Histories*.[53] In his description of an embassy to king Guntram, Gregory began the chapter with his own summons by Childebert and arrival at Guntram's court, and ended the chapter with the departure of himself and his fellow envoys, laden with gifts, from the court.[54] In some cases, as in the departure of the Persarmenian envoys for Tiberius' court at the end of *Hist*. IV.40, the making or seeking of *amicitia* seemed to herald a bright future. Perhaps more often, however, Gregory emphasized the fragility of an *amicitia* or the potential for duplicity in a relationship, as in his accounts of the friendships of Clovis.

Amicitia was a word with many shades of meaning—in focusing on its use in diplomatic contexts, this chapter illuminated the ideas behind its use. For Gregory, *amicitia* was a tool rulers used to bolster their positions—and often it was a ruler in a defensive position who sought to make and maintain such a relationship. But all of the friendly alliances Gregory describes do not last, and we are left to wonder whether he thought this legacy of the late antique past was wholly a good thing.

Private Records of Official Diplomacy: The Franco-Byzantine Letters in the Austrasian Epistolar Collection

Bruno Dumézil

Epistolae Austrasicae 14

The humble Fortunatus to the bishop Magneric, holy lord, father in Christ, admirable by his apostolic merits.

Summit of honors, Father of the Fathers, High Priest, flower of the precious pontifical rank, you whom the rewards given under the title of faith raise to the pinnacle, head of the Church by gift of God, you who are the disciple of the eminent Nicetius, good Magneric, you whose greatness performs the presage of your name, illustrated by your holy merit, formed by such a great master, you replace it, making fruitful the seat of his works. Generously and docilely preserving his holy memory, minister acting according to the rite, here you become master. You are considered the worthy successor of your pious master; of him remain both an heir and a bearer of fruit. The father grew up after his death and made you grow up; when he wins the sky, you win the supreme seat. You are the pupil who, in place of your predecessor, feeds the flock and the flock does not suffer ills, as long as it benefits from your wealth. You are desirable for your brothers, pleasant for your subordinates; you are an even dearer pastor for the people by the love you inspire it. In you, the hungry has his bread, the traveler his roof, the naked man his garment, the exhausted his rest, the stranger his hope. In doing these works, take good care, venerable bishop, to return to the double the talents that have been entrusted to you.[1] By praying also, sweet devotee, for Fortunatus, and giving me the hope of forgiveness, may you receive the palm, father. End.[2]

What is the relation between the panegyric of a bishop of Trier and the negotiation of an alliance between the Merovingians and Byzantium?

A major part of our knowledge on diplomatic relationships between sixth-century Austrasia and the East relies on an epistolary collection, known as the *Austrasian Letters* (*Epistolae Austrasicae*).³ This collection is transmitted by a single, composite manuscript (Vatican, Biblioteca Apostolica Vaticana, lat. 869), of which it occupies only the first thirty folios.⁴ According to Bernhard Bischoff's philological analysis, the codicological unit containing the "Austrasian Letters" was produced in the monastery of Lorsch during the first third of the ninth century.⁵ Yet, questions such as when those letters were gathered for the first time, who was behind this project, and what its aim was, are still open for debate.

The letters themselves were written between the end of the fifth and the last decade of the sixth century, which is our sole *terminus post quem*. The *terminus ante quem* is given by our copy of the manuscript, which, as we have just noted, is dated to the first third of the ninth century. Every point in time between these two dates seems possible. And indeed, several scholars in the past offered various hypothetical dates. In his edition for the *Monumenta*, Wilhelm Gundlach had suggested that the *Epistolae Austrasicae* was assembled by an Austrasian courtier, who was active in the region of Metz during the second half of the 580s.⁶ Throughout the twentieth century, the general scholarly tendency was to associate this collection of letters with the famous formularies of the Merovingian period, and to regard it as a literary model for future use.⁷ At the beginning of the twenty-first century, Elena Malaspina, following Pierre Goubert, proposed a slightly later date for the compilation of this collection, dating it to the mid 590s, but without presenting a firm view on the literary nature of the letters in question.⁸ More recently, Graham Barrett and George Woudhuysen proposed a completely novel reading of this collection in an important article that was published in the journal *Early Medieval Europe*. In their paper, Barrett and Woudhuysen suggest that the *Epistolae Austrasicae* was a Carolingian compilation of historical nature that was put together in the monastery of Lorsch, using some records that were kept in Trier.⁹ In what follows, I should like to reflect on a few elements in Barrett and Woudhuysen's theory.

First, there is the question of location. An entry in the catalog of the library of Lorsch, that was written around 830, reads: "a book of letters by different bishops and kings, which I found in Trier, gathered in a single volume (*in uno codice*)," to which another hand added "forty-three."¹⁰ Barrett and Woudhuysen's analysis of this much discussed entry seems accurate. The Lorsch entry does not suggest that the letters from Trier were found in one volume. It only indicates that the library of Lorsch owned a collection of letters in one volume. On the other hand, this entry does not say that the letters from Trier were an arbitrary collection of unrelated separate pieces. In other words, it is impossible to infer whether the letters from Trier were an archive of unrelated letters or a coherent compilation of letters. Barrett and Woudhuysen also suggest that a detailed analysis of the *Epistolae Austrasicae* may show that the compiler had used several previous collections, whose existence could be postulated based on the use of the words *Explicit* or *Finit* at the end of each entry.[11] This, one should stress, accords extremely well with what we know about the gathering of other letter collections.[12] Some micro-collections, like the ones envisioned by Barrett and Woudhuysen, were amassed into a single compilation at a fairly early stage of transmission, as was probably the case with the *Visigothic Letters*.[13] Others were combined into a single collection rather late. To give just one example, the micro-collections of Ennodius of Pavia, as shown by Stephane Gioanni, were gathered into a single volume only at the end of the eighth century.[14] By the way, it is worth noting that the library of Lorsch owned its own small letter collection of Ennodius *in uno codice*.[15] In the case of the *Austrasian Letters*, the great variety in ending words (*Finit*, *Explicit* and such) does not support the hypothesis that the various micro-collections were gathered into a single compilation in one go.

Another convincing argument put forward by Barrett and Woudhuysen is that the *Austrasian Letters* are not a collection of formulaic or "model" letters. They explain that the notion of "model letters" is quite meaningless, and that such a mixed selection of texts could certainly not fall into the category of a "handbook."[16] One could, however, be more skeptical when Barrett and Woudhuysen juxtapose the *Austrasian Letters* with Marculf's *Formularies* in order to demonstrate that the latter were heavily worked on and decontextualized in order to make them formulaic and timeless. It is true that the *Austrasian Letters* were not stripped of all contextual information, but there are some signs of simplification. For example, both letters 35 and 36 begin with the words *simili prologo* (with a similar prologue), which can be explained by a will to save effort and materials. This practice could also be found it the micro-collection of Burgar of Septimania that was assembled in the 630s.[17] Indeed, individual names were not erased from the *Austrasian Letters*, especially when the names of ambassadors are concerned. But, does that imply that whoever collected the letters had envisioned the *Epistolae Austrasicae* as a historical document? In the case of Cassiodorus' *Variae*, which was originally designed as a formulary—even if it is certainly much more than that[18]—individual names were not erased. Similarly, in the *Formulary of Sens*, which is dated to seventh century,[19] one can find a strange micro-collection of letters that preserves various personal names as a model for *insultatoria* (list of insults) full of spite.[20] Hence, keeping the names of people and of places in the letters is not necessarily a clear sign of Carolingian historical awareness.

The *terminus post quem* for the compilation of the *Epistolae Austrasicae* is another problem. The latest documents in this *corpus* are letters 40 and 41, which cannot be dated precisely. Nevertheless, letter 41 was written by Romanus, the Exarch of Ravenna between 589/590 and 595/597, and therefore can be dated roughly to that period.[21] Barrett and Woudhuysen note that "peace established, the great Italian motor of diplomatic exchange between the Franks and the Empire came spluttering to a halt, explaining why the *E[pistolae] A[ustrasicae]*, the second half of which focuses on these intricate negotiations, cease where they do."[22] However, Byzantine sources suggest that diplomatic exchange between Francia and Byzantium did not cease after this peace.[23] Furthermore, papal documents demonstrate that legates were traveling freely between the Frankish and Byzantine courts, and that the question of Lombard (and Avar) threat was far from settled.[24] Hence, the *Epistolae Austrasicae*'s *terminus post quem* has nothing to do with an imaginary halt in diplomatic exchange; rather it has to do with the collector's own choice, or with the lack of material.

Another possible argument for the Carolingian date is the fact that Gregory of Tours does not mention the Austrasian collection, not even the letters to Nicetius of Trier, although he composed a *vita* of Nicetius.[25] But Gregory does quote the first sentence from the Austrasian collection's first letter of Nicetius,[26] which implies that Gregory had access to a micro-collection of Nicetius' letters when writing his *Histories*.

As far as the place of compilation is concerned, Barrett and Woudhuysen have shown that a great number of letters can be linked with Trier rather than Metz, as suggested by Gundlach. I agree with their observation,[27] and would strengthen it by pointing to the links between Dynamius of Marseille and Magneric of Trier,[28] which allows us to associate the corpus of the *Epistolae Austrasicae* with that city.[29] But Barrett and Woudhuysen's next argument is more difficult to follow: "The collection may stop where it does because Trier had fewer letters that were of interest to the Carolingians from after 600 than from before."[30] This is plausible, because after Magneric the bishops of Trier seem to have been less active.[31] But this, one should stress, may be a false impression. Whereas most of the deeds of Magneric are recorded in the works of Gregory of Tours and Venantius Fortunatus, the deeds of the late bishops of Trier (from the 590s onwards) were almost completely forgotten. This, however, must not be taken to imply that they did not write at all, especially those who served under King Theodebert II. It is reasonable to assume that if the ninth-century church of

Trier owned archives from the sixth century, it must have possessed even more documents from the seventh and the eighth centuries. If this is the case, how is it that there are no letters from the beginning of the 590s in the *Austrasian Letters*?

To sustain the idea of a Carolingian work, Barrett and Woudhuysen put great emphasis on the epistolographic interest in Lorsch. Indeed, in the monastery's library catalogue from the 830s, the *Austrasian Letters* are registered next to letters by Seneca, Sidonius Apollinaris and Ennodius of Pavia. But none of these collections seem to have been made by the monks of Lorsch, and so the *Austrasian Letters* would be their sole epistolary masterpiece. Moreover, if the collector of the letters had access to the original letters, how could he make such appalling errors? To give just one example, the title of letter 40 announces a "letter from the Emperor [of Byzantium] to King Childebert," whereas everything in this letter indicates that it was in fact sent by the Exarch of Ravenna to a queen, probably Queen Brunhild, the mother of King Childebert II.[32]

The most problematic point remains the *capitulatio*. In the Lorsch manuscript of the Austrasian collection, the list of letters at the beginning of the collection was written with care, even elegance, but it is full of mistakes. Entries for letters 18, 30, 42, 46 and 48 are completely missing, whereas many others are false or over-shortened. Barrett and Woudhuysen did not fail to notice this fault, and explained it in the following way: "The most plausible reconstruction is that it was made, imperfectly, after the transcription of the first forty-seven letters, and then *EA* 48 was added as an appendix to the collection but never entered into the index."[33] Although this supposition makes sense for letter 48, it does not explain how the compiler of this collection could forget so many of the other letters. Moreover, the same hand that had copied the *capitulatio* also copied the first eight folios of the *Epistolae Austrasicae*. It seems untenable, then, that the *capitulatio* was copied at a later stage by someone who had already forgotten part of the collection. It is more likely that the monk of Lorsch was copying an exemplar that already had a *capitulatio*, and that the author of this *capitulatio* was using an already modified version of the original letters, which would account for the mistakes and the misunderstandings. Hence, one can postulate at least two earlier versions of this collection of letters before the one found in Trier. There were probably fewer letters in one of these earlier versions, since the words *finit feliciter* at the end of letter 47 clearly indicate that one of these earlier versions ended there. It may well be that letter 48 was added after the initial compilation, or even after the *capitulatio* was added, since it does not appear there.

When were the *Austrasian Letters* gathered for the first time? One should agree with Barrett and Woudhuysen that it would be dangerous to dismiss the idea of a Carolingian work, knowing that the letters of Avitus of Vienne, Gregory the Great or even Ennodius of Pavia were also gathered at a later stage.[34] But some arguments should be raised in favor of an early date. The letters' stratigraphy seems strange. Texts from the end of the fifth century are very few, they increase in number progressively during the sixth century, and at least twenty-three letters are dated between 580 and 591. The series stops suddenly at this date. It would seem surprising that a late collection, using letters gathered here and there by chance, would have such a limited and awkward chronological distribution.

If one assumes that the *Epistolae Austrasicae* was assembled earlier than the Carolingian period, where did this take place? Even if the letters did not come from a single source, it is obvious that more than half of the private letters mention people from the region of Trier.[35] Furthermore, since Childebert II and Brunhild were often residing in the Moselle valley, official letters may have been produced in this area as well. We also know that, on certain occasions, the bishop of Trier traveled by boat to the royal court.[36] As for the lay aristocrats, many private letters and official *dictatores* in the *Austrasian Letters* seem to involve aristocrats who were active at the Austrasian court during the 560s up to the 590s.[37] We know this faction of aristocrats very well from the writings of Venantius Fortunatus and Gregory of Tours. This pro-Burgundian group included many diplomats,[38] and until 581 its main figure seems to have been Count Gogo, who had negotiated the wedding between King Sigibert I and the Visigothic princess Brunhild. We know that this group was politically weaker between 581 and 583, when Egidius of Reims was the leading figure in Austrasia.[39] None of the letters preserved in the Austrasian collection can be dated to these three years, whereas the 590s are well-documented by letters 25 to 47.

A tempting but unverifiable hypothesis would be that the collection's first compiler was an Austrasian from the aristocratic, pro-Burgundian faction, who was active in the area of Trier, and was working during the last decade of the sixth century. The best candidate would be Bishop Magneric of Trier.[40] During the 580s, he served as a diplomatic counsellor to Queen Brunhild, so he would have had access to diplomatic letters exchanged with Byzantium, and maybe took part in their redaction. From the year 583 onwards he served as the new head of the pro-Burgundian faction. When he negotiated the Treaty of Andelot in 587,[41] his people obtained the rehabilitation of Rector Dynamius of Marseille, one of the lay aristocrats who contributed to the *Austrasian Letters*.[42] Magneric disappeared in the beginning of the 590s, which may explain the abrupt end of the collection.

To this one may add that Venantius Fortunatus, an old friend of Gogo, knew Magneric very well and even sent him a verse panegyric.[43] This poem was almost unknown in the early Middle Ages and was not part of the medieval collections of Fortunatus' *Carmina*, not even of the collection Σa, a selection of Fortunatus' poetry that was gathered by an Austrasian courtier.[44] And yet, we find this short text in the *Austrasian Letters*, which would suggest that the compiler of the *Epistolae Austrasicae* had a particular interest in this literary work.[45] If Magneric of Trier, or one of his secretaries working after his death, made the collection, it becomes easy to explain why the panegyric is found there.[46] Otherwise, how could we explain the fact that a monk of Lorsch would be interested in this letter, whose style and subject are at odds with the rest of the collection?

If we suppose that someone in Magneric's circle gathered the collection, it could also explain the great number of letters written in Reims. When Egidius of Reims, head of the pro-Chilperic faction, was deposed by a council that was convened by Childebert II in November 590, he was replaced by Romulf, son of Duke Lupus of Champagne.[47] Lupus' family had a prominent position among the pro-Burgundian aristocratic families; after all, Dynamius and Lupus were close friends, and Romulf was probably a descendant of Bishop Remigius of Reims.[48] So, at the beginning of the 590s, those around Magneric had both access to the archives of Reims, and good reasons to flatter an important ally by including four texts written by Romulf's illustrious ancestor in the collection.

Even if we cannot ascertain that Magneric had compiled the collection, an early date accounts better for the way in which the letters were gathered. The *Epistolae Austrasicae* consist of personal letters, letters of local importance, and letters from within an inner aristocratic network. Some letters are models for private correspondence, a few mention the name of useful friends or followers, and many could be used again during future negotiations with Byzantium or with the Lombards. The whole collection reflects a great unity in epistolary practices. The difference between a private letter and a diplomatic exchange is tenuous, since the man who dictated the letters in both cases was the same. Between a friendly note and an official letter, there is but a thin difference in style that this collection exposes, masters and duplicates. But, one should stress, no effort was made to turn these letters into historical records. It could have been possible. During the second half of the sixth century, in southern Gaul, the compiler of the *Collectio Corbeiensis* chose to arrange his material (conciliar canons, decretals and royal letters) in chronological order.[49] Similarly, the collector of the *Epistolae Arelatensis* made the same choice when ordering his material chronologically in order to demonstrate the pivotal role of Arles in the relations between Rome and Gaul.⁵⁰ Moreover, during the Carolingian period, the chronologically ordered canon law collections reflect a tendency to historicize legal material.⁵¹ This did not happen in the *Austrasian Letters*. If, as we suggest, the first compiler of the *Austrasian Letters* worked around the 590s, he did not work as a collector, looking for all the correspondence of the same author, nor was he looking for outstanding masterpieces. He did not work as an historian, since his aim was not to record the deeds of a certain bishopric; and the collection cannot be regarded as an *ars dictaminis*, since its interest lies not only in its style.

To sum up, it seems that the *Austrasian Letters* were collected for a powerful figure, whose areas of interest were at the same time political, diplomatic, literary and personal. Furthermore, we can attribute the initiative to Magneric of Trier, or maybe to one of his followers, who was hoping to succeed Magneric shortly after his death. According to this hypothesis, the chronology of compilation would have been as follows. During the sixth century, a series of individual letters were assembled into micro-collections, among which were a micro-collection of Remigius of Reims' letters, one of Theodebert's, and the twenty-three diplomatic letters from the 580s.⁵² Shortly after 590, these micro-collections were combined into a single collection, probably in Trier, and shortly afterwards a *capitulatio* was added to this collection. This *capitulatio* already had many mistakes, and therefore suggests that the original letters were not available anymore. At a late stage, letter 48, which is not mentioned in the *capitulatio*, was discovered and added to the collection. It is also possible that some of the four missing letters were added at this point in time. Finally, in the first third of the ninth century, a monk from Lorsch discovered this collection, and made a copy of it. This could not have been the same monk who added letter 48 to the collection, since he would probably have corrected the *capitulatio*.

No doubt it is possible to imagine another course of events, in which most of the process took place in Lorsch. Even if that was the case, still the material that was found in Trier was neither an archive, nor a collection of *membra disiecta* from a glorious past, but rather an already coherent corpus. Hence, there is no reason to doubt the global authenticity of the *Austrasian Letters*. A lot had happened between the original composition of these letters and the production of the Vatican manuscript of the *Epistolae Austrasicae*. They were copied three or four times during that period, and as attested by the extensive *marginalia* and corrections, they attracted the attention of numerous scholars throughout the Middle Ages and the early modern period. By discussing these letters today, and by making some mistakes of interpretation, we simply continue a long-established tradition.

6

The Language of Sixth-century Frankish Diplomacy

Yaniv Fox

Epistolae Austrasicae 42

In the name of our Lord Jesus Christ, the Emperor Caesar Flavius Maurice Tiberius, faithful in Christ, clement, most high, beneficent, pacific, Alamannic, Gothic, Antic, Alanic, Vandalic, Herulic, Gepidic, African, pious, fortunate, illustrious, victor and triumphant, forever Augustus, to Childebert, vir gloriosus, king of the Franks.

(Kal. Sept. 585?)[1]

1. Your Glory's letter, delivered to us by Jocundus the bishop and Chotro the chamberlain, has indicated to us that you have maintained your father's amicable and affectionate intentions toward us and our most sacred empire. This is found in writing to Your Clemency in the abundant words of other legations. **2.** And it appears to us astonishing that, having affirmed the right intent regarding the former unity of the Frankish nation and Roman rule, no effort has thus far been made by Your Eminence in accordance with this friendship, that is nonetheless expressed in writing, and signed by priests, and sealed with terrible oaths, yet with too much time having passed and without any perceived effect. **3.** And if this is so, why do you tire your indispensable legates over so much distance by land and sea in vain and without the necessary response, boasting childish speech, without producing anything of utility? In keeping with our imperial benevolence, we have received your aforementioned ambassadors, even though we knew not whether they were sent by you in earnest, and to that, which was reported by them with gentle whispers, we gave the adequate response, that by your other legations you have already made manifest. **4.** And we wish you, if you desire to have our friendship, that surely and without delay you examine everything, and do not only speak with words, but fulfill in virile fashion, as behooves a king, what you have said, so as to similarly secure and expect our pious benevolence. It would therefore suit Your Glory to effect, at least now, that which was assured in writing between us, so that by this occasion the unity of your people and our most fortunate republic will be fulfilled ever more, and no controversy will arise between us. Not for the sake of enmity were the above mentioned agreements entered into, but so that a firm and complete friendship would persevere.

Written by Manuel

May God protect you for many years, from a most Christian and most loving parent.

Given in the Kalends of September in Constantinople, by the divine emperor Maurice Tiberius forever Augustus, and after the consulate of the same, year 1.

As any search through the *Histories* of Gregory of Tours quickly reveals, the Franks employed all manner of methods in communicating with their neighbors. Gregory reports on dozens of embassies, legations, and other similar efforts, in which envoys were dispatched to pass on or retrieve information, compact agreements, sue for peace, and threaten war. To these, one must add religious efforts of all shapes and sizes, undertaken by individuals and church delegations from Gaul, with the intent of proselytizing, reforming, and restructuring religious communities of subordinate peoples, or with obtaining relics and guidance from sources of perceived religious authority. The aggregate of this effort, though doubtless indicative of the Franks' foreign horizons, coexists somewhat uncomfortably with our own notions of what constitutes a coherent and sustained foreign policy.

Certainly, the fact that the Franks had several courts at once—a number that fluctuated in the sixth century between one and four—adds another layer of complexity to an already difficult question.[2] The degree to which the courts of these *Teilreiche* constituted entities independent of one another is contingent upon a dynamic set of circumstances: the relative seniority of their kings, their positions in regional alliances, pre-existing inheritance arrangements, and so on. Gregory was constantly aware of the tangled webs of interconnectedness that extended between the Merovingian courts, whose intrigues form a ubiquitous element of his prose.

A second element that bears remembering is that the king (or, on occasion, queen) of the Franks functioned as the voice of the state. It is he who speaks to us through edicts, capitularies, and, in our case, diplomatic epistles. The extant corpus of diplomatic letters certainly reflects this fact; although it is essentially meant to function as a dispatch between political entities, it very often mimics interpersonal communication, with all its intrinsic nuances.

One consequence of this is that diplomatic letters can adopt a variety of tones. At times, their voice is cool and measured; on other occasions, they exhibit a wide range of emotion: admonitory, cajoling, sycophantic, or angry. Recent scholarship has paid much attention to the performative dimensions of royal "emotion," and its uses as a tool of rulership.[3] From the vase of Soissons to the heated spats of Fredegund and Rigunth,[4] the kings and queens of the *Histories* are often described as being overcome by emotion. It is a view that has left its mark in the critical appraisals they received from historians in the past, and understandably, modern scholars interested in rehabilitating the Merovingians saw a need to interpret the complex semiotics of royal emotion as overwhelmingly rational means to an end.

Of course, kings did, at times, genuinely act out of fear, anger, a need for validation or, in other words, emotion. Whether any of this has left an echo on the written record is another question. It is not that the sources sidestep the issue, but rather that we are seldom able to discern whether the emotional language is there to convey genuine sentiment, or, as recent scholarship suggests, to produce a certain result in the intended reader. Separating the individual writing the letter from his or her epistolary persona is therefore a challenging task. This is especially true of some of the letters we shall examine, which forcefully explore emotional themes.

The letter that opens this chapter is concerned with a set of unfulfilled strategic commitments. It nevertheless uses an emotionally evocative tone, inviting us to envisage a father, the Byzantine emperor Maurice, berating his disobedient child, King Childebert II. The sender calls upon the recipient to "man up," put aside childish behavior, and make good on his promise. Knowing full well that what we are reading is not a conversation between two individuals but an exchange between bureaucracies about the deployment of troops to the Italian theater to engage the Lombards, the language necessarily changes its meaning.[5] Almost perforce, it is transformed either into coded language or into rhetorical trope.

We would probably be correct to interpret Maurice's missive as a cleverly crafted attempt to personalize a strategic question. Other, more personal, letters included in this correspondence are not so straightforward. In the following chapter, I propose to look at the language used in letters between the court of Childebert II and the Byzantines in the 580s and early 590s. The language used in this exchange reflects two very different perspectives. Notions of Christian charity, familial affection, piety and righteousness were employed by both chanceries with equal proficiency, yet they were meant to convey very different sentiments for either side. Moreover, as I will attempt to show, we should not dismiss the idea that some of these letters contain genuine expressions of emotion.

*

By the time the Franks began to use diplomacy in earnest, the kingdoms on their diplomatic itinerary were overwhelmingly Christian. Not all shared the Franks' orthodoxy, to be sure. Some, like the Visigoths, were outright Arians, while others, like the Lombards, were perhaps intentionally ambiguous,[6] yet the symbolism of Christian language would have resounded more or less clearly in the courts that received Frankish legations.

Looking at diplomacy, Childebert II is an interesting king to follow, for several reasons. Throughout most of his reign, the evidence for Austrasia's frequent contacts with the Byzantines and Lombards is much better than for parallel regions. Austrasia is said to have held special importance for the Empire, and in this sense Childebert was already building on a legacy established in the days of Sigibert I, his father.[7]

Childebert's relationship with other Merovingian kings also provides an interesting vantage point on foreign affairs, which were on many levels informed by the internal dynamics of the three kingdoms. In this, a decisive role was played by Childebert's uncle, Guntram, whose own relationship with Byzantium, which oscillated between begrudging acceptance and open recalcitrance, counterbalanced Austrasia's more receptive attitude towards the Empire's advances.

Over all of these contacts hovers the conquest of Italy by the Lombards, beginning in 568. The establishment of the Lombards in Italy meant not only the loss of territories which the Byzantines had wrested from the Ostrogoths only several years earlier, at enormous cost; it also heralded a reconfiguration of Frankish attitudes towards Italy. The Lombards were important diplomatic partners to both Franks and Byzantines before they entered Italy, yet their advance presented both with a host of new challenges and opportunities.[8]

Ricochets from the chaotic state of affairs in the Apennine peninsula began hitting Gaul almost immediately, as Lombard military detachments crossed the Alps with growing frequency, disrupting the border region with Guntram's Burgundy.[9] While the immediate purpose of these maneuvers was probably to obtain plunder and captives, the fact that Marius of Avenches had raiding parties entering the *finitima loca Galliarum* already in 569 might suggest that the Lombards were testing the limits of Frankish tolerance, perhaps with the intent of redrawing the map in Provence, already chronically unstable because of infighting between Sigibert and Guntram.[10]

Naturally, the Merovingians were inclined to oppose this development, presenting an opportunity for cooperation with the Byzantines. Many of the delegations shuttling back and forth between Metz and Constantinople had to do with Italy, and since the Franks and Byzantines were united not only in strategic interest, but also in faith, one is tempted to search for some expression of this in the *Epistolae Austrasicae* and other pieces of relevant evidence.[11]

Indeed, the *Austrasian Letters* are a good place to start, as roughly a third of the entire collection bears witness to Byzantine-Austrasian relations under Childebert and his mother, Brunhild. Yet plans for Italy occupy less space in this collection than one might expect. Much of the correspondence reflects Frankish concern with the fate of the young Athanagild, product of the marriage between Ingund, Childebert's sister, and Hermenegild, the rebellious Visigothic prince. Athanagild was held in Constantinople after both he and his mother fell into Byzantine hands, and after Ingund had died in Carthage.[12] It is this group of Frankish letters that is richest in emotional language. It is also the one which demonstrates most clearly the complementary roles played by emotion in the Frankish letters and religion in the Byzantine ones.

As they stand, the *Austrasian Letters* hardly constitute a systematic compendium of Merovingian foreign policy. As Barrett and Woudhuysen have recently argued, the collection we have today may have emerged from a literary context very much removed from the Merovingian chanceries that initially produced its constituent parts.[13] Whether we subscribe to this notion of a later composition, or to the explanation presented by Bruno Dumézil in this volume,[14] it is evident that the collection bears the markings of a prolonged and layered process of curation. Both explanations seem to agree, however, that the *Austrasian Letters* provide a somewhat piecemeal account of the diplomatic relations between the Byzantines and the Franks.[15]

What the collection does contain is an assortment of letters, ranging from those sent by Bishop Remigius of Reims to Clovis and to several ecclesiastical colleagues,[16] through correspondence between Theudebert I and Emperor Justinian, to the already mentioned block of documents chronicling the exchanges between Childebert II, his mother, and a list of dignitaries in Byzantium, Italy, and Gaul.[17] The most prominent imperial figure in the latter part of the collection is the emperor, Maurice, to whom are addressed two letters directly. We may safely assume that the Frankish epistles addressed to the emperor's mother-in-law, members of his entourage, and subordinate officials in the Italian exarchate, also considered him to be foremost on the list of intended readers.

Already in the salutation to the letters addressed to Emperor Maurice, religious overtones are present: he is, alongside his more secular-sounding titles of *triumphator* and *gloriosus*, also referred to as pious and paternal. This should, no doubt, be understood as politesse and proper epistolary protocol, yet the use of such language in the preface is repeated throughout the text itself, which is, to quote Simon Loseby, "saturated with religious references."

In his subtle analysis of Gregory of Tours' Italian and Byzantine narratives, Loseby argues that, compared to the attitudes expressed in the *Austrasian Letters*, the *Histories* exhibit "discrepancies [...] in content and tone."[18] While the bishop of Tours is said to offer a morally neutral, at times even critical, perspective of the Frankish intervention in Italy, the *Austrasian Letters* zealously reflect the exhortations of the imperial court and the Italian episcopate. To establish this, he cites two letters by Childebert and Brunhild to the emperor and to other Byzantine personages, and a corresponding missive from the Italian exarch, Romanus.

Indeed, Childebert's appeal to Maurice in letter 25 is tastefully interspersed with pious expressions: one *qui placet Domino*, a *divinitate propitia*, and another *inspirante Domino* for good measure.[19] So is letter 29, sent by Brunhild to Anastasia, which contains one *tribuente Domino* and another *si Christus effectum tribuit*.[20] Letter 31, addressed to John, the Constantinopolitan patriarch, stands out as being more explicit in its usage of religious terminology.[21] Once again, we encounter interjections of *praestante Domino*, alongside sycophantic acknowledgments of John's apostolic honor and good works. Yet, were we to remove these flourishes, the text would ring just as clearly in its message, if not in its decorum. The religious language is there because it fits the linguistic register deemed appropriate in such texts, not because it serves any discursive function. When the intended recipient of the letter is a clergyman, the usage of religious phrases becomes predictably more pronounced, yet its content seldom departs from platitudes, probably intended to lull the addressee into a more receptive mood.

In fact, most of the letters addressed to the Byzantines are, for lack of a better description, devoid of much substance. This is not very surprising, since it would have been required, for purposes of protocol, to read aloud the formal letters borne by ambassadors, probably in the presence of the entire court. The more operative dimensions of the embassies that carried the letters would doubtless have been discussed in private.[22] Nevertheless, the tone is underwhelming considering it is meant to reflect the mindset of a king gearing up to go to war.

The same, however, may not be said of the Byzantine employment of epistolary language, religious or otherwise. Firstly, we are struck by its explicit attempt to cajole the Franks into action by appealing to their sense of religious identity. Letter 40, sent by Romanus the exarch of Italy to Childebert, urges the Frankish king to exert every effort to prevent the shedding of Christian blood and to protect the clergy, and does so by invoking both parties' shared love for the orthodox faith.[23] Childebert's piety stands in clear opposition to the iniquity of the Lombards, who are described as *nefandissimi* and, naturally, as *inimici Dei*.[24]

The same narrative thrust continues in the subsequent letter, in which Romanus regards Frankish military intervention in Italy to be divinely ordained. Strikingly, the Italian populace is referred to as *christiana gens*, in dire need of the protection only Frankish arms can afford. Stripped bare of their religious rationale, Romanus' letters simply fall apart; what remains of an emotional and articulate call to arms is a terse and factual report of troop movements and meetings between generals. Proof that the Byzantines saw religious language as a means of galvanizing the Franks may be deduced by the conspicuous absence of such terminology in Letter 42, which, as we saw earlier, contains a short-tempered reprimand from Emperor Maurice.

The emperor, who has, by now, tired of Frankish embassies bearing empty promises, admonishes King Childebert and threatens to withdraw his friendship.[25] Not once is the shared faith of the two parties invoked, nor the heretical practices of their common adversary. In fact, religious language is only used once, in the closing sentence—"May God protect you for many years, from a most Christian and most loving parent"[26]—clearly with the intent of accentuating the hierarchical differences between the two. One can only imagine the faces in the audience had this text been recited publicly. In some respects, then, Letter 42 is an admission of failure on the Byzantines' part. Their efforts to excite the Franks into a religiously motivated campaign have borne little fruit, so a different persuasive strategy, in the form of an emotional admonishment, was attempted.

Gregory, as he himself reports, was privy to the deliberations in the Austrasian court concerning the relationship with the Lombards and the Empire. He was, moreover, well-versed in diplomatic etiquette, as the person chosen to represent Childebert before his uncle.[27] Gregory provides an exhaustive description of the embassy to Guntram, which replicates a familiar dynamic from the *Austrasian Letters*. Much like the emperor, Guntram had seniority over Childebert, and expressed his disappointment and anger on account of unfulfilled promises. Childebert conveyed his eagerness, either with letters or ambassadors, to placate his interlocutor by promising to make good on his word.

Yet nowhere in Gregory's narrative do the Lombards invoke the kind of vitriol found in abundance in the official correspondence emanating from Byzantium. The Lombards emerge in the *Histories* as cooperative and sensible, and are thus able to dissuade the Franks, on more than one occasion, from following through with their plans. Had he wished, Gregory could have made the Lombards out to be a murderous bunch,[28] and his refusal to do so is even more extraordinary given the less-than-exemplary state of their religious orthodoxy.

It seems, therefore, that Gregory's reserved treatment of Childebert's Italian adventures is not so much a departure from the tone found in the *Austrasian Letters*, as a continuation of its implicit line of reasoning. The Austrasians were willing—lackadaisically—to consider intervening in Italy, first because they were bribed with exorbitant amounts of Byzantine money, and then when they were pressured into doing so by the capture of Athanagild, of whom, tellingly, Gregory breathes not a word. Yet as soon as some difficulty arises, or an opportunity for peaceful resolution presents itself, Frankish resolve seems to vanish.[29]

I would here argue that the *Histories*, unencumbered by the diplomatic constraints that seem to weigh so heavily on the *Austrasian Letters*, provide a closer approximation of the prevailing winds in Metz with regard to Italy, which were, at best, lukewarm. The *Austrasian Letters* are certainly telling the Byzantines what they want to hear, but they do so by adhering to a language that remains uncommitted, and whose religious layer serves to qualify, not to nail down. In other words, the Byzantines are asking: "are you going to live up to your word as Christians?" to which the Franks answer: "God willing..."

To test this, we must turn our attentions to letter 46, which is the only letter sent by Childebert to express a different tone entirely.[30] Addressed to Archbishop Lawrence of Milan, or rather, "Patriarch Lawrence," to quote the text directly,[31] the letter makes use of very strong, unequivocal language in describing the Lombards and their religious affinities. In fact, it has been noted as one of the rare Frankish expressions of criticism on the subject of the Lombards' heretical practices. While it is not entirely clear whether the Franks were here alluding to Arianism or to the Tricapitoline schism, given Lawrence's theological reconciliation with Rome some years earlier, Arianism seems to be the safer bet.

The letter, probably dating from 585, contains an appeal to Lawrence, who had been operating out of the safety of Byzantine-held Genoa. In it, Childebert requests assurances that the exarch, Smaragdus of Ravenna, lend his support to the Frankish invasion by deploying his own troops against the enemy. As noted by Balzaretti, the letter also suggests that Lawrence had access to troops independently of his connections with the exarch, making him a key figure as far as the Franks were concerned.³² Given his ecclesiastical credentials, his command of military assets, and his dislike of the Lombards, referring to them as a *gens execrabilis* and denigrating their faith as false and unjust would seem a prudent strategy, especially when coupled with the letter's obvious adulation. That the previous Austrasian invasion, which we know ended with an anticlimactic acceptance of Lombard tribute, should be described in the letter as a dramatic fulfillment of the emperor's wishes, complements its general tendency for hyperbole.

Depending on Gregory's somewhat jumbled recounting of Childebert's Italian initiatives, the letter should probably be seen as accompanying the second campaign, which, we learn, was nothing short of a fiasco. Discord quickly broke out between the dukes sent to carry out the attack, and the campaign was discontinued.³³ As J. B. Bury noted in his classical study on the later Roman Empire, this might even have happened before the army reached the Alps.³⁴

In this regard, the decision to include two bits of information—that the invasion was undertaken as the result of Byzantine demands that Childebert refund the 50,000 *solidi* he had already received and that Ingund was rumored to be held in Constantinople—cannot be coincidental.³⁵ Gregory was not especially loquacious about these matters to begin with, but he was apparently willing to divulge this much, as well as to state that in the past, Maurice's demands that the money be returned were casually dismissed.³⁶

All of this adds up to an understanding that the Franks were never very serious about Italy and had probably earmarked Maurice's money for different purposes altogether. They only began to entertain the thought of an invasion when their own speculations about Ingund and Athanagild's whereabouts weighed in. The neutral language, in both the *Histories* and the *Austrasian Letters*, bears witness to the tepidness of the Frankish approach. Once Childebert decided to mount the second campaign, however, it became necessary to secure Byzantine assistance on the ground. Letter 46, which explicitly asks of its recipients to advance against the Lombards in anticipation of a Frankish invasion that has yet to materialize, employs more colorful language, but it does so exactly because it seeks to solicit, not evade, military commitment.

The most highly charged emotional rhetoric is, of course, reserved for those letters aimed at obtaining the release of the young Athanagild. Here themes of longing and grief are explored in depth, demonstrating that, for the Franks, the letters' tone was anything but haphazard. Gillett observed that the evocative language of the Athanagild letters was aimed not solely at the emperor, but at a host of influential recipients.³⁷ This cumulative argumentative effort was intended to bring about a reversal in the Byzantines' policy, not least because the dramatic effect produced by reading these letters in public would have pressured the court, transforming the issue into a moral one. Still, Gillett believes that emotional considerations took second place to more pragmatic ones, and that the letters were meant, first and foremost, to advertise the issue, not to generate *pathos*.[38]

The letters were crafted to resound with a list of recipients who had the emperor's ear. Once those were sufficiently convinced, they would have presumably made their case to the emperor, arguing that Maurice's image as a just ruler would be jeopardized by continuing to hold on to Athanagild. Be that as it may, we must accede that any such argumentation would only have been effective if, at some point, it awakened the empathy of its audience. That, I would argue, was the whole point, and also the reason why they would have been dramatically performed. Granted, the emperor, the empress, or any of the recipients further down the line could have remained aloof from the letters' exhortations. But for any of this to be interpreted as a moral issue, it must have been immediately apparent that to keep Athanagild captive was somehow wrong, if only to the peripheral listeners at court.

My point here is that the epistolary language of the Merovingians could have been both calculated and genuinely reflective, emotionally. To interpret it as strictly strategic only makes sense if it were code for some other, separate, objective. This would perhaps be an appropriate reading of Guntram's attempt to scapegoat Reccared with the deaths of Ingund and Hermenegild.[39] Considering his own Spanish entanglements, Guntram's angry posturing comes off as performative and premeditated, although admittedly we have only Gregory's word to go by. Brunhild and Childebert's case, on the other hand, is not so easily pigeonholed.[40]

So long as the recovery of Athanagild was the object of the letter writers' desires, such descriptive language was probably an approximate representation of Brunhild's emotional state of longing. Barring this, the only remaining possibility would have been that the Franks really wanted Athanagild back, but not for the reasons they were stating. Yet we simply have no reason to assume this, since Athanagild's value as anything other than an object of emotional attachment would have been negligible. Once his father was killed and his uncle, Reccared, took the reins of power, Athanagild's prospects of inheriting the Visigothic throne diminished significantly. His potential for filling some future role in a Frankish context would seem even more implausible, considering that Childebert's designs for inheritance would have included his own sons—Theuderic and Theudebert—and not his nephew, however dear Athanagild may have been to his heart.

What, then, would have been the point of securing him, if we adopt a utilitarian view of Frankish policy on this question? Gillett offers two options—a Frankish unease with his captivity, and an attempt to neutralize Maurice's leverage by transforming the Athanagild question from a strategic into a moral one. Both could well be true, although, at least with regard to the second solution, a better way to counter Maurice's pressure would simply have been to refuse to play along. Of course, the fact that the Austrasians persisted in their efforts demonstrates that for them, it was an emotional issue all along.

That the Merovingian family would have found the idea of one of their own being held captive objectionable is certainly plausible. Yet, one must ask whether Athanagild, at any point in his short life, qualified as a Merovingian. As Wood and others have argued, the Frankish royal family was more a conceptual structure than a biological one.[41] Chlothild, Radegund, and even Brunhild herself were foreigners who successfully assumed a Merovingian identity; none would doubt that they were indeed just that—Chlothild was the *materfamilias* of the entire royal clan, Radegund its model saint.[42] Brunhild's later role as the *bête noir* of numerous chronicles and hagiographies notwithstanding, she was nothing if not a quintessential Merovingian queen.[43] It is perhaps testimony not only to Brunhild's emotional nature, but also to her subtle understanding of what made a Merovingian, that Theudebert II eventually found himself the target of her wrath. In a famous episode of the *Chronicle of Fredegar*, the aged queen encouraged her grandson Theuderic to declare war on his brother by convincing him that Theudebert was sired not by Childebert but by the gardener, a stratagem that worked all too well.[44] Why, then, should we assume that Athanagild would be anything but a Visigothic prince, given that he had never set foot in Gaul?

This leaves one final option: Brunhild was not acting to protect the integrity of Merovingian honor, but as a grieving parent.[45] It is true that Brunhild never met the boy in person, yet one can easily empathize with a heartbroken mother, watching helplessly as her daughter is carried off, subjected to various indignities, and finally allowed to die. It is also perfectly conceivable that she would have found some measure of solace in the return of her daughter's child.[46] If the letters are effective, it is only because Brunhild's maternal plight so naturally gains our compassion. Gillett is certainly correct to claim that the language is stylized, but not to the point of somehow masking its candor.

The phrasing choices of the Athanagild letters, while admittedly drawn from time-honored rhetorical repertoires, are thus best taken at their word. Whether they are expressing urgency or tepidness, they are, at the very least, honest insofar as they aim to reproduce some facsimile of the desires of their senders.

*

The next installment in this drama came with the betrothal of Childebert's remaining sister, Chlodosuintha. Initially promised to the Lombard king, Authari, she was eventually offered as a bride to Reccared.[47] The reasoning behind this, argues Gregory, was that Childebert recognized the Visigoths as Catholics. It is unclear whether we are meant to infer from this that the Lombards were not Catholics, or that this had any bearing on Childebert's decision-making process. Given the extensive treatment of Reccared's conversion, it seems likely that Gregory's intent was to highlight the transformation taking place in Spain, not to direct any criticism at the Lombards, about whose religious practices he is remarkably taciturn. In any event, the Austrasian *volte-face* was followed shortly by a third Frankish invasion in Italy, which yielded even poorer results than previous ones had done.

The catastrophic outcome of the third campaign is suspect, because unlike previous and subsequent invasions, it is completely lacking in detail. While Gregory opens with Childebert's decision to opt for Reccared, this perhaps had more to do with the prospect of an alliance between Austrasia and Spain and the Visigothic offer of ten thousand *solidi*, two considerations that Gregory reports elsewhere.[48] In any event, the situation with the Lombards did not change in any way that would warrant the attack, so its context becomes very difficult to reconstruct. As far as Gregory was concerned, however, the pertinent fact remained that Reccared was now a Catholic, marking a clear break with the Goths' heretical—and much maligned—past.

*

In conclusion, it is possible to say that the *Histories* remain resistant to the Byzantine argumentation that sought to conceive of military involvement in Italy as a confessional obligation, as indeed Loseby has observed. This, I would add, reflects not only Gregory's narrative agenda, but also his intimate acquaintance with the strategic objectives of the Austrasians.

It is also clear that Childebert's half-hearted Italian initiatives, which, in retrospect, achieved very little, were not motivated by a desire to expunge religious heresy. This attitude is corroborated in the *Austrasian Letters*. The Franks' reserved use of religious terminology echoes Byzantine rhetoric, but only insofar as it allows the Franks to agree wholeheartedly, without stating explicitly what it is they are agreeing to. Only when they find themselves in need of military support do they suddenly become interested in the spiritual wellbeing of Italian provincials.

In the Athanagild letters, Frankish equivocation and *realpolitik* move aside to reveal a different facet of Merovingian diplomacy. While their rhetoric is constructed with utmost care, it is the universal nature of the emotions expressed within that makes them relatable. Loss and grief were readily decipherable modes of emotional appeal, especially when framed as the plea of one bereaved mother to another. If the letters stood a chance of resonating with their intended audiences, it would only be because they successfully evoked genuine empathy. Considering the context of their composition, it certainly appears that under their classicizing exterior they carry more than a trace of emotional truth.

Whether their aim was eventually achieved is unknown, although it is unlikely that Athanagild found his way to Gaul. Nor can the Byzantine entreaties be said to have been especially successful in motivating the Franks to dislodge the Lombards from Italy. In this, Frankish stylistic acumen and Byzantine sophistication are truly on par with one another.

Part Three

Bridging the Seas: Law and Religion

7

Mediterranean Homesick Blues: Human Trafficking in the Merovingian *Leges*[1]

Lukas Bothe

Lex Salica 39.2-4 *Concerning kidnapping*[2]

[2] If a foreign slave has been kidnapped and taken overseas (*trans mare*) and if he is found there by his master and names in the public court (*mallus publicus*) the man by whom he was kidnapped in his own country (*in patria*), he ought to gather three witnesses there. Again, when the slave has been recalled from across the sea, he must again name [the kidnapper] in another court meeting (*mallus*), and again three suitable witnesses must be consulted. At a third court meeting, however, he ought to do the same, so that nine witnesses swear that they heard the slave speak consistently (*semper equaliter*) against the kidnapper (*plagiator*) in three court meetings. And afterwards he who kidnapped him, known as denounced werewolf in court language (*mallobergo mallo wiridarium hoc est*), shall be held liable for 1,400 *denarii*, which make 35 *solidi*. Admit such slave's confession for up to three kidnappers (*plagiatores*), yet under the condition that he must provide the names of the men and of the villas consistently.

[3] But if anyone kidnaps and sells a freeman and afterwards he is returned to his own country (*in patria*), known as steeling from the country in court language (*mallobergo chalde ficho*), let him be held liable for 100 *solidi*.

[4] If anyone sells a freeman and afterwards he is not returned to his property in his own country (*in patria ad propria*), and there is no definite proof, let oathtakers swear as if for homicide. If he cannot find oathtakers, known as abduction of a freeman in court language (*mallobergo frio falcono*), let him be held liable for 8,000 *denarii*, which make 200 *solidi*.

Lex Ribuaria 17 (16) [Concerning a captured man or freewoman]

If a freeman sells another Ribuarian freeman abroad (*extra solum*) and cannot bring him back, let him be held liable for 600 *solidi*, or let him swear with seventy-two [oathtakers]. And if he does bring him back into the country (*in solum*), let him be held liable for 200 *solidi*. It is resolved that this be observed similarly concerning a freewoman.[3]

Two Merovingian laws on kidnapping and the Roman *Crimen Plagii*

Two laws from the two major Frankish law books, the *Lex Salica* (*c.* 500) and the *Lex Ribuaria* (*c.* 633), address the problem of kidnapping and human trafficking in some detail and demand varying penalties. The Ribuarian provision was almost certainly modeled on the earlier Salic one. Apparently, the casuistry of the venerable *Lex Salica* was no longer required and was hence replaced by the pragmatic catchall clause of the *Lex Ribuaria*, which also raised the legal fine significantly. This article examines the legislative history of both laws. It argues that each law was informed by obscure historical contexts, while textual elaboration and choice of sanctions probably relied on the appropriation of *crimen plagii* (kidnapping) from Roman law.

Such processes of appropriation are quite common in early medieval law, if not always regarding legal consequences but certainly the elements of an offense. Rustling of herds is a case in point; in Roman law the crime of *abigeatus* (qualified cattle rustling) was qualified either by a certain amount of stolen livestock or repeat offenses and was subject to severe punishments such as forced labor in the mines (*metallum*), or death in the arena (*ad bestias*).[4] According to Hermann Nehlsen, *abigeatus* infiltrated Visigothic, Burgundian, and ultimately Frankish law via the *Pauli sententiae*.[5] In the *Lex Ribuaria* rustling of herds is qualified by a fixed amount of stolen livestock and punished the same as murder, homicide by arson and indeed kidnapping with the equivalent of three wergilds.[6] The extraordinarily high fine of 600 *solidi* due in each case marks these offenses as crimes proper. That is to say, the fine goes beyond the needs of *compositio* (dispute settlement by compensation), and aims to neutralize the offender, which was quite in tune with Roman law's penal approach.

Regulations that deal with kidnapping and human trafficking are legion in the Merovingian *leges*,[7] and they appear to rest upon common sources.[8] First among the models for the Ribuarian title is *Lex Salica* 39 concerning kidnapping. Its Latin title *de plagiatoribus* implies reception and appropriation of Roman law's concept of *plagium*, extensively dealt with in the undated *Lex Fabia de plagiariis* (probably originating from the early first century BC).[9] According to Theodor Mommsen, *plagium* referred to the fraudulent assumption of the right of dominion either over a Roman citizen or his freedman against his own will, or over a slave against the owner's will.[10] The Fabian law thus protected the freedom and property rights of Roman citizens alone, and the actions provided for by statute reflect this caveat. Either the victim's free status was determined or—if a slave was concerned—the kidnapper was sued for theft. The *Lex Fabia* mandated that every citizen had the right to file a case before the praetor, resulting in a fine of 50,000 sesterces to the benefit of the state. Penal consequences gradually toughened until Constantine finally established the death penalty for kidnappers in 315.[11]

Frankish law's approach to kidnapping is quite reminiscent of Roman *plagium*, as the grading of penalties for slaves and freemen implies. Kidnapping of slaves was implicitly subsumed under *Lex Salica*'s theft legislation, as the 35 *solidi* fine for a slave kidnapped and sold across the sea in *Lex Salica* 39.2 was also due for slaves killed or stolen under less heinous circumstances.[12] However, before that fine could be extracted, a complicated legal procedure was used to determine the kidnapper. If a slave was taken overseas and found there by his former master, he was required to denounce his kidnapper with a total of nine witnesses in three subsequent court meetings, puzzlingly on both sides of the sea. How realistic was such a process? Ian Wood suggests that this law should be viewed in the context of Frankish overlordship exercised over the south coast of England, and thus he acknowledges the ambitious Frankish claim to enforce its power in courts on both sides of the Channel.[13] Considering the assumed small-scale approach of the law, Harald Siems wonders whether *trans mare* could simply refer to "seaborne transportation" rather than actually mean "overseas."[14] In any case, one needs to explain the legal reasoning behind the phrase. The whole idea of selling an abductee overseas rested upon the notion that it made his or her return unlikely, and thus entailed near-impunity for the abductor. According to the archbishop of Constantinople, John Chrysostom (*c.* 347–407), kidnapped children were often brought to distant shores, a strategic but cruel tactic applied by illegal slave traders around 400 in order to minimize chances of being discovered, as Kyle Harper stresses.[15]

Frankish hegemony over England as assumed by Wood may well provide a reasonable context for the Salic provision,[16] even though Siems' skepticism about its practicability is equally justified. After all, both authors account for legal predecessors from which laws like this drew.[17] In an article on the spread of the Theodosian code in Gaul, Wood suspects that the Salic provision was perhaps influenced by legislation similar to the 33rd novel of Valentinian III dating to January 31, 451 (discussed later),[18] and Siems follows up that same proposition in detail.[19] Yet, a Roman origin and a North Sea context of the Salian provision do not exclude each other. If true, the pair would indeed constitute a prime example for the reception and appropriation of Roman law in early medieval Gaul. Valentinian's novel refers to a famine that plagued the Italian peninsula in 450 and forced many people to sell their own children into slavery.[20] The sale into transmarine or extraterritorial regions mentioned in the law must therefore refer to a Mediterranean context. In moralizing language, the emperor declares that the distress sales were invalid and commands that buyers be recompensed by a twenty percent margin. Anyone violating the imperial decree in the future would forfeit six ounces of gold—the equivalent of 36 *solidi*! Perhaps it is only a coincidence that the Salic fine for kidnapping an alien slave closely resembles the Roman fine for selling one's own children to slavery. But while Valentinian's novel relates specifically to parents forced to sell their children into slavery and therefore aims to safeguard Roman families, these details are stripped from the imperial law for its reuse in the *Lex Salica*, which penalizes the sale of any slave *trans mare*. The Merovingian legislators appropriated parts of the norm and transplanted it into a new legal and geographical context, namely the protection of slave holders' property rights against illegal sales across the North Sea. It is remarkable how comfortably the Franks appropriated Roman imperial legislation and utilized it for their own ends.

The third and fourth clauses of *Lex Salica* 39 reveal that for a kidnapped freeman, the fine was increased to 100 or 200 *solidi*, depending on whether the kidnapper was able to return the victim to his home country (*in patria ad propriam*). Obviously, these provisions follow a different legal reasoning, and the Ribuarian provisions were modeled according to it. Among the many possible models for the Ribuarian provision on captured men and freewomen, its editors also count an undated royal decree (*antiqua*) from the *Lex Visigothorum*.[21] *Lex Visigothorum* VII.3.3 demands that the abductor of a free child, who was kidnapped and sold into slavery, should in turn be handed over to the child's nearest relatives, who may choose either to kill or sell him; alternatively, the relatives could extract 300 *solidi* from the kidnapper as a homicide compensation.

The applicability of the child's wergild is justified by the notion that sale by the parents or kidnapping were crimes as serious as homicide. Visigothic law literally equates *plagium* and *homicidium*, which seems to be confirmed in Salic law where the sale of a freeman is punished by his wergild and oathtakers are demanded to swear "as if for homicide."[22] The *Lex Ribuaria* goes even further and implicitly puts kidnapping and human trafficking on the same level as murder, calling for a triple wergild of 600 *solidi* or seventy-two oathhelpers.[23] As this law was adopted and adapted, the penalties for illegal slavery became increasingly harsh. This suggests that illegal slavery was an increasing concern across the fifth and seventh centuries.

A possible context for the increased fear of illegal enslavement may be the emergence of Samo's kingdom somewhere in modern day Bohemia and Moravia around the year 623/624. The so-called *Chronicle of Fredegar* reports that Samo's Slavs repeatedly raided Thuringia and the other Austrasian *pagi*, eventually leading to the establishment of young Sigibert III's sub-kingdom in Austrasia.[24] It is probably in this same context that the *Lex Ribuaria* was compiled. Some of its most distinctive provisions were perhaps ad hoc reactions to the very threat that led to the establishment of the kingdom and the compilation of the *Lex*. On the other hand, the increase of fines was likely influenced by the ongoing appropriation of Roman law in the Frankish kingdoms. The Merovingians had to deal with Roman law in Burgundy and elsewhere south of the Loire, where the majority of their subjects lived according to Roman law and thus considered *plagium* a capital crime.[25] It is now widely acknowledged that the compilation of the *Lex Ribuaria* was not so much a codification of the alleged customs of the Rhineland Franks but rather a skillful revision of existing legislation.[26] When the *Lex Ribuaria* was compiled in or around 633, the Merovingian kingdoms looked back at a chain of royal decrees that had been added to the core of Frankish law, the *Lex Salica*, over the course of the sixth century. Roman and Burgundian law had influenced some of these decrees but, more importantly, they also played a role in the compilation of the *Lex Ribuaria*. All Austrasian kings from Childebert II onwards had close ties with Burgundy, and may have drawn on Burgundian scholars for the production of the *Lex Ribuaria*. Childebert II employed Guntram's Burgundian *referendarius*, Asclepiodotus, who was in all likelihood the eponymic prefect of Provence,[27] and who was certainly trained in Roman law.[28] Both Chlothar II and his son Dagobert I had claims in Burgundy, and Fredegar relates that both kings intervened in Burgundian legal affairs.[29] It is, therefore, only logical to assume that their or their counsellor's acquaintance with Burgundian and Roman law is also reflected in Austrasian legislation.

As far as the Ribuarian law on captured men and freewomen is concerned, the compilers relied on various Roman and Romano-Burgundian sources in order to revise *Lex Salica*'s kidnapping title. Valentinian III's Italian novel prohibiting the sale of enslaved children to transmarine territories was probably known in Austrasia as part of Alaric's *Breviary* and presumably already informed the Salic model of the Ribuarian provision.[30] The same is true for the Visigothic *Antiqua* VII.3.3, which equated enslavement with homicide and thus considered wergild payment an appropriate sanction for the crime.[31] This notion was already embedded in *Lex Salica* 39.3–4. The conspicuous tripling of the wergild in *Lex Ribuaria* 17, however, reflects the uncompromising approach of Roman law to *plagium* as a capital crime, which dates back to Constantine's tightening of the Fabian law on kidnapping.[32] Constantine's law of 315 established the death penalty for kidnapping but, with its references to public spectacles and gladiatorial shows, was unfit for seventh-century Austrasia with its affinity to wergild and *compositio*. Nevertheless, its interpretation was incorporated in the *Lex Romana Burgundionum*, which in turn may well have had some influence on the Ribuarian provision:

> Title 4. Concerning sales and thefts
>
> [1] If someone heinously kidnapped someone (*in plagii scelere*) and is convicted for that crime, whether it was a freeborn or a slave whom he presumed to sell, he shall suffer capital punishment (*capite puniatur*), according to the Law of Theodosius, book 9, Concerning the Fabian Law, addressed at Domitius Celsus, Vicar of Africa.[33]

The *Lex Romana Burgundionum* is less comprehensive than Alaric's *Breviary* and its text relies on juristic commentaries rather than on the actual laws from the *Codex Theodosianus*, while its structure essentially parallels the *Lex Burgundionum*.[34] About a century after its compilation, the *Lex Romana Burgundionum* appears to still have been associated with contemporary Roman legal practice. Based on unambiguous interpretations of the law, the *Lex Romana Burgundionum* had more of a practical attitude than Alaric's *Breviary* and was therefore more likely to be consulted when the stance of Roman law was required. By contrasting the 200 *solidi* wergild fixed in *Lex Salica* 39.4 with the absolute necessity of the death penalty demanded by Romano-Burgundian law, the compilers of the *Lex Ribuaria* apparently reconciled the two alternative kidnapping sanctions in the triple wergild of 600 *solidi*. In the logic of the dominant composition system, the heavy fine approached capital punishment in its severity. After all, inability to pay such threefold wergild liability entailed either inter-generational indebtedness or personal debt slavery.[35]

The attested shift from compensation to quasi-penal sanction may be attributed to unique regulatory requirements around the year 633 that forced legislators and compilers to grapple with preceding acts of legislation. From the earlier evidence it appears that various and successive processes of legislation and appropriation must have taken place between the first Roman laws on *plagium* and the Ribuarian provision on captured men and freewomen in the seventh century. However, the long-term legal development was neither linear nor teleological. Each intermediate stage had its own causes and context. This is true for the *Fabian Law* on kidnappings, which was probably occasioned by the crisis of the Roman Republic in the first century BC. Similarly, the Ribuarian title on captured men and freewomen might have been inspired by the threatening raids of Samo's Slavs into Austrasia in the 630s. Similarly, likely contexts can be postulated for Valentinian III's novel of January 451, the Salic provision on kidnapping and selling slaves *trans mare*, and for other laws containing related legislation.[36] Although only some of these laws directly influenced later laws, the Roman *crimen plagii* was ultimately behind all later legislation on kidnapping. Despite the historical uniqueness of each law, they all respond to the threat of slavery and the existence of slave markets. In the remainder of this paper, I should like to examine the above-cited provisions on kidnapping and human trafficking from a broader Mediterranean perspective, the theme of this book.

Transmarine slave trade in historiography and its traces in legislation from the early medieval Frankish kingdoms

In his 2002 article entitled "New Light on the Dark Ages: How the Slave Trade Fuelled the Carolingian Economy," Michael McCormick asserts that the Carolingians engaged in the Mediterranean slave trade from the mid-eighth century onwards, supplying the Muslim Caliphate with European slaves in exchange for oriental luxuries and cash in gold.[37] This notion, already put forward by McCormick in his *The Origins of the European Economy*, alters rather than replaces one of the most influential historical narratives of the twentieth century, the so-called Pirenne thesis.[38] According to Henri Pirenne, the decline of the ancient Mediterranean economy was due to the Arab expansion in the seventh century.[39] The rise of Muslim rule in the Levant and in North Africa not only interrupted the established long-distance trade routes across the Roman *mare nostrum*, but it also destroyed the cultural unity of the Mediterranean basin. As

Bonnie Effros suggests, Pirenne's thesis took shape under the influence of contemporary Orientalist stereotypes and colonial discourses.[40] However, in Pirenne's view the alleged clash of cultures in the Mediterranean sealed the somewhat delayed end of the Roman world as much as it prompted the reorientation of a downsized European economy towards the Atlantic coast, from where it slowly began to re-emerge in subsequent centuries.[41]

McCormick bases his reappraisal of the Pirenne thesis on advancement in modern historiography: "So everything about the early medieval economy looks different today from the way it looked to our predecessors. Everything that is, except Mediterranean shipping."[42] Relying on both recent archaeological and numismatic finds, as well as on written sources, McCormick focuses on communications and commerce rather than on commerce alone.[43] McCormick shows that long distance trade across the Mediterranean actually increased over roughly the same period Pirenne had argued for a decline.

Calculating that the inflow of Eastern luxuries must have been accompanied by an outflow of wealth from Europe, McCormick spends little time pondering on other goods such as weapons, furs, or timber that European merchants might have brought to the Arab world. McCormick concludes that only slaves could have been so profitable an export to out-value oriental luxury goods, such as spices, drugs, silk, or gold. As the Arab economy was recovering from the last wave of Bubonic plague just after the mid-eighth century, slaves were extremely valuable.[44] According to McCormick, the emerging city of Venice became the major gateway for the transfer of slaves from Europe to the Caliphate from the second half of the eighth century onwards.[45] True to his title, McCormick's interest was not in the slave trade itself but rather in its long-term consequences for the nascent European economy. Since "Europe financed the early growth of its commercial economy by selling Europeans as slaves to the Arab world," McCormick concludes, we must reconsider the conventional narrative of "the rise of the European economy."[46]

Although McCormick's findings appear somewhat sensational, his emphasis on the Mediterranean slave trade recalls previous arguments. Pirenne himself devoted a couple of pages to the slave trade in Gaul and in the Tyrrhenian Sea,[47] stressing the enduring importance of slavery in household matters and agriculture after the fifth century. He cited a number of sources from the sixth and seventh centuries that indicate the ubiquity of *mancipia* at the time and he suggested the supply must have come from Britain, the North, and the Slavonic territories to the east of the Frankish kingdoms. He even mentioned Samo, who according to the *Chronicle of Fredegar* came to the "Slavs called the Wends" as a merchant (*negucians*) and was, most probably, a slave trader himself. Slaves presumably raided from the fringes of the Frankish kingdoms were driven to Narbonne and Marseille, from where they were shipped to Italy and beyond by the same Jewish and Syrian merchants who were responsible for the import of Mediterranean commodities. Pirenne concluded that the enormous circulation of gold in Gaul implies a considerable amount of export of vestments, textiles, timber, and especially slaves. In fact, McCormick's biggest conclusion is to extend to the Carolingian age what Pirenne had already established for the Merovingian period.

Whatever the ambiguities in either thesis, both scholars stress the importance of the transmarine slave trade as evidence for long-distance trade. In his initial account of Roman continuity in the sixth century, that is, the widely accepted first part of the Pirenne thesis, Pirenne stressed the key role of Marseille, from where European slaves were shipped across the Mediterranean in exchange for oil, papyrus, and gold. Although Venice appears to have superseded Marseille as the chief slave port during the eighth century, both ports linked the Frankish kingdoms with the rest of the Mediterranean at some point in the Early Middle Ages. Hence, both ports owed some of their prosperity to the slave trade. One must wonder where all these slaves were taken from, and how the apparently vibrant Mediterranean slave trade relates to the legislation on kidnapping and illegal human trafficking discussed earlier.

Pirenne collected some evidence on the slave trade from Merovingian sources, and Dietrich Claude rehearsed these sources in his brief account of the slave trade in the early medieval Western Mediterranean.[48] Very little is known about the origin of slaves sold in Gallic markets during the Merovingian period. Gregory of Tours, for example, mentions a man traveling to Italy on a ship full of heathens, which might have been a slave ship, but he gives no clue as to their origin.[49] In a letter to Emperor Maurice, Gregory the Great complains about many enslaved Romans who were sold to the Franks by the Lombards.[50] In another letter, Gregory orders the priest Candidus to buy young *Angeli* in Gaul, aged seventeen or eighteen, to be given to monasteries.[51] The *Vita Eligii*, dating from the first half of the seventh century, recounts that Eligius bought numerous slaves at Marseille and freed "all alike, Romans, Gauls, Britons and Moors but particularly Saxons who were as numerous as sheep at that time, expelled from their own land and scattered everywhere."[52] The *Vita Boniti* (late seventh century) reports much the same, although it withholds the ethnicity of the freed captives.[53] There are a few other sources, but in general, information on the origin of slaves is rather scarce. Since we do not hear much about slaves from the Frankish heartlands, Claude suggested that the majority of slaves sold in Gaul came from the periphery of the Merovingian kingdoms. Assuming that mass enslavement was in most cases the result of wars and famines, Claude further concluded that these regionally and temporally restricted phenomena account for the seemingly paradoxical fact that some countries needed to both import and export slaves.[54] However, the Frankish laws against kidnapping and human trafficking provide an insight into a previously neglected aspect of early medieval slavery, though perhaps only in loose relation to the Mediterranean slave trade that drew so much attention by economic historians.

For obvious geographical reasons, neither the *Lex Salica* nor the *Lex Ribuaria* explicitly refer to the Mediterranean slave trade; however, their emphasis on the forbidden export of enslaved people suggests that ramifications of the Mediterranean slave trade were perceptible throughout the Frankish kingdoms and especially in its rougher frontier regions. Like the two Frankish *leges*, the laws of the Alamans and Bavarians contain similar provisions against the sale of kidnapped freemen and women.[55] Apart from that, the *Lex Alamannorum* prohibits the sale of slaves outside its borders while at the same time allowing slave owners to command freely over the fate of their slaves within the duchy:

> [1] Let no one sell slaves [*mancipia*] outside the province, unless it is done by the order of the duke. [2] Within the province, when it is necessary let each man have the power of deciding [the fate] of his slave according to law. However, let him not have the power of holding him in captivity outside the province. If, however, anyone does this and thereafter is convicted according to our decree that applies to all Alamans, and if anyone wishes to transgress this order, let him lose the price he assigned to his own slave, and, in addition, let him make compensation of a *fredus,* which the law requires.[56]

According to this law, the owner's power of disposition over their slaves was uncontested as long as they respected ducal authority over export regulations. Under which circumstances could the duke of Alemannia be interested in selling slaves across the duchy's border, and, does this relate to the occasional ransom of war captives? Alternatively, does this quite singular provision even hint at an officially sanctioned slave trade with the Mediterranean slave ports across the Alps? We will hardly know the answer to these questions unless some new evidence is unearthed. However, it seems that the initial prohibition to sell slaves outside the province was never really intended to protect the interest of the unfree population, but rather to secure the economic interest of individual slaveholders and of the duchy as a whole, which was in danger of thinning out its labor force. Bearing in mind the above-mentioned appropriation of Roman *plagium*, this interpretation makes sense, since the *Lex Fabia* was also framed to protect either the personal freedom or the property rights of Roman citizens. Thus, the prohibition of selling slaves outside the province protected ownership over slaves that was crucial for the duchy's economic potential. The *Lex Alamannorum* is quite explicit in this respect, as it lists the tributes and services expected from the church's *servi* and *coloni* in some detail.[57] Bearing in mind that the Alemannic and Bavarian duchies' primary function was to guard the Merovingian kingdoms' southeastern frontier,[58] and if the workforce were unprotected, it might result in the duchy's inability to fulfill their military duties.

The prohibition on kidnapping and selling free persons, on the other hand, protected the personal freedom and social status of the more privileged population in Alemannia. In the *Lex Alamannorum*, the penalties imposed for the sale of freemen and freewomen echo those of the Frankish *leges* discussed earlier. Whenever the vendor was able to bring back the enslaved person and restore his or her freedom, the penalty would be moderate; otherwise, compensation would amount to a full wergild.[59] Sales within the Alemannic province entailed only lighter penalties.[60] The *Lex Baiuvariorum* does not distinguish between internal and external sales, but similarly halves the wergild if the abductor was able to bring back the victim and restore his or her freedom, over and above a public fine of 40 *solidi*. If the victim was not returned, the *Lex Baiuvariorum* requires the vendor to lose his freedom on account of his inability to pay the wergild.[61] These examples from the fringes of the Merovingian kingdoms reveal a clear case of double standards. While legislators generally ruled against the trafficking of free persons and especially penalized for their transport across boundaries, the everyday trade in "regular" slaves remained largely untouched. The slave trade was clearly an important part of the kingdom's estate-based economy, and was promoted insofar as it did not present a threat to the elites.

Additionally, it was undesirable to sell Christian slaves to Jews or pagans from a religious point of view as the danger of apostasy loomed large.[62] Hence, canon 13 of the Synod of Clichy (626/627) banned the sale of Christians to Jews and pagans, reinforcing the ban with a threat of excommunication and annulment of such a sale.[63] The ninth canon of the Synod of Châlons (c. 650) similarly forbade selling *mancipia* outside Clovis II's kingdom in order to prevent Christian slaves from falling into the hands of pagans or, even worse, Jews.[64] Following Roman law, other canons targeted Jews who might convert or circumcise Christian slaves.[65] Even though the impetus behind these canons was the prevention of apostasy, the primary interest of Jewish and non-Jewish slave traders was profit rather than faith. Thus, slave traders had to make trade-offs between the salvation of souls, impending penal consequences, and genuine business interests. In general, repeated emphasis against selling Christians and exporting slaves and enslaved free persons suggests that profits were substantial enough for slave traders to take that risk.[66]

Conclusion

The laws make clear that kidnapping and human trafficking were endemic throughout the Merovingian and Carolingian period, and attempts were regularly made to prevent the workforce from being crippled, or Christians from being converted away from Christianity; however, this is only part of the story. Pirenne and McCormick's description of the transmarine slave trade may therefore represent only the most extreme extent of early medieval slavery, when external demand determined supply. The study of the legal sources immediately suggests that the ramifications of a vibrant Mediterranean slave trade were tangible at least at the Frankish frontier to the east and south-east, if not also in the heartlands further to the west. Within the Merovingian kingdoms, a large network of regional slave markets must have existed. These markets supplied both local and trans-regional demands and probably absorbed kidnapped slaves and free persons alike. It is difficult to determine how many people were actually shipped across the Mediterranean at any given time, and whether this figure changed dramatically in either way by or because of the Arab expansion. Pirenne's primary assumption that the Roman slave economy survived into the sixth and seventh centuries seems as valid today as it was in 1937. McCormick's take on the increased export of slaves to the Caliphate adds another layer to the Pirenne thesis, since it reflects another economic consequence of the political changes around the Mediterranean. Although McCormick's thesis appears to contradict Pirenne's thesis, it actually confirms Pirenne's emphasis on the ability of the Arab expansion to change the Mediterranean economy permanently. McCormick's critics focused on his externalization bias. By placing the "blame" for the Carolingian slave trade on soaring demand in the Caliphate, McCormick reduced the moral responsibility of European slave traders to a minimum.[67] Alice Rio recently downplayed the Franks' involvement in the Mediterranean slave trade but still admitted that the Franks and *Francia* as a transit zone may well have profited from the slave trade in indirect ways (e.g. through taxation or the provision of eunuchs).[68]

The evidence from the Merovingian *leges* recapitulated here suggests that very little had changed on the ground between the fifth and eighth centuries.

Hundreds of thousands of people were uprooted and sold into slavery around the Mediterranean and north of the Alps. While the transition from antique slavery to medieval serfdom has been debated time and again,[69] there is no way of denying that throughout the Early Middle Ages genuine slaves, that is, persons born unfree, were treated and traded like goods rather than human beings. It is also worth mentioning that early medieval *servi* often changed their masters together with the land they ploughed, leaving questions of legal status to the study of polyptychs and *urbaria* rather than to the study of legislative texts.[70] Nevertheless, the Merovingian *leges* are full of references to slavery and the slave trade, and the fact that most *leges* contain such slave legislation[71] demonstrates that slaves constituted a significant part of early medieval populations.

Legislators' continued efforts to ban kidnapping and human trafficking suggest that the natural reproduction of the slave population alone was insufficient to meet the demand of unfree labor at home and abroad.[72] Recent works on ancient slavery controversially discuss the extent to which natural reproduction, warfare, exposure of infants and child abduction contributed to the Roman slave supply that needed an annual influx of up to 300,000 men and women a year.[73] Since large-scale slave trade was far from over by the seventh century, one may assume a similar variety of sources for the continuous supply of slaves during the Merovingian period. The recurrent prohibition of sales into extraterritorial regions bears witness to the permanent threat posed by human trafficking within the Merovingian kingdoms. The sale of a slave *trans mare* in *Lex Salica* 39.2 is just one special case that would not make sense in the land-locked territories of Austrasia, where we find sales *extra solum* or *provinciam* instead. The pragmatic motives for each law were certainly rooted in contemporary and often regional affairs, but legislators and compilers evidently engaged with the heritage of the Roman imperial law preserved in the *Codex Theodosianus*, the Visigothic *Breviary*, and the Burgundian *Lex Romana*. On the one hand, the Merovingian *leges* reflect imminent military threats, such as the one posed by Samo's kingdom, as well as underlying causes, such as the Mediterranean slave trade. On the other hand, legal concepts like the inalienability of freedom for the free and property rights of slave owners remain indebted to Roman *plagium*, as attested by the rubric of *Lex Salica* 39 on kidnapping, *de plagiatoribus*. The history of the two laws discussed in this article shows how confidently the Merovingians appropriated Roman law and how daunting kidnapping and human trafficking remained for societies around the Mediterranean basin well into the Early Middle Ages.

8

The Fifth Council of Orléans and the Reception of the "Three Chapters Controversy" in Merovingian Gaul[1]

Till Stüber

Letter from Pope Vigilius to Bishop Aurelianus of Arles, AD 550

We have received the letter of Your Fraternity the day before the Ides of July,[2] Anastasius delivered it to us. We give thanks to the divine clemency, as we read that your care for matters of faith and for our opinion fully corresponds with (your) holy duties. Thus, on all days of your life, the Word of God complies well with your condign charity, as it is written: "I did choose thee out of all to be a priest, that thou ascend to my altar and bring a great name before me."[3]

Therefore it is necessary that we alleviate your loving efforts with a short report, for the time being, as far as this is possible, taking into account the current circumstances: Be assured in every possible way that we have not admitted anything that was found to be contrary to the rulings of our predecessors or to the holy faith [...] of the four synods, that is Nicaea, Constantinople, Ephesus I and Chalcedon – this is far from what we have done! [...] Your Fraternity, who is known to be Vicar of the Apostolic See on behalf of us, therefore may keep all bishops informed that they should not get misled by anyone, neither by counterfeit documents, feigned words nor by legates (*aut falsis scriptis aut mendacibus verbis aut nuntiis*). [...]

Your Fraternity may also see to it that you cease not to ask our glorious son, King Childebert, zealous for Christendom, who is known to show his full veneration towards the Apostolic See, over which God wants us to preside, that he, as we are confident, devoutly care for the Church of God, which is in many things destitute. Since the Goths, as we heard, have intruded into the city of Rome with their king, he [Childebert I] may deign to write him [Totila], lest he interfere with our church, causing detriment, since he adheres to an alien faith (*quippe velut aliene legis*).⁴ He [Totila] may thus not wage anything, for any reason, causing perturbation to the Catholic Church. For it is proper for a Catholic king like him [Childebert I] to defend with all his strength the faith and the church, where God wanted him to be baptized.⁵

In April 550, Pope Vigilius, at that time resident in Constantinople, sent the legate Anastasius to Arles. This legate, a cleric from the Church of Arles, had arrived in the imperial city the previous year. Returning to his homeland, he carried a papal letter, some lines from which are quoted above. It appears that Anastasius had been sent to the East because Aurelianus, the bishop of Arles and the Apostolic Vicar in Gaul, was concerned about the pope's orthodoxy. In his letter, the pope apparently attempted to allay these concerns by declaring that he did not say anything against the belief of his predecessors or against the rulings of the four ecumenical councils. Nevertheless, the pope's answer was not sufficient, at least in the eyes of some of his contemporaries. In his letter, Vigilius made use of a rhetorical strategy that was popular among late antique clerics, that is, questioning of one's orthodox beliefs was not answered with specific reference to the details of the reproach, but was rather rebuffed by asserting the mutual acceptance of respected theological authorities.⁶ Hence, Vigilius' letter does not provide us with any clear information on the concerns that worried Aurelianus and prompted him to send an envoy from Arles to Constantinople, some 2,000 kilometers away. Only by looking closer at the contemporary context does it become clear that the Gallic embassy must have been concerned with the Three Chapter crisis, a theological controversy initiated by the imperial court of Constantinople, which had spread across the entire Mediterranean by the mid sixth century.

Vigilius had traveled to Constantinople in 546/7, amidst Emperor Justinian's military campaign in Italy. If the account of the *Liber Pontificalis* is to be trusted, he did not leave Rome voluntarily, but was forced to do so by imperial troops.⁷ Having arrived at the capital, the pope became involved in the Christological controversies prevalent in the eastern Mediterranean. In April 548, a year before the Arlesian embassy was sent to the imperial city, Vigilius had given in to Justinian's pressure and publicly condemned the so-called Three Chapters, that is, the writings of three theologians whom many Eastern clerics considered Nestorians.⁸ Since these three theologians were—at least in part—approved by the Council of Chalcedon, numerous clerics in Northern Italy and Africa perceived Vigilius' condemnation of the Three Chapters as an attack on their orthodox faith. Vigilius' stance on the Three Chapters thus proved to be disastrous, leading to a schism that plagued the Latin Church well into the seventh century.⁹

While Vigilius' attitude towards the Three Chapters met manifest opposition throughout the Latin West, the position of the Frankish Church is less clear. The only collective response to the controversy was formulated by the Fifth Council of Orléans of 549, wherein clerics from seventy-one bishoprics of all three Merovingian kingdoms were assembled.¹⁰ Aurelianus' role in convening this council was prominent, as is attested by the fact that his signature appears in second place, after Bishop Sacerdos of Lyon.¹¹ It is possible that Aurelianus had sent Anastasius to Constantinople in preparation for the council, but by the time the bishops assembled on October 28, 549, Anastasius had not yet returned to Gaul.

Apparently, the bishops attached some importance to doctrinal matter, since the conciliar acts begin with a statement relating to the Three Chapters controversy:

> And thus the impious sect once founded by Eutyches, the sacrilegious originator, conscious of his evil, and departing from the living fount of the Catholic faith, as well as whatever was set forward by the similarly venomous and impious Nestorius, both of which sects the Apostolic See condemns, so too we execrate them, their founders and followers and we anathematize and condemn them by the power of this present constitution, preaching the right and apostolic order of faith in the name of Christ.¹²

At first glance, this doctrinal statement neither seems to be clear nor exceedingly spectacular. On the one hand, it does not explicitly mention the Three Chapters, and on the other hand, the condemnation of Eutyches and Nestorius—their names standing for two extreme Christological points of view—was more or less the only point the opponents and the advocates of the Three Chapters could easily agree upon.¹³ However, as the bishops explicitly refer to the Apostolic See, at first glance, one might interpret their verdict as supporting Vigilius and his condemnation of the Three Chapters.¹⁴

That the episcopal ruling of Orléans should rather be understood as a stand *against* the condemnation of the Three Chapters has been convincingly demonstrated by Ian Wood, who relied on a contemporary letter by Nicetius, the metropolitan bishop of Trier, to Emperor Justinian.¹⁵ This letter is of special interest in this context—first, because it mentions the *Nestorii et Euticii* [...] *iam anthematizata* [...] *secta*;¹⁶ and second, because Nicetius was one of the bishops who signed the canons of the Fifth Council of Orléans.¹⁷

We therefore may suppose that Nicetius and the other bishops present at Orléans had a common understanding of the doctrines of both heresiarchs. However, our sources suggest that the Gallic bishops were poorly informed on the contents of the heresies they had anathematized. It seems that they failed to notice that in the Eastern debates the names of Nestorius and Eutyches stood for two radically opposed Christological concepts.[18] It appears that when Nicetius asked Justinian to abstain from the heresies of Nestorius and Eutyches, he assumed that a single person could support both doctrines.[19] In his wordy epistle, Nicetius barely comments on the theology of these heresies, believing that the supporters of Nestorius and Eutyches regarded Christ as *purus homo,* only human.[20] Whereas this view corresponds to what the followers of Nestorius were commonly associated with,[21] it was by no means applicable to either Eutyches or the Monophysites. Leaving aside these theological aspects, it is crucial to note that the bishops at Orléans did not consider their anathema as a confirmation of the official doctrine propagated by the imperial court, but as the exact opposite. Were it different, Nicetius' fervid Philippic would be unintelligible, since he depicts Justinian as a follower of both heresiarchs and attacks him for precisely this reason.[22]

Bearing in mind that the Gallic bishops considered the condemnation of the Three Chapters as a heretical act, it is quite surprising that they referred to the papacy in order to justify their own position, since the incumbent successor of St. Peter had only recently condemned the Three Chapters himself. Given the fact that Anastasius had not yet returned from Constantinople, it is possible that the mention of the Apostolic See reflects a decelerated flow of information from the East to the West.[23] Furthermore, the bishops who convened in Orléans retained the possibility of implicitly invoking the position of former popes—notably Leo the Great—whose orthodoxy concerning this matter was considered orthodox beyond all doubt.[24]

As the issue was regarded as a challenge to the true faith, it is not surprising that it was a highly sensitive matter with the potential to polarize the Frankish episcopate, since the bishops considered themselves as defenders of the true faith and ecclesiastical unity. However, as there are no contemporary sources referring to the Fifth Council of Orléans, the interesting question whether the need to adopt a unanimous position did in fact polarize the episcopate, cannot be answered with certainty. That the conciliar acts themselves do not contain any traces of discussions or dissent among the assembled pontiffs is hardly surprising, as Gallic conciliar pronouncements usually aimed to convey an image of unchallenged episcopal unity. There are, nevertheless, two later sources that mention the council while suggesting that there may have been some degree of dissent among the participants. As will be seen, both sources are unfortunately too problematic to infer further details about that possibility.

The first source is the *Liber Vitae Patrum* by Gregory of Tours. In his *vita* of Gallus of Clermont, Gregory reports that Childebert I had assembled a *magnus episcoporum conventus* at Orléans,[25] to treat the case of Marcus, the local bishop. Marcus had been driven into exile because of allegations left unspecified by Gregory.[26] According to Gregory, the assembled bishops ruled that Marcus be restored to his see, as the accusations brought up against him were judged unfounded (*vacuum*). Curiously, however, the signature of the "host bishop" is nevertheless absent from all of the manuscripts preserving the subscription lists of the Council of Orléans.[27]

Even more problematic is the second source, a passage from the *Life* of Bishop Domitianus of Tongres, one of the participants at Orléans.[28] In their "Histoire des conciles," Hefele and Leclercq quote this *vita*, providing a lively account of the conciliar proceedings.[29] According to the unknown author, the reason for convening the *concilium generale* at Orléans was the *hæresis Ariana,* prevalent in the *Aurelianorum provincia* at that time. The assembly hosted a debate between supporters of the heresy and the orthodox, while the latter eventually managed to convince most of the heretics. The *vita* purports that the few who remained unrelenting were subsequently driven to exile.[30] Given that the conciliar acts attest the presence of Domitianus of Tongres, while they do not, as a matter of course, provide any reference to the "Arian heresy" mentioned in the *vita*, the quoted report may sound like a remote but independent testimonial of events having taken place at the council. However, more recent research has called this interpretation into question. According to the conclusive studies by Philippe George,[31] the *vita* edited by Henschen (abbreviated as "VD 2" by George) depends on an older *Vita Domitiani* (= VD 1), left unpublished by the Bollandists. While the older *vita*—George dates it to the second half of the eleventh century— deals extensively with the struggle against heretics at Orléans, it does not call them "Arians," nor does it give them any other label. Given the dependence of the two *vitae*, the specification *hæresis Ariana* in VD 2 thus appears to be an arbitrary addition by the younger hagiographer. But why, in the first place, did the author of VD 1 link the Council of Orléans to heresy? As the *Gesta pontificum Tungrensium sive Leodicensium* of Heriger of Lobbes († 1007)—the earliest known narrative source on Domitianus—only provide a short reference to the conciliar acts of Orléans without any mention of heretics, George suggests that the hagiographer may have been inspired by another, more recent synod at Orléans.[32] This synod assembled in 1022 had in fact condemned heretics to be burnt at the stake.[33] While the specific traits of the heresy portrayed in VD 1 may well have been modeled after the recent heresy of Orléans, as suggested by George, his assumption that the link between Domitianus and heterodoxy had been deliberately contrived by the older hagiographer seems less plausible to me. Seen against the background of the condemnation of *nefariae sectae* at Orléans in 549, the possibility of an older tradition, a *Vita Domitiani vetustissima*,[34] must, in my opinion, be left open to further consideration.

Leaving aside the question whether the Three Chapters did polarize the Gallo-Frankish episcopate or not—the mentioned sources provide hints that support this possibility—it is clear that the bishops did not have to cope with a solely theological matter. Thus, their decision had also political implications, affecting Frankish-Byzantine relations and diplomacy. After all, the prelates took issue with the official dogmatic position propagated by the imperial court. To my mind, this political dimension of the Three Chapters controversy is reflected in the diplomatic activities of the Merovingian royal courts. One should note that the bishop of Trier's attack against Justinian was written by an influential metropolitan in the Austrasian kingdom of Theudebald, who was still a minor and under the influence of powerful magnates and ecclesiastics.[35] For example, during his reign, Nicetius had convened under the auspices of the minor king an episcopal council at the city of Toul to deal with incest charges that were brought against Frankish magnates.[36] Moreover, the fact that diplomatic letters of the Austrasian court survive in a collection of letters also containing the letters of Nicetius,[37] suggests that the harsh words directed at Justinian were not merely the literary outpourings of an odd maverick,[38] and they were well in line with the official diplomatic stance adopted by the Austrasian court. Given that at the beginning of the 550s the Gothic war in Italy was far from decided, this correlation also had a political significance. In fact, Nicetius' adamant anti-Byzantine position is confirmed by Procopius' statements on the Austrasian-Ostrogothic alliance.[39] Here, Procopius not only criticizes Theudebert's (d. 547/8) engagement with the Byzantines, but he also puts forward similar accusations against Theudebald. He mentions an agreement between Theudebert and Totila, demanding that the monarchs mutually guarantee their respective territories in Italy. Procopius also reports on a disappointed Byzantine embassy to Theudebald's court in 548/9, which left empty-handed. Given that Theudebert's son and successor, Theudebald, had only recently been appointed king, Justinian apparently hoped to convince the teenage king to abandon the Italian policies his father had so successfully pursued.[40] If Procopius is to be trusted, the Byzantine envoy even asked the Merovingian to hand over some territories, which had been illegitimately (οὐδὲν αὐτῷ προσῆκον) annexed by

Theudebert, to the Roman Empire. Furthermore, Theudebald was asked to lend military support to the Byzantines against the Ostrogoths (ὁμαιχμία).⁴¹

The diplomatic huff caused by Theudebald's brusque refusal can also be gleaned from a letter sent by the Austrasian king to Justinian. Its composition should be understood in the context of the embassy mentioned by Procopius.⁴² In his letter, Theudebald complains that Justinian's envoys said "many things opprobrious" against his deceased father, and defends himself by stating that he, Theudebert, had never behaved unfaithfully towards the emperors or the kings.⁴³ Seen against this background, Theudebald's assertions that he remained interested in "inviolable treaties" and *amicitiae* with Byzantium seem to be placatory remarks that did not smooth over the fact that both correspondents entertained contradictory political interests.⁴⁴

It is important to note that when compared with the maneuvers of the Austrasian court, the foreign policy of Childebert of Paris appears to have been much more conciliatory towards Byzantium.⁴⁵ This may have been due to the fact that Childebert I did not want the Austrasians to become overly powerful. Although Childebert did not actively participate in the Gothic war, his refusal to ally with Totila betrays a rather hostile attitude towards the Ostrogothic ruler.⁴⁶ Furthermore, Pope Vigilius' letters to the bishop of Arles show that the Byzantines hoped to take advantage of their hitherto successful ecclesiastical cooperation with Childebert for military purposes. From the early fifth century onwards, the so-called Apostolic Vicariate of Arles tied southern Gaul to the papacy.⁴⁷ In the days of Vigilius, when the pope was detained in imperial custody, Constantinople discovered the political potential of this institution. Since the pontificate of Caesarius of Arles (502–542), the popes had bestowed on their vicars the pallium, an honorary *insignium* originally worn by Roman magistrates.⁴⁸ At first the popes appear to have bestowed the pallium of their own accord, however, after Justinian's troops had entered Italy the situation changed dramatically.⁴⁹ On 18 October, 543, Vigilius informed Bishop Auxanius (542/3–546), Caesarius' successor, that he would only be able to concede the pallium after receiving the emperor's authorization. This was followed by two years of negotiations between Rome and Constantinople which involved King Childebert.⁵⁰ Auxanius died shortly after the successful conclusion of these negotiations, and so the procedure was repeated when Aurelianus (546–551/3) requested the pallium. In his confirmation letter to Aurelianus, the pope explicitly noted that bequeathing the pallium accords with the wishes of King Childebert, who had negotiated with the imperial couple in order to get their permission. Vigilius also urged Aurelianus to ensure that the *gratiae initae federa* between Childebert and

Justinian should be preserved.[51] It is reasonable to assume that these negotiations took such a long time because Justinian wanted to make sure that Childebert was ready to support the Byzantines in one way or another. In this regard, it seems significant that the letter to Aurelianus left the papal chancery alongside another letter, addressed to all the bishops in Childebert's realm ("*universis episcopis, qui sub regno gloriosissimi filii nostri, Childeberti regis, sunt per Gallias constituti*").[52] The main purpose of this letter was to emphasize the authority and superiority of Vigilius and his local representative, the bishop of Arles, over all the bishops of Childebert's realm.

By the same token, in Vigilius' letter quoted at the outset of this paper, political and ecclesiastical issues were not treated separately. On the one hand, Vigilius tried to bolster his own orthodoxy, asserting as we have seen, that he would adhere to the writings of his predecessors and to the four ecumenical Synods. Furthermore, he would condemn those who called "the faith of Saint Cyril[53] [...] impious."[54] Notwithstanding this unambiguous side swipe at the Nestorians, Vigilius tellingly refrained from mentioning the Three Chapters explicitly. Neither did he comment on his own *Iudicatum,* by which he had publicly condemned the Three Chapters two years before. Nevertheless, Vigilius' position clearly implies that at the time some of the Merovingian bishops had already adopted contradictory views regarding the pope's orthodoxy. Vigilius used this opportunity to urge Aurelianus to take his duties as a papal vicar seriously. The bishop was thus instructed to convince his Gallic colleagues of the orthodoxy of the current Roman position. On the other hand, Aurelianus was also prompted to ask Childebert I to threaten the Arian king Totila, as a proper Catholic ruler should do.[55] Hence, it should come as no surprise that Childebert was the addressee of the pope's requests, and not Theudebald.

Seen against this background, it seems to be no accident that at the same time, when Vigilius—via the bishop of Arles—contacted Childebert and his episcopate, there were parallel lines of communication (via Milan) connecting Constantinople and Theudebald's court in Reims. It is noteworthy in this context that a particular manuscript, nowadays in Berlin's *Staatsbibliothek*, the so-called *Codex Remensis* (Phill. 1743), contains a letter that explicitly refers to the letters written by Vigilius to Aurelianus of Arles.[56] However, the issues in this letter are presented in a fundamentally different manner compared to their description in the papal letters. Significantly, the letter from the *Codex Remensis* was not included in any of the letter collections that originated from the bishopric of Arles.[57] The letter was sent by some Milanese clerics to a group of Frankish envoys, informing them about recent developments in Constantinople. As has been suggested in the past, these Frankish envoys may be identified with an official embassy sent to Justinian by the Austrasian king.[58]

The letter itself can be dated to the end of 551.[59] It cautions the envoys about lies and deceptions spread by the Byzantine court. The clerics explicitly mention one Anastasius, who was none other than the Provençal legate we have encountered at the beginning of this paper. Anastasius is said to have been bribed to convince the Gallic bishops to condemn the Three Chapters, which the Milanese clerics considered to be a complete annulment of the "holy Synod of Chalcedon."[60] Serving this purpose, Anastasius, according to the clerics, sent letters in the name of the pope, failing to call a spade a spade, and instead dealing with "many other issues" and stating "that [the most holy Pope] is guarding and preserving the Catholic faith and the respect of the four synods according to the tradition of the fathers."[61] Apparently, the letter that Anastasius brought to the bishop of Arles fits extremely well with this description.[62] Significantly, the author of this letter warned his readers against people like the Milanese clerics, as they were spreading "counterfeit documents and feigned words" asserting that Vigilius had abandoned the true faith.

For their part, the Milanese clerics also wanted to ensure that the Austrasian embassy was informed of the dishonorable conditions under which Vigilius and the other prelates were kept in Constantinople. They gave a detailed account of recent events, and after invoking the Last Judgement, the legates were advised to convince the bishops of Provence to reject any new reports from Constantinople.[63] It is evident that the Milanese clerics tried to entice Theudebald's legates to influence the bishops in Childebert's realm to oppose Justinian's religious policy. In particular, they tried to reach the bishop of Arles, the pope's official mouthpiece in Gaul. Hence, the means of transmitting information had to be selected very carefully. After all, acquiring new information was always precarious, as it could easily be manipulated.[64]

Certainly, it is not a mere coincidence that the Milanese clerics regarded the Austrasian embassy as being trustworthy enough to support their cause, particularly as a direct line of communication ran from Milan to Trier, whose bishop, Nicetius, we have already encountered. It is worthwhile noting that over a longer period of time, Nicetius corresponded with Florianus, abbot of a monastery in the diocese of Milan.[65] In a letter that, according to Bruno Dumézil, should be read in connection with the Milanese letter to the legates discussed earlier, Florianus asks Nicetius to pray for Bishop Datius, who stayed at Constantinople between 539 and 552.[66] Datius is also repeatedly mentioned in the letter of the Milanese clergy. Again, the background for this letter seems to be the Three Chapter crisis, as suggested by the fact that Ennodius of Pavia, godfather of Florianus, is given the epithet *Nestoriae* [sic!] *fulmen, Euticis extinctor*.[67]

*

To sum up, our sources are too scanty to support the assumption that there were dogmatic undercurrents in the Merovingian kingdoms that were related to their respective diplomatic activities with regard to Byzantium. However, the sources suggest that theological and church-related knowledge was more likely to be transmitted if it aligned with the political aims of the respective rulers. Furthermore, it appears that in addition to the ecclesiastical initiatives taken by Childebert of Paris, the Austrasian court was equally interested in dogmatic issues that were fervently debated at the time across the Mediterranean. That the bishops at Orléans nevertheless managed to articulate a unified response, which was hostile to the stance of the Imperial court, demonstrates that they felt a very strong urge to express dogmatic unity. That they did so despite conflicting political interests of the Merovingian kings,[68] implies that the corporate power of the Merovingian episcopate was still considerable in the sixth century. Considering that the Fifth Council of Orléans remained for over sixty years the last episcopal assembly that gathered bishops from all over the Frankish realms,[69] one may wonder whether this period of ecclesiastical particularism was not, at least partly, the result of various royal interests.[70] While collaboration with the episcopate was certainly a prerequisite for a successful kingship, the Merovingian monarchs were rather careful not to initiate or support episcopal gatherings that exceeded the boundaries of their own kingdoms.[71]

9

Reconciling Disturbed Sacred Space: The Ordo for "Reconciling an Altar Where a Murder Has Been Committed" in the *Sacramentary of Gellone* in Its Cultural Context

Rob Meens

Reconciliation of an altar at which a murder has been committed
To God, the forgiver of crimes, to God, the cleanser of impurity, to God who has purified the world, hardened through sins from the beginning, through the splendor of his coming, we humbly pray, dear brothers, that he may assist us as a powerful fighter with the guiles of the raging devil in order that if his poisoned cunning has made something in us soiled and corrupted through his daily persecutions, what has become polluted through the devil's fraud will become purified through celestial compassion because as it is his to shatter what is whole and perfect, so it belongs to our creator to restore what has lapsed and to make steadfast what is unstable. Through our lord [...]

God whose goodness does not have a beginning nor an end,[1] who, filled with piety, chooses to restore in us what has gone lost rather than to slay what will perish and who, if negligence will have polluted something, or anger perpetrated something wrong, or drunkenness troubled something, or if lust perverted something, through grace preserves so that you would rather purify through grace than strike it by fury and who, the prudent creator of your work, chooses rather to erect what is lying low[2] than to punish that which should be damned; we beseech you with prayers that, appeased, you will benevolently accept the shelter of your tabernacle and that through the infusion of celestial grace you will cleanse your altar that was polluted through the fraud of the enemy who cuts to pieces, and that you will possess it in a purified state. May in the future all spiritual vileness be absent, may the envy of the ancient serpent be eliminated and extinguished and may the throngs of the devil with their frauds be driven away. Let him take away with him the stain that he brought about, let him be condemned to perennial punishments and gather with him the seeds of his works so that these may perish. Let no guilt of the elapsed contagion from now on do any harm, let nothing remain that is polluted through the fraud of the enemy, when it is cleansed through the infusion of your spirit. Let the pure simplicity of your church and the brightness of innocence that has been defiled, after receiving grace return to its glory. And may the crowd of the people that congregate here experience that their prayers when being presented, will be fulfilled. Through [our Lord . . .].[3]

This chapter will depart from two prayers. These prayers were said in order to restore the purity of an altar after a person had been killed there. They were therefore part of a process of restoration and reconciliation responding to a serious crisis in a Christian community caused by violence and bloodshed. This contribution will look at these prayers in their historical context in order to better understand their significance. It will therefore look into the sacramentary in which they are found and into the concepts of holiness attached to altars and churches at the time. It will become clear that these prayers mark a significant change in the development of the sanctity of the church building and the altar in the late Merovingian and early Carolingian period.

The prayers are found in a Mass book written in the late eighth century possibly somewhere in the diocese of Meaux, not very far from Paris. Although this Mass book, now known as the Sacramentary of Gellone, therefore dates from the period after the Carolingians usurped royal power among the Franks, it has been regarded as a work marking the transition from Merovingian to Carolingian ecclesiastical culture, particularly from an art historical point of view.[4] The work is known from a single manuscript, now in Paris, a manuscript famous for its rich illuminations.[5] It comprises prayers and benedictions to be used by a bishop. Since the manuscript demonstrates links with Cambrai, it was probably composed for its bishop, possibly to be identified with Hildoard (790–816), who is known for his liturgical interests. Soon after the sacramentary had been composed, it must have traveled, possibly by the agency of Benedict of Aniane, to Aquitaine, where it was employed in the monastery of Gellone (St. Guilhem le Désert) near Benedict's home monastery in Aniane. From this monastery it received its name, the Gellone sacramentary, although its origins clearly lie, as we have seen, much further north.

The Gellone Sacramentary is the earliest representative of a wider group of sacramentaries, which are now generally known as the eighth-century Gelasian Sacramentaries.[6] The prayers for the rededication of a defiled altar are also found in two other representatives of this group, the Sacramentary of Angoulême and the one from Autun.⁷ This group comprises some fourteen sacramentaries that combine elements from the Gelasian and Gregorian sacramentaries and probably go back to an archetype that may have been conceived at the monastery of Flavigny during the reign of the first king from the Carolingian dynasty, Pippin.⁸ They contain Roman liturgical prayers in combination with Frankish material that liturgists refer to as "Gallican." One of the rites that liturgists regard as Frankish, and therefore Merovingian, is the consecration rite for churches that we find in them.⁹ There is no evidence indicating that in the late antique or early Merovingian period churches were consecrated through a particular liturgical performance. The earliest liturgical evidence for such rites is to be found in the late Merovingian and early Carolingian sacramentaries. Such rites were the result of several tendencies. There is a close connection with the dedication of the altar.

In the early Christian period the first celebration of the eucharist made an altar special and gave it a kind of sacredness. The councils of Agde (506) and Epaone (517) speak of a ritual of anointment with chrism.¹⁰ At the council of Orléans (511) the bishops allowed the consecration of a church that had been used by heretics, in this case Arians, something which the Burgundian bishops assembling in Epaone a little bit later (517) would not permit. It is not clear, however, how such a consecration would look.¹¹ Although we can see some ritual acts which conveyed a specific quality to the altar and the church building, in late antiquity and the early Merovingian period the sanctity of the church found most of its expression in the community of the faithful gathering there. The *ecclesia*, the church, was in the first place a gathering of people, and much less a material thing like a building. Such a view is, for example, propounded in the sermons that Caesarius of Arles preached on the occasion of the dedication of an altar, where he stressed that although the altar was made of stone, and the church made of wood and bricks and they were made holy through an act involving unction and benediction, for God the holiness of the temples of the hearts and bodies of the believers was what mattered most.¹²

The Gellone Sacramentary contains one of the earliest specimens of the rite for the consecration of a church building. This rite is based on an earlier one found in the Old Gelasian Sacramentary. The Old Gelasian Sacramentary, a work blending Roman and Merovingian material, survives in a manuscript written around the middle of the eighth century, and derived its Roman material from a Roman liturgical book composed between 628 and 715.¹³ Its Roman core was enriched with Merovingian liturgical traditions and the prayers and Mass texts for the dedication of a church that are to be found in this work, belong to these Merovingian enrichments. The Old Gelasian Sacramentary thus contains the earliest prayers for the liturgical dedication of a church.[14] Although the prayers refer to the dedication of the basilica, they mostly focus on the consecration of the altar, thus demonstrating its importance. Moreover, it is only in the context of the consecration of the altar that something of a ritual is described: the altar should be touched in its four corners with a mixture of water and wine and should be sprinkled seven times. The rest of the liquid should then be poured at the base of the altar. Incense should be offered to give it a most sweet smell. In addition, the sacramentary provides prayers for the consecration of three objects closely associated with the altar: the paten, the chalice, and the chrismal.[15]

In the Sacramentary of Gellone, and in two closely related sacramentaries, the Sacramentary of Angoulême and the Sacramentary of Autun, the core found in the Old Gelasian Sacramentary was developed further. The Gellone added formulas that exorcized alien, unholy and polluting substances from the building and beseeched the Lord to send a holy angel to protect all the visitors of the place. It thus stressed the purity of the church space and the need to keep it free from any form of pollution.[16] The Angoulême Sacramentary includes a detailed description of the ritual that is to be followed by the priests and clerics involved in the process. The ritual stresses the importance of the relics that are to be included in the altar, and thus has a similar focus on the altar as the Old Gelasian. It also describes how the priests and clerics should go through the whole church building making the sign of the cross with chrism.[17] The Sacramentary of Autun can be seen as a culmination of these trends, resulting in an elaborate description of the dedication ritual, involving exorcisms, a circuit of the church, a sprinkling of the wall and the pavement, thus stressing the building itself and the space. To emphasize the space even more, an alphabet had to be written on the pavement of the church.[18]

From the evidence provided in these liturgical books, one can conclude that from around the middle of the eighth century in Francia evidence survives of a ritual for the consecration of a church. The core of the ritual is found in the Old Gelasian Sacramentary and then was taken further in a number of eighth-century Gelasian Sacramentaries. In these rituals the altar remained the focus of church dedication, but increasingly the building itself was subjected to a process of sacralization. We can observe that the focus moves from a stress on the community of believers, as we have seen it in the sermons of Caesarius of Arles, to the building itself. Attention is being paid to the altar, the most important liturgical utensils, and to the walls and pavement of the building. This sacralization of space was accompanied by a growing emphasis on the purity of the building. The church needed to be exorcized before dedication and had to be guarded from impure contagions. This increasing attention being paid to the concept of the church as a sacred building has recently been analyzed in interesting detail by Miriam Czock. From her analysis of liturgical sources, conciliar legislation, and penitential books, she was able to establish that it was only in the eighth century that the idea of the church building as a sacred place became entrenched in Gaul.[19] Czock discerns three major developments contributing to this idea of the church as a holy place. First there is the close relationship between the altar and relics. The practice of placing relics in altars led to a growing reverence for the altar. Then there is the late Roman practice of sanctuary that was adopted in Merovingian secular and ecclesiastical legislation. The legislation demarcated the church building and surrounding areas as a space in which a refugee was not to be harmed and thus a space was defined which had to remain free of violence and shedding of blood. Thirdly, we can observe an attempt to keep the church apart from people and things that were regarded as unclean. Particularly in penitential literature that was introduced in Francia from insular sources and found an eager reception there, we encounter many rules intended to keep the church building free from pollution, thus demonstrating in effect a certain reverence for the building as such.

These three developments came together in the eighth century, resulting not only in the emergence of a ritual for church dedication as we find it in the Gellone Sacramentary, but also in the creation of the ritual that we started with: the ritual for the reconciliation of an altar where a murder had been committed. In the following I will briefly sketch these three developments, in order to better understand the ritual in the Gellone Sacramentary.

First, there is the question of relics and altars. The Fifth Council of Carthage (401) required that altars in the countryside that contained no relics of martyrs had to be destroyed, thus establishing a close connection between relics and altars.[20] It was only at the second council of Nicaea (787) that it was decreed that every altar should house a relic, but in the fifth and sixth centuries a close connection between altars and relics was generally established. Such a connection is also evident in Merovingian Gaul. Gregory of Tours, for example, takes great care to provide relics for an oratorium that his predecessor Eufronius had used as storeroom and that Gregory then consecrated in honor of Martin and several other saints.[21] The custom to build a church over graves of martyrs and saints, again a case exemplified in Tours, where the basilica built on top of the grave of St. Martin grew into a major religious site in the Merovingian kingdom, added another layer to the connection between the altar and relics.

The sanctity of the church was further enhanced by legal developments. The sacred bodies resting in churches not only attracted people seeking healing from diseases or protection against misfortunes, but they also attracted men and women escaping the persecuting power of the emperor, the king or their representatives. In the early fifth century the Roman emperors had issued legislation recognizing the practice of people seeking asylum in church buildings, and these rules had been incorporated into the *Codex Theodosianus*, a text that circulated in Merovingian Gaul.[22] In 511 the Merovingian king Clovis called for a general council to be held in Orléans. This council ruled that murderers, adulterers and thieves seeking refuge in a church, its surrounding courtyard or the house of the priest, were not to be harmed. Clovis' successor, Chlothar I, corroborated the decisions reached at the council. That these legal provisions were an answer to existing practices is demonstrated by the work of Gregory of Tours, who mentions many men in dire straits seeking safety in a church, and in particular described the difficult situations in which he could find himself when people had sought refuge in the basilica of St. Martin in Tours.[23] The right of sanctuary, which was at least partly inspired by a concern to protect the purity of the church building, could paradoxically also lead to a defilement of a church. In some cases, the fact that someone sought refuge in a church led to serious confrontations and sometimes even bloodshed in a church.[24]

Merovingian bishops, apparently, did not worry a lot about the purity of the church building. Apart from the topic of church asylum, they issued no rules concerning the purity of the church space. We do find such rules, however, in penitential literature that was introduced into Merovingian Francia from the end of the sixth century. Particularly the penitentials attributed to Theodore, the seventh-century archbishop of Canterbury, abound with rules prohibiting entrance to a church to people that were for some reason or another considered to be impure. Theodore ruled, for example, that someone who had killed another person on the order of his lord, should stay away from church for 40 days.[25] It seems therefore that shedding blood, even without any form of personal responsibility, was irreconcilable with entering a church. Sex, or perhaps semen, was also regarded as problematic in regard to visiting a church as the following rules suggest. Newlywed persons had to stay away from church for 30 days, probably because of the association of a wedding and sexual intercourse.[26] A man should wash before entering a church after having had sex with his wife.[27] A cleric who slept in church and had an involuntary seminal emission there had to do penance for three days.[28] Women were also regarded as impure when they menstruated or had given birth. Theodore ruled that menstruating women—lay women and nuns—should not enter a church or take part in Holy Communion.[29] Women entering a church after having given birth but before they were purified from blood, a period lasting for forty days according to Theodore, should do penance for three weeks.[30] The issue of entering a church in a state of impurity caused by sex, menstruation or childbirth, had already been a topic of concern in the earliest days of the English Church, as is evident from the responses of Gregory the Great to queries from Augustine of Canterbury, gathered in the so-called *Libellus Responsionum*.[31] Theodore's penitential rulings were well-known in later Merovingian Francia. In the first half of the eighth century they were added to the Merovingian canon law collection, known as the *Collectio Vetus Gallica*, when monks from the monastery of Corbie reworked this systematic canon law collection that had originated in Lyon somewhere around the year 600.[32]

The Old Gelasian Sacramentary is now preserved in the Vatican, but part of the original manuscript has been separated and is now kept in Paris. Quite a few eighth-century Gelasian sacramentaries are combined with penitential books. This is also true for the Old Gelasian Sacramentary. The Paris section of the codex contains an early Frankish penitential that derives most of its material from the penitential of Columbanus, the Irish *peregrinus*, who arrived in Gaul around 590 and who not only founded a number of monasteries but also introduced Irish penitential books. In the penitential that was originally connected to the manuscript of the Old Gelasian Sacramentary and is known as the *Paenitentiale Parisiense simplex*, there is an intriguing sentence prohibiting to have sex in a church.[33] This is quite unusual for early penitential books, but there is a parallel in the ninth-century *Paenitentiale Vindobonense C*, in a series of sentences that is probably deriving from an early insular text.[34] Particularly noticeable is the lifelong penance that is being prescribed, indicating the seriousness of the offense.

The three factors just mentioned, the close relationship between relics, altars and churches, the importance of the legally defined right of asylum and the penitential regulations safeguarding the purity of the church, all seem to have contributed to the development of a liturgical ritual for the consecration of a church and that for the re-consecration of a church that had been defiled by bloodshed, that we have seen emerging in the Old Gelasian Sacramentary and its early, eighth-century successors. The eighth-century Gelasian Sacramentaries demonstrate other signs of being influenced by conceptions of the pure and the impure as we encounter them in insular and early Frankish penitential literature. The Gellone Sacramentary, for example, contains a prayer for those who have eaten carrion, the consumption of which was prohibited in penitential literature because of its impurity.³⁵ The prayer for someone who was being vexed by a demon, uses exactly the same words to describe such a person as Theodore's penitential.³⁶ The Gellone Sacramentary contains an exorcism prayer for a well which has been contaminated by negligence. Contamination of a well is a theme that is regularly discussed in penitential literature.³⁷

If we look at the ritual in the Gellone Sacramentary, we can detect the concern for purity. The two prayers abound with terms related to forms of uncleanness, such as *sordes, maculatus, corruptus* and *pollutus*. On the other hand we encounter many terms related to purification: *mundare, purificare, purgare, restituere*.³⁸ The first prayer is less concerned with the altar or the church building and focuses on the state of mind of the believers, while the second talks explicitly about the altar and the place where it is housed (*tabernaculi receptaculum*). At the end the second prayer mentions the pure simplicity of the church that needs to be restored, which might be deliberately ambiguous in that it can refer to the community of believers as well as to the church building.

Although the rubric clearly states that the ritual is meant for being used when an altar had been defiled by murder, such an act is not explicitly addressed in the prayers. Several kinds of sins are mentioned that might have contributed to the defilement of the altar, such as anger, drunkenness and lust. That such sins can lead to violence seems evident in these cases, but the prayer also refers to negligence in this context, which is harder to link with violence. Possibly this is related to another way in which an altar can be polluted, i.e. through the neglectful handling of the host. Again, this is a topic that receives ample attention in penitential literature. The seventh-century Irish penitential of Cummean, for example, contains a long chapter dealing with such cases. It discusses the case when mice eat from the eucharist, when worms are found in it, when the eucharist loses its taste and color because it was not properly stored. It also discusses negligent ways of handling the host by the priest in cases where the eucharist is dropped, when it can no longer be found, when wine is spilled from the chalice and other forms of negligent behavior. Particular concern is also expressed when someone after consuming the eucharist has to vomit, thus exposing the eucharist to even more serious forms of defilement, such as being lapped up by dogs.³⁹ In the context of the connection between the sacramentary and conceptions of purity that we find in penitential books, it seems that the ritual as we find it in the Gellone Sacramentary may also have been meant to be used in other circumstances when an altar had been defiled. The formulations of the prayers are certainly general enough to be usefully employed on other occasions, for apart from the title it received the prayers contain no specific references to murder or bloodshed.

The non-specificity of the prayers may have had other advantages as well. They do not address explicitly the actual deeds that caused the defilement of the altar and by implication the church building, but only speak about the root causes of the infraction in rather general terms: the vices of negligence, anger, drinking and lust, as well as the ruses of the devil. Such non-specificity, perhaps, functioned as a means of avoiding having to address specific acts and thus existing conflicts and persons. We can assume that violence taking place in a church upset the local community. Murdering someone in church probably caused great social upheaval, fueling forms of local discord and division, that might lead to vengeance and feud. The prayers seem to evade to tackle such existing problems in the community head-on and instead stress the community of the faithful in their pure simplicity and innocent splendor. By emphasizing the deeper causes of a specific act of violence, the prayers were able to shun explicitly addressing conflicting issues and to stress the restored innocence of the community. How exactly the rifts within a community were healed remains unclear, but the prayers suggest that the liturgy of purification was the outcome of a process of negotiation, sealing a conclusion, so to speak, rather than being an essential part of the negotiations themselves. The liturgy probably functioned primarily as a way of demonstrating the restored unity of the Christian community, and at such a moment it could be inconvenient to address specific issues and thus persons. If someone was killed in a church this was a breach of the right of sanctuary, and in such cases the priest or bishop was probably involved in the protection of the refugee and the process of mediation in order to settle the issue at hand.[40] As the person presiding over the liturgy of purification, it was the bishop, or perhaps on a local level the priest, who was a central figure in the ritual demonstratively proclaiming the reconciliation.

We have seen how a ritual of purification for a defiled altar survives in two sacramentaries composed at the end of the eighth century. The ritual probably had a local Frankish origin and may go back to the late Merovingian period. The concepts of the church as a sacred space certainly does. The right of sanctuary and the custom of building churches on top of holy graves are moreover unquestionably major components of the Merovingian world, as is violence near an altar. Historiographical texts demonstrate that already before the late eighth century, people were being killed in churches. Although concepts of the church as a holy place may have been less pronounced before the first half of the eighth century—when, as we have seen, insular notions strengthened existing Merovingian tendencies—spilling blood within a church was seen as a serious offense. The work of Gregory of Tours, although mentioning quite a few cases of bloodshed in churches, does not provide any evidence for a liturgical rite of reconciliation for a church or an altar that had been defiled in such a way. Gregory's work does demonstrate, however, that breaches of the right of sanctuary were not taken lightly, and conciliar legislation suggests the same.[41] This raises the question of how people dealt with such problems before the period for which we have evidence for the existence of such rites.

We have seen that the Old Gelasian Sacramentary contains the earliest evidence for the existence of a ritual for the dedication of a church, and that in an earlier period the first Mass being sung over an altar constituted an act of consecration. In the case of blood being shed at an altar, the first liturgical celebration after such an event must also have had special significance. It would have functioned as a kind of reestablishment and reinforcement of pre-existing relations within the community, although in fact these relations might, of course, have changed because of what had happened. The liturgical celebrant, the local priest or bishop, presiding over such a celebration must somehow have appeased the community and restored the proper order, thereby at least symbolically healing existing rifts within the community. The first liturgical celebration after the defilement of a church, therefore, can be seen as a parallel to the first Mass through which an altar, and to a certain extent the church building, were normally "consecrated," if one can use this word in this context. The sources speak mostly of dedication. We do not know how this went about in practice although the anointing of an altar with chrism seems to have been an important aspect of it. One can imagine that a similar ritual was used when a church had been polluted by bloodshed, but any evidence supporting such a proposition is lacking. Once a more formal form of church dedication had developed, the need for a ritual of rededicating a church after it had been violated was apparently felt quite quickly. The ordo for the rededication of a defiled altar that we find in the Gellone Sacramentary should be seen as the response to this need.

10

Imitation and Rejection of Eastern Practices in Merovingian Gaul: Gregory of Tours and Vulfilaic the Stylite of Trier

Tamar Rotman

Gregory of Tours, *Histories* VIII.15

"[...] I [Vulfilaic] also set up a column on which I remained standing barefooted while suffering great torments. When winter came, as it usually does, the weather was so cold that I was frostbitten, its severe frost caused my toenails to fall off, and the rain that fell on my beard froze and hung down from it like melted candle-wax." It is said that this region frequently bears harsh winters.

As we were engaging in conversation, I [Gregory] interrogated him about what he had eaten and drunk and how he had destroyed the idols on that mountain. He answered: "For food and drink I had little bread and vegetables with some water. Many people from neighboring villages began to flock to me and I constantly warned them that Diana and her idol are powerless, that the cult they seem to have practiced in their honor is worthless and that the songs they had sung while they were drunk were unworthy as well. Instead, they should better have been giving a glorious sacrifice to God almighty, the creator of heaven and earth. [...]"[1]

Introduction

In one of his many expeditions around Gaul, the famous sixth-century bishop, Gregory of Tours, arrived at Carignan and met there a certain Vulfilaic who was at the time a deacon and a member of a monastery nearby. Gregory was curious to hear about Vulfilaic's biography: how had a Lombard like him arrived in Gaul? how and when was he converted to Christianity? and how did he become a member of the Gallic clergy? Vulfilaic hesitated and refused to answer Gregory's queries. But after some persuasion, including a promise to never reveal what he would tell Gregory, Vulfilaic was willing to give an account of his life, which Gregory later recorded in the eighth book of the *Histories*, regardless of the promise he made to Vulfilaic.[2]

According to that account, Vulfilaic had shown an interest in Christianity and its saints already as a child, and one saint interested him in particular—Martin of Tours. Although he did not know exactly who Martin was or what good deeds he had done, Vulfilaic worshipped him nonetheless.[3] In his youth, Vulfilaic became a disciple of abbot Aredius of Limoges, who encouraged him to pay a visit to the shrine of Saint Martin in Tours. Vulfilaic took his advice, traveled to Tours, and then decided to stay in Gaul and settle in Trier. Not long after, he discovered that the local inhabitants in that area were worshiping an idol of the Roman goddess Diana. He immediately climbed upon a pillar, and imitating Simeon the Stylite, he sat on top of the pillar. Vulfilaic remained there barefooted. When winter came, he told Gregory, it was so cold that his toenails fell off and the rain that fell on his beard was frozen.[4]

During his time on the pillar, Vulfilaic preached to the people passing by in an attempt to convince them to destroy the idol of Diana. Gradually, he gathered some followers who eventually were convinced to demolish the statue. Excited by his success, Vulfilaic climbed down from the pillar and went to a nearby church in order to pray and ask for God's assistance. He then joined his followers and together they destroyed the idol. Vulfilaic returned to his house and there he discovered that his body was severely injured. He returned to the church, anointed himself with an oil he once brought from the shrine of Saint Martin, and, miraculously, he was cured overnight.[5] Vulfilaic understood this miracle as an omen that he should return to his pillar, but it was not that easy. As soon as he moved towards the pillar, several bishops approached him, telling him that he should not do this because "It is not right what you are trying to do. Such an obscure person as you cannot be compared with Simeon of Antioch, who sat on a column."[6] They urged him to climb down from his column, saying that it would be better for him to join "the brethren whom you have gathered around you."[7] Vulfilaic accepted their request without an argument. He explained to Gregory that he had to listen to the bishops because it is considered a sin to disobey them. Shortly afterwards, Vulfilaic's column was demolished (just like Diana's idol was), and even though it saddened Vulfilaic, he never tried to sit upon another pillar again. He explained that such an action would be considered as an act of disobedience to the bishops and, hence, a sin.[8]

The encounter between Gregory and Vulfilaic did not receive much attention in modern scholarship, even though it is a unique story that gives us a rare glimpse of the ways in which eastern stories and religious practices had reached Gaul and were received there. In the late 1970s Hubert Collin discussed the episode of Vulfilaic in a study on the origins of the cults of Diana and Vulfilaic in Gaul.⁹ Collin, however, used Gregory's account in the *Histories* as a hagiographical record that gives essential biographical information about Vulfilaic, while ignoring the broader context of the story and its role within the *Histories*. Collin did not question Vulfilaic's interactions with the local clergy, he did not examine the phenomenon of "stylitism" (that is, the practice of being a stylite) in Gaul, and he did not wonder why Gregory had chosen to include such a story in his *Histories*. In the early 1980s Walter Goffart mentioned Vulfilaic in his article on foreigners in the *Histories* of Gregory of Tours. But Goffart, so it seems, was only interested in the Lombard origins of Vulfilaic, and he did not question his short career as a stylite and the various implications of the story.¹⁰

A decade later, Yitzhak Hen mentioned this incident in a broader discussion of the survival of paganism in Merovingian Gaul.¹¹ Hen described Vulfilaic as a "disturbed person" who caused such a commotion that the local inhabitants of the region had to ask their bishops to interfere and convince Vulfilaic to step down of his column. The destruction of the pillar, according to Hen, occurred because the people of Trier were "horrified by the possibility that Vulfilaic might return to his column."¹² This analysis of the incident is not completely accurate and it simplifies a far more complicated affair. Indeed, the possibility that Vulfilaic would return to his old stylite ways horrified some people. Yet, they were not the simple inhabitants of Trier as Hen suggested. Instead, as I intend to argue here, they were the Gallic bishops who felt that their episcopal authority was in danger because of Vulfilaic's acts. Similarly, Conrad Leyser suggested the reaction of the bishops to Vulfilaic's attempt to become a stylite was a result of their fear for their authority.¹³ Vulfilaic, however, was not Leyser's main interest and he used his story in order to bring forth the broader issue of Christian cultures in Merovingian Gaul. I wish to discuss the story of Vulfilaic from a different angle and to examine it as a reflection of Merovingian attitudes towards the Byzantine East.

As noted earlier, the bishops reasoned their request by comparing Vulfilaic to Simeon Stylites. Therefore, it is necessary to look into the role of Simeon Stylites in the story and to survey the possible ways in which his fame and cult had reached Gaul. Moreover, comparing the religious, social, and political role of Simeon Stylites and his fellow holy men in the eastern parts of the post-Roman world with the role of the Merovingian clergy (and more precisely, that of the episcopacy) may explain the vehement rejection of Vulfilaic's attempt to become a stylite.

Simeon Stylites in Merovingian Gaul

Simeon Stylites lived in Syria during the fifth century. He is considered to be one of the first Christian stylites, and no doubt he is the most famous of them all. He was highly regarded by the local communities that surrounded him already in his lifetime, and he was venerated as a saint after his death. His popularity spread far and wide, and his fame had even reached Gaul.[14] Gregory of Tours recorded an account of Simeon in his *Glory of the Confessors*, where he relates that after Simeon was converted to Christianity he climbed upon a column and stayed there. No woman was allowed to visit or look at him, not even his own mother,[15] and even after his death women were still forbidden to approach his pillar or to enter his church. This prohibition did not stop one woman from disguising herself in a man's clothes, thinking that she could deceive the saint, trick God and enter the church. The moment she stepped into the church she fell down and was struck dead.[16]

Gregory's account in the *Glory of the Confessors* refers to an incident that took place in the Byzantine East, and hence it does not reflect Gallic attitudes towards Simeon Stylites. Furthermore, there is no evidence of an active cult in honor of Simeon in sixth-century Gaul, when Gregory wrote his books. As far as we can tell, no church was dedicated to him throughout Gaul, nor were his relics circulating around the Merovingian kingdoms.[17] Nevertheless, it appears from Gregory's accounts in the *Histories* and in the *Glory of the Confessors* that Simeon was well known in Gaul and his important role as a holy man was perfectly understood and acknowledged.

The account of Simeon Stylites in the *Glory of the Confessors* accords with other accounts of Syrian and other eastern saints and martyrs that Gregory included in his second miracle collection, the book of the *Glory of the Martyrs*.[18] Like Simeon Stylites, most of these non-Gallic saints were not venerated in Gaul.[19] Whereas their inclusion in Gregory's hagiographical collections may seem quite unusual, it nevertheless indicates that during Late Antiquity and the Early Middle Ages, stories, relics, and sometimes cults and religious practices from the East circulated around the post-Roman Christian West. Throughout his historiographical and hagiographical writings, Gregory reveals the different ways in which these practices had reached the West: merchants, pilgrims, ecclesiastical and secular envoys and immigrants were all plausible agents of cults of saints and religious practices. Thus, even though the foreign saints mentioned by Gregory in his works were not necessarily worshipped and venerated in Gaul, the fact that he mentioned them in the first place indicates that they were known and their holy power was acknowledged by people in the West.[20]

The spread of Simeon's sacred reputation and influence in Gaul is also apparent in Gregory's account of Vulfilaic. It is mentioned explicitly in the bishops' argument against Vulfilaic's attempt to become a stylite and in the way Gregory characterized Vulfilaic. At the beginning of his account Gregory tries to create some resemblance between Vulfilaic and Simeon Stylites that relies on their choice to become stylites. As the quotation at the beginning of this paper indicates, after Vulfilaic described the reasons that led him to climb upon the pillar, Gregory asked him specific questions about his life on the column: he wondered what Vulfilaic ate and drank and how he managed to convince people to follow him and destroy the pagan idol with him. In return, Vulfilaic described the little food and water he had, and then gave a lengthy description of his followers and the destruction of the statue of Diana.

Writing about Vulfilaic in this manner enabled Gregory to depict him as a zealous ascetic, who, like Simeon, gathered people around him and gained power and authority. Gregory was able to create such a comparison between the Syrian stylite and his Gallic imitator because his audience was already familiar with the story of Simeon Stylites. As will be shown next, the social and religious role of the eastern holy men is the key for our understanding of the Merovingian episcopal response to Vulfilaic.

Indeed, as Gregory's account of Simeon Stylites in the *Glory of the Confessors* and the various accounts in the *Glory of the Martyrs* reveal, the Gallic clergy, who was responsible for the religious conduct of its flock, was willing to retell miraculous and hagiographical stories about eastern saints and martyrs, and sometimes even to import and install relics of non-Gallic saints in local shrines. Yet they were not always thrilled to support or accept local attempts to imitate the deeds of eastern holy men, as the story of Vulfilaic clearly demonstrates. The bishops who approached Vulfilaic showed great respect to Simeon Stylites. From their response to Vulfilaic's actions it appears that they believed Simeon was indeed a holy man, to whom a man like Vulfilaic simply could not be compared. But Vulfilaic's lack of holiness was not the only reason the bishops had rejected his attempts to imitate Simeon Stylites. I would suggest that their disapproval was also a result of their fear that by imitating Simeon Stylites, Vulfilaic might jeopardize their own episcopal authority. Perhaps this is why Vulfilaic explains to Gregory what he had probably heard from the bishops themselves—he had to listen to them because disobeying the bishops is considered to be a sin. By stating that, Vulfilaic acknowledges the episcopal superiority over him, a statement which also emphasizes the strength of the episcopal authority.

The rise and function of the Merovingian holy man

The tension between Vulfilaic and the bishops should be examined against the broader background of the political, religious and cultural transformations of the post-Roman world. Peter Brown had already discussed the role of the holy men in late antique Syria.[21] According to Brown, holy men like Simeon Stylites were zealous Christians who preferred living their lives as ascetics. Most of them did so in isolation, either in the desert or in enclosed compounds, which secured the little food and water they needed to keep themselves alive. Some of these holy men were more eccentric than others, and the people who lived near them adored their religious perseverance and their unusual lifestyle. Gradually, the holy men attracted pilgrims and followers. In his survey, Brown points out that these holy men were usually outsiders, without any social, political or religious affiliation with the people living nearby. Consequently, they were perfectly suited to serve as mediators and consultants for the communities around them.[22] Indeed, in late antique Syria, when the traditional social and administrative networks of the Roman Empire were slowly disintegrating, these holy men took upon themselves some of the roles of the traditional patrons and subsequently gained important and influential positions.[23] Their influence touched upon religious matters, but, most importantly, they played a crucial role as political and social mediators. In other words, they exercised an immense influence on almost all daily matters.

The disintegration of the traditional modes of authority and social stratification affected the entire Roman world, and Gaul was no different. Whereas in the East individual holy men had bridged to some extent the administrative gap by adopting religious and secular functions, in Gaul it was the church and its institutions that took control. The Gallo-Roman elite was quick to realize that the church had a lot to offer in terms of power and control. Hence, descendants of Gallo-Roman senatorial families took over numerous ecclesiastical positions, gaining a new way to preserve their supremacy in both religious and civil spheres. As a result, the Gallic ecclesiastical elite became an exclusive group.[24] In order to become a bishop, for instance, one had to receive the proper education, know the "right people" and have some social relations with other, more influential persons. One also had to have some support from the local community one served. During the sixth century, as the Merovingian kings established their authority and kingship, the bishops were gradually losing theirs.[25] Therefore, they had to secure any remaining control they still had and ensure that their episcopal authority was not compromised.

When Vulfilaic climbed upon the column, preaching to the people passing by, encouraging them to leave their old pagan practices, and convert to Christianity—he challenged the responsibilities of the local clergy. By telling Vulfilaic that he could never truly imitate Simeon, they acknowledged their awareness of the various functions and responsibilities Simeon had over the people who gathered around him. They perfectly realized that although he was not a member of the local clergy, Simeon had preached to the people, encouraging them to improve their Christian ways, and more significantly, had functioned as a mediator in secular matters. In other words, they understood that Simeon's role in Syria was similar to their role in Gaul. This may explain the bishops' uncompromised reaction to Vulfilaic's actions, classifying his disobedience as a sin.

In order to secure their position and their episcopal authority the bishops tried to prevent Vulfilaic from becoming a holy man like Simeon. Their argument against Vulfilaic emphasizes that. First, they made sure that neither he nor anyone else would think that Vulfilaic and Simeon were alike. Whereas Simeon may be venerated as a saint, Vulfilaic must not be seen as a holy figure and therefore should not be venerated as a living saint. Second, they reinforced their authority by bidding Vulfilaic to obey and intimidating him with a religious threat—he must obey the bishops, otherwise he would be considered a sinner that ought to be punished not only by them, but by God himself.

Power and authority: the case of Gregory of Tours

Gregory had very good reasons to include a story that emphasizes the authority of the Gallic bishops. His appointment to the episcopal see was not warmly welcomed by the people and the clergy of Tours, to say the least. He was appointed by King Sigibert I, who did not consult the people or the clergy of Tours beforehand as expected. The reasons for that are complicated and not fully understood, but no doubt that the delicate geo-political circumstances of Tours at that time were part of it. Although ruled by Sigibert, the king of Austrasia, Tours was actually an enclave within the Neustrian kingdom of Chilperic. The bishoprics around Tours were loyal to Chilperic, as was the vast majority of the religious and secular elite of Tours itself. They opted for a bishop who shared their political interests and loyalties; Sigibert, on the other hand, who was thinking on various ways to strengthen his rule in the region, appointed an outsider whom he could trust. Hence, Gregory was chosen.[26] Indeed, Gregory had very little political influence in Tours. Even though he claimed that he was related to all but five of Tours' previous bishops,[27] in reality Gregory's family had more influence in the Auvergne and Lyon rather than in the Touraine.[28] Furthermore, Gregory's ordination took place in the cathedral of Reims instead of Tours.[29] Celebrating the ordination outside Tours was against the fifth canon of the Fourth Synod of Orléans (541), according to which a newly elected bishop must be ordained in his new church or, at least, in the same province he was meant to serve.[30] The irregularity of Gregory's ordination may have given his opponents another way to portray him as an illegitimate bishop, who hardly had any influence in and relation to Tours and who was ordained against the canon rule. All in all, it is not surprising that the local elites of Tours saw Gregory as a foreign intruder and perceived his appointment as an external imposition on their local affairs.[31]

These circumstances led to Gregory's constant need to justify his appointment and secure his position and episcopal authority. One way to do that was through promotion of cults of saints, most notably that of Saint Martin of Tours. Martin was one of the most celebrated saints in Merovingian Gaul and the fact that the center of his cult was set in Tours made him even more important there. Therefore, it was necessary for the bishop of Tours to keep commemorating Martin and promote his cult. Gregory understood that very well, and consequently Martin is mentioned numerous times in the *Histories*. Gregory also dedicated to Martin an entire hagiographical treatise in four books, which is, in fact, the longest hagiographical work he had written.[32] His accounts of Martin and his deeds in both the *Histories* and in the *Vita Martini* glorify the saint and relate the magnificent miracles he had performed, among them some miracles that Gregory himself or one of his relatives had experienced.[33] By doing so, Gregory stressed the fact that he was a protégé of Saint Martin, and hence portrayed himself as a pious man. Most importantly, it proved to Gregory's audience that the most prestigious saint of Tours protected Gregory and accepted his appointment as the new bishop of the town. Thus, by emphasizing the patronage of Martin, Gregory made a heroic attempt to gain support from the inhabitants of Tours.

Gregory, however, did more than that in order to reinforce his episcopal authority. He also used Martin's reputation and popularity in order to promote cults of other saints, who were important to him personally. An excellent case in point is the cult of the martyr Julian of Brioude, Gregory's other patron saint. Gregory dedicated a whole book to Julian. It was not as long as his *Vita Martini*, but it is nevertheless one of Gregory's longest hagiographical works.[34] Gregory relates the martyrdom of Julian and describes the miracles that he had performed, including some miracles that Gregory and his relatives had experienced and witnessed.[35] Just like his books on Martin of Tours, here too, writing about miracles enabled Gregory to display his special connection with the saint. Yet, unlike Martin, Julian was not a popular or a well-known saint in Tours, and as far as we can tell there was no cult in his honor there. Hence Gregory had to establish Julian's cult in Tours, connecting Martin and Julian through relics.

According to Gregory, on his way back from Reims to Tours after his ordination, he stopped at Clermont, paid a visit at the shrine of Julian, from where he picked up some relics of Julian that were later installed in the altar of Saint Martin's basilica in Tours.[36] After the deposition of these relics a possessed man began shouting:

> "Martin! Why have you joined yourself to Julian? Why did you invite him to this place? Your presence was enough of a torment for us; now you have invited someone like yourself to increase the torture! Why do you do this? Why do you and Julian persecute us so?"[37]

Gregory uses the possessed man in order to stress the holiness of the saints. This is, of course, a common hagiographical *topos* that was used by Gregory and by many hagiographers throughout the Middle Ages.[38] The possessed man does not only emphasize Julian's holy power, he also emphasizes Martin's acceptance of Julian. The statement of the possessed man serves Gregory to portray himself as a good and zealous bishop, who increases the divine protection over Tours by bringing the relics of Julian and establishing his cult in the town. Moreover, by accepting Julian, Martin also accepts the person who brought him to Tours, that is, Gregory himself. The message to the people of Tours is clear—if their most important and most beloved saint is willing to accept Gregory as the bishop of Tours, they must accept him as well.

Gregory had exploited Martin's popularity for his own needs in another, perhaps less obvious, way. I would suggest that Gregory's account about Vulfilaic should be read with the cult of Saint Martin in mind. Already at the beginning of this account, Gregory mentions that Vulfilaic had built a church in which he installed relics of Saint Martin.[39] By doing so Gregory creates the first association between Martin and Vulfilaic. He furthers his own conversation with Vulfilaic as a Martinian narrative. Vulfilaic tells Gregory that as a little child he had heard about Martin of Tours and subsequently began to worship him, even though he knew very little about the saint.[40] The conversation ends with several miracle stories performed by Martin of Tours that Vulfilaic relates to Gregory.[41]

Gregory, however, does more than weaving Martin's presence into Vulfilaic's biography. He also compares Vulfilaic to Martin. Like Martin, Vulfilaic was also a foreigner, and like Martin he was inspired by a Gallic priest—in Martin's case it was Hilary of Poitiers and in Vulfilaic's it was Aredius of Limoges.[42] Moreover, both adopted an ascetic way of life. But whereas Martin's asceticism and foreign origins won him his popularity and fame throughout Gaul already in his lifetime, in Vulfilaic's case they were the very reasons because of which the Gallic bishops asked him to step off his column.

The similarities between Vulfilaic and Martin were meant to portray Vulfilaic in a positive way and show that even though he had upset the clergy, he was still a righteous man, whose words should be taken seriously. In other words, Martin gave Vulfilaic credibility, and that was essential to the message Gregory wanted to convey through the story of Vulfilaic. For Gregory, the most important part of the story is Vulfilaic's acknowledgment of episcopal authority and the realization that disobeying the bishops is a sin. Vulfilaic was forgiven for his behavior, but the entire incident was a clear warning to anyone who defies the bishops.

Whereas in *Histories* and his hagiographies Gregory explains why he deserves to be the bishop of Tours, the story of Vulfilaic clarifies that no one should undermine Gregory's authority as a bishop. Whoever defies Gregory and refuses to follow his orders would be considered a sinner and therefore will be punished—just like Vulfilaic would have been considered a sinner if he had insisted on being a stylite. It seems, then, that the Vulfilaic affair was Gregory's way to discuss episcopal authority, to emphasize its importance and to secure his own episcopal position.

Conclusion

I should like to end this discussion with what may be an even more intriguing lesson to be gained from the story of Vulfilaic. Gregory includes various accounts of the East in both his historiographical and hagiographical works; some of these accounts discuss political events,[43] others report on religious matters, such as miracles that were performed by eastern saints, which, more often than not, took place in the East. All of these accounts demonstrate Gregory's familiarity with the Byzantine past and with some current political developments. The account of Vulfilaic, on the other hand, reveals something else that is more relevant to the "here" and "now" of Gregory's life, rather than the Byzantine, or even the Merovingian, past. Nevertheless, the story of this "strange" man, who decided one day to climb upon a pillar and preach to the people passing by, clarifies more than anything else that not only ideas and stories from the Byzantine East were circulating around the Merovingian Kingdoms, but also that Merovingian authors and clergymen, like Gregory of Tours himself, had some understanding of contemporary Byzantine culture and religious practices. The Gallic bishops were worried because Vulfilaic, with his eccentric behavior, represented the political, religious and social function of holy men in the eastern Mediterranean, such as Simeon Stylites. Gregory used that knowledge for his own purposes and in order to strengthen his own authority as the bishop of Tours.

To sum up, the story of Vulfilaic exemplifies the multifaceted relations between the West and the East. Reading it against a broader cultural, religious and somewhat personal context helps us to reach a better understanding of Merovingian culture and society, as well as its religious practices and perceptions. Furthermore, it also exhibits Gregory's unique anecdotal and complex style of writing. Reading the story with Gregory's personal history in mind, reveals that he molded the account of Vulfilaic the Stylite for his own needs. This clarifies once again that any anecdote in Gregory's writings is there for a reason (sometimes, a personal one), and it is for us to find out what Gregory intended to convey with each and every one of these accounts.

Part Four

Shifting Perspectives: Emperors, Tributes and Propaganda

11

Magnus et Verus Christianus: The Portrayal of Emperor Tiberius II in Gregory of Tours[1]

Pia Lucas

Passages from Gregory of Tours, *Histories*[2]

IV.40

After emperor Justinian had died in the city of Constantinople, Justin came to the reign, a man devoted in all things to avarice, a despiser of the poor, a despoiler of the senators, who was so full of greed that he ordered chests of iron to be made, in which he heaped up pounds of minted gold. It is also said that he lapsed into the Pelagian heresy. For after a short time, he was driven out of his mind and chose Tiberius as Caesar to defend his provinces, a just man, generous in almsgiving, balanced in judgment, winning victories, and, what supersedes all other good qualities, a most true Christian. [...]

V.19

[...] And as he [Caesar Tiberius] spent much of the treasure that Justin had heaped up on the poor, the empress [Sophia] scolded him frequently that he would bring the state to poverty, saying: "What I have collected in many years, you scatter about in a short time." To this he used to respond: "Our treasury will not lack anything, as long as the poor receive alms, and the captives are ransomed. For this is indeed the great treasure, as the Lord says: 'Collect your treasure in heaven, where neither rust nor moths doth corrupt, and where thieves do not dig it out nor steal it.' [Mt. 6:20] Therefore, let us collect for the poor in heaven from what God has given [us], so that the Lord thinks us worthy of being increased in this world." And because he was, as we said, a great and true Christian, as long as he cheerfully distributed alms to the poor, the Lord gave him ever more and more. [...]

V.30

While these things were happening in Gaul, Justin, after completing the eighteenth year[3] of his reign, ended his life in the insanity which he had contracted. After he was buried, Tiberius seized power, which he had in fact embraced long ago. But when the people expected that he would proceed to the circus according to local custom, and they were planning to lay a trap for him on behalf of Justinian [whom they wanted to replace him], who was understood to be Justin's nephew, he [Tiberius] proceeded to the holy places instead. When he had finished his prayers, he summoned the pope of the city, and entered the palace with the consuls and the prefects. Then, clothed in purple, crowned with a diadem and sitting on the imperial throne, he was confirmed to the reign among great acclaim. When the conspirators, who were hiding at the circus, learned what had happened, they were confused by shame and went away without having achieved any result. They could not harm the man who had put his hope in God. [...]

VI.30

In this year emperor Tiberius left this world, leaving his people in great sadness about his passing. He was most benevolent, inclined to almsgiving, just in judgement, cautious in judging; he despised no one, but embraced everyone in his good will. Loving everyone, he was himself loved by all. [...]

The Eastern Roman emperor Tiberius (574/8–582) cuts a fine figure in the *Histories* of the bishop of Tours. Not only is he the main protagonist in several extensive passages, longer than any references to other non-Merovingian rulers, he also surpasses all other mentioned sovereigns in terms of merit and character. The famous Justinian (527–565) is only accorded a few short entries, wherein he is rarely named explicitly, and all mentions are either neutral in tone or slightly negative. One austere sentence records his death.[4] Tiberius' successor Maurice (582–602) is granted a little more space by Gregory, but in contrast to Tiberius, there are barely any entries that reveal much about his qualities or the character of his rule.[5] Tiberius' predecessor Justin II (565–578) is depicted in a very negative manner and seems to be molded as a direct antithesis to Tiberius himself.[6]

In order to analyze and understand why Gregory of Tours painted such a bright picture of Tiberius, it is necessary to place his assessment in a broader context. To what extent was Gregory's judgment related to sources that were available to him? What could and did he know about the East? How does the bishop's perspective on the relationship between the Empire and the Merovingian kingdoms figure into the equation? And what function does this Eastern Roman emperor fulfill in the grand narrative of the *Histories*?

Objects, people and stories on the move—channels of communication

The ongoing long-distance trade between sixth-century Gaul and the Mediterranean had been pointed out by Pirenne,[7] and confirmed with some modifications by numerous subsequent historians, most notably Michael McCormick.[8] It is also attested in Gregory's own works. Not only does he refer to Syrian merchants in Gaul several times, he also mentions products from the Eastern regions in passing as a matter of course. He expected readers to be aware of the outstanding quality of wine from Gaza, he compares the complexion of an ill man to Saffron, or instinctively points to papyrus as the obvious writing material, and Marseille as the port where it would be imported.[9] Further evidence for "things that traveled"[10] from the East to Gaul comes from the relic collection at Sens, where the relic labels, referring back to acquisitions from the sixth century in their earliest layer, show a large proportion of relics from the Holy Land as well as the Byzantine East.[11] Gregory himself sent his own deacons around the world, and they came back with relics and the narratives accompanying them.[12] He met relic merchants, pilgrims and clerics from faraway lands who told him stories, not only about religious subjects, but also about political events. Bishop Simon of Armenia probably informed him about the Persian attack on Apamea and Antioch, as well as about the earthquake that destroyed the latter.[13] Gregory also tells us about embassies to Visigothic Spain and the Byzantine court, and although he only mentions his conversations with envoys from Spain explicitly, there is no reason to believe that he did not have the opportunity to meet Byzantine envoys or members of the returning Frankish embassies, as well.[14] The bishop of Tours himself was quite involved in political affairs, and served as an envoy in the service of King Childebert II to his uncle Guntram's court in Burgundy.[15] Hence, there was no lack of opportunities for the transfer of information through oral channels.[16]

It is noteworthy that Gregory is considered by Byzantinists as a well-informed author on at least some Eastern matters.[17] His description of events concerning the imperial court, such as the role of the Hippodrome in the investiture of new emperors (which Tiberius deliberately eschews), demonstrates enough knowledge of Byzantine customs and practices to make his account plausible.[18]

Averil Cameron even contemplates a common written source which Gregory and two Eastern contemporaries, Evagrius Scholasticus (d. c. 594) and John of Ephesus (d. c. 588), may have used, since the works of all three contain close parallels.[19] Foremost among these are the characterizations of the emperors Justin II and Tiberius. Justin's greed for money, that he often attained unjustly, and his avarice, are an excellent case in point. The same is true of Tiberius' reputation as a generous, just and merciful ruler.[20] Whatever this potential common source might have been, it raises the question of language, as Gregory did not know Greek or Syrian. He did, however, use an Eastern written source as a model in another case, the *Legend of the Seven Sleepers of Ephesus*. As he informs us, he retold their story in Latin with the help of a Syrian named John, suggesting that translators from Greek and Syriac were available in the West.[21]

Although it cannot be proven that such a common written source existed, we seem to be dealing with information and stories that were circulating widely among contemporaries in the East. It is also feasible that such tales had already found a more or less fixed form in oral communication. Whichever is correct, the existence of a certain tradition does not explain why Gregory chose to follow this depiction of the emperors. In order to gain a better understanding of the reasons for the author's selection and way of representation, it is helpful to take a closer look at Gregory's position regarding the *imperium*.

Dealings with the Empire in the *Histories*

What does Gregory tell his readers, and where do his interests lie in the portrayal of the Empire? Throughout his work, religious subjects—miracles, saints and holy places—dominate the narrative. In the *Histories*, most of the information Gregory provides is painted with a Christian tint. The few emperors of the past mentioned by name in the first book all appear in a Christian context, mostly in relation to the persecutions of the early church.[22] The role of Christian emperors in promoting the Christian faith was marginalized, and even in the case of Constantine, his pro-Christian policy was outshone by Helena's finding of the Cross. Similarly, Theodosius' efforts to establish orthodoxy are not brought up at all, Gregory merely stated that he put all his hope in God.[23] Moreover, current political affairs and events in the East are also referred to in a religious guise. For example, the report on the already mentioned earthquake in Antioch echoes the destruction of Sodom, and the beginning of the Persian war is associated with the Christian revolt in Armenia, ignoring the fact that Justin had refused to pay the Persians the tribute agreed upon.[24]

On the other hand, we find almost nothing in Gregory's text on the religious disputes in the East. He briefly alludes to the Monophysite heresy in fifth-century Constantinople, but he breathes not a word about the Three Chapters controversy.[25] Similarly, the assessment of Tiberius and Justin II has nothing to do with their religious policies. Tiberius is called "a most true Christian" (*virissimum christianum*) based on his personal qualities, and Justin is simply a heretic without reference to any actions or policies.[26] This latter assertion is strange and not mentioned in other sources. It might be implicitly connected to political decisions, after all. As Averil Cameron has shown long ago, Justin intentionally pursued an ambiguous religious policy, trying (unsuccessfully) to reconcile the orthodox, Chalcedonian bishops and the Monophysites.[27] Gregory's comment could reflect a garbled account of Justin's attempts at reconciliation with the Monophysites that had reached Gaul. But we will look further for Gregory's reasons to include Justin II's alleged heretical tendencies in the next section. Just as religious policies were left out, so were other Byzantine political maneuvers or relations with its neighbors. Gregory only records a single victory against the Persians, which, quite tellingly, took place during Tiberius' reign.[28] The Avars are not mentioned at all in the Byzantine context.

When the Empire of Gregory's own days comes into focus, it is generally with regard to its involvement in the West, mostly concerning either the Franks or the Visigoths. Already in the days of Justinian, the Empire's aim had been to keep a foothold in Spain, and to enlist Frankish help in Italy against the Ostrogoths. After 568, the foe to be expelled from Italy was the Lombards. Still, the attempts to obtain support from the Franks continued, despite the lessons the Empire might have learned from king Theudebert's self-serving intervention which resulted in significant, albeit only temporary, gains for the Franks.[29] After these were lost under his son Theudebald, the Franks were reluctant to get properly involved in Italy despite sporadic Lombard incursions into Gaul itself.

Although some scholars have stated that the Franks showed a certain reverence towards the emperors, or even that they accepted some sort of preeminence of the Empire, there is no indication in Gregory's writing that he or his contemporaries in Gaul perceived Byzantium as a superior political power or as protector of the Christian faith.[30] It is clear that there was a certain cultural appeal in the Byzantine East and in the traditions of the Roman Empire, as can be gleaned from the minting of pseudo-imperial coinage, or from the conscious *imitatio imperii* in the self-depiction of Merovingian rulers, who mostly abided by the formal conventions of diplomatic exchange, even if they pursued independent policies.[31] However, from the *Histories*, we get the impression of equality. Although Gregory still calls the Eastern empire "res publica" without geographical demarcations,[32] this must not be taken to imply any supremacy over, or legitimate claims to, the Western *regna*. When referring to Theudebert, Gregory never suggests that the appropriated lands in Italy should have belonged to the Empire.[33] Instead, he uses the Italian campaigns to enhance Theudebert's fame and glory as a king. In his narrative, all victories fall under his reign, and all losses belong to that of his disagreeable son Theudebald.[34] Gregory's emphasis on the good fortune of Theudebert's duke Buccelenus, and his wistful comment after Theudebald's losses that no one was ever able to win these lands back, does not point to a sympathetic attitude towards the Empire's interests.[35] Instead, immediately before this episode, when writing about the Visigoths and the former imperial possessions in Spain, Gregory even proclaims that the empire had "wickedly occupied" the cities there.[36] In Gregory's mind, there is no imperial prerogative over the West.

It is true that there is no deprecating depiction of the Byzantines in general,[37] but we cannot really speak of an image of "the Byzantines" as a coherent group in Gregory's works. Particularly the positive portrait of Tiberius should not be confused with a general positive image of the Empire as a whole, as a quick look at his depiction of the other emperors reveals.[38]

Another remarkable fact is that Gregory, despite his preoccupation with the fight against Arianism, never emphasizes the common orthodoxy of the Empire and the Franks, in a world where all other *gentes* were considered Arians. This common ground had been pointed out by Pope Pelagius II, as well as in the diplomatic exchange with the Empire; but Gregory did not draw attention to it.[39] This is particularly conspicuous if one regards the arrival of a relic of the True Cross in Gaul. A part of the True Cross resided in Constantinople since early in Justin's reign.[40] Although a piece of this relic was sent to Gaul by the imperial couple, Sophia and Justin, they are not implied in its transfer at all. In Gregory's text, all honor goes to the former queen Radegund. Gregory does not even make clear whether the relic was brought to her convent from Jerusalem or Constantinople.[41] It is inconceivable that the bishop of Tours did not know. He was close to the court of King Sigibert, to whom Radegund appealed for support before requesting the relic,[42] he knew Radegund herself and subsequently held her funeral,[43] and their mutual close friend Venantius Fortunatus wrote a poem in thanks to the imperial couple (569), praising their orthodoxy and their generosity.[44] Furthermore, Gregory's own predecessor, Eufronius of Tours, received the relic and deposited it with all honors in Poitiers.[45] Despite these facts, Gregory evidently had no interest in depicting Justin as a champion of the faith.

This relic gift has recently been connected to an embassy from King Sigibert to Justin,[46] which aimed at a formal peace around 568.[47] This embassy has usually been dated to 571, but the scholar who put this date forward for the first time, Ernst Stein, never intended this to be more than a suggestion, as it cannot be accurately confirmed by the sources.[48] The most prestigious relic of the cross would hardly have been handed over to Sigibert's stepmother, with the king's intervention on Radegund's behalf, before peace had been achieved. According to Cameron, the gift was made early in Justin's reign, in context of his affirmation of orthodoxy after Justinian's escapades, and she dates the relic request to 568, and the poem by Venantius Fortunatus to the year 569.[49] Dating the embassy to this period instead of to 571 seems particularly plausible as Justin II did have a fresh reason to acquire a Frankish ally in 568, after the Lombards invaded Italy in the spring of the very same year.

Over the next thirty years, the emperors tried to find ways to induce the Franks to engage in the Italian campaigns, with little success. We know that Tiberius, who served as Caesar under Justin from 574, received several appeals for help against the Lombards from Rome, but, bound to the Eastern front, he could no longer afford to send men to Italy, especially after a disastrous campaign in 575. Instead, he gave financial help and suggested to coax Lombard dukes to switch sides or to get the Franks to intervene.[50] Against this background, scholars have seen Tiberius' (or his successor Maurice's) hand behind two upheavals in the West around 580, that is, the revolt of the Visigothic prince Hermenegild against his father,[51] and the so-called Gundovald affair, the details and aims of which are still debated.[52] Hermenegild enlisted the help of imperial troops in Spain against his father, King Leovigild, and Gundovald, who claimed to be another son of King Chlothar I, came to Gaul from the court of Constantinople, where he had spent a large part of his adult life. This much is clear from Gregory's narrative.[53] Other than that, his report barely implies Byzantine involvement. But, as far as the Gundovald affair is concerned, scholars have recognized Byzantine funding in the treasure that the pretender brought with him, and they have pointed out the Byzantine interest in a candidate that would support their cause in Italy.[54] It is interesting that Gregory does not bring up Tiberius' name explicitly in the telling of these events, and the larger part of the narrative unfolds without a specific reference to Byzantine involvement.[55] Some historians assume that it was not Tiberius, but Maurice who had provided imperial support,[56] but a careful reconstruction of the chronology makes this highly unlikely.[57] The reports on Hermenegild are restrained in a similar way. In Gregory's text, the initiative for the alliance with Byzantium seems to come from the prince. The emphasis lies on the imperial governor or the generals with whom the pact was made, not on Tiberius himself.[58] Therefore, in spite of the long passages on Tiberius, the reader is left with the impression that he was quite uninvolved in actual politics.

Christian rulers, heretics and sinners

Portrayed in this way, almost completely detached from political affairs, Tiberius remains monodimensional, a veritable "cardboard-character."[59] Showing Tiberius as abandoning an orthodox prince for his Arian father, or as contributing to the horrible civil wars in Gaul that Gregory vehemently condemned, would have destroyed the image of the *magnus et verus Christianus*. His co-emperor Justin II was portrayed as a dark counterpart. Wherever Tiberius is just and generous, Justin makes unjust gains and greedily keeps all to himself. He cannot protect his provinces due to his madness, whereas Tiberius is successful in war, and, most strikingly, Justin is a heretic, whereas Tiberius is a "true Christian." In this respect, it is worthwhile recalling that none of the Eastern sources mention Justin's heresy.[60] In Gregory's text, his lapse into Pelagianism is soon followed by madness, and he uses this type of sequentiality frequently to express divine punishment, so that one could describe this storytelling principle as "narrative justice." This pattern, which was popular among Christian authors such as Eusebius and Orosius, can also be found in Evagrius and John of Ephesus, although they give other reasons for the emperor's insanity. Whereas Evagrius connects it to the emperor's failures in the Persian war, John presents it as God's punishment for the persecution of Monophysites.[61] Gregory's choice of causality is also connected to the strange silence on the True Cross. After all, mentioning that it was a gift given by a heretical madman would have blemished the acquisition of this most venerable of relics. More importantly, reporting this pious act would have run against what Gregory intended with his presentation of Justin. In the *Histories*, both Tiberius and Justin are just vignettes, but they serve an important function. Justin not only offers a negative foil for Tiberius, he also shares many traits with a Merovingian king with whom the bishop of Tours had a strained relationship, that is, Chilperic I.[62] In his vicious obituary, Gregory accuses Chilperic of unjustly accumulating wealth and of despising the poor.[63] As we shall see, Gregory also attributes heretical tendencies to him. In this regard,

Justin's divine punishment, already described in book IV, serves as a disguised prolepsis for the sake of the reader—the similarly depicted Merovingian king would also meet his deserved punishment in Gregory's narrative.[64]

Gregory's attitude towards Chilperic has been discussed extensively in modern scholarship. Some believe that Gregory portrayed this king more positively in the passages shortly before narrating his death,[65] but although he is not everywhere painted as black as in the obituary itself, his list of bad deeds is long. He killed his first wife because of his love to Fredegund, the most hateful character in the *Histories*;[66] he wickedly pursued bishops, such as Praetextatus of Rouen, whom Gregory tried to defend, he even physically tortured clerics on one occasion.[67] His armies left devastation everywhere, and the only time he tried to stop them, he failed.[68] Several times he violated the sanctuary of the church, something that did not even happen in the times of pagans or heretics, as Gregory tells his readers.[69] The poor suffered under his extraordinary taxation, and his daughter's bridal procession, in which he violently forced people to participate, led only to grief.[70] According to Gregory, his good deeds are few and far between. The first and only time he is reported to have given alms to the poor is when he understood his last remaining sons' deaths as divine vengeance for his own greed and injustice, and when another son was born, he was so relieved that he freed prisoners and remitted all debts.[71] Soon thereafter, his good behavior lapsed again.[72] It seems as if books V and VI of the *Histories* were written to come to a head with Chilperic's horrible death, because several visions anticipate the king's death.[73] The juxtaposition of Tiberius and Chilperic is a rhetorical device,[74] in which justice and generosity towards the poor are the most obvious reference points. Gregory uses the most explicit language in his obituaries. Tiberius' death was lamented by all people, for "loving everyone, he was loved by all," but Chilperic died deserted by everyone, because "he truly loved no one, and he was loved by none."[75] Further, the Merovingian king is depicted as consciously emulating acts which may have been considered imperial prerogatives—a form of *imitatio imperii*[76]—but, as Gregory insists, he failed in them all. He tried to be a cultural leader, to change the written language by introducing Greek(!) letters, and to write his own poems, but Gregory describes these efforts as unlearned and awkward.[77] He attempted to take a leading role in church affairs, but had no understanding of theology and unwittingly fell into heresy. Gregory's debate with a tenacious Arian envoy from Visigothic Spain is narrated just before Gregory's own discussion with the king, and the choice of words strengthens the similarity with the obstinate heretic.[78] Furthermore, Chilperic attempted to convert Jews, but in a personal debate, the Jew's arguments left him speechless and Gregory had to step in. When narrating his other attempts of converting Jews, Gregory only focuses on the failures of this endeavor.[79] Chilperic built a circus and proudly made golden plates in honor of the Franks, in a feeble copy of the gold medallions commemorating the "Glory of the Romans" which Tiberius sent him.[80] The connection of Tiberius with gold recalls to the reader earlier scenes in which the emperor's generosity to the poor is applauded. This offers an implicit comparison to Chilperic, who proudly showed the golden objects to Gregory.[81] The Merovingian king merely looks at their shiny surface, as if this was a sign for being a successful ruler in itself. In Gregory's portrayal, Chilperic strives to imitate imperial glory by emulating the wrong actions: all he should have tried to do was act like a "true Christian"—this was what had made Tiberius a successful ruler, not gold and circuses.

Gregory illustrates this Christian ideal through anecdotes. For example, he seems to rearrange a passage from an unknown source that is found in a very similar outline in John of Ephesus,[82] in which Sophia scolds Tiberius for scattering the money she and Justin had amassed. Although praising Tiberius' generosity in other passages, here John complains that Tiberius had squandered money instead of giving it to the poor. Gregory, on the other hand, links this story to the emperor's charity instead. We cannot tell which of the two authors diverged from the common source (be it written or oral), but it is rather obvious that Gregory contextualized Sophia's speech in a way that would fit his aims and objectives concerning Tiberius. He lets the emperor explain to Sophia that there is no point in heaping treasures in this world, and has him quote Mt. 6:20, concluding that one should collect treasure in heaven by giving to the poor on earth. According to Gregory, since Tiberius always followed this principle and gave willingly, God constantly provided him with treasure to spend.

The subject of lust for material gain (*cupiditas*),[83] and its opposite, generosity towards the poor and the church, are recurrent topics in Gregory's narrative. When he deplores the woes of the civil wars in the preface to book V, he also points at their cause—the overflowing royal treasuries and the kings' perpetual lust for more, even for the possessions of others. In an earlier passage on the sufferings caused by war, Gregory asserts that unlike their ancestors, contemporaneous people were stealing even from the churches and did not respect the bishops.[84] Interestingly, Gregory does not only express this causal reasoning in auctorial remarks, but has some of his protagonists repeat these views. The first is Fredegund, who, in a uniquely lucid moment, acknowledges that her sons' illness was a divine punishment. Connecting the lessons of Tiberius' dialog with Sophia and the already mentioned preface to book V, she echoes

Gregory's words about overflowing treasuries, and states that she and Chilperic needed to stop heaping up treasures, not knowing for whom they collected it. As a result of their greed and injustice towards the poor, they would lose their sons.[85] Similarly, King Guntram wrathfully berates his army for plundering, and declares that victory would only be granted if people heeded the actions of their forebears: building instead of plundering churches, and honoring the saints and the clerics.[86] Among these forefathers were, of course, King Clovis, who vehemently forbade his army from plundering church property,[87] and Theudebert, who, like Tiberius, exemplified the qualities of a model Christian ruler, although he was not universally good. Yet he was just, honored the bishops, gave to the churches and helped the poor.[88] To some extent, these were the qualities that Gregory expected of a good Christian in general,[89] but they were particularly fundamental in rulers whose actions could determine the fate of kingdoms and individuals alike.[90] In this regard, how Gregory depicts Tiberius is not only a comment on his negative mirror-image, King Chilperic, but also on other kings in the *Histories*, most notably Guntram. Although some scholars tend to focus on Gregory calling Guntram "bonus rex,"[91] he was "no hero."[92] The bishop of Tours does not conceal his bad sides. Like so many kings, he chose horrible wives and he lost his sons because of his own sins (just like Chilperic). Although he respected the church in general, he sometimes disregarded the right of sanctuary and pursued individual bishops. Particularly after the Gundovald affair, he was generally distrustful.[93] In fact, this list does not read much better than the list of Chilperic's flaws. But this image is counterbalanced by a more positive assessment than Chilperic ever receives in the *Histories*. One could see Gregory's representation of King Guntram as a *peccator*, who is aware of his sins, repents and tries to better himself. Despite several relapses, he is on a learning curve that peaks in the middle of book IX. Although he did persecute bishops who were involved in the Gundovald affair, he stopped these actions when he became ill (which Gregory presents as a punishment from God), and he is generally depicted as respecting the bishops.[94] Gregory further illustrates this point when describing his own dealings with the king. While Chilperic is mostly shown to refuse the advice of the bishop of Tours, his brother is twice depicted in close accord with Gregory.[95] It is worth remembering that Gregory stresses the good relations with the bishops in the case of Tiberius, as well, especially when he shows him accompanied by the patriarch of Constantinople in the crucial act of succession.[96] Chilperic's antagonism towards the bishops, on the other hand, is censored again in his obituary, and reinforced in the visions that both Gregory and Guntram have of the deceased king. In these visions, he is either sketched as a bishop of the Antichrist, or as being condemned to damnation by three bishops of Guntram's *regnum*.[97] The shared visions underscore the common stance of Gregory and the king, and the importance of heeding the bishops.

Unlike Chilperic, Guntram is likened to a priest or a bishop in taking care of his people during the plague.[98] While the crimes of Chilperic's armies are reported without extenuating circumstances, Guntram gets the chance to distance himself from the wrongdoings of his generals and soldiers. His speech shows that he understood how God worked—without promoting the church and honoring the saints and the bishops, there could be no victory.[99] In the same passage, the accused *duces* attribute to King Guntram all the qualities that Gregory considers essential in a good Christian ruler, such as benevolence, fear of God, love for the church, reverence for the bishops, and generosity towards the poor. Guntram shares Tiberius' most preeminent qualities and is frequently shown distributing his treasures to the needy.[100] As Guntram himself realized, in contrast to his brother, the condition for a fortunate reign was to put one's hope and trust in God. This was already true for Theodosius, and this is why, in the narrative of the *Histories*, Guntram wins his wars, just like Tiberius, who gained so much in the only recorded victory over the Persians that "even human greed (*cupiditas*) was satisfied," although he himself never showed cupidity.[101] Chilperic, on the other hand, who lusted for gains in his civil war efforts, never understood God's role, and therefore was doomed to lose.[102] As a result of their trust in God, Guntram and Tiberius merited to win treasures that they could distribute to the poor.[103] Although Guntram was wary of assassination (not without reason) and went everywhere with armed guards, except into the church, it was his trust in holy places that saved him several times.[104] Tiberius, too, escaped several plots against him by putting his trust in God, most importantly at his investiture, when he went to the holy places to pray instead of going to the Hippodrome. In contrast, when under pressure during the civil wars, Chilperic did not go to any holy place, but preferred to imitate the pagan emperors by building a circus. Only one assassination attempt against him is recorded, but nothing saved him from it.[105] But the most important parallel between Tiberius and Guntram are the miracles connected to them. They were granted to just these two Christian rulers in Gregory's text, and enabled them to take even better care of their people. Treasures were revealed to Tiberius so that he would be able to support the poor, whereas a thread of Guntram's cloak was used to cure a child afflicted with the plague.[106] Gregory explicitly tells us that he firmly believes the story of this miracle, since Guntram had held vigils, fasted and had been even more charitable than usual. After this panegyric, we scarcely hear of Guntram, who was still a far from perfect ruler. Gregory never gives a concluding judgment, as he chose to omit his death entirely from his narrative.[107]

It is apparent that the only ruler who is depicted without fault by Gregory of Tours is one who was geographically rather distant. Guntram, on the other hand, is not merely a vignette, but a "real" king with good and bad features. To a lesser extent, this is also true for Chilperic. One could argue that the reason is simply that both Merovingian kings lived in close proximity to Gregory himself, and he had to deal with them on a regular basis, so that he knew more about them than about the Eastern Roman emperors. However, Gregory's knowledge of the Byzantine world aligns with Eastern sources, and the example of the True Cross shows that he had more knowledge at hand than he let his readers know. It was the way he aimed to portray these rulers that determined how he selected and arranged his information, not lack of knowledge. Justin and Tiberius were not judged by Gregory against the achievements of their actual reigns and policies. They were distant enough to warrant only cursory and one-sided portraits in a history centering on Frankish Gaul. Gregory used their image to mold them as a parallel reference point for his representation of their Merovingian counterparts. The image of both Guntram and Chilperic in the *Histories* interact with the positive and negative models of these emperors, and this juxtaposition acts as a comment on the Merovingian rulers' performance. Painting Justin and Tiberius black and white enabled Gregory to lecture his readers on the benefits of true Christian rulership.

12

When Contemporary History Is Caught Up by the Immediate Present: Fredegar's Proleptic Depiction of Emperor Constans II

Stefan Esders

Fredegar, *Chronicon* IV.81

This year the emperor Constantine died. Constans, his son, still of minor age, was raised to the Empire on the decision of the senate. This empire was in his time very heavily devastated by the Saracens. Jerusalem was captured by the Saracens, and the remaining cities were razed. Upper and lower Egypt was invaded by the Saracens; Alexandria was taken and plundered. The whole of Africa was devastated and occupied by the Saracens for a while; and there the patrician Gregory was killed by the Saracens. Only Constantinople with the province of Thrace and a few islands, and also the province of Rome remained under imperial control, for the greatest part of the whole Empire was severely worn down by the Saracens. Finally, also the emperor Constans, constricted and cornered, became a tributary of the Saracens, so that merely Constantinople and a handful of provinces and islands were reserved under his control. For about three years and, as it is reported, even longer, Constans filled the treasury of the Saracens with one thousand gold solidi a day. But eventually, after strength had been recovered, Constans, to some extent regaining the empire, refused to pay the tribute to the Saracens. How this came about and happened I shall report in its proper sequence under the year when it was made good and I shall not cease to write, until, God willing, I finish about these and other matters what is desired, all of which that I know to be true I shall include in this book.[1]

The *Chronicle of Fredegar* is among the first extant narrative accounts on the seventh-century Arab expansion.[2] It is particularly interesting as the author clearly witnessed the breathtaking rapidity of Arab invasions which caused the Roman Empire to fight for its very existence. This had consequences for the structure of his narrative, which presented Frankish history as part of an entangled Mediterranean history, framed according to a chronology of Merovingian rulers.[3] When it reached the early 640s, the author decided to break out of his chronological framework. In some sort of prolepsis, he gave a telescoped account of East Roman history under Emperor Constans II (642-668) that led his readers to experience a number of crucial events that happened in the 650s, among them the first naval attacks of the Saracens which eventually led to the first siege of Constantinople. Moreover, in the following chapter, the author also gave a prospective treatment of Visigothic history from the death of King Chintila (639) to that of King Chindasvinth (653), whose brutal reign concluded with the king's peaceful death and his son Reccesvinth's succession to the throne.[4] Having provided these previews of events in the 650s, the author returns to narrate Frankish history of the early 640s in the following chapter, but his narrative breaks off soon after.

In the Chronicle's fourth book, there are several occasions wherein Fredegar briefly anticipates events that took place later in time,[5] but his deviation from the narrative in the chapters concerning Eastern Rome and Spain appears to be a complex issue.[6] In what follows, an attempt will be made to explain this rupture by taking into account both the author's historiographical agenda and the political events he observed. It appears highly significant that the author decided to break free of his chronological scheme for the first time when narrating East Roman and Visigothic history, that is, "non-Frankish" history. This crucial point reveals much about Fredegar's Mediterranean perspective on seventh-century history, which embraced Frankish history as part of a wider world.

1. Fredegar's narrative sequence of seventh-century East Roman history

Reports on seventh-century Roman imperial history are presented by "Fredegar"[7] as part of two narrative "clusters," both centered around Eastern Rome's wars with its external enemies under the emperors Heraclius and Constans II. Though it seems suggestive that the author followed the same source for his narrative on eastern Mediterranean events,[8] it must be emphasized that he sought to structure these two accounts along different narratological lines.

Fredegar's narrative on the reign of Emperor Heraclius follows a clear design. It starts with Phocas and ends with Heraclius' ignominious death in 641, after the emperor committed incest, gave up the Christian faith, and eventually died of a fever.[9] Fredegar's main rhetorical device in narrating Heraclius' rise and fall is a tale of an astrological prediction received by Heraclius, asserting that his empire would be devastated by a circumcised people.[10] Misguided, the emperor interprets this as a reference to the Jews whom he persecuted, only to realize that the prediction in oracular manner referred to the Saracens, on whose invasions Fredegar reports soon after. Heraclius' blindness prevented him from drawing the right conclusions from the horoscope, as is revealed by his death. In particular, the charges put forward that he became an Eutychian heretic and eventually even apostatized clearly echo the Lateran Synod of 649, in which the religious dogma of Monothelitism, as propagated by Heraclius and Constans, was banned as heretical. There are several versions of the horoscope story, appearing in a number of different eastern sources. Most of these texts were written in Arabic and situate the story in Palestine, which may indeed be the place from which the story had originated. In the aftermath of the death of the patriarch Sophronius, several adherents of Monothelitism were appointed bishops in Palestine, as is reported in some detail by Bishop Stephen of Dora, legate of the apostolic see of Rome at the Lateran Synod.[11] If this supposition is correct, we may assume that Fredegar took over a narrative framework handed over to him in order to give a coherent account of Heraclius' reign. According to Fredegar's narrative, which ends up with the complete disaster caused by the emperor's personal and religious perverse behaviors, parallel developments took place in the reign of the Frankish king Dagobert, who had concluded a major treaty with Heraclius in 629 or shortly thereafter. Given the narrative plot, which clearly presupposes the Lateran synod's decisions on Monothelitism and on Heraclius' *Ecthesis* of 638, by which the emperor had promulgated the new dogma, Fredegar appears to have taken notice of the narrative through networks that connected him with Rome in the 650s, while he seems to have written his own report of Heraclius' and Dagobert's reigns soon after.

Even more striking is the fact that Fredegar's narrative on the reign of Constans II is very different in character from his first report on the Arab expansion under Heraclius. This becomes clear from its narrative structure, which lacks a "story" comparable to that of Heraclius.[12] In this case, the account of Constans largely follows a geographical scheme of Arab expansion, starting with Palestine and Egypt, before moving on to North Africa, which brings things as close as possible to Gaul. Another geographical line draws attention to the fact that only Constantinople, Thrace and a few islands, as well as Rome, remained under imperial control, and the narrator deals in some detail with the huge Byzantine tribute payments to the Arabs, which Constans discontinued after the Roman recovery.

Another major difference concerns religion. In the depiction of how Constans II massively lost ground against the Saracens, there is not the slightest critique of his religious policies. Such an omission appears as striking, as it was precisely Constans II's *typos* of 648, a law forbidding public debate on the issue of Monothelitism that had been condemned by the Lateran synod of 649. Moreover, the emperor's rigorous arrest of Maximus Confessor and Pope Martin I and their condemnation for high treason effectively brought the collapse of Rome's opposition to Monothelitism in 653.[13] This silence is difficult to explain: Did Fredegar think that it would be best to keep silent on this issue, as the crisis of the Roman Empire acquired an existential dimension following the Arab invasions by sea? Was this a delicate topic, given the possibility that the Austrasian and Neustrian courts pursued different policies with regard to the Lateran synod?[14] Or was he writing later than assumed, and therefore was aware of Emperor Constans' plans to move to southern Italy, where he arrived in 662 and took residence until his murder in 668? At any rate, this observation strengthens the impression that the prolepsis was caused by an extraordinary situation, both political and personal, as Fredegar was not sure whether he would be able to finish his works in chronological order.

2. The Arab conquest of Palestine and Egypt

"Jerusalem was captured by the Saracens, and the remaining cities were razed."

Fredegar's report on Heraclius' reign culminates in a description of a major and decisive battle which the Romans lost. Although Fredegar does not mention specific place names and his topographical knowledge of the Near East appears rather limited, it seems clear that he was referring to the battle of Yarmouk, which took place in August 636.[15] This is presented by Fredegar as the turning-point in Heraclius' reign. The chapter on Constans seems to resume this narrative, but its chronology is far from reliable, as the Arab conquest of Jerusalem most likely happened in April 638, whereas Fredegar dates it to the reign of Constans II.[16] Was this simply a mistake or was there any rationale behind Fredegar's incorrect attribution?

It appears that in the chapter on Constans, Fredegar was interested in giving a succinct account of the Arab conquests, from Palestine through Egypt and up to North Africa. Hence, it would make sense to attribute the conquest of Jerusalem to Constans' reign in order to present it as yet another important step in a series of Arab conquests, which took place right after:

"Upper and Lower Egypt was invaded by the Saracens [and] Alexandria was taken and plundered."

It is interesting to note that Fredegar differentiates between the two major Egyptian provinces of Upper and Lower Egypt, which seems to suggest that it must have mattered to his source of information. The conquest of Egypt with the capture of Alexandria is usually dated to 642, although there is evidence that in 645/6 Byzantine forces managed to reconquer Alexandria for a year, before it was lost again to the Arabs.[17] Fredegar does not seem to be concerned with this, nor does he provide any further information on Egypt, on its huge economic importance for Eastern Rome's tax income, or on the religious struggles that took place there on the eve of the conquest.[18] This seems to confirm the impression that Fredegar was only interested in giving a short survey of the Arab conquests, not realizing that their conquest was religiously motivated and was about to bring a religious change to the conquered territories. Nevertheless, some religious bias may have tinted his narrative of the conquest. In particular, one should not underestimate the importance of the conquest of Jerusalem, as it played a role in apocalyptical terms as the beginning of the end of time. Such eschatological dimensions are not very explicit in Fredegar's chronicle, but there are some hints which suggest that Fredegar must have been aware of what was going on.[19] There is also evidence from Visigothic Spain that suggests how the conquest of Jerusalem was perceived in the West.[20] The apocalypse did not take place, of course, but apocalypticism and the eschatology of empire could equally serve as a justification of political measures, since they could serve as an important narrative device to structure a sequence of historical events.[21] It is clear that in his chapter on Constans II, Fredegar articulates some hope of an immediate reconquest as part of a military conflict that had already been interpreted by many seventh-century contemporaries as "final."[22]

3. North Africa and the revolt of the exarch Gregory

"The whole of Africa was devastated and occupied by the Saracens for a while; and there the patrician Gregory was killed by the Saracens."

It is well known that the Arab takeover of Egypt in 642 paved the way for the conquest of Cyrenaica in 645 and then of the Latin provinces of North Africa immediately thereafter.[23] These provinces were of enormous strategic importance for the Roman Empire and also closely connected to the Heraclean dynasty.[24]

Again, Fredegar is silent on this point, but interestingly he mentions the defeat and death of Gregory the exarch (whom he calls *patricius*). But once again the modern reader is bewildered by the fact that half of the story about Gregory is missing.[25] There is no mention of Gregory's usurpation of imperial office,[26] probably in 645, nor any mention that he pursued a religious policy directed against Monothelitism as imperial dogma.[27] As in the case of the battle of Yarmouk, Fredegar is not interested in naming Sufetula (Sbteila in modern Tunisia), where Gregory took residence and suffered his disastrous defeat in 647, which proved to be a turning-point in the history of North Africa.[28]

On the other hand, the expression *paululum* (for a while)[29] matters here, since it seems to suggest that Fredegar knew and felt secure enough to state that the Saracens had withdrawn from Africa and no longer posed a threat at the time when he was writing. This indicates a fairly precise knowledge of African affairs, for it is only Arab sources that tell us that a treaty was concluded after the battle, with a huge tribute to be paid to the Saracens for their withdrawal.[30] Fredegar thus saw the Arab invasion of North Africa as a brief intermezzo, only to state in the next sentence that relatively confined areas of the Empire remained permanently under imperial control. That he did not mention any religious dimension when narrating the North African story may also have to do with the collapse of the anti-Monothelite opposition in Rome in 653, which had been heavily supported by the African Church,[31] and possibly even by some parties in Visigothic Spain.[32] Again, this reading is very different from his account on Heraclius that could only make sense at the time of writing, in the later 650s.

4. The Arab attack on Constantinople

"Only Constantinople with the province of Thrace and a few islands, and also the province of Rome remained under imperial control, for the greatest part of the whole Empire was severely worn down by the Saracens. Finally also the emperor Constans, constricted and cornered, became a tributary of the Saracens, so that merely Constantinople and a handful of provinces and islands were reserved under his control. For about three years and, as it is reported, even longer, Constans filled the treasury of the Saracens with one thousand gold solidi a day. But eventually, after strength had been recovered, Constans, to some extent regaining the empire, refused to pay the tribute to the Saracens."

It deserves to be emphasized that the attack mentioned by Fredegar was indeed the first Arab attack on the East Roman capital undertaken by sea,[33] as the commander Mu'āwiya, who would later become caliph, persuaded the third Caliph 'Uthmān (644-656) to build a fleet for that purpose,[34] apparently using the resources of recently conquered Egypt.[35] In 649, a Saracen fleet plundered Cyprus and deported a huge number of captives,[36] whereas Constantinople had to pay an enormous tribute for their withdrawal—this appears to be the treaty to which Fredegar was referring.[37] In the meantime, the Arabs could use these tributes to build their fleet, while peace with Constantinople allowed them to focus on their efforts to destroy the Persian Empire. In 654 Mu'āwiya turned against Constantinople once more and this time he could beat the Roman navy in a sea battle near the Phoenix Mountains on the Lycian coast.[38] Although most of these events are largely known from Byzantine sources, Fredegar's account seems to be remarkable in four respects: first, he seems to have had a rough idea of the geographical dimensions of Arab control over the sea; second, he may have known that there was an Arab attack on Constantinople, which is otherwise only known from a miraculous anecdote in the Armenian chronicle attributed to Sebeos;[39] third, he did know that Constans was successful in freeing the Empire of the tribute payments after three (or more) years; and finally, he was aware of the fact that Constans was successful, at least "to some extent" (*aliquantisper*), in his attempted *reconquista*. That the peace-treaties concluded between the Arabs and Constans had lasted only three years is also attested by Sebeos,[40] who, being one of the few sources to take a positive stance towards the heretical ruler Constans, reports a disastrous defeat suffered by the Arab fleet near Chalcedon. That was a major turning-point in the history of the Arab-Constantinopolitan affair, since it forced the Arabs forces to withdraw, and allowed Constantinople to recover. It is known that Constans went on an expedition against the Slavs, who settled north of the Danube, immediately after the Arab defeat, as a result of which he transferred them to Anatolia as military settlers.[41] Meanwhile, in 658/659, Mu'āwiya felt it necessary to agree to another treaty, which forced him to pay a tribute to Constantinople; and soon afterwards Constans went on a campaign against Armenia.[42] Fredegar's report on these affairs suggests that he must have had some very detailed source of information, which our extant Eastern sources—notoriously fragmentary and difficult to interpret for the reign of Constans II—did not have. Furthermore, all the non-Arab sources that we have fail to explain another turning-point in this course of events, that is, the murder of the third Caliph 'Uthmān in Medina in 656. This assassination started a fierce faction-fighting for succession between the family of Muhammad's son-in-law, 'Alī ibn Abī Tālib, and the Syria-based Umayyad family, which forced both parties to concentrate on this internal conflict for some time.[43]

"For about three years and, as it is reported, even longer, Constans filled the treasury of the Saracens with one thousand gold solidi a day."

A closer look at the wording of the above cited sentence suggests that Fredegar must have known much more than he reveals in his narrative. We know from the *Chronicle* of the Byzantine historian Theophanes that Constans II indeed launched a counter attack in northern Syria shortly after 656. As a consequence, and due to the inner-Arabic conflicts, Muʿāwiya had to pay tributes to the Roman side. Interestingly enough, according to Theophanes this treaty stipulated as tribute the same payments which Fredegar reports the Romans had been previously paying to the Arabs, that is, 1,000 gold *solidi* a day, along with a horse and a slave.[44] It is Fredegar's *Chronicle* alone that refers to this tribute as part of the treaty of 649/50.[45] This seems to suggest that the numbers presented by Fredegar are realistic, since other sources also refer to a tribute of this size (to be paid by the Saracens) as part of a treaty concluded in 685.[46]

It is noteworthy that according to Fredegar the military conflicts between Romans and Arabs culminated in the payment of huge tributes in gold. What must have struck the Frankish author is the sheer sum of these tributes, which were significantly higher than all other tributes he reports upon,[47] such as the Lombards' tribute to the Franks, which was merely 12,000 *solidi* per year.[48] We may assume that Fredegar was well aware of the hugely debased value of gold coins in Gaul at his time,[49] (which eventually led to the Merovingians abandoning the minting of gold coins shortly after 670),[50] and that there were no gold mines in Gaul. His emphasis on the huge tributes of thousands of gold *solidi* paid by Constantinople to the Arabs is conspicuous, since it did not require detailed economic knowledge to understand what this practically meant—large sums of *solidi* now flew into the *thesaurus Saracenorum*, that is, effectively into the military economy of the Empire's most forceful enemy.

5. Historiographer and observer of a world crisis

To modern readers, Fredegar's originality and appeal as a historian lies in the fact that he sought to narrate the history of the Frankish kingdoms as part of a Mediterranean history, and indeed, a world history. This differs remarkably from and can be read as a counternarrative to his source Gregory of Tours, whose historiographical vision channeled the history of Christianity into the world of Christian Gaul.[51] Fredegar, by contrast, sought to argue against any view of history that saw the Mediterranean world falling apart. As Andreas Fischer has convincingly demonstrated, Fredegar used various narrative techniques to synchronize the histories of the Frankish, the Visigothic kingdoms, and the East Roman Empire. His sequence of chapters on Constans II, on Chindasvind, and on Clovis II becomes coherent through Fredegar's use of analogy. The first aspect to be found in all three chapters is an emphasis on rulers of minor age, leading to some reflections upon the inherent perils of these situations and on the limits of aristocratic power. A second *leitmotiv* that connects the chapters on the emperor and the Frankish and Visigothic kings is financial matters, in particular tributes, treasures and money. These topics, as sagaciously observed by Fredegar, played an important role in the Frankish politics of the 650s and possibly even the 660s, when he was writing his *Chronicle*.[52] In most recent scholarship Fredegar is thus highly appreciated as an author, who, despite his poor command of Latin, appears to have had much more information at hand than his simple sentences seem to suggest, and who used rhetorical techniques, such as analogy and synchronicity, to enhance his narrative and create a high degree of coherence.[53]

The chapter at the center of this paper fits into this picture. Although a prolepsis can also be used as a literary device, as some sort of "cliffhanger story," Fredegar's use of it appears to be different. This becomes clear in the way he personally addresses his readers, anticipating that contrary to his previous announcement, he may not be able to finish the history in the chronological manner in which he had narrated it up to the year 641. The fragmentary style in which his work abruptly ends proves him right. The result is a remarkable leap forward to a crucial moment in world history, written by an author who was distant from these events in geographical terms, but had a keen interest in the Mediterranean implications of the history of his own time. Rare words like *paululum* and *aliquantisper* indicate how sensitively and gradually Fredegar registered the course of events and how carefully he sought to characterize even shorter periods of just a few years as echoing the wavering fortune of historical process. The events detailed in these chapters reveal a unique snapshot in time, written in a situation when it could not be foreseen to which direction these important events would eventually set the course of world history.

13

Byzantium, the Merovingians, and the Hog: A Passage of Theophanes' *Chronicle* Revisited[1]

Federico Montinaro

The Chronicle of Theophanes Confessor

[AM 6216, AD 723/4]

Leo, 8th year
Isam, leader of the Arabs (19 years), 1st year
Germanus, 10th year
John, 19th year

I am now going to tell the story of the blessed Stephen, Pope of Rome, how he fled to the land of the Franks and was saved.

This celebrated man Stephen suffered many ills at the hands of Astulphos, king of the Lombards. He sought refuge among the Franks at the time of Pipin [sic], who was majordomo and chief of the administration of all the affairs of the Frankish nation: for it was their custom that their lord, that is their king, would reign by virtue of heredity, but take no part in the administration and do nothing except eat and drink inordinately. He would live at home and on 1 May would preside over the whole nation to greet them and to receive their greetings and customary gifts and to give them gifts in return, and then would live by himself until the following May. He has a majordomo, as the man is called, who administers all the affairs according to the king's and the nation's wishes. The descendants of that line were called Kristatai, which means "hairy backs": for, like pigs, they had bristles sprouting from their back.

Now, the aforementioned Stephen, compelled by the cruelty and senselessness of Astulphos, obtained the latter's permission to proceed to the Frankish country to do whatever he was able. When he arrived, he performed the investiture of Pipin, a man who was then greatly esteemed and was also administrator of public affairs on the king's behalf; who, furthermore, had fought the Arabs who had crossed from Africa to Spain, the same who have held Spain until now, and attempted to make war even against the Franks. The said Pipin opposed them with his host; he killed the commander of the enemy, Abderachman, as well as a countless multitude of them by the river Eridanos, and drew his nation's admiration and love, not only for this deed, but also on account of his other qualities. He was the first to rule his nation not by virtue of heredity, the said Stephen having absolved him of his oath to the king, tonsured his predecessor and confined him honourably in a comfortable monastery. This Pipin had two sons, the brothers Karoulos and Karoulomagnos.[2]

The above cited passage is taken from the Greek *Chronicle* traditionally attributed to the monk Theophanes the Confessor (d. 817 or 818), a celebrated victim of the iconoclastic persecution under Emperor Leo V. The *Chronicle* covers more than five centuries of Byzantine and Near Eastern history, from Diocletian's accession in 284 down to 813, and is, for the latter part, a source of exceptional value. Together with a group of later West-Syrian chronicles, it belongs to the few texts that preserve bits of the earliest narrative source on the great Arab conquests of the seventh century, and it incorporates several contemporary accounts of middle Byzantine history, among them the author's eyewitness account. The *Chronicle* was certainly completed between 813 and 815. The chronicler strongly condemns the eight-century iconoclasts, but he ignores Leo V's own iconoclastic turn during the latter years of his reign (see below) and depicts him positively. In that respect, the work is a true monument of iconodule resistance.[3] Similarly, although perhaps less conspicuously in view of its eastern focus, the *Chronicle* provides the first, rather comprehensive, Byzantine account of the *Völkerwanderung*.

For its fifth- and early sixth-century ethnography, Theophanes' *Chronicle* is largely dependent upon the eyewitness account of Procopius of Caesarea, and for the later sixth century it relies upon the work of Theophylact Simocatta.[4] For the eighth century onwards it preserves independent and to some extent unique information about the Franks, who, following Charlemagne's coronation, were more visible internationally. If one ignores for a moment the occasional reports on diplomatic exchanges between the Franks and Byzantium, the information on the Franks is concentrated in two entries, under the Alexandrian *Anni mundi* 6216 (723/724) and 6289 (796/797). The first entry, which is cited at the beginning of this paper, begins with an odd excursus on the end of Merovingian rule.[5]

This excursus is chronologically misplaced. Pippin, as we know, was king of the Franks from 751 to his death in 768; Stephen was pope between 752 and 757; and Aistulf reigned from 749 to 756. Furthermore, Pippin's pontifical investiture at Saint-Denis is firmly dated by Western sources to July, 754. At the end of this entry the author appears to insert a few lines on the accession of Caliph Hishām b. ʿAbd al-Malik (724–743) and an extremely concise reference to Stephen's flight to Francia: "Stephen, the Pope of Rome, sought refuge with the Franks."[6] Still more confusing is the fact that in the Latin translation (*c*. 870) by Anastasius the Librarian, the Head of archives and secretary to many popes, the excursus is found under the (equally wrong) *Annus mundi* 6234, which corresponds in Theophanes' reckoning to 741/2.[7] The reasons for that are unclear. These inconsistencies seemed enough to Theophanes' nineteenth-century editor, Carl de Boor, to suggest that the short mention of the pope's flight represented in fact the original entry, while the excursus was a later *scholion* which eventually found its way into Theophanes' original text.[8] This notion was prudently retained by Cyril Mango in his introduction and commentary to the English translation (cited above).

Mango suggested that the Greek-speaking monastic community of Rome was the immediate oral source for the Frankish material in the *Chronicle*. This assertion is strengthened by an unnoticed detail in the passage cited at the beginning of this chapter. The chronicler awkwardly speaks of Stephen II as being "compelled by the cruelty and senselessness" of the Lombard king Aistulf, but he also states immediately afterwards that he obtained the latter's "permission" to travel to Francia, seemingly in order to seek protection against the very same king. The apparently nonsensical sequence can only be understood in light of the more complete narrative of the *Liber pontificalis*, which records a meeting in Pavia shortly after the Lombard occupation of Ravenna. On this occasion, the pope defied the wicked monarch by asking his explicit permission to travel to Francia in order to meet Pippin. Aistulf was infuriated by this request, but after a few futile attempts to talk the pope out of his plans, he gave him leave (*tunc absolutus est ab eo*).[9] Hence, a uniquely Roman version of the events reached Constantinople through Greek mediation.

Modern historians were struck by the patent resemblance between the account of the Merovingians in Theophanes' *Chronicle* and the opening chapters in Einhard's *Life of Charlemagne*. The latter work was composed sometime between 817 and 836, with a more precise dating in 828 or 829 being today preferred.[10] Indeed, one finds in Einhard's text the very structure of the Greek source, for it too displays an excursus presenting the Merovingian kings as "lazy," emphasizing the power of the *major domus*, and referring briefly to the Frankish-Arab clashes in southern Gaul. Einhard also shares with Theophanes one peculiar mistake, namely the attribution of the deposition of Childeric III to pope Stephen rather than to his predecessor, Zachary.[11] Some scholars, as we shall see, have gone so far as to suggest that Einhard was depending on a Byzantine source when describing the late Merovingians. Others, who stressed the differences between Theophanes and Einhard, have argued instead that both Einhard and Theophanes relied on a common source. There are, to be sure, too many differences between the two accounts, so that no real textual dependence in any direction can be postulated.[12]

Yet the most conspicuous mistake in Theophanes' *Chronicle* appears in its depiction of Pippin, rather than Pippin's father, Charles Martel, as the successful commander who led the Frankish army in 732. Einhard relates the same events in this context, but speaks correctly of Charles Martel.[13] The mistake in Theophanes' *Chronicle*, however, has a parallel, hitherto overlooked, in another Frankish source, the *Deeds of the Bishops of Auxerre*, which was composed in the 870s. At the beginning of the biography of Hainmar, who was the bishop of Auxerre at the times of Charles Martel, one reads the following:

> Once he was appointed bishop, Hainmar held the office for fifteen years. He was a very vital man, not less distinguished by the nobility of his birth and very rich with property as well. For his secular authority increased to the point that he held the power of a duke over almost the entire territory of Burgundy. Now it so happened that at that time Pippin, the son of Charles the Elder, had to move to Aquitaine in response to the plea of Odo, the duke of Aquitaine, against Haimo, the king of Saragossa, who had married Odo's daughter Lampagia and then broke the nuptial vows. They met at the place called Iberra and started to fight; then Hainmar rushed with his men upon the Saracens, brought them to their knees in a supreme slaughter and was victorious, together with his king and Christ's favour.[14]

Michel Rouche has argued that the source of this fantastic account was oral and local, consisting of something like a proto-*Chanson de Roland*.[15] Similarly, at least one more unusual piece of information in Theophanes' *Chronicle*, that is, the penetration of 'Abd ar-Raḥman's troops as far as the river Rhône, is to be found in the *Annals of Moissac*, completed in 828.[16] In other words, it seems that Theophanes' account reflects a plethora of Western sources highly informed by Carolingian propaganda. In order to understand *when* and *where* these sources may have been put together one has to broaden the perspective.

Another entry in Theophanes' *Chronicle* that also betrays a Frankish source of information is the account of Charlemagne's imperial coronation on Christmas 800, which, in Theophanes' chronology, is to be found at the very end of the entry for the *Annus mundi* 6289, or 796/7:

In the same year, too, the relatives of the blessed Pope Adrian in Rome roused up the people and rebelled against Pope Leo, whom they arrested and blinded. They did not manage, however, to extinguish his sight altogether because those who were blinding him were merciful and took pity on him. He sought refuge with Charles, king of the Franks, who took bitter revenge on his enemies and restored him to his throne, Rome falling from that time onwards under the authority of the Franks. Repaying his debt to Charles, Leo crowned him emperor of the Romans in the church of the holy apostle Peter after anointing him with oil from head to foot and investing him with imperial robes and a crown on 25 December, indiction 9.[17]

This is not the place to rehearse the prodigious bibliography on the historic significance of Charlemagne's coronation of 800. Nor is it the place to dwell on the textual problems raised by this passage, which are further complicated by the parallel transmission in Latin and in Syriac. Suffice it to say that in spite of some difficulties, it seems that the Greek text of Theophanes' *Chronicle* must have been the source of all other extant reports.[18] Crucial for my argument is the fact that the account of Charlemagne's coronation shares some important features with Theophanes' Merovingian excursus. First, it is not concerned directly with the Franks, but purports to narrate the story of a pope's flight from Rome under the protection of a Carolingian king, who then receives some sort of investiture. Second, the entry is misplaced within the *Chronicle*'s own chronological frame. The attempt to kill Leo and the pope's flight to Francia, two well documented events, only occurred in 799.[19] Finally, the same events are recorded concisely by Theophanes under *Annus mundi* 6293. Hence, Theophanes' concise account is incorporated into the narrative in the right chronology of events, whereas the longer passage is, most probably, a later addition.

It should be noted that a little earlier in the narrative, in the entry for the *Annus mundi* 6289, one finds a two-line note on Pope Adrian's death and Leo's election (which in fact happened in late 795) squeezed between events that had happened in the East. Among these is Empress Irene's blinding and ousting her son Constantine VI, which is therefore juxtaposed with a similar attack on the pope.[20] The events in Constantinople led to an unprecedented situation, in which a woman ruled alone. Carolingian propaganda soon used this precedent as an argument against the legitimacy of the Eastern Roman Empire.[21] Hence, one finds here the same degree of Carolingian bias which we have encountered in the Merovingian excursus. It is hard to see how anybody else than the author of the Merovingian excursus under *Annus mundi* 6216 could have penned the entry for 6289.

The coronation account contains one piece of information that commentators have often dismissed as a mistake, namely, the reference to Charlemagne's imperial anointment, which appears to follow some medical models.[22] An error in the older editions of the *Liber pontificalis* had indeed transformed the royal anointment of one of Charlemagne's sons into Charlemagne's own imperial one, but this was cleared up by Louis Duchesne in his 1892 edition. Moreover, in his commentary on the imperial anointment of 800, Duchesne claimed that "aucun auteur occidental n'y fait la moindre allusion,"[23] a position that was silently accepted by Mango. Yet, this claim is emphatically wrong. Charlemagne's imperial anointment does indeed pop up in the biography of Charlemagne's younger son and successor, Louis the Pious, which was composed by the auxiliary bishop of Trier, Thegan, in 837.

Thegan's work opens with a short genealogy of the Carolingians, which ends with a statement to that effect that Pope Stephen *consecravit et unxit* Pippin *in regem*, whereas more recently pope Leo *consecravit et unxit* Pippin's son Charles *ad imperatorem*. Later Thegan repeats this very same formula—*unxit et consecravit ad imperatorem*—when describing the second imperial coronation and anointing of his own protagonist, Louis the Pious, by Pope Stephen IV.[24] This formula, one should note, borrows from a scene in Leviticus (8:13), in which Moses anointed Aaron and his sons. Thegan's testimony, which was overlooked by Byzantinists, prevents us from dismissing altogether the information in Theophanes' *Chronicle* as a mere mistake. Nevertheless, scholars in the past were hesitant to take the story of Charlemagne's imperial anointment seriously.[25]

It is quite remarkable that both the *Liber pontificalis* and the *Royal Frankish Annals* are silent about the exact ceremony of Charlemagne's coronation, as is Einhard. Similarly, the *Annals of Fulda* are not explicit when describing Louis' imperial anointment. Robert-Henri Bautier has argued that the term *consecratio* in the contemporary *Annals of Lorsch* alludes, in accordance with later use, to Charlemagne's anointment of 800.[26] Although it is doubtful whether Charlemagne was actually anointed by Pope Leo as part of his coronation in 800, there can be little doubt that by 837, as reflected in Thegan's account, the anointment was perceived as a crucial component of the rite. Obviously, Thegan presents the anointment as a fundamental feature of the imperial coronation of his day, and provides it accordingly with a historical background. In this respect, even if he did find a reference to Charlemagne's anointment in some official protocols, he certainly belonged to a group of historians who fashioned Charlemagne's memory so as to fit the aims and objectives of Louis the Pious' court.[27]

As we have already noted, there are plenty of indications that Theophanes' *Chronicle* was completed before Leo V unveiled his iconoclast religious policy. This shift in imperial ideology appears to have taken the public somewhat by surprise, with the *de facto* deposition of the Patriarch Nikephoros, dated by hagiographical sources to March 13 or 20, 815, and the iconoclast synod at Saint Sophia a few weeks later, which was convened by the emperor himself and by the new patriarch, Theodotos.[28] Yet, at least one later addition was made to the *Chronicle*. This addition rightly specifies the duration of Nikephoros' patriarchate as nine years, and it was inserted in the relevant chronological rubric, under *Annus mundi* 6298, following the chronicler's general practice of mentioning this kind of information upon accessions.[29] As Mango and others have pointed out, it is hardly conceivable that an anti-iconoclast work such as the *Chronicle* of Theophanes could have enjoyed significant circulation before the official restoration of icons in 843, leaving plenty of time for modifications to take place in the text. There is no reason to assume that the addition in this case was made much later than the completion of the *Chronicle* itself or by anybody else than its author. This is also the case with the Merovingian excursus and the coronation account.

The (real or fictional) ceremony of 800 was only recorded in the West in terms similar to those found in Theophanes' *Chronicle* in the 830s, when a dynastic crisis imposed a new quest for legitimacy at the Frankish court. It is, however, likely to have caught the attention of the Greek monks of Rome, whom, following Mango, I have regarded as the source for the Frankish information in the *Chronicle*, before that. This transfer of knowledge from the West to Constantinople took place, most probably, between Charlemagne's death in January 814 and Louis the Pious' consecration by Pope Stephen IV in October 816, during which period the bond between Rome and Aachen was strengthened. According to the *Liber pontificalis*, Pope Leo's attackers, who had been exiled to Francia by Charlemagne, were pardoned and allowed to return to Rome with the pope on his way back from Reims.[30]

In sum, the Frankish material under *Anni mundi* 6216 and 6289 must indeed be regarded as a set of updates appended to the original text of Theophanes' *Chronicle* in the form of *scholia*. Nevertheless, these updates, I would submit, were added by the same author who was responsible for the rest of the work, shortly after its completion, and at the same time as the update acknowledging Nikephoros' deposition under *Annus mundi* 6298, most probably in late 816 or in 817. At that time, Stephen IV's journey to Francia evoked, for multiple reasons, the memory of both his eighth-century namesake and his immediate predecessor, Leo III. Moreover, by 817, the above-mentioned parallels with Einhard's *Life of Charlemagne* may simply betray Theophanes' indirect acquaintance with that work, if one retains the earliest possible date for its composition, rather than vice versa, as implausibly surmised by Godefroid Kurth.[31] Be that as it may, the author of the *Chronicle*, for reasons unknown to us but which would fit the portrait of Theophanes the Confessor as a sick man towards the end of his life, refrained from rewriting the early years of Leo V's reign or from continuing the narrative after 813.[32]

In conclusion, a few remarks concerning the most famous item in the Merovingian excursus are in order, namely the claim that the Merovingians were characterized by a row of bristles sprouting from the spine, which made them look like hogs. This enigmatic description was dismissed in the past as a lamentable misunderstanding of some references to hair style that made the Merovingians known as the "long-haired" kings,[33] similar to the one made by Einhard when he speaks of *crine profuso*. Yet the description in the *Chronicle* finds a striking textual parallel in the Old French *Chanson de Roland*, in a *laisse* that describes the various peoples lead by the Emir of Babylon, Baligant:

> Chevalers unt a merveillus esforz:
> En la menur .L. milie en out.
> La premere est de cels de Butentrot,
> E l'altre aprés de Micenes as chefs gros;
> Sur les eschines qu'il unt en mi les dos
> Cil sunt seiét ensement cume porc.[34]

> They have a formidable force of knights,
> There are fifty thousand in the smaller division.
> The first is made up of men from Butentrot,
> And the one that comes after, of large-headed men from Misnes:
> On their spines, along the length of their backs,
> They have bristles like pigs.[35]

Henri Grégoire first brought this parallel to the attention of Byzantinists as part of a complex hypothesis on the date of the *Chanson*.[36] He argued that the *Chanson*'s description of the Micenes or Misnes depends ultimately on Theophanes' characterization of the Merovingians, obviously through the Latin translation of the *Chronicle* by Anastasius. Indeed Anastasius' translation of Theophanes' *Chronicle* and earlier Greek chronicles, commonly known as the *Historia tripartita*, enjoyed a wide circulation in the West and influenced the western perception of early Islam before the Crusaders.[37] Grégoire further identified the legendary Micenes with the *Nemitzoi* (Czech *Němec*), or German mercenaries of eleventh-century Byzantine sources.[38] It is also possible, however, that the description of a bristled people was already embedded in something close to the proto-*Chanson de Roland* envisaged by Rouche, the focus of which were the events of Poitiers, and an echo of which reached Constantinople via Rome around 816.

Conclusion

Stefan Esders and Yitzhak Hen

In his posthumous ground-breaking study *Mohammed and Charlemagne*, the Belgian historian Henri Pirenne wrote that "under the Merovingians the Frankish kingdom was a power which filled an international role, and was guided by an unvarying policy; which was, to install itself securely on the shores of the Mediterranean."[1] Pirenne's work has been subject to endless criticism and revisions since its publication. Yet, the influence of the Pirenne thesis on many a generation of scholars was immense, not the least because Pirenne had established the terms of reference for the debate over the transformation of the Roman world and the emergence of medieval Europe.[2] For Pirenne, the Merovingian kingdoms were part and parcel of a larger Mediterranean world, at least before "Islam had shattered the Mediterranean unity which the Germanic invasions had left intact."[3]

Notwithstanding Pirenne's initial observations, and albeit the fact that the Merovingian kingdoms were, perhaps, the most powerful and long-lasting polity of the post-Roman world, their politics and culture were often interpreted as provincial phenomena. Like the history of most post-Roman barbarian kingdoms, Merovingian history was looked at through a narrow prism of local affairs and developments, detached from the broader disintegrating Roman Empire. This partial attitude towards the barbarian kingdoms of the post-Roman West, however, is gradually giving way to a new and more comprehensive approach. After decades of research, it became commonplace that the so-called Barbarian Invasions and the subsequent establishment of barbarian kingdoms on Roman soil were, by and large, a Roman phenomenon that took place in a Roman geo-political orbit, centered around the Mediterranean, that is, the Roman *mare nostrum*.[4] The Merovingian kingdoms were no different.

The aim of the various papers assembled in this volume was to break free of the traditional views on the course of Merovingian history, and to study the

Merovingian kingdoms of the Early Middle Ages in a broader Mediterranean context. Our working hypothesis has been that apart from being post-Roman barbarian kingdoms, deeply rooted in the traditions and practices of the western Roman Empire, the Merovingian kingdoms had complicated and multi-layered social, cultural and political relations with their barbarian neighbors, as well as with their eastern Mediterranean counterparts, that is, the Byzantine Empire and the Umayyad Caliphate. By focusing on some well-known written sources, most of which were composed or disseminated under Merovingian rule, the papers in this volume sought to contextualize Merovingian history by implementing a more Mediterranean perspective, or at least a perspective that aims to transcend the political frontiers of the Merovingian kingdoms.

The papers in this volume elucidate, each in its own way, how deeply entrenched the Merovingians were in a pan-Mediterranean political, religious, economic and intellectual framework, and how, on the other hand, global Mediterranean circumstances left their imprint on Merovingian affairs. Even events, which, at face value, seem like minor "internal" affairs, had some important international aspects. An excellent case in point is the so-called Gundovald affair, whose Byzantine support exposed the shaken ground on which Merovingian legitimacy rested in the sixth century. The fact that Gundovald could combine his alleged Merovingian claims with Byzantine political support (and money), illustrates the extent to which the sources for Merovingian legitimacy were not exclusively internal. Rather, they were embedded in a more comprehensive political ideology that regarded the Merovingian kingdoms as yet another "kingdom of the Empire."[5]

It seems clear from the ongoing discussion in the various papers collected here that the textual resources on which Merovingian politics and culture relied were originally produced and designed within an expansive framework that extended geographical boundaries, that is the Roman Empire, or at least some extensive relevant parts of it. No doubt, these resources were, in some sense, regionalized through a sophisticated process of grafting and adaptation.[6] And yet, their original geographical bias was evident well after the Roman Empire as a political entity had ceased to exist in the west. In particular, religious texts forced their audiences to imagine historical and contemporary landscapes that reached far beyond the *here* and *now*.[7] Texts, artefacts and stories that were imported to Gaul by pilgrims, official delegates, merchants, immigrants and refugees contributed immensely to a wide-ranging perception and to the formation of a creative imagination that involved much more than the immediate setting in which one lived, but rather encompassed the entire *mare nostrum* of the late antique world.

Against the broader Mediterranean perspective that the papers in this volume adopt, it appears that the dichotomy of "East versus West" is untenable. There were numerous political players in the Mediterranean basin, and each contributed his or her share to the game. Much time and effort were invested in the past in the study of individual kingdoms, such as Visigothic Spain, Frankish Gaul, Lombard Italy, or Anglo-Saxon Britain, not the least because these kingdoms were perceived as precursors of modern state formation in Europe.[8] We would submit that much more research that compares the various post-Roman barbarian kingdoms to each other and studies their interaction with one another and with their eastern counterparts is needed. Otherwise early medieval studies are under threat of becoming schematic. We hope that the papers in this volume will encourage some scholars and students to pursue this challenge.

Notes

Introduction

1 *Hist.* VI.6, p. 272. This deaf-mute pilgrim did not have to continue his journey to Rome, since he was healed by Hospicius himself.
2 Erin T. Dailey, *Queens, Consorts, Concubines: Gregory of Tours and Women of the Merovingian Elite* (Leiden/Boston: Brill, 2015); Jamie Kreiner, *The Social Life of Hagiography in the Merovingian Kingdom* (Cambridge: Cambridge University Press, 2014); Yaniv Fox, *Power and Religion in Merovingian Gaul: Columbanian Monasticism and the Formation of the Frankish Aristocracy* (Cambridge: Cambridge University Press, 2014); Helmut Reimitz, *History, Frankish Identity and the Framing of Western Ethnicity, 550–850* (Cambridge: Cambridge University Press, 2015).
3 Alexander C. Murray (ed.), *A Companion to Gregory of Tours* (Leiden: Brill, 2016).
4 Isabel Moreira and Bonnie Effros (eds.), *Oxford Handbook of the Merovingian World*, (Oxford: Oxford University Press, expected for 2019).
5 Michael McCormick, *Origins of the European Economy: Communications and Commerce, A.D. 300–900* (Cambridge: Cambridge University Press, 2002); Chris Wickham, *The Inheritance of Rome: A History of Europe from 400 to 1000* (London: Allen Lane, 2009); Peter Brown, *Society and the Holy in Late Antiquity* (Berkeley: University of California Press, 1982); Andreas Fischer and Ian N. Wood (eds.), *Western Perspectives on the Mediterranean: Cultural Transfer in Late Antiquity and the Early Middle Ages, 400–800 AD* (London: Bloomsbury, 2012).
6 Averil Cameron, *Byzantine Matters* (Princeton: Princeton University Press, 2014).
7 Similar in scope and aim is the forthcoming volume: Stefan Esders, Yaniv Fox, Yitzhak Hen and Laury Sarti (eds.), *East and West in the Early Middle Ages: The Merovingian Kingdoms in Mediterranean Perspective* (Cambridge: Cambridge University Press, 2019), as it shares the supraregional perspective and the interest in cultural exchange.

1 History, Geography, and the Notion of *Mare Nostrum* in the Early Medieval West

1 *Expositio totius mundi et gentium*, cc. 55 and 58, ed. and trans. Jean Rougé, SC 124 (Paris: Cerf, 1966), 192–5 and 196–9 respectively. The English translation is my

own. For an older English translation of the entire treatise, see Alexander Vassiliev, "*Expositio totius mundi*: an anonymous geographic treatise of the fourth century A.D.," *Seminarium Kondakovianum* 8 (1936): 1–39.
2. Sallust, *De bello Iugurthino*, cc. 17–18, ed. Leighton D. Reynolds (Oxford: Clarendon Press, 1991), 68–70.
3. Julius Caesar, *De bello Gallico*, I.1, ed. Otto Seel (Leipzig: Teubner, 1961), 8–9.
4. Appian of Alexandria, *Roman History*, praef. 1–5, ed. Horace White, vol. 1 (Cambridge, MA and London: Harvard University Press, 1912), 2–9.
5. Tacitus, *De origine et situ Germanorum*, c. 1, ed. Michael Winterbottom (Oxford: Clarendon Press, 1975), 37–8.
6. See, for example, Natalia Lozovsky, *The Earth is Our Book: Geographical Knowledge in the Latin West ca. 400–1000* (Ann Arbor: University of Michigan Press, 2000), and see there for further references. See also the various papers in *Geography and Ethnography: Perceptions of the World in pre-Modern Societies*, eds. Kurt A. Raaflaub and Richard J.A. Talbert (Chichester: Wiley-Blackwell, 2010).
7. On all these historical narratives, see David Rohrbacher, *The Historians of Late Antiquity* (London and New York: Routledge, 2002); Brian Croke, "Late antique historiography, 250–650 CE," in *A Companion to Greek and Roman Historiography*, ed. John Marincola (Oxford: Blackwell, 2007), 567–81; idem, "Historiography," in *The Oxford Handbook of Late Antiquity*, ed. Scott F. Johnson (Oxford: Oxford University press, 2012), 405–36; David Woods, "Late Antique historiography: a brief history of time," in *A Companion to Late Antiquity*, ed. Philip Rousseau (Oxford: Wiley-Blackwell, 2007), 357–71. See also the various papers in *Greek and Roman Historiography in Late Antiquity*, ed. Gabriele Marasco (Leiden: Brill, 2003).
8. On the Christian historical narratives, see Hervé Inglebert, *Interpretatio christiana: les mutations des savoirs (cosmographie, géographie, ethnographie, histoire) dans l'Antiquité chrétienne* (Paris: Institut d'études augustiniennes, 2001). See also Croke, "Late antique historiography," and idem, "Historiography," and see there for further bibliography.
9. Orosius, *Historiarum adversum paganos libri VII*, I.2, ed. Karl Zangemeister, CSEL 5 (Vienna: G. Olms, 1882), 9–40.
10. Jordanes, *De origine actibusque Getarum*, I.4, ed. Theodor Mommsen, MGH SS Auct. ant. V.1 (Berlin: Weidmann, 1882), 54–66.
11. Isidore of Seville, *Historia Gothorum, Vandalorum et Sueborum*, ed. and trans. C. Rogríguez Alonso, *Las historias de los Godos, Vandalos y Suevos de Isidoro de Sevilla* (León: Centro de Estudios e Investigación "San Isidoro," 1975); see in particular the so-called *Laus Spaniae* ("The praise of Spain").
12. The amount of literature on the so-called Barbarian Invasions is enormous and cannot be listed here. For some succinct introductions, see Guy Halsall, *Barbarian Migrations and the Roman West, 376–568* (Cambridge: Cambridge University Press,

2007); Edward James, *Europe's Barbarians, AD 200–600* (Harlow: Pearson-Longman, 2009), and see there for further bibliography.

13 Andrew D. Merrills, *History and Geography in Late Antiquity* (Cambridge: Cambridge University Press, 2005).
14 Merrills, *History and Geography*, 11.
15 The best study of the *Expositio* is still Rougé's introduction to his SC edition; see *Expositio*, 7–137. See also Jesse E. Woodman, "The Expositio totius mundi et gentiium: Its Geography and Its Language," (PhD diss., Ohio State University, Columbus, 1964); F. Martelli, *Introduzione alla "Expositio totius mundi." Analisi etnografica e tematiche politiche in un'opera anonima del IV secolo* (Bologna: Giorgio Barghigiani, 1982); Hans-Joachim Drexhage, "Die *Expositio totius mundi et gentium*: eine Handelsgeographie aus dem 4. Jh. n. Chr., eingeleitet, übersetzt und mit einführender Literatur (Kap. XXII-LXVII) versehen," *Münstersche Beiträge zur antiken Handelsgeschichte* 2 (1983): 3–41.
16 *Expositio*, pp. 57–69; Peter Mittag, "Zu den Quellen der *Expositio totius mundi et gentium*. Ein neuer Periplus?," *Hermes* 134 (2006): 338–51.
17 *Expositio*, 70–82; Mittag, "Zu den Quellen."
18 See *Expositio*, 89–91.
19 *Vetus orbis descriptio*, ed. Jacques Godefroy (Geneva: P. Chouet, 1628).
20 *Expositio*, c. 28, p. 160. On the date of the *Expositio*, see *Expositio*, 9–26.
21 Gabriele Marasco, "L'*Expositio totius mundi et gentium* e la politica religiosa di Constanzo II," *Ancient Society* 27 (1996): 183–203.
22 See Ammianus Marcellinus, *Res Gestae*, XXV.7.9-11, ed. John C. Rolfe, vol. 2 (Cambridge, MA and London: Harvard University Press, 1940), 532–5.
23 The Greek version did not survive. On the language of the *Expositio*, see Alfred Klotz, "Über die *Expositio totius mundi et gentium*," *Philologus* 65 (1906): 97–127; *Expositio*, pp. 89–103; Tibor Grüll, "*Expositio totius mundi et gentium*: a peculiar work on the commerce of [the] Roman Empire from the mid-fourth century – compiled by a Syrian textile dealer?," in *Studies in Economic and Social History of the Ancient Near East in Memory of Péter Vargyas*, ed. Zoltán Csbai (Budapest: L'Harmattan, 2014), 629–42, at 630.
24 See *Expositio*, 27–38.
25 *Expositio*, c. 22, p. 156.
26 Grüll, "*Expositio totius mundi et gentium*," 631.
27 See Giusto Traina, "Mapping the new empire: a geographical look at the fourth century," in *East and West in the Roman Empire of the Fourth Century: An End to Unity*, eds. Roald Dijkstra, Sanne van Poppel and Daniëlle Slootjes (Leiden and Boston: Brill, 2015), 49–62.
28 See Grüll, "*Expositio totius mundi et gentium*," 635–7.
29 See *Expositio*, 27–38; Grüll, "*Expositio totius mundi et gentium*," 634–5.

30 *Expositio*, 48–55.
31 See, for example, Ramsay MacMullen, *Christianizing the Roman Empire, A.D. 100–400* (New Haven and London: Yale University Press, 1984); Philip Rousseau, *The Early Christian Centuries* (London and New York: Longman, 2002); Peter Brown, *The Rise of Western Christendom: Triumph and Diversity, A.D. 200–1000*, 3rd ed. (Oxford: Blackwell, 2013).
32 On these attributions, see *Expositio*, 48–55.
33 *Expositio*, c. 3, p. 142.
34 See Grüll, "*Expositio totius mundi et gentium*," 637–9.
35 *Expositio*, 101–3. On the culture of Ostrogothic Italy under Theoderic the Great, see Yitzhak Hen, *Roman Barbarians: The Royal Court and Culture in the Early Medieval West* (Basingstoke: Palgrave-Macmillan, 2007), 27–58, and see there for further bibliography. See also the various papers in *A Companion to Ostrogothic Italy*, eds. Jonathan J. Arnold, Shane Bjornlie and Kristina Sessa (Leiden and Boston: Brill, 2016).
36 On the Latin of the *Expositio*, see *Expositio*, 89–103, and compare with the Latin of the *Edictum Theoderici* and the so-called *Anonymus Valesianus*. On the Latin of the *Anonymus Valesianus*, see J.N. Adams, *The Text and Language of a Vulgar Latin Chronicle (Anonymus Valesianus II)* (London: Institute of Classical Studies, 1976). On the *Edictum Theoderici*, see Sean D.W. Lafferty, *Law and Society in the Age of Theoderic the Great: A Study of the* Edictum Theoderici (Cambridge: Cambridge University Press, 2013).
37 *Ravennatis anonymi Cosmographia*, IV.13, 19, 29 and 42, ed. Joseph Schnetz, rev. eds. (Stuttgart: Teubner, 1990), 53, 56, 65 and 78 respectively. See also Franz Staab, "Ostrogothic geographers at the court of Theoderic the Great: a study of some sources of the Anonymous Cosmographer of Ravenna," *Viator* 7 (1976): 27–64.
38 On the *Descriptio*, see *Expositio*, 104–27.
39 In some cases, it seems as if Orosius is giving a free translation of the *Expositio*'s Greek text; see *Expositio*, 46–47. On Orosius' geographical section, see Merrills, *History and Geography*, 35–99.
40 On Cassiodorus and his writings, the starting point is James J. O'Donnell, *Cassiodorus* (Berkeley: University of California Press, 1979). See also Hen, *Roman Barbarians*, 39–58; Shane Bjornlie, *Politics and Tradition Between Rome, Ravenna and Constantinople: A Study of Cassiodorus and the* Variae, *527–554* (Cambridge: Cambridge University Press, 2013).
41 This is not the place to go in detail into the endless debate about the relations between Cassiodorus' original composition and that of Jordanes. For some references, see Brian Croke, "Cassiodorus and the *Getica* of Jordanes," *Classical Philology* 82 (1987): 117–34; Arne S. Christensen, *Cassiodorus, Jordanes and the History of the Goths. Studies in a Migration Myth* (Copenhagen: Museum Tusculanum Press, 2002).

42 On Jordanes' geographical digressions, see Merrills, *History and Geography*, 100–69.
43 Hen, *Roman Barbarians*, 39–58; Bjornlie, *Politics and Tradition*, passim.
44 Hen, *Roman Barbarians*, 45–9.
45 Hen, *Roman Barbarians*, 39–58. See also Jonathan J. Arnold, *Theoderic and the Roman Imperial Restoration* (Cambridge: Cambridge University Press, 2014).
46 See O'Donnell, *Cassiodorus*, 36–46; Hen, *Roman Barbarians*, 47–9.
47 W. H. C. Frend, *The Rise of the Monophysite Movement* (Cambridge: Cambridge University Press, 1972), 143–54; Patrick Amory, *People and Identity in Ostrogothic Italy, 489–554* (Cambridge: Cambridge University Press, 1997), 203–16; Jan-Markus Kötter, *Zwischen Kaisern und Aposteln: Das Akakianische Schisma (484–519) als kirchlicher Ordnungskonflikt der Spätantike* (Stuttgart: Franz Steiner Verlag, 2013).
48 Cassiodorus, *Orationum reliquiae*, 1, ed. Ludwig Traube, MGH SS Auct. ant. XII (Berlin: Weidmann, 1894), 466.
49 The most common edition is *Ordo generis Cassiodororum*, ed. Theodor Mommsen, MGH SS Auct. ant. XII (Berlin: Weidmann, 1894), vi. For a more recent edition, see Alain Galonnier, "*Anecdoton Holderi* ou *Ordo generis Cassiodororum*: Introduction, édition, traduction et commentaire," *Antiquité tardive* 4 (1996), 299–312. I cite the English translation by Samuel J. B. Barnish, *Cassiodorus: Variae* (Liverpool: Liverpool University Press, 1992), xxxvi-xxxvii.
50 Cassiodorus, *Variae*, IX.25.5, ed. Åke J. Fridh, CCSL 96 (Turnhout: Brepols, 1973), 379.
51 On all the Frankish sources, see now Helmut Reimitz, *History, Frankish Identity and the Framing of Western Ethnicity, 550–850* (Cambridge: Cambridge University Press, 2015).
52 See also Peter van Nuffelen, *Orosius and the Rhetoric of History* (Oxford: Oxford University Press, 2012).

2 True Differences: Gregory of Tours' Account of the Council of Mâcon (585)

1 *Hist.* VIII.20, pp. 386–7. Other English translations can be found in Alexander C. Murray, *Gregory of Tours, The Merovingians* (Peterborough, Ontario: Broadview Press, 2006), 183; *Gregory of Tours, History of the Franks*, transl. Lewis Thorpe (London: Penguin, 1974), 451–3 and *The History of the Franks*, transl. Ormonde M. Dalton (Oxford: Clarendon Press, 1927), 344–5.
2 On the 2nd synod of Mâcon, see Odette Pontal, *Die Synoden im Merowingerreich* (Paderborn: Schöningh, 1986), 161–7; Ian N. Wood, *The Merovingian Kingdoms, 481–751* (London: Longman, 1993), 106; Stefan Esders, *Römische Rechtstradition*

und merowingisches Königtum. Zum Rechtscharakter politischer Herrschaft in Burgund im 6. und 7. Jahrhundert (Göttingen: Vandenhoeck & Ruprecht, 1997) 296–316; Aloys Suntrup, *Studien zur politischen Theologie im frühmittelalterlichen Okzident: Die Aussage konziliarer Texte des gallischen und iberischen Raumes* (Münster: Aschendorff, 2001), 103–9; Sebastian Scholz, *Die Merowinger* (Stuttgart: Kohlhammer, 2015), 154–60.

3 On the participants and their regional distribution see Pontal, *Die Synoden*, 162–3. See also the illustrations in Michel Rouche, *L'Aquitaine des Wisigoths aux Arabes, 418–781: naissance d'une region* (Paris: École des Hautes Études en Sciences Sociales, 1979), 81; and in Bruno Dumézil, *La reine Brunehaut* (Paris: Fayard, 2008), 536.

4 Pontal, *Synoden*, 156–9.

5 On the divisions see Eugen Ewig, "Die fränkischen Teilungen und Teilreiche (511–613)," in idem, *Spätantikes und fränkisches Gallien: Gesammelte Schriften (1952–1973)* (Munich: Artemis, 1979) I, 114–71, at 142–7; Marc Widdowson, "Merovingian Partitions. A 'Genealogical Charter'?" *Early Medieval Europe* 17 (2009), 1–22.

6 Walter Goffart, "Byzantine Policy in the West under Tiberius II and Maurice. The pretenders Hermenegild and Gundovald (579–585)," *Traditio* 13 (1957), 73–118; Bernard S. Bachrach, *The Anatomy of a Little War. A Diplomatic and Military History of the Gundovald Affair (568–586)* (Boulder: Westview Press, 1994); Constantin Zuckerman, "Qui a rappelé en Gaule le Ballomer Gundovald?," *Francia* 25 (1998), 1–18; Marc Widdowson, "Gundovald, 'Ballomer' and the Politics of Identity," *Revue Belge de Philologie et d'histoire* 86 (2008), 607–22; Walter Goffart, "The Frankish Pretender Gundovald, 582–585. A Crisis of Merovingian Blood," *Francia* 39 (2012), 1–27. Most historians assume today that Gundovald was a Merovingian.

7 *Hist.* VII.34, pp. 354–5; IX.28, pp. 446–7 and IX.32, pp. 451–4. See Zuckerman, "Qui a rappelé," 7. Zuckerman's assumptions have been questioned by Goffart, "Frankish pretender," and Dumézil, *Brunehaut*, 266. However, Brunhild was the only person who could have an interest in inviting an adult Merovingian to Gaul at that time, which paralleled her earlier plans to marry Chilperic's son Merowech in 576 (*Hist.* V.18, pp. 216–25), see Till Stüber, "Der inkriminierte Bischof. Verratsvorwürfe und politische Prozesse gegen Bischöfe im westgotischen und fränkischen Gallien (466–614)" (PhD, Freie Universität Berlin, 2017), 260–2; Julia Hofmann, "The men who would be kings. Challenges to royal authority in the Frankish kingdoms, c. 500–700" (PhD diss., Oxford University, 2008), 151–87.

8 Karl Ubl, *Inzestverbot und Gesetzgebung. Die Konstruktion eines Verbrechens (300–1100)* (Berlin and New York: De Gruyter, 2008), 176–82.

9 On the Praetextatus case see Esders, *Römische Rechtstradition*, 443–8; Nira Gradowicz-Pancer, "Femmes royales et violences anti-épiscopales à l'époque mérovingienne: Frédégonde et le meurtre de l'évêque Prétextat," in *Bischofsmord im*

Mittelalter – Murder of Bishops, eds. Natalie Fryde and Dirk Reitz (Göttingen: Vandenhoeck & Ruprecht, 2003), 37–50; Bernhard Jussen, *Patenschaft und Adoption im frühen Mittelalter*, (Göttingen: Vandenhoeck & Ruprecht, 1991), 177–98; Philippe Buc, *Dangers of Ritual. Between Early Medieval Texts and Social Scientific Theory* (Princeton: Princeton University Press, 2001), 88–106; Helmut Reimitz, "Historicizing Rome. Gregory of Tours and the Roman past," in *Transforming the Early Medieval World. Studies in Honor of Ian N. Wood*, ed. Kivilicim Yavuz (forthcoming); Michael Glatthaar, "Der Edictus Chilperichs I. und die Reichsversammlung von Paris (577)," *Deutsches Archiv für Erforschung des Mittelalters* 73 (2017), 1–74, at 15–8, 27–8, 30 and 32, Stüber, *Der inkriminierte Bischof*, forthcoming.

10 *Hist.* VII.34, pp. 354–5; IX.28, pp. 446–7 and IX.32, pp. 451–4.
11 On Gregory and his works see now the essays in Alexander Callander Murray (ed.), *A Companion to Gregory of Tours* (Leiden: Brill, 2016), with bibliography; for Gregory's *Histories* in the panorama of Merovingian historiography see Helmut Reimitz, "The history of historiography in the Merovingian kingdoms," in Bonnie Effros and Isabel Moreira (eds.), *The Oxford History of the Merovingian World* (Oxford: Oxford University Press, forthcoming), with further references.
12 *Hist.* VIII.2, pp. 371–2.
13 *Hist.* VIII.2, pp. 371–2.
14 *Hist.* VIII.7, pp. 375–6.
15 *Hist.* VIII.12, pp. 378–9.
16 *Hist.* VI.24, pp. 291–2; VII.11, p. 333 and VII.24, p. 344; VIII.13, pp. 379–80. On Theodore, see Stüber, *Der inkriminierte Bischof*, 249–69; on Dynamius see Walter Berschin, "Dinamius Patricius von Marseille († nach 597)," in idem, *Mittellateinische Studien* (Heidelberg: Mattes, 2005), 9–16; Bruno Dumézil, "Le patrice Dynamius et son réseau: culture aristocratique et transformation des pouvoirs autour de Lérins dans la seconde moitié du VIe siècle," in: Yann Codou and Michel Lauwers (eds.), *Lérins, une île sainte dans l'Occident médiéval* (Turnhout: Brepols, 2009), 167–94.
17 See Stüber, *Der inkriminierte Bischof*, forthcoming.
18 It is not absolutely certain but very likely that the council of Mâcon was the council that Gregory had mentioned earlier as the one scheduled for October 23.
19 On this Nicetius, see Karin Selle-Hosbach, *Prosopographie der merowingischen Amsträger von 511–613* (Bonn, 1974), no. 157.
20 On this see Godefroid Kurth, "Le concile de Mâcon et l'âme des femmes," *Revue des questions historiques* 51 (1892), 556–60 [reprinted in idem, *Études franques*, vol. 1 (Paris: Honoré Champion, 1919), 161–68], and more recently Katharina Bracht, "Can women be called 'man'? On the background of a discussion led at the 2nd Council of Mâcon (585 AD)," *Acta patristica et byzantina* 17 (2006), 144–54.
21 *Hist.* VII.16, pp. 337–8.

22 *Hist.* V.18, pp. 216–25.
23 *Hist.* VIII.20, p. 387.
24 Cf. above, n. 11, and below n. 31.
25 The synodal acts of Mâcon are edited in two standard editions: MGH Conc. I, pp. 163–73; *Concilia Galliae A. 511–A. 695*, ed. Carlo de Clercq, CCSL 148a (Turnhout: Brepols, 1963), pp. 237–50. A French translation can be found in Jean Gaudemet and Brigitte Basdevant, *Les canons des conciles mérovingiens* (Paris: Cerf, 1989), II, 454–85; a German translation in Josef Limmer, *Konzilien und Synoden im spätantiken Gallien von 314–696 nach Christi Geburt* (Frankfurt am Main: Peter Lang, 2004) 287–96; parts of it in English in: Alexander C. Murray, *From Roman to Merovingian Gaul . A reader* (Peterborough, Ontario: Broadview, 2000), 572–4.
26 2nd synod of Mâcon (585): MGH Conc. I, p. 173; CCSL 148a, p. 250; cf. Pontal, *Synoden*, 162–3.
27 2nd synod of Mâcon II, c. 7: MGH Conc. I, pp. 167–8; CCSL 148a, p. 242.
28 Stefan Esders and Helmut Reimitz, "After Gundovald, before Pseudo-Isidore: Episcopal Jurisdiction, Clerical Privilege, and the Uses of Roman Law in the Frankish Kingdoms," *Early Medieval Europe* (forthcoming).
29 2nd synod of Mâcon II, c. 18: MGH Conc. I, p. 171; CCSL 148a, p. 246. See Ubl, *Inzestverbot und Gesetzgebung*, 166–7.
30 2nd synod of Mâcon II, c. 5: MGH Conc. I, p. 166–7; CCSL 148a, p. 241. See Ernst Perels, *Die kirchlichen Zehnten im karolingischen Reiche* (Berlin: Weidmann, 1904), 14–7; Ivo Fasiori, "Storia della decima dall'editto di Milano (313) al secondo Concilio di Mâcon (585)," *Vetera Christianorum* 23 (1986), 39–61; Ubl, *Inzestverbot und Gesetzgebung*, 173.
31 2nd synod of Mâcon II, c. 6: MGH Conc. I, p. 167; CCSL 148a, pp. 241–2. Beda Kleinschmidt, "Das bischöfliche Rationale und der 6. Kanon der Synode von Macon," *Historisches Jahrbuch* 27 (1906), 799–803.
32 2nd synod of Mâcon II, c. 13: MGH Conc. I, p. 170; CCSL 148a, p. 245.
33 2nd synod of Mâcon II, c. 15: MGH Conc. I, p. 170; CCSL 148a, p. 246. See on this Michael McCormick, *Eternal Victory. Triumphal Rulership in Late Antiquity, Byzantium, and the Early Medieval West* (Cambridge: Cambridge University Press, 1986), 329–30; on the Roman background, see Esders, *Römische Rechtstradition*, 302–4; see also Ubl, *Inzestverbot und Gesetzgebung*, 167.
34 On Gallic bishops' knowledge of Roman law and their referring to it in the sixth century see Engbert Jan Jonkers, "Application of Roman Law by Councils in the Sixth Century," *Tijdschrift voor Rechtsgeschiedenis* 20 (1952), 340–3 and in particular Detlef Liebs, *Römische Jurisprudenz in Gallien (2. bis 8. Jahrhundert)*. Freiburger rechtsgeschichtliche Abhandlungen N. F. 38 (Berlin: Duncker & Humbolt, 2002).
35 Martin Heinzelmann, *Gregory of Tours. History and Society in the Sixth Century*, trans. Chris Caroll (Cambridge: Cambridge University Press, 2001); Walter Goffart,

Narrators of Barbarian History (AD 550–800). Jordanes, Gregory of Tours, Bede and Paul the Deacon, 2nd edn (Princeton: Princeton University Press, 2005), and cf. now the essays and bibliography in *A Companion to Gregory of Tours*, ed. Murray.

36 See, Ian N. Wood, "Topographies of Holy Power in Sixth-Century Gaul," in Mayke de Jong, Frans Theuws and Carine van Rhijn (eds.), *Topographies of Power in the Early Middle Ages* (Leiden: Brill, 2001), 137–54; Ian N. Wood, "Constructing cults in early Medieval France. Local saints and churches in Burgundy and the Auvergne 400–1000," in Richard Sharpe and Alan Thacker (eds.), *Local Saints and Local Churches in the Early Medieval West* (Oxford: Oxford University Press, 2002), 155–87; idem, "The individuality of Gregory of Tours" in idem and Kathleen Mitchell (eds.), *The World of Gregory of Tours* (Leiden, Boston and Cologne: Brill, 2002), 29–46.

37 On Priscus, see Martin Heinzelmann, *Bischofsherrschaft in Gallien. Zur Kontinuität römischer Führungsschichten vom 4. bis zum 7. Jahrhundert. Soziale, prosopographische und bildungsgeschichtliche Aspekte* (München: Thorbecke, 1976), 176–9.

38 *VP* VIII, pp. 240–52. For an English translation see Gregory of Tours, *Life of the Fathers*, trans. Edward James, 2nd edition (Liverpool: Liverpool University Press, 1991), 49–64.

39 *Hist.* IV.36, pp. 168–9.

40 *Hist.* IV.36, pp. 168–9.

41 Heinzelmann, *Bischofsherrschaft*, 177 with n. 538.

42 Heinzelmann, *Bischofsherrschaft*, 177–8.

43 *Corpus Inscriptionum Latinarum (CIL)* 13: *Inscriptiones trium Galliarum et Germaniarum Latinae*, eds. Otto Hirschfeld and Carl Zangemeister, pars I, fasc. 1, *Inscriptiones Aquitaniae et Lugdunensis*, ed. Otto Hirschfeld (Berlin: De Gruyter, 1899, repr. 1966), no. 2399.

44 Peter Brown, *Society and the Holy in Late Antiquity* (Berkeley: California University Press, 1982), 245.

45 On the date see Heinzelmann, *Bischofsherrschaft*, 172.

46 "[…] *iurgia dispiciens suspiciensque deum*[…]," CIL 13, no. 2400, see also Gregory of Tours' account on Nicetius in his *Vita Patrum* VIII.3, pp. 243–44 about a conflict with the count of Lyon Armentarius who overruled Nicetius.

47 Esders and Reimitz, "Episcopal Iurisdiction."

48 Cf. above, p. 23

49 An overview over the different views provides Alexander C. Murray, "Chronology and composition of the Histories of Gregory of Tours," *Journal of Late Antiquity* 1 (2008), 157–74, but cf. still Heinzelmann, *Gregory of Tours*, and Wood, *Gregory of Tours* who, for different reasons, imagine Gregory's work on the *Histories* as a project that concerned Gregory for a much longer period.

50 G. Halsall, "Nero and Herod? The death of Chilperic and Gregory's writing of history," in Kathleen Mitchell and Ian N. Wood (eds.), *The World of Gregory of Tours*

(Leiden: Brill, 2002), 337–50; for Chilperic as a model of a bad king, see Heinzelmann, *Gregory of Tours*, 41–51.
51　*Hist.* V.18, pp. 216–25.
52　Arnaldo Momigliano, "The origins of ecclesiastical historiography," in idem, *The Classical Foundations of Modern Historiography*, (Berkeley, California; University of California Press, 1992), 132–56, at 140.
53　*Hist.* VIII.41, p. 407–8.
54　Esders and Reimitz, "Episcopal Jurisdiction."
55　Helmut Reimitz, "Genre and Identity in Merovingian Historiography," in: Gerda Heydemann and Helmut Reimitz (eds.), *Historiography and Identity*, vol 2: *Post-Roman Multiplicity* (Turnhout: Brepols, forthcoming).
56　Umberto Eco, *Lector in fabula. Cooperazione interpretatativa nei testi narrativi* (Milano: Bompiani, 1979), cf. the collection of translated essays in Umberto Eco, *The role of the Reader. Explorations in the Semiotics of Texts* (Bloomington: Indiana University Press, 1984).
57　Peter Brown, "Gregory of Tours. Introduction," in Kathleen Mitchell and Ian N. Wood (eds.), *The World of Gregory of Tours* (Leiden: Brill, 2002), 1–28, here at 19.

3   East and West from a Visigothic Perspective: How and Why Were Frankish Brides Negotiated in the Late Sixth Century?

1　I would like to thank the members of the GIF project for their useful comments on an earlier version of this paper.
2　*Hist.* IX.15–16, pp. 429–31.
3　*Concilios visigóticos e hispano-romanos*, ed. José Vives (Barcelona: Instituto Enrique Flórez, 1963), 116 [hereafter, *Concilios*].
4　*Hist.* IX.15, pp. 429–30.
5　*Hist.* IX.15: "conpunctus miseratione divina," (p. 429).
6　See the article by Yaniv Fox in this volume.
7　Walter Goffart, "Byzantine Policy in the West under Tiberius II and Maurice: The Pretenders Hermenegild and Gundovald (578–585)," *Traditio* 13 (1957): 73–118; Walter Goffart, "The Frankish Pretender Gundovald, 582–85. A Crisis of Merovingian Blood," *Francia* 39 (2012): 1–27.
8　Using the terms "Austrasia" and "Neustria" is problematic, since the latter is mentioned for the first time in the so-called *Chronicle of Fredegar*. *Austrasii* already appears in Gregory of Tours' *Histories* (*Hist.* V.14, pp. 207–13, at 213). For reasons of readability and to help to distinguish the parties involved I will resort to those terms.

9 Martina Hartmann, *Die Königin im frühen Mittelalter* (Stuttgart: Kohlhammer, 2009), 74–5.
10 Janet L. Nelson, "A propos des femmes royales dans les rapports entre le monde wisigothique et le monde franc à l'Époque de Reccared," in *Concilio III. de Toledo. XIV Centenario, 589–1989*, ed. Arzobispado de Toledo con la colaboracibon de Caja Toledo (Toledo: Arzobispado de Toledo, 1991), 465–76, here 468; Ian Wood, *The Merovingian Kingdoms 450–751* (London and New York: Longman, 1993), 170.
11 Wood, *Merovingian Kingdoms*, 170.
12 *Hist.* V.38, pp. 243–5, here 244. It is most likely that one of the conditions for this marriage was Ingund's conversion, as her mother had already converted when she had moved from Spain to Austrasia. See *Hist.* IV.27–28, pp. 160–1; see also Paul Goubert, "Byzance et l'Espagne wisigothique (554–711)," *Études byzantines* 2 (1944): 5–78, here 20; Bruno Dumézil, "La différence confessionnelle dans les couples du haut moyenâge: facteur de stabilité ou motif de rupture? (Ve–VIIIe siècle)," in *Répudiation, séparation, divorce dans l'Occident médiéval*, ed. Emmanuelle Santinelli (Valenciennes: Presses universitaires de Valenciennes, 2007), 257–73, here 264.
13 On the dating of this uprising see, for example, Roger Collins, "Gregory of Tours and Spain," in *A Companion to Gregory of Tours*, ed. Alexander C. Murray (Leiden: Brill, 2015), 498–515, here 507–9. Collins discusses the dating problem that derives from the different chronologies in Gregory of Tours and John of Biclarum. *Iohannis Abbatis Biclarensis Chronica*, ed. Theodor Mommsen, *MGH SS Auct. ant.* 11, pp. 163–220 [hereafter, Joh. Bicl., *Chron.*], here ad a. 579.3, p. 215. On the uprising in general, see also Bruno Dumézil, "Le meurtre du père: jugements contrastés sur la révolte d'Herménégild," in *Splendor Reginae. Passions, genre et famille. Mélanges en l'honneur de Régine Le Jan*, eds. Laurent Jégou, Sylvie Joye, Thomas Lienhard and Jens Schneider (Turnhout: Brepols, 2015), 29–38.
14 Joh. Bicl., *Chron.*, ad a. 579.3, p. 215. For a different translation of this famous phrase, see Knut Schäferdiek who does not believe that Goisuinth supported Hermenegild and her granddaughter: Knut Schäferdiek, *Die Kirche in den Reichen der Westgoten und Suewen bis zur Errichtung der westgotischen katholischen Staatskirche* (Berlin: De Gruyter, 1967), 147: see also Collins, "Gregory of Tours and Spain," 22, who argues that Hermenegild and his wife reconciled with Goisuinth before the uprising. On the general reasons for Hermenegild to rise against his father, see Margarita Vallejo Girvés, *La Hispania y Bizancio. Una relación desconocida* (Madrid: Ediciones Akal, 2012), here 235–62.
15 Despite its bulkiness, this concept, as used by Janet Nelson, is quite helpful for distinguishing between the various diplomatic parties involved. See Nelson, "A propos des femmes," 472.
16 *Hist.* V.40, pp. 247–8, here 247. This envoy was Bishop Elafius of Châlons.
17 *Hist.* IX.24, pp. 443–4. See Nelson, "A propos des femmes," 473; see also Schäferdiek, *Die Kirche*, 141–42.

18 See below.
19 See *Hist.* VI.43, pp. 314–16.
20 See above.
21 See below.
22 *Hist.* V.43, pp. 249–52, VI.18, pp. 287–8, VI.29, pp. 295–7, VI.33, p. 304, VI.34, pp. 304–5, VI.40, pp. 310–13.
23 Joh. Bicl., *Chron.*, ad a. 580.2, p. 216; Gregory calls this new dogma a perfidious trick. *Hist.* V.38, pp. 243–5, V.43, pp. 249–52, VI.40, pp. 310–13. See Peter J. Heather, *The Goths* (Oxford: Blackwell Publishing, 1996), 280; Markus Mülke, "Romana religio oder catholica fides? Der Westgotenkönig Leovigild und das arianische Reichskonzil von 580 n. Chr. in Toledo," *Frühmittelalterliche Studien* 43 (2009): 53–69. Manuel Koch, *Ethnische Identität im Entstehungsprozess des spanischen Westgotenreiches* (Berlin: De Gruyter, 2012), 213.
24 Joh. Bicl., *Chron.*, ad a. 580.1, p. 216.
25 *Hist.* V.44, pp. 252–4.
26 Isidore of Seville, *Historia de regibus Gothorum, Vandalorum et Suevorum*, ed. Theodor Mommsen, *MGH SS Auct. ant.* 11, 46–7, pp. 285–6 [hereafter, Isidore, *Hist. Goth.*]; Isidore implies both: Agila was either killed by his own men because they were afraid of the Byzantine troops that may have entered Spain under the pretext that they would support Agila; or Athanagild was trying to establish his position by calling Byzantine troops for help, but he could not get rid of them after the defeat of Agila.
27 Christine Delaplace, "L''affaire Gondovald' et le dispositif défensif de l'Aquitaine wisigothique et franque," *Aquitania* 25 (2009): 199–211, here 206.
28 On the relationship between the Lombards and the Empire see Walter Pohl, "The Empire and the Lombards: Treaties and Negotiations in the Sixth Century," in *Kingdoms of the Empire: The Integration of Barbarians in Late Antiquity*, ed. Walter Pohl (Leiden, New York and Köln: Brill, 1997), 75–134.
29 Such as applying diplomatic means and interfering in the internal affairs of its enemies. On the (changing) strategy see Goffart, "Byzantine Policy," 73–4; Jamie Wood, "Defending Byzantine Spain: Frontiers and Diplomacy," *Early Medieval Europe* 18, 3 (2010): 292–319, here 310; Margarita Vallejo Girvés, "Byzantine Spain and the African Exarchate. An Administrative Perspective," *Jahrbuch der Österreichischen Byzantinistik* 49 (1999): 13–23.
30 *Hist.* V.38, pp. 243–5, here 245.
31 *Hist.* VI.43, pp. 314–16.
32 *Hist.* VIII.28, pp. 390–1; Joh. Bicl., *Chron.*, ad a. 585.3, p. 217.
33 Wood, "Defending Byzantine Spain," 311; Vallejo Girvés, *La Hispania y Bizancio*, 241.
34 *Hist.* VI.43, pp. 314–16.

35 *Hist.* VI.42, p. 314. Compare Vallejo Girvés, *La Hispania y Bizancio*, 241; and the article by Yaniv Fox in this volume.
36 Regarding the usurpation, see Bernard S. Bachrach, *The Anatomy of a Little War. A Diplomatic and Military History of the Gundovald Affair (568–586)* (Boulder: Westview Press, 1994); Walter Goffart, "Frankish Pretender." Whether Gundovald was Chlothar's son cannot be proved without doubt.
37 Delaplace, "L'affaire Gondovald'," 206. She assumes he might have stayed on Corsica or Sardinia.
38 On Ingund's and Athanagild II's fate, see *Hist.* VI.43, pp. 314–16 VIII.18, pp. 384–5, VIII.21, pp. 387–8, VIII.28, pp. 390–1, IX.16, pp. 430–1.
39 *Hist.* VI.40, pp. 310–13, here p. 310.
40 *Hist.* VI.34, pp. 304–5, VI.40, pp. 310–313. See Bachrach, *Anatomy*, 82.
41 *Hist.* VII.9, p. 331.
42 *Hist.* VI.45, pp. 317–19, VII.9, p. 331, VII.39, pp. 362–3.
43 Bachrach, *Anatomy*, 101; Delaplace, "L'affaire Gondovald'," 207; Goffart, "Frankish Pretender," 20.
44 *Hist.* IX.28, pp. 446–47.
45 Goffart, "Frankish Pretender," 20; Delaplace argues differently: Delaplace, "L'affaire Gondovald'," 205.
46 Goffart, "Frankish Pretender," 20–21. Similar arguments were raised by Bachrach and Delaplace. See Bachrach, *Anatomy*, 101; Delaplace, "L'affaire Gondovald'," 207.
47 *Hist.* VI.2, p. 266; VI.11, pp. 280–82. See Robert Folz, "Sur l'inspirateur du pacte d'Andelot: Gontran roi de Bourgogne," *Les Cahiers haut-marnais* 175 (1988): 14–20.
48 Eugen Ewig, *Die Merowinger und das Imperium* (Düsseldorf: Westdeutscher Verlag, 1983), 32.
49 *Hist.* VI.33, p. 304.
50 *Hist.* VIII.28, pp. 390–1.
51 *Hist.* VIII.28, pp. 390–1, VIII.30, pp. 393–7, VIII.35, p. 404, VIII.38, p. 405, IX.1, pp. 414–15, IX.7, pp. 420–1, IX.15–16, pp. 429–31.
52 Joh. Bicl., *Chron.*, ad a. 586.2, p. 217; conversion: ad a. 587.5, p. 218; *Hist.* IX.15, pp. 429–430; Isidore, *Hist. Goth.*, 52, pp. 288–9.
53 *Hist.* VIII.28, pp. 390–1, VIII.30, pp. 393–7, VIII.35, p. 404, VIII.38, p. 405.
54 *Hist.* IX.15–16, pp. 429–31.
55 *Hist.* IX.16, pp. 430–31.
56 Bachrach, *Anatomy*, 69–83; Dumézil, *Brunehaut*, 202–8.
57 *Hist.* IX.20, pp. 434–41. On the Treaty of Andelot see Anna M. Drabek, "Der Merowingervertrag von Andelot aus dem Jahr 587," *Mitteilungen des Instituts für Österreichische Geschichtsforschung* 78 (1970): 34–41.

58 In *Hist.* IX.1, p. 414–15, Gregory describes that they reconciled, which was necessary because Goisuinth had supported his brother Hermenegild against Leovigild as suggested by John of Biclaro. Joh. Bicl., *Chron.*, ad a. 579.3, p. 215. See above.
59 *Hist.* IX.16, p. 431.
60 *Hist.* IX.25, pp. 444–5.
61 *Hist.* VI.42, p. 314, Joh. Bicl., *Chron.*, ad a. 584.4, p. 217; See Goffart, "Frankish Pretender," 15; and Delaplace, "L'affaire Gondovald'," 205.
62 *Hist.* VIII.28, pp. 390–1.
63 For Brunhild's correspondence with Constantinople on this matter, see *EA* 27, p. 139. On the rhetoric of these letters, see Andrew Gillett, "Love and Grief in Post-Imperial Diplomacy: The Letters of Brunhild," in *Power and Emotions in the Roman World and Late Antiquity* eds. Denijel Dizno and Barbara Sidwell (Piscataway (NJ): Gorgias Press, 2010), 127–65; and the article by Yaniv Fox in this volume.
64 *Hist.* IX.25, pp. 444–5.
65 *Concilios*, 116: "Ego Baddo gloriosa regina hanc fidem, quam credidi et suscepi, mea manu de toto corde subscribsi"; on Baddo, see for example José Orlandis, "Baddo, gloriosa regina," in *De Tertullien aux Mozarabes: Antiquité tardive et christianisme ancien: mélanges offerts à Jacques Fontaine à l'occasion de son 70e anniversaire par ses élèves, amis et collègues*, eds. Louis Holtz and Jean-Claude Fredouille (Paris: Institut d'études augustiniennes, 1992), 83–91.
66 For differing depictions and dating of these uprisings, see *Hist.* IX.15, p. 430; IX.31, p. 450; Joh. Bicl., *Chron.*, ad a. 589.2, p. 218 and 590.1, p. 219; see Andrew T. Fear, trans., *Lives of the Visigothic Fathers* (Liverpool: Liverpool University Press, 1997).
67 Isidore, *Hist. Goth.*, 53, pp. 289–90; Joh. Bicl., *Chron.*, ad a. 589.2, p. 218 and 590.1, p. 219; *Hist.* IX.15, p. 430, IX.31–32, pp. 450–1. This argument depends on a comparison of the chronology of events in these three authors.
68 See Edward A. Thompson, "The Conversion of the Visigoths to Catholicism," *Nottingham Medieval Studies* 4 (1960), 4–35; Roger Collins, "King Leovigild and the Conversion of the Visigoths," in *Law, Culture and Regionalism in Early Medieval Spain*, ed. Roger Collins (Aldershot: Variorum, 1992), 1–12; Heather: *The Goths*.
69 He also continued his father's *imitatio imperii* that, in the case of Leovigild, manifested itself in minting coins, founding cities, such as Victoriacum or Reccopolis, issuing the *Codex revisus*, using imperial insignia, recognizing his sons as co-rulers, and convening synods. See Isidore, *Hist. Goth.*, 51, p. 208; Christoph Eger, "Zur Imperialisierung des westgotischen Königtums aus archäologischer Sicht," in *Spolien im Umkreis der Macht: Akten der Tagung in Toledo vom 21.–22.09.2006*, eds. Thomas G. Schattner and Fernando Valdés Fernández (Mainz: P. von Zabern, 2009), 151–69, here 169. Dietrich Claude, *Geschichte der Westgoten* (Stuttgart: Kohlhammer, 1970), 72; see also idem, *Adel, Kirche und Königtum im Westgotenreich* (Sigmaringen:

Thorbecke, 1971); idem, "Gentile und territoriale Staatsideen im Westgotenreich," *Frühmittelalterliche Studien* 6 (1972): 1–38; Peter Linehan, *History and the Historians of Medieval Spain* (Oxford: Clarendon Press, 1993), 22; Koch, *Ethnische Identität*, 190; Mülke, "Romana religio oder catholica fides?," 62; Karl F. Stroheker, *Germanentum und Spätantike* (Zurich: Artemis, 1965), 134–91.

70 Franz Görres, "Rekared der Katholische (586–601). Neue kirchen- und culturgeschichtliche Forschungen auf dem Gebiete des Vormittelalters," *Zeitschrift für wissenschaftliche Theologie* 42 (1899): 270–322.

4 Friendship and Diplomacy in the *Histories* of Gregory of Tours

1   *Hist.* IX.20, pp. 439–40
2   Koenraad Verboven, *The Economy of Friends: Economic Aspects of Amicitia and Patronage in the Late Republic* (Brussels: Latomus, 2002), 35. For an excellent survey of *amicitia* in the Roman tradition, see David Konstan, *Friendship in the Classical World* (Cambridge: Cambridge University Press, 1997), 122–48.
3   Eva Österberg, *Friendship and Love, Ethics and Politics Studies in Mediaeval and Early Modern History* (Budapest; New York: Central European University Press, 2010), 52–3.
4   Verena Epp, *Amicitia: zur Geschichte personaler, sozialer, politischer und geistlicher Beziehungen im frühen Mittelalter* (Stuttgart: Anton Hiersemann, 1999), 299.
5   Epp, *Amicitia*, 2–3.
6   Peter Brown, *Through the Eye of a Needle* (Princeton: Princeton University Press, 2012), 393–94; see also Epp, *Amicitia*, 302–3. On friendship at the late antique imperial courts, see John Matthews, *Western Aristocracies and Imperial Court* (Oxford: Clarendon Press, 1990), 254–5.
7   Konstan, *Friendship in the Classical World*, 172–3.
8   Antonella Liuzzo Scorpo, *Friendship in Medieval Iberia: Historical, Legal, and Literary Perspectives* (Burlington: Ashgate, 2014), 200.
9   Alexander Murray, "Chronology and the Composition of the *Histories* of Gregory of Tours," *Journal of Late Antiquity* 1, no. 1 (2008): 158.
10 Murray, "Chronology," 161.
11 *Hist.* III.15, pp. 112–16; *Hist.* IV.11, p. 142; *Hist.* IV.46, p. 181; *Hist.* VI.36, p. 307; *Hist.* VII.47, p. 366; *Hist.* IX.19, p. 432; *Hist.* X.1, p. 479; *Hist.* X.14, p. 500.
12 *Hist.* IV. 46, pp. 180–3.
13 *Hist.* IV.47, pp. 183–4; for a detailed discussion see Erich Auerbach, *Mimesis the Representation of Reality in Western Literature*, trans. Willard R. Trask, (Princeton: Princeton University Press, 1968), 77–83.

14 Gerd Althoff, *Family, Friends, and Followers: Political and Social Bonds in Early Medieval Europe*, trans. Christopher Carroll, (Cambridge: Cambridge University Press), 71.
15 *Hist.* IX.19, pp. 432–4.
16 *Hist.* III.15, pp. 112–16.
17 *Hist.* X.1, pp. 477–81. On the title *apocrisiarius*, which encompassed a diplomatic role, see Andrew Gillett, *Envoys and Political Communication in the Late Antique West, 411–533* (Cambridge: Cambridge University Press, 2003), 266–7.
18 For example, *Hist.* IV. 23. On oathtaking as a structural device in narrative see Stefan Esders, "'Avenger of all perjury' in Constantinople, Ravenna and Metz. St Polyeuctus, Sigibert I and the Division of Charibert's Kingdom in 568," in *Western Perspectives on the Mediterranean. Cultural Transfer in Late Antiquity and the Early Middle Ages (400–800)* ed. Andreas Fischer and Ian Wood (London: Bloomsbury, 2014), 22–3, n. 49; and on oaths in general id., "Late Roman Military Law in the Bavarian Code," clio@themis. *Revue électronique d'histoire du droit* 10 (2016): 4.
19 Paul Barnwell, "War and Peace: Historiography and Seventh Century Embassies," *Early Medieval Europe* 6, no. 2 (1997): 128–9. Examples of use of the word *amicitia* for diplomacy within the Merovingian kingdoms include: *Hist.* V.18, p. 222; *Hist.* V.39, p. 247; *Hist.* VII.38, p. 360; *Hist.* IX.20, p. 439; *Hist.* X.19, pp. 510–11; *Hist.* X.28, pp. 520–2.
20 Gillett, *Envoys and Political Communication in the Late Antique West*, 267–8.
21 Three times in book two (*Hist.* II.35, p. 84; *Hist.* II.40, pp. 89–91; and *Hist.* II.4, pp. 39–40); four times in book four (*Hist.* IV.23, pp. 155–6 and three times in *Hist.* IV.40, pp. 171–3); three times in book five (*Hist.* V.18, pp. 216–25 Hist.V.38, pp. 243–5 and *Hist.* V.39, pp. 245–7); once in book six (*Hist.* VI.43, pp. 314–16); once in book seven (*Hist.* VII.38, pp. 359–62); twice in book nine (*Hist.* IX.29, pp. 44–8 and *Hist.* IX.20, pp. 434–41); and three times in book ten (*Hist.* X.19, pp. 510–13 and *Hist.* X.28, pp. 520–2).
22 Ian Wood, "Gregory of Tours and Clovis," *Revue Belge de Philologie et d'Histoire* 63 (1985): 249–72, reprinted in *Debating the Middle Ages* eds. L.K. Little and B.H. Rosenwein, (Oxford: Blackwell, 1998), 73–91.
23 *Hist.* II.35, p. 84; *Hist.* IV.23, pp. 155–6; and *Hist.* IX.29, pp. 447–8.
24 *Hist.* II.40, pp. 89–91.
25 *Hist.* II.35, p. 84.
26 Herwig Wolfram, *History of the Goths* trans. Thomas J. Dunlop (Berkley; London: University of California Press), 192 n. 181.
27 Wolfram, *History of the Goths*, 192.
28 Ralph Mathisen, "The First Franco-Visigothic War," in *The Battle of Vouillé, 507 CE: Where France Began* eds. Ralph Mathisen and Danuta Shanzer (Berlin: De Gruyter, 2012), 6. Historians vary on the dates of this meeting: Mathisen prefers just after 500; Wolfram gives the date as 502. Wolfram, *History of the Goths*, 192.

29 *Hist.* II.40, pp. 89–91.
30 *Hist.* II.41, pp. 91–2. Penny MacGeorge, *Late Roman Warlords* (Oxford: Oxford University Press), 128, n. 71.
31 The problems with Gregory's chronology of the reign of Clovis are many and complicated; a cogent overview is offered by Danuta Shanzer, "Foreword" in *The Battle of Vouillé, 507 CE: Where France Began* eds. Ralph Mathisen and Danuta Shanzer, viii–ix. The destruction of Ragnachar is described in *Hist.* II.42.
32 *Hist.* IV.23, pp. 155–6.
33 *Hist.* IX.29, p. 447: "Sit amicitia inter nos, et non pereamus ac dissolvamus certum ditioni tuae tributum. Ac ubicumque necessarium contra inimicus fuerit, ferre auxilium non pegebit."
34 *Hist.* IX.29, pp. 447–8.
35 Margaret Mullett, "The Language of Diplomacy," In *Byzantine Diplomacy* eds. Jonathan Shepard and Simon Franklin (Aldershot: Variorum Reprints, 1992), pp. 203–16; and Gillet, *Envoys and Political Communication in the Late Antique West*, 4.
36 The most recent edition is Elena Malaspina, *Il liber epistolarum della cancelleria Austrasica (Sec. V–VI)* (Rome: Herder, 2001). On the making and purpose of the collection, see Graham Barrett and George Woudhuysen, "Assembling the Austrasian Letters at Trier and Lorsch," *Early Medieval Europe*, 24, no. 1 (2016): 3–57.
37 On these letters, see Bruno Dumézil's and Yaniv Fox's contributions in this volume and also Bruno Dumézil and Thomas Lienhard, "Les 'Lettres austrasiennes': Dire, cacher, transmettre les informations diplomatiques au haut Moyen Âge," in *Les relations diplomatiques au Moyen Âge. Formes et enjeux* eds. Marie-Céline Isaia and Armand Jamme, (Paris: Publications de la Sorbonne, 2011), 69–80.
38 Specifically, *EA* 18; 30; 33; 37; 39; 42; pp. 132–4; 172–4; 178; 184–6; 188–90; 202–4.
39 *Celsitudinis Vestrae agnoscentes dignitatem meritis inlustram, oportunum duximus distinare vel litterarum conloquia, quorum per longa intervalla non adhibetur praesentia. EA* 36, lines 1–6, p. 184.
40 *Hist.* IX.28, pp. 446–7.
41 On envoys, see Bruno Dumézil, "Les ambassadeurs occidentaux au VIe siècle: recrutement, usages et modes de distinction d'une élite de représentation à l'étranger," in *Théorie et pratiques des élites au Haut Moyen Age: Conception, perception et réalisation sociale*, eds. François Bougard, Hans-Werner Goetz, and Régine Le Jan (Turnhout: Brepols, 2011), 243–60.
42 *Hist.* IV.40, pp. 171–3. On Gregory's portrait of Tiberius, see Pia Lucas' chapter in this volume.
43 Firminus' activities as count are described three times: *Hist.* IV.13, *Hist.* IV.30, and *Hist.* IV.35. The other envoy, Warinar the Frank, is only mentioned in relation to the embassy described in *Hist.* IV.40, pp. 171–3.

44 Averil Cameron, "On the Byzantine Sources of Gregory of Tours," *Journal of Theological Studies* 26, no. 2 (1975): 421–6, reprinted in *Continuity and Change in Sixth-century Byzantium* (London: Variorum Reprints, 1981). The passage is translated in Geoffrey Greatrex and Samuel N. C. Lieu, *The Roman Eastern Frontier and the Persian Wars AD 363–628* (London: Routledge, 2002), 139. On the subject of similarities between Gregory and Evagrius, see Valerie A. Caries, "Evagrius Scholasticus and Gregory of Tours: A Literary Comparison" (PhD diss., University of California, Berkley, 1976).

45 For a recent revision to the chronology of contemporary events, see Mischa Meier, "Die Translatio des Christusbildes von Kamulianai und der Kreuzreliquie von Apameia nach Konstantinopel unter Justin II. Ein übersehenes Datierungsproblem" *Zeitschrift für antikes Christentum* 7 (2003): 237–50.

46 Walter Goffart, "Foreigners in Gregory of Tours," *Florilegium* 4 (1982): 98, n. 25. For commentary on this episode, see Greatrex and Lieu, *The Roman Eastern Frontier and the Persian Wars AD 363–628*, 281, n. 26–28.

47 Gregory himself comments on his sources in the prologue to Book Two of the *Histories*; see Andrew Cain, "Miracles, martyrs, and Arians: Gregory of Tours sources for his account of the Vandal Kingdom," *Vigiliae* 59, no. 5 (2005): 424–5. Gregory refers to Syrian merchants who settled in Gaul *Hist.* VII.31, pp. 350–2 and *Hist.* X.26, p. 519, and his own deacon seems to have been his source of information about the inauguration of Gregory the Great as pope, as he describes in *Hist.* X.1, pp, 477–81. As noted by Paul Barnwell, in "War and Peace: Historiography and Seventh Century Embassies," *Early Medieval Europe* 6, no. 2 (1997): 128–9, Gregory mentions over sixty diplomatic events in the *Histories*, and it seems possible that he had information from envoys returned from Byzantium in *Hist.* IV.40. He was himself a royal envoy on several occasions. On bishops as envoys see Gillett, *Envoys and Political Communication in the Late Antique West*, 113–71; on their travels see Jamie Kreiner, "About the Bishop: the Economy of Government in Post-Roman Gaul," *Speculum* 86 (2011): 336–7, 340–1.

48 Anna M. Drabek, "Der Merowingervertrag von Andelot aus dem Jahr 567," *Mitteilungen des Instituts für Österreichische Geschichtsforschung* 78 (1970): 34–41; Wolfgang Hermann Fritze, "Die fränkische Schwurfreundschaft der Merowingerzeit" *Zeitschrift der Savigny-Stiftung für Rechtsgeschichte* 71 (1954): 96.

49 Althoff, *Family, Friends and Followers*, 68–9. This emphasis on *caritas* also appears in *Hist.* IX.16, pp. 430–1, to describe the alliance Reccared sought after he became a Catholic.

50 Drabek, "Der Merowingervertrag von Andelot aus dem Jahr 567," 34. The diplomatic meeting and its results is introduced in *Hist.* IX.11, p. 426, the text of the treaty is in *Hist.* IX.20, pp. 434–41.

51 Althoff, *Family, Friends and Followers*, 69–70.

52 *Hist.* X.28, pp. 520–2.

53 Gillett, *Envoys and Political Communication in the Late Antique West*, 267–8.
54 *Hist.* IX.20, pp. 434–41.

5 Private Records of Official Diplomacy: The Franco-Byzantine Letters in the Austrasian Epistolar Collection

1 Cf. Mt. 25: 14–30.
2 *EA*, 14, p. 14.
3 For its edition, see Elena Malaspina, *Il* Liber epistolarum *della cancellaria austrasica* (Rome: Herder, 2001).
4 Paul Goubert, *Byzance avant l'Islam, tome second, Byzance et l'Occident sous les successeurs de Justinien, vol. 1, Byzance et les Francs*, (Paris: Picard, 1955), 170–1; Malaspina, *Il* Liber epistolarum *della cancellaria austrasica*, 27–8; W. J. Anderson, "Vatic. Ottob. lat. 1210 and Vatican Palat. lat. 869 ff. 62–69," *Revue Bénédictine* 43 (1931): 104–5. Preparing this paper, I could not use the important study of Gernot Michael Müller, "Briefkultur im merowingischen Gallien. Zu Konzeption und Funktion der Epistulae Austrasicae," in *Zwischen Alltagskommunikation und literarischer Identitätsbildung. Studien zur lateinischen Epistolographie in Spätantike und Frühmittelalter*, ed. Gernot Michael Müller (Stuttgart: Franz Steiner Verlag, 2018), 302–52.
5 Bernhard Bischoff, *Die Abtei Lorsch im Spiegel ihrer Handschriften* (Lorsch: Laurissa, 1989), 51.
6 Wilhelm Gundlach, "Die Sammlung der Epistolae Austrasicae," *Neues Archiv der Gesellschaft für ältere deutsche Geschichtskunde* 13 (1888): 365–87.
7 Pierre Riché, *Éducation et culture dans l'Occident barbare*, vi^e–viie siècle (Paris: Seuil, 1962), 265–7.
8 Malaspina, *Il* Liber epistolarum *della cancellaria austrasica*, 7–9.
9 Graham Barrett and George Woudhuysen, "Assembling the Austrasian Letters at Trier and Lorsch," *Early Medieval Europe* 24, no. 1 (2016): 3–57. Also, on Ep. 2: Graham Barrett and George Woudhuysen, "Remigius and the 'Important News' of Clovis rewritten," *Antiquité tardive* 24 (2016): 471–500.
10 Angelika Häse (ed.), *Mittelalterliche Bücherverzeichnisse aus Kloster Lorsch* (Wiesbaden: Harrassowitz, 2002), 98: "Liber epistularum diuersorum patrum et regum, quas Treueris inueni, in uno codice."
11 Barrett and Woudhuysen, "Assembling the Austrasian Letters," 27–31.
12 Cristiana Sogno, Bradley K. Storin and Edward J. Watts (eds.), *Late Antique Letter Collections: A Critical Introduction and Reference Guide* (Oakland: University of California Press, 2017), 5–6.

13 *Epistolae Wisigothicae*, ed. Johannes [Juan] Gil, *Miscellanea Wisigothica*, 2nd ed. (Sevilla: Universidad de Sevilla, 1991); Salvador Iranzo Abellán, "La epistolografía hispana de época visigótica," in *Artes ad humanitatem*, II, eds. Esperança Borrel Vidal and Lambert Ferreres Pérez, (Barcelona: Secció Catalana de la SEEC, 2010), 87-96.
14 Stephane Gioanni, *Ennode de Pavie, Lettres, Livres I et II*, (Paris: Les Belles Lettres, 2006), XCLI-CLIV.
15 This codex is in Brussels, Bibliothèque Royale de Belgique, Ms. 9845-9848.
16 About this notion of a "handbook of style" see Ian N. Wood, "Letters and Letter Collections from Antiquity to the Middle Ages: The Prose Works of Avitus of Vienne," in *The Culture of Christendom: Essays in Medieval History in Commemoration of Denis T. Bethell*, ed. Marc A. Meyer (London: Bloomsbury, 1993), 42.
17 *Epistolae Wisigothicae*, 10, 11 and 12, ed. Juan GIL *Miscellanea Wisigothica* (Sevilla: Universidad de Sevilla, 1972), 30-36.
18 Shane Bjornlie, "What Have Elephants to Do with Sixth-Century Politics? A Reappraisal of the 'Official' Governmental Dossier of Cassiodorus," *Journal of Late Antiquity* 2, no. 1 (2009): 143-71.
19 Alice Rio, *Legal Practice and the Written Word in the Early Middle Ages: Frankish Formulae, c. 500-1000* (Cambridge: Cambridge University Press, 2009), 121-6.
20 Gerardus J. J. Walstra, *Les cinq épîtres rimées dans l'appendice des Formules de Sens* (Leiden: Brill, 1962); Yitzhak Hen, "Changing Places: Marculf, Chrodobert and the Wife of Grimoald," *Revue belge de philologie et d'histoire* 90 (2012): 225-43.
21 John R. Martindale, *The Prosopography of the Later Roman Empire*, III (Cambridge: Cambridge University Press, 1992) 1092-3; Charles Pietri and Luce Pietri (eds.), *Prosopographie chrétienne du Bas-Empire*, vol. II: *Italie (313-604)* (Rome: Ecole française de Rome, 1999), 1905-6.
22 Barrett and Woudhuysen, "Assembling the Austrasian Letters," 12.
23 Théophylacte Simocatta, VI, 3, 6-8, transl. Michael Whitby et Mary Whitby, *The History of Theophylact Simocatta* (Oxford: Clarendon Press, 1986), 162.
24 For example, Gregory the Great, *Ep.* VIII. 4, ed. Dag Norberg (Turnhout: Brepols, 1982), 518-21.
25 *VP*, XVII, pp. 277-83.
26 *Hist.*, II.31, pp. 77-8.
27 Barrett and Woudhuysen, "Assembling the Austrasian Letters," 12-14.
28 On their relation, see below p. [6].
29 Bruno Dumézil, "Le patrice Dynamius et son réseau: culture aristocratique et transformation des pouvoirs autour de Lérins dans la seconde moitié du VIe siècle," in *Lérins, une île sainte de l'Antiquité au Moyen Âge*, eds. Yann Codou and Michel Lauwers (Turnhout: Brepols, 2009), 167-94.
30 Barrett and Woudhuysen, "Assembling the Austrasian Letters," 37.

31　Nancy Gauthier, *L'évangélisation dans les pays de Moselle. La province romaine de Première Belgique entre Antiquité et Moyen-Age (IIIème-VIIIème siècles)*, (Paris: De Boccard, 1980), 189-204.
32　Bruno Dumézil, *La reine Brunehaut* (Paris: Fayard, 2008), 281-2.
33　Barrett and Woudhuysen, "Assembling the Austrasian Letters," 44.
34　Elena Malaspina and Marc Reydellet, *Avit de Vienne, Lettres* (Paris: Les Belles Lettres, 2016), LXIX-LXXXI; Bruno Judic "La production et la diffusion du Registre des lettres de Grégoire le Grand," in *Actes des congrès de la Société des historiens médiévistes de l'enseignement supérieur public, 32e congrès* (Paris: Publications de la Sorbonne, 2002) 71-87; Stéphane Gioanni, *Ennode of Pavie, Lettres, Tome I* (Paris: Les Belles Lettres, 2006), CXLI-CXLVI.
35　*EA*, 5-8, 11 and 14, pp. 74-97, 112-16 and 120-3.
36　*VP*, XVII.5, pp. 282-3.
37　*EA*, 12, 13, 16, 17 and 22, pp. 116-19, 126-31.
38　Bruno Dumézil, "Gogo et ses amis: écriture, échanges et ambitions dans un réseau aristocratique de la fin du VIe siècle," *Revue Historique* 643 (2007): 553-93.
39　Luce Pietri et Marc Heijmans (eds.), *Prosopographie chrétienne du Bas-Empire*, IV, *Gaule (314-614)* (Paris: Association des amis du Centre d'histoire et civilisation de Byzance, 2013), 614-18.
40　Pietri/Heijmans, *Prosopographie chrétienne*, 1223-4.
41　*Hist.*, IX.10, pp. 424-6.
42　*EA*, 12 and 17, pp. 116-17 and 128-31; *Hist.*, IX.11, p. 426.
43　*EA*, 14, pp. 120-3.
44　R. Koebner, *Venantius Fortunatus. Seine Persönlichkeit und seine Stellung in der geistigen Kultur des Merowinger-Reiches* (Leipzig and Berlin: Teubner, 1915), 128-37; Marc Reydellet, *Venance Fortunat, Poèmes, I* (Paris: Les Belles Lettres, 1994), LXXVII-LXXVIII.
45　*EA*, 14, pp. 120-3.
46　At the beginning of the eleventh century, the poem was also used in the *Vita Magnerici* (§50-51), written by Eberwin of St. Martin of Trier *Vita Magnerici, AA SS, Iul.* VI, pp. 183-91.
47　*Hist.*, X.19, pp. 510-13.
48　Martin Heinzelmann, "L'aristocratie et les évêchés entre Loire et Rhin jusqu'à la fin du VIIe siècle," *Revue d'Histoire de l'Église de France* 62 (1976): 87.
49　David Ganz, *Corbie in the Carolingian renaissance* (Sigmaringen: Thorbecke, 1990), 40.
50　*Epistolae Arelatenses genuinae*, in Wilhelm Gundlach (ed.), MGH Epp. III (Berlin, 1882), 5-83.
51　Rosamund McKitterick, *History and Memory in the Carolingian World* (Cambridge: Cambridge University Press, 2004), 255.
52　*EA*, 1-4, 19-20, 25-47, pp. 58-73, 134-9, 164-217.

6 The Language of Sixth-century Frankish Diplomacy

1. This article is supported by the I-CORE program of the Planning and Budgeting Committee of the Israeli Committee for Higher Education and the Israel Science Foundation (ISF) Grant no. 1754. I would like to thank Stefan Esders and the editors for their comments and suggestions. The edition of the *Epistolae Austrasicae* used throughout is Malaspina's [hereafter, *EA*]. Translation my own, aided by Malaspina's Italian translation. *EA* 42, pp. 202–4.
2. See Eugen Ewig, *Die fränkischen Teilungen und Teilreiche (511–613)* (Wiesbaden: F. Steiner, 1953); Mark Widdowson, "Merovingian Partitions: A 'Genealogical Charter'?," *Early Medieval Europe* 17, no. 1 (2009): 1–17.
3. For a very partial list, see Barbara H. Rosenwein, *Emotional Communities in the Early Middle Ages* (Ithaca and London: Cornell University Press, 2007); Gerd Althoff, "*Ira regis*: A History of Royal Anger," in *Anger's Past: The Social Uses of Emotion in the Middle Ages*, ed. Barbara H. Rosenwein (Ithaca and London: Cornell University Press, 1998), 59–74; Maximilian Diesenberger, "Hair, Sacrality and Symbolic Capital in the Frankish Kingdoms," in *The Construction of Communities in the Early Middle Ages: Texts, Resources and Artefacts*, eds. Richard Corradini, Maximilian Diesenberger, and Helmut Reimitz (Leiden and Boston: Brill, 2003), 173–212; Matthew Innes, "'He Never Even Allowed His White Teeth to be Bared in Laughter': The Politics of Humour in the Carolingian Renaissance," in *Humour, History and Politics in Late Antiquity and the Early Middle Ages*, ed. Guy Halsall (Cambridge: Cambridge University Press, 2002), 131–56; Nira Gradowicz-Pancer, "De-Gendering Female Violence: Merovingian Female Honour as an 'Exchange of Violence'," *Early Medieval Europe* 11, no. 1 (2002): 1–18.
4. Gregory of Tours, *Hist.* II.27, pp. 72–3, and IX.34, pp. 454–5, respectively.
5. On the letter collections and "feelings," see Averil Cameron, "Defining the Holy Man," in *The Cult of Saints in Late Antiquity and the Middle Ages*, eds. Paul Antony Hayward and James Howard-Johnston (Oxford: Oxford University Press, 1999), 27–44, at 40, questioning their ability to reflect genuine emotion. Specifically, for the *Epistulae Austrasicae*, see Rosenwein, *Emotional Communities*, 115. The most comprehensive and indispensable treatment remains Andrew Gillett, "Love and Grief in Post-Imperial Diplomacy: The Letters of Brunhild," in *Power and Emotions in the Roman World and Late Antiquity*, eds. Barbara Sidwell and Danijel Dzino (Piscataway NJ: Gorgias Press, 2010), 127–65. On *amicitia* in epistolary culture, see Hope D. Williard, "Letter-Writing and Literary Culture in Merovingian Gaul," *European Review of History: Revue européenne d'histoire* 21, no. 5 (2014): 691–710 and her contribution to this volume.
6. On the Lombards' religion, see Walter Pohl, "Deliberate Ambiguity: The Langobards and Christianity," in *Christianizing Peoples and Converting Individuals*, eds. Guyda Armstrong and Ian N. Wood (Turnhout: Brepols, 2000), 47–60; also, Steven Fanning, "Langobard Arianism Reconsidered," *Speculum* 56, no. 2 (1981): 241–58.

7   As evidenced by *EA* 42: "... amicalem quidem voluntatem et paternum affectum circa nos atque sacratissimam rempublicam nostram conservare vos indicant," p. 202. Paul Goubert, *Byzance avant l'Islam, tome seconde: Byzance et l'occident sous les successeurs de Justinien* (Paris: Éditions A. et J. Picard et Cie, 1956), 17–19; Walter Goffart, "Byzantine Policy in the West under Tiberius II and Maurice: The Pretenders Hermenegild and Gundovald (579–585)," *Traditio* 13 (1957): 73–118.

8   On the complex nature of the relationship between the Lombards and the Empire prior to and after 568, with some discussion of the Frankish context, see Walter Pohl, "The Empire and the Lombards: Treaties and Negotiations in the Sixth Century," in *Kingdoms of the Empire: The Integration of Barbarians in Late Antiquity*, ed. Walter Pohl (Leiden, New York and Köln, 1997), 75–134.

9   Gregory of Tours, *Hist*. IV.42, pp. 174–7.

10 Marius of Avenches, *Chronicum*, in Justin Favrod, ed. and trans., *La chronique de Marius d'Avenches (455 – 581), Texte, traduction et commentaire* (Lausanne: Université de Lausanne, 1991), 82, *s.a.* 569: "Eo anno etiam in finitima loca Galliarum ingredi praesumpserunt ubi multitudo captivorum gen/tis ipsius venundati sunt" (That year they attempted to enter the boundaries of Gaul, where they could buy a multitude of captives from these peoples). The Franks' Bavarian policies were intimately linked to these developments. On this, see Carl I. Hammer, "Early Merovingian Bavaria: A Late Antique Italian Perspective," *Journal of Late Antiquity* 4, no. 2 (2011): 217–44 and idem, "*De gestis Langobardorum*: Queen Theodelinda and Langobard Royal Tradition," *Frühmittelalterliche Studien* 48, no. 1 (2015): 237–60. I wish to thank Carl Hammer for sending me copies of these papers.

11 This attitude is certainly present in the writings of Agathias. See Agathias, *The Histories*, eds. Hans-Georg Beck, Athanasios Kambylis and Rudolf Keydell, Corpus fontium historiae Byzantinae, vol. IIa (Berlin: De Gruyter, 1975), I, 2.4, 11 and Averil Cameron, "Agathias on the early Merovingians," *Annali della Scuola Normale Superiore di Pisa, Classe di Lettere e Filosofia* 2, no. 37 (1968): 95–140, at 136–9.

12 See Edward James, "Gregory of Tours, the Visigoths and Spain," in *Cross, Crescent and Conversion: Studies on Medieval Spain and Christendom in Memory of Richard Fletcher*, eds. Simon Barton and Peter Linehan (Leiden and Boston: Brill, 2008), 43–64, at 56; Wolfram Drews, "Hermenegild's Rebellion and Conversion – Merovingian and Byzantine Connections," in *East and West in the Early Middle Ages: The Merovingian Kingdoms in Mediterranean Perspective*, eds. Stefan Esders, Yaniv Fox, Yitzhak Hen, and Laury Sarti (Cambridge: Cambridge University Press, 2019).

13 Graham Barrett and George Woudhuysen, "Assembling the Austrasian Letters at Trier and Lorsch," *Early Medieval Europe* 24, no. 1 (2016): 3–57.

14 See Bruno Dumézil's contribution in this volume, pp. 55–62.

15 Andrew Gillett, "Ethnography and Imperium in the Sixth Century: Frankish and Byzantine Rhetoric in the *Epistolae Austrasicae*," in *Basileia: Essays on Imperium and*

Culture in Honour of E.M. and M.J. Jeffreys, eds. Geoffrey Nathan and Linda Garland (Brisbane: Australian Association for Byzantine Studies, 2011), 67–81, at 70.

16. For a new edition and a re-contextualization of the famous letter, see now Graham Barrett and George Woudhuysen, "Remigius and the 'Important News' of Clovis Rewritten," *Antiquité Tardive* 24 (2016): 471–500.

17. Michael McCormick, "Epistolae Austrasicae," in *The Oxford Dictionary of Byzantium*, ed. Aleksandr Petrovich Kazhdan, 3 vols. (Oxford: Oxford University Press, 1991), vol. 1, 717–8.

18. Loseby, "Gregory of Tours, Italy, and the Empire," 492.

19. *EA* 25, pp. 164–6.

20. *EA* 29, pp. 170–2.

21. *EA* 31, pp. 174–6.

22. Gillett, "Ethnography and Imperium," 71.

23. *EA* 40, pp. 190–6.

24. On the ethnic cargo attached to *nefandissimus* in Byzantine propaganda, see Gillett, "Ethnography and Imperium," 73. Compare to Pope Gregory the Great's *nefandissima Langobardorum gens*, in his *Registrum epistularum*, ed. Dag L. Norberg, *Corpus Christianorum Series latina*, vols. 140–140A (Turnhout: Brepols, 1982), V.38, p. 22.

25. *EA* 42, pp. 202–4.

26. *EA* 42, p. 204: "Divinitas te servet per multos annos, parens christianissimae atque amantissime."

27. Gregory of Tours, *Hist.* IX.20, pp. 434–41.

28. As indeed he does, in his account of Hospitius. See Gregory of Tours, *Hist.* VI.6, pp. 272–6. On this episode, see Julia Hillner, *Prison, Punishment and Penance in Late Antiquity* (Cambridge: Cambridge University Press, 2015), 271.

29. On Gregory's dire view of Justin II and on the undesirability of close relations with the Byzantines, see Helmut Reimitz, "*Pax inter utramque gentem:* the Merovingians, Byzantium and the History of Frankish Identity in the Last Decades of the Sixth Century," in *East and West in the Early Middle Ages: The Merovingian Kingdoms in Mediterranean Perspective*, eds. Stefan Esders, Yaniv Fox, Yitzhak Hen, and Laury Sarti (Cambridge: Cambridge University Press, 2019).

30. *EA* 46, pp. 212–14.

31. *EA* 46, p. 212: "Incipit ad Patriarcam Laurentio de Domni nomen."

32. Ross Balzaretti, *Dark Age Liguria: Regional Identity and Local Power, c. 400 – 1020* (London and New York: Bloomsbury, 2013), 93.

33. Gregory of Tours, *Hist.* VIII.18, pp. 384–5.

34. John Bagnell Bury, *A History of the Later Roman Empire: From Arcadius to to Irene (395 AD to 800 AD)*, 2 vols. (London and New York: Macmillan and Co., 1889), vol. 2, 164.

35 For a clear analysis of these tributes and their functions, see A. Fischer, "Money for Nothing: Franks, Byzantines and Lombards in the Sixth and Seventh Centuries," in *East and West in the Early Middle Ages: The Merovingian Kingdoms in Mediterranean Perspective*, eds. Stefan Esders, Yaniv Fox, Yitzhak Hen and Laury Sarti (Cambridge: Cambridge University Press, 2019).
36 Gregory of Tours, *Hist.* VI.42, p. 314.
37 Gillet, "Love and Grief," 150–7.
38 Gillett, "Love and Grief," 158.
39 Gregory of Tours, *Hist.* IX.16, pp. 430–1. Gillett, "Love and Grief," 159, n. 61. On Gregory's cautious approach to Guntram, see Guy Halsall, "Nero and Herod? The Death of Chilperic and Gregory of Tours' Writing of History," in *The World of Gregory of Tours*, eds. Kathleen Mitchell and Ian N. Wood (Leiden: Brill, 2002), pp. 337–50. Also, compare this to the Austrasian-Neustrian-Visigothic alliance against Theuderic II after his rejection of Ermenberga. See Fredegar *Chron.* IV.31, p. 132.
40 For some discussion of Guntram's strategic considerations, see Yaniv Fox, "New *honores* for a Region Transformed: The Patriciate in Post-Roman Gaul," *Revue Belge de Philologie et d'Histoire* 93 (2015): 249–86.
41 Ian N. Wood, "Deconstructing the Merovingian Family," in *The Construction of Communities in the Early Middle Ages: Texts, Resources, Artefacts*, eds. Richard Corradini, Maximilian Diesenberger and Helmut Reimitz (Leiden and Boston: Brill, 2003), 149–72; Erin T. Dailey, "Gregory of Tours, Fredegund, and the Paternity of Chlothar II: Strategies of Legitimation in the Merovingian Kingdoms," *Journal of Late Antiquity* 7, no. 1 (2014): 3–27.
42 For Chlothild, see Erin T. Dailey, *Queens, Consorts, Concubines: Gregory of Tours and the Women of the Merovingian Elite*, Mnemosyne Supplements, vol. 381 (Leiden and Boston: Brill, 2015), 39–44; On the cult of Radegund, see Brian Brennan, "St Radegund and the Early Development of Her Cult at Poitiers," *Journal of Religious History* 13, no. 4 (1985): 340–54.
43 On her portrayal, see Y. Fox, "The Bishop and the Monk: Desiderius of Vienne and the Columbanian Movement," *Early Medieval Europe* 20, no. 2 (2012): 176–94.
44 Fredegar *Chron.* IV.27, p. 131.
45 For an interesting, though admittedly improbable, suggestion that the letters were snuck into the package, see Vida A. Tyrrell, *Merovingian Letters and Letter Writers*, Unpublished doctoral dissertation (Center for Medieval Studies, University of Toronto, 2012), 30.
46 Compare to the expressions of grief in the exchange of letters between Einhard and Lupus of Ferrières, that, while couched in elite literary norms and a pious Christian worldview, break free of the genre's constraints. See Lupus of Ferrières, *Letters*, ed. and trans. Graydon W. Regenos (The Hague: Martinus Nijhoff, 1966), eps. 2–4,

pp. 4–14; Frederick S. Paxton, "Vocabularies of Grief and Consolation in Ninth-Century Francia," Annual Meeting of the Medieval Academy of America, Chicago (2009). Presentation.

47 Gregory of Tours, *Hist.* IX.25, pp. 444–5. Compare Anna Gehler-Rachůnek's contribution to this volume.

48 Ian N. Wood, *The Merovingian Kingdoms, 450 – 751* (London and New York: Longman, 1994), 172–3.

7 Mediterranean Homesick Blues: Human Trafficking in the Merovingian *Leges*

1 I would like to thank the editors for all their efforts, the German-Israeli Foundation for funding the project, and the participants of the 2016 seminar in Beer-Sheva for a fruitful discussion. Similarly, I would like to thank the German Science Foundation DFG for funding the SFB 700 "Governance in Areas of Limited Statehood" in which context this article originated. Last but not least, many thanks to Michael Eber and Pia Lucas for shortening suggestions and to Ellora Bennett and Courtnay Konshuh for language advice.

2 *Pactus legis Salicae* 39 *De plagiatoribus*, ed. K. A. Eckhardt, MGH LL nat. Germ. 4, 1 (Hanover: Hahn 1962), 142–45; translation based on Ian Wood, "Disputes in late-fifth and sixth century Gaul: some problems," in *The Settlement of Disputes in Early Medieval Europe*, eds. Wendy Davies and Paul Fouracre (Cambridge: Cambridge University Press, 1986), 21–2; and Theodore John Rivers, *Laws of the Salian and Ripuarian Franks* (New York: AMS Press, 1986), 82–3.

3 *Lex Ribuaria* 17 (16), [*De captivato homine vel femina ingenua*], eds. F. Beyerle / R. Buchner, MGH LL nat. Germ. 3,2 (Hanover: Hahn, 1954), 80; translation based on Rivers, *Salian and Ripuarian Franks*, 176.

4 Theodor Mommsen, *Römisches Strafrecht* (Leipzig: Duncker, 1899), 775–76 fn. 5–10 & fn. 1–3.

5 Hermann Nehlsen, *Sklavenrecht zwischen Antike und Mittelalter: Germanisches und römisches Recht in den germanischen Rechtsaufzeichnungen I: Ostgoten, Westgoten, Franken, Langobarden* (Göttingen: Musterschmidt, 1972), 116–18; The *Pauli sententiae* were part of the Visigothic Breviary of the Theodosian Code, the most comprehensive collection of Roman law available in the Western kingdoms throughout the Merovingian period.

6 *Lex Ribuaria* 16 [*De homino mordrido*]; 17 [*De captivato homine vel femina ingenua*]; 18 [*De incendio*]; 19 [*De sonestis*], 80–1.

7 *Lex Salica* 39, 142–5; *Lex Ribuaria* 17, 80; *Lex Alamannorum* 45/46–47/48, ed. K. Lehmann, MGH LL nat. Germ. 5, 1 (Hanover: Hahn, 1966), 105–7; *Lex*

Baiwariorum 9, 4, ed. E. von Schwind, MGH LL nat. Germ. 5,2 (Hanover: Hahn, 1926), 370–1; for discussion see Harald Siems, *Handel und Wucher im Spiegel frühmittelalterlicher Rechtsquellen* (Hanover: Hahn, 1992), 23–7.

8 Arnold Ehrhardt, "Rechtsvergleichende Studien zum antiken Sklavenrecht I: Wergeld und Schadenersatz," *Zeitschrift der Savigny-Stiftung für Rechtsgeschichte: Romanistische Abteilung* 68, no. 1 (1951): 74–130, here 102 fn. 86; cf. also Siems, *Handel und Wucher*, 28–9.

9 Dig. 48.15.

10 Mommsen, *Strafrecht*, 780 fn. 5–7 passim.

11 C. Th. 9.18.1.

12 *Lex Salica* 10.1 *De servis vel mancipiis furatis*, 50–1.

13 Wood, "Disputes," 21–2.

14 Siems, *Handel und Wucher*, 24–5.

15 Kyle Harper, *Slavery in the Late Roman World AD 275–425*, (Cambridge: Cambridge University Press, 2011), 81; cf. John Chrysostom, Mut. Nom. I.1 (Migne, PG 51:115).

16 Cf. Ian Wood, *The Merovingian North Sea* (Alingsås: Viktoria bokförlag, 1983); Ian Wood, "Frankish Hegemony in England," in *The Age of Sutton Hoo. The Seventh Century in North-Western Europe*, ed. Martin Carver (Woodbrigde: Boydell Press, 1992), 235–41.

17 Wood, "Hegemony," 238–9; Siems, *Handel und Wucher*, 28–9.

18 Ian Wood, "The Code in Merovingian Gaul," in *The Theodosian Code. Studies in the Imperial Law of Late Antiquity*, eds. Jill Harries and Ian Wood (London: Duckworth, 1993), 161–77, here 175 fn. 137.

19 Siems, *Handel und Wucher*, 29.

20 *Novellarum Valentiniani* 33.1 (Haenel 32; Brev. 3, 11) *De Parentibus qui filios distraxerunt et ne ingenui barbaris venundentur neque ad transmarina ducantur. (451 Ian. 31); Lex Romana Visigothorum*, ed. G.F. Haenel (Leipzig: Teubner, 1849), 290–2.

21 *Lex Visigothorum* VII.3.3 *Antiqua. De ingenuorum filiis plagiatis*, ed. Zeumer, MGH LL nat. Germ 1 (Hanover and Leipzig: Hahn, 1902), 298–9.

22 *Pactus legis Salicae* 39.4 *De plagiatoribus*, 144: "[…] sicut pro occiso iuratores donet […]."

23 *Lex Ribuaria* 16–17, p. 80.

24 Fredegar *Chron*. IV.75, pp. 158–9.

25 Cf. Stefan Esders, "Roman law as an identity marker in post-Roman Gaul (5th-9th centuries)," in *Transformations of Romanness. Early Medieval Regions and Identities*, eds. Walter Pohl, Clemens Gantner, Cinzia Grifoni, Marianne Pollheimer-Mohaupt (Berlin: DeGruyter, 2018), 325–44.

26 Cf. Heiner Lück, Art. Lex Ribuaria', in *HRG*² Vol. *III*, 902–908; http://www.hrgdigital.de/HRG.lex_ribuaria digital (accessed May 10, 2017).

27 Cf. "Asclepiodotus 3&4," in *PLRE III: A.D. 527–641*, 1 (Cambridge: Cambridge University Press, 1992), 134–5.
28 Cf. Karl Ubl, *Inzestverbot und Gesetzgebung. Die Konstruktion eines Verbrechens (300–1100)* (Berlin-New York: De Gruyter, 2008), 182–183; Ian Wood, "Roman Law in the Barbarian Kingdoms," in *Rome and the North*, eds. Alvar Ellegård and Gunilla Åkerström-Hougen (Jonsered: Åström, 1996), 5–14, here 11; Detlef Liebs, *Römische Jurisprudenz in Gallien (2.-8. Jahrhundert)* (Berlin: Duncker & Humblot, 2002), 75–9.
29 Fredegar *Chron.* IV.44 for Chlothar II and Fredegar *Chron.* IV.58 for Dagobert, pp. 142–3 and 149–50.
30 Nov. Val. 33.1 (Haenel, 290–292); cf. Wood, "Code in Gaul," 175 fn. 137; cf. Siems, *Handel und Wucher*, 29.
31 *Lex Visigothorum* VII.3.3 *Antiqua*, 298–9; cf. Siems, *Handel und Wucher*, 29 f.
32 *Codex Theodosianus* 9.18.5 AD LEGEM FABIAM ... – August 1, 315. INTERPRETATION: If any person should steal the children of others and take them anywhere at all, whether he be freeborn or slave, he shall be punished by death (transl. C. Pharr, *The Theodosian Code and Novels, and the Sirmondian Constitutions*, Princeton: Princeton University Press, 1952, 240).
33 *Lex Romana Burgundionum* 4, 1, ed. R. von Salis, MGH LL nat. Germ. 2, 1 (Hanover: Hahn, 1892), 127 (transl. Bothe).
34 Detlef Liebs, "Art. Lex Romana Burgundionum," *HRG*² Vol. III (2016), 908–12; www.HRGdigital.de/HRG.lex_romana_burgundionum (accessed August 16, 2018).
35 Cf. *Lex Ribuaria* 12.2, p. 78: "Whenever the 600 *solidi* are required, let him swear in similar manner with seventy-two [oath-takers]. If that man is so poor that he cannot pay, let his descendants pay up to three generations [after him]." (transl. Rivers, *Salian and Ripuarian Franks*, 175); – *Capitulare legi Ribuariae additum* a. 803 c. 3, ed. Boretius, MGH Capit. I (Hannover: Hahn, 1883), no. 41, 117: *Regarding cap. 12*; "That a freeman, who cannot pay some legal fine and has no warrantors either, be permitted to pledge himself to the person, whose debtor he is, until he repays the fine he owes." (transl. Bothe).
36 Cf. Michael Wissemann, "Eine gesetzliche Beschränkung des Menschenhandels," *Münstersche Beiträge zur antiken Handelsgeschichte* 3 (1984), 88–90; from a letter by Augustine (ep. 10+ [Divjak]), Wisseman reconstructs a now lost law enacted by Honorius between 401–05, which prohibited the export of slaves from Africa to transmarine provinces and allegedly claimed to punish the merchants with proscription and exile.
37 Michael McCormick, "New Light on the Dark Ages: How the slave trade fuelled the Carolingian economy," *Past and Present* 177, no. 1 (2002), 17–54.

38　Bonnie Effros, "The Enduring Attraction of the Pirenne Thesis," *Speculum* 92, no. 1 (2017): 184–208, 199–200.
39　Henri Pirenne, *Mahomet et Charlemagne* (Paris: Nouvelle Société d'éditions, 1937, repr. 1961).
40　Effros, "Attraction," 192 and 207.
41　Pirenne, *Mahomet et Charlemagne*, 138, 175, 178–81.
42　McCormick, "Slave Trade," 24.
43　Michael McCormick, *The Origins of the European Economy. Communications and Commerce AD 300–900* (Cambridge: Cambridge University Press, 2001), esp. 733–77.
44　McCormick 2002, "Slave Trade," 40–3.
45　McCormick, "Slave Trade," 43–52; cf. also McCormick, *Origins*, 763–71.
46　McCormick, *Origins*, 53–4.
47　Pirenne, *Mahomet et Charlemagne*, 53–5 passim.
48　Dietrich Claude, *Der Handel im westlichen Mittelmeer während des Frühmittelalters* (Göttingen: Vandenhoeck und Ruprecht, 1985), 95–9 passim.
49　*VP* XVI.5, p. 282.
50　*Gregorii I Registrum* V.36, eds. Ewald / Hartmann, MGH Epp. 1 (Hanover: Hahn, 1891), 317–18.
51　*Gregorii I Registrum* VI.10, pp. 388–9.
52　*Vita Eligii* I.10, ed. Krusch, MGH SS rer. Merov. IV (Hanover and Leipzig: Hahn, 1902), 677 (transl. McNamara 1997 [2001, 144]; https://sourcebooks.fordham.edu/basis/eligius.asp, accessed August 16, 2018).
53　*Vita Boniti* c. 25, ed. MGH SS rer. Merov. VI (Hanover and Leipzig: Hahn, 1913), 132.
54　Claude, *Handel*, 99.
55　*Lex Alamannorum* 45/46–47/48, pp. 105–7; *Lex Baiwariorum* IX.4, pp. 370–1.
56　*Lex Alamannorum* 37, p. 97 (transl. Thedore John Rivers, *Laws of the Alamans and Bavarians*, Philadelphia, University of Pennsylvania Press, 1977), 79.
57　*Lex Alamannorum* 11/12–12/13, pp. 82–4.
58　Cf. Stefan Esders, "Late Roman Military Law in the Bavarian Code," *Clio@themis. Revue électronique d'histoire du droit* 10, accessed June 16, 2016: http://www.cliothemis.com/IMG/pdf/3-_Esders-2.pdf.
59　*Lex Alamannorum* 45/46 *De libero, qui liberum extra terminos vendiderit* & 46/47 *De eo, qui feminam ingenuam extra marcam vendiderit*, 105–6.
60　*Lex Alamannorum* 47/48 *De eo, qui liberum hominem vel feminam liberam infra provinciam vendiderit*, 107.
61　*Lex Baiwariorum* IX, 4 *Si liberum hominem furaverit*, 370–71. That the vendor should lose his freedom is a claim almost certainly appropriated from Visigothic law, the influence of which on the *Lex Baiwariorum* is well-attested; cf. Isabella

Fastrich-Sutty, *Die Rezeption westgotischen Rechts in der Lex Baiwariorum* (Cologne: Heymann, 2001).

62 Cf. Edgar Loening, *Geschichte des deutschen Kirchenrechts. Bd. 2: Das Kirchenrecht im Reich der Merowinger* (Strasbourg: Trübener, 1878), 53–55 & 227–8; cf. also Hartmut Hoffmann, "Kirche und Sklaverei im frühen Mittelalter," *DA* 42 (1986), 1–24, here 14–16.

63 *Concilium Clippiacense* 626 aut 627 Sept. 27 c. 13, ed. Maassen, MGH Concilia Aevi Merovingici (Hannover: Hahn, 1893), 199.

64 *Concilium Cabilonense* A. 639–654 Oct. 24 c. 9, ed. Maassen, MGH Concilia Aevi Merovingici (Hannover: Hahn, 1893), 210.

65 Loening, *Kirchenrecht*, 53–4; referring to Nov. Theod. II, tit. 3 § 4, and canon 31 of the 4th Council of Orleans, (*Concilium Aurelianense* 541 Mai 14, ed. Maassen, MGH Concilia Aevi Merovingici, 94).

66 Cf. also McCormick, "Slave Trade," 47–8.

67 Cf. David Wyatt, *Slaves and Warriors in Medieval Britain and Ireland, 800–1200* (Leiden: Brill, 2009), 21–2; Revisionists on the other hand find fault with even that minimum; cf. Joachim Henning, "Slavery or Freedom? The causes of early medieval Europe's economic advancement," *EME* 13, no. 3 (2003): 269–77.

68 Alice Rio, *Slavery after Rome 500–1100* (Oxford: Oxford University Press, 2017), 24–8.

69 Classic studies are: Marc Bloch, "Comment et pourquoi finit l'esclavage antique," in Idem, *Melanges historiques*, 2 vols., vol. 1 (Paris: S.E.V.P.E.N., 1963), 261–86; Charles Verlinden, *L'esclavage dans l'Europe médiévale* (Bruges: De Tempel, 1977); Frantisek Graus, "Die Gewalt bei den Anfängen des Feudalismus," *Jahrbuch für Wirtschaftsgeschichte* 1 (1961): 61–156; Hoffmann, "Kirche und Sklaverei"; cf. most recently Rio, *Slavery*.

70 Cf. Rio, Slavery, 215–45.

71 Cf. Nehlsen, *Sklavenrecht*; cf. also Ehrhardt, "Sklavenrecht I."

72 Cf. Hoffmann, "Kirche und Sklaverei," 23, suggesting that the *mancipia* of Frankish estates (*Grundherrschaften*) reproduced themselves naturally.

73 E.g. W. V. Harris, "Child exposure in the Roman Empire," *Journal of Roman Studies* 84 (1994): 1–22; Harper, *Late Antique Slavery*, 67–8; Walter Scheidel, "The Roman Slave Supply," in *Cambridge World History of Slavery, Vol. 1 The Ancient Mediterranean*, eds. Keith Bradley and Paul Cartledge (Cambridge: Cambridge University Press, 2011), 287–310.

8 The Fifth Council of Orléans and the Reception of the "Three Chapters Controversy" in Merovingian Gaul

1 This paper is based on a talk given at the "International Medieval Congress" in Leeds on July 4, 2016. Special thanks are due to the four editors of this volume for their many helpful remarks and improvements to the text. I am particularly indebted to Ellora Bennett who corrected my English and saved me from numerous teutonisms originally contained in the manuscript. All remaining mistakes are, needless to say, my own.
2 July 14, 549.
3 1 Sam. 2:28.
4 Or rather, correspondingly, "as it is common among Arians"?
5 See *Epistola Arelatensis* 45 (29 April 550: JK 925), transl. Stüber; for the Latin original, see the edition by Wilhelm Gundlach, in his: MGH Epp. 3,1, pp. 67–68. In the following, the *Epistolae Arelatenses* will be quoted according to Gundlach's edition.
6 That this practice can be linked to structural features of the late antique *Reichskirche* is shown by the excellent discussion in Jan-Markus Kötter, "Die Suche nach der kirchlichen Ordnung: Gedanken zu grundlegenden Funktionsweisen der spätantiken Reichskirche," *Historische Zeitschrift* 298 (2014): 22–3.
7 *Liber Pontificalis, Vita Vigilii* in *Le Liber Pontificalis. Texte, introduction et commentaire*. Vol. 1, ed. Louis Duchesne (Paris: Ernest Thorin, 1886), 297. See the discussion in Jeffrey Richards, *The Popes and the Papacy in the Early Middle Ages: 476-752* (London: Routledge, 1979), 143–4.
8 On the role of the papacy in the Three Chapters controversy, see Richards, *The Popes,* 139–161 and the detailed, still valuable account by Erich Caspar, *Geschichte des Papsttums von den Anfängen bis zur Höhe der Weltherrschaft. Vol. 2: Das Papsttum unter byzantinischer Herrschaft* (Tübingen: J. C. B. Mohr, 1933), 234–305. On Vigilius, see especially Claire Sotinel, "Autorité pontificale et pouvoir impérial sous le règne de Justinien: le pape Vigile," *Mélanges de l'Ecole française de Rome. Antiquité* 104 (1992): 439–63.
9 Robert A. Markus and Claire Sotinel, "Epilogue" in *The Crisis of the Oikoumene: The Three Chapters and the Failed Quest for Unity in the Sixth-Century Mediterranean*, eds. Celia Chazelle and Catherine Cubitt (Turnhout: Brepols, 2007), 277–8.
10 Jean Gaudemet and Brigitte Basdevant, *Les canons des conciles mérovingiens (VIe–VIIe siècles)*. Vol. 1 (Paris: Éditions du Cerf, 1989), 297.
11 Cf. MGH Conc. 1, pp. 108–9.
12 See *Concilium Aurelianense* (a. 549), canon 1, translated by Ian N. Wood, "The Franks and Papal Theology, 550–660" in *The Crisis of the Oikoumene: The Three Chapters and the Failed Quest for Unity in the Sixth-Century Mediterranean*, eds.

Celia Chazelle and Catherine Cubitt (Turnhout: Brepols, 2007), 223–4. For the Latin text, see MGH Conc. 1, p. 101.
13 Nancy Gauthier, *L'évangélisation des pays de la Moselle* (Paris: De Boccard, 1980), 176.
14 This seems to be the interpretation by Gaudemet/Basdevant, *Les Canons*, 302, n. 1.
15 Wood, *The Franks*, 225–26. On Nicetius' letter, see also Hans A. Pohlsander, "A Call to Repentance. Bishop Nicetius of Trier to the Emperor Justinian" in *Byzantion* 70 (2000): 457–73.
16 *EA* 7.3, p. 82.
17 MGH Conc. 1, p. 109.
18 On their respective christologies, see Henry Chadwick, *The Church in Ancient Society: From Galilee to Gregory the Great* (Oxford: Oxford University Press, 2001), 527–35 (Nestorius) and 553–6 (Eutyches).
19 Bruno Dumézil and Thomas Lienhard, "Les *Lettres austrasiennes*: dire, cacher, transmettre les informations diplomatiques au haut Moyen Âge" in *Les relations diplomatiques au Moyen Âge: Formes et enjeux*, ed. Thierry Kouamé (Paris: Publications de la Sorbonne, 2011), 74.
20 *EA* 7.3 and 7.4, p. 82.
21 Richard M. Price, "The Three Chapters Controversy and the Council of Chalcedon" in *The Crisis of the Oikoumene: The Three Chapters and the Failed Quest for Unity in the Sixth-Century Mediterranean*, eds. Celia Chazelle and Catherine Cubitt (Turnhout: Brepols, 2007), 26.
22 *EA* 7.8, p. 84/6: "Speak not in your heart: 'I have done it, I have done it! I have triumphed, I have triumphed!' (*Feci, feci! vici, vici!*) You are vanquished and bound (*victus es et vinctus*), for you are a son of the devil and an enemy of justice. Let it be known to you that the whole of Italy, entire Africa, Spain, and unified Gaul (*Gallia coniuncta*) have anathematized your name, while deploring your perdition. And if you do not destroy what you taught and publicly exclaim: 'I have erred, I have erred, I have sinned! Anathema to Nestorius! Anathema to Eutyches!', you shall, as they were, be delivered to eternal torment." Transl. Stüber.
23 Eugen Ewig, *Die Merowinger und das Imperium* (Opladen: Westdeutscher Verlag, 1983), 22–3 n. 89.
24 Asserting the orthodoxy of one's own position by emphasizing the accordance with the papacy and, hence, with "the entire Church," was a practice already known in southern Gaul in the days of Caesarius of Arles, who was Aurelianus' predecessor; on this, see Étienne Delaruelle, "L'Église romaine et ses relations avec l'Église franque jusqu'en 800," in *Le Chiese nei regni dell'Europa occidentale e i loro rapporti con Roma sino all'800* (Spoleto: Centro italiano di studi sull'alto medioevo, 1960), 153.
25 This gathering is to be identified with the Fifth Council, cf. Odette Pontal, *Die Synoden im Merowingerreich* (Paderborn: Ferdinand Schöningh, 1986), 94.

26 LV 6.5, p. 233: "incriminato ab iniquis [...] et in exilium truso."
27 MGH Conc. 1, pp. 108–12.
28 BHL 2255.
29 Karl Joseph von Hefele and Henri Leclercq, *Histoire des conciles d'après les documents originaux*. Vol. 3.1 (Paris: Letouzey et Ané, 1909), 158–9.
30 The *Vita S. Domitiani episcopi Traiectensis* is edited by Godefroid Henschen in: *Acta Sanctorum Maii*. Vol. 2 (Antwerpen: Michel Cnobbaert, 1680), pp. 146–7.
31 Godefroid Henschen, "Vies et miracles de Saint Domitien: Évêque de Tongres-Maastricht (535–549)," *Analecta Bollandiana* 103 (1985): 305–54 and 119 (2001): 5–32.
32 George, *Vies et miracles*, 309–14.
33 On this synod, see Huguette Taviani-Carozzi, "Une histoire 'édifiante': L'hérésie d'Orléans en 1022" in *Faire l'évènement au Moyen Âge*, ed. Claude Carozzi and ead. (Aix-en-Provence: Publications de l'Université de Provence 2007), 275–98.
34 The existence of such a *vita* is not ruled out by George, *Vies et miracles*, 25–6.
35 On Nicetius' position, see Michel Rouche, *L'Aquitaine des Wisigoths aux Arabes 418–781: Naissance d'une région* (Paris: Jean Touzot, 1979), 427–28. That the young Austrasian king was easily influenced by his episcopate is also suggested by Gregory of Tours, *Hist*. IV 6, p. 139 where an episcopal candidate is told by his potential future colleagues: "veni, consenti nobis, et benedicentes consecremus te ad episcopatum. rex vero parvulus est, et si qua tibi adscribitur culpa, nos suscipientes te sub defensione nostra, cum proceribus et primis regni Theodovaldi regis agemus, ne tibi ulla excitetur iniuria." Other evidence is found in *EA* 6, 78–81.
36 On this synod, see Karl Ubl, *Inzestverbot und Gesetzgebung. Die Konstruktion eines Verbrechens (300–1100)* (Berlin: De Gruyter, 2008), 147–8.
37 The letters are solely preserved in a ninth-century manuscript from Lorsch, Pal. lat. 869, kept today at the Biblioteca Apostolica Vaticana. On the *Epistolae Austrasicae*, see Bruno Dumézil's contribution to this volume.
38 Pohlsander, *Call to Repentance*, 460.
39 Procop., *Bell. Goth*. IV.24, pp. 617–23.
40 Ewig, *Die Merowinger*, 21.
41 Procop., *Bell. Goth*. IV.24, pp. 618–19; on this, see also Erich Zöllner, *Geschichte der Franken bis zur Mitte des sechsten Jahrhunderts* (München: C. H. Beck, 1970), 91.
42 Editors of the *Epistolae Austrasicae* have dated this letter (no. 18) to the years 547 or 548/9 respectively (see Graham Barrett and George Woudhuysen, "Assembling the Austrasian Letters at Trier and Lorsch," *Early Medieval Europe* 24, no. 1 (2016): 54). On the chronology, see Eduard Schwartz, *Vigiliusbriefe* (München: C. H. Beck, 1940), 28–29 n. 2. The embassy of Leontius, the one mentioned by Procopius (*De bello Gothorum* IV.24), has to be dated after the embassy of John and Missorius,

subject of Theudebald's aforementioned letter. Both embassies seem to have been dedicated to the same subject, see Ewig, *Die Merowinger*, 21–22.

43 *EA* 18.3 and 18.4, pp. 132–4.

44 *EA* 18.5, p. 134. That these friendly declarations possibly did not prevent Theudebald from sending his *dux* Lanthacarius against the Byzantines, is shown by an entry in the chronicle of Marius of Avenches, ad a. 548: "eo anno Lanthacarius dux Francorum in bello Romano transfossus obiit," (edited in: Justin Favrod, *La chronique de Marius d'Avenches (455–581)* (Lausanne: Université de Lausanne, 1993), 74. It is also possible, however, that Lanthacarius had still been sent by Theudebert. The chronology here is uncertain (see Bruno Krusch, in: MGH SS rer. Merov. 7, p. 487).

45 On Childebert's relations to Byzantium, see Ewig, *Die Merowinger*, 14–25.

46 Procop., *Bell. Goth.* III.37, p. 436. Following Zöllner, *Geschichte der Franken*, 97, Totila's embassy to Childebert's royal court at Paris is to be dated either to 549 or to 550, it is thus concurrent with the Fifth Council of Orléans.

47 On the history of the Apostolic Vicariate of Arles, see Georg Langgärtner, *Die Gallienpolitik der Päpste im 5. und 6. Jahrhundert: Eine Studie über den apostolischen Vikariat von Arles* (Bonn: Hanstein, 1964). Langgärtner's work, being too legalistic at times, can be supplemented by the helpful studies of Ralph W. Mathisen, *Ecclesiastical Factionalism and Religious Controversy in Fifth-Century Gaul* (Washington D. C.: Catholic University of America Press, 1989) and Martin Heinzelmann, *Bischofsherrschaft in Gallien: Zur Kontinuität römischer Führungsschichten vom 4. bis zum 7. Jahrhundert* (Zurich: Artemis Verlag, 1976), 73–84.

48 William E. Klingshirn, *Caesarius of Arles: The Making of a Christian Community in Late Antique Gaul* (Cambridge: Cambridge University Press, 1994), 130. On the *pallium*, see also the detailed analysis of Joseph Braun S. J., *Die liturgische Gewandung im Occident und Orient: Nach Ursprung und Entwicklung, Verwendung und Symbolik* (Freiburg i. Brsg.: Herdersche Verlagsbuchhandlung, 1907), 620–76.

49 This has been concluded by Caspar, *Geschichte des Papsttums*, 235–238, followed by Delaruelle, *L'Église romaine*, 151–52. Langgärtner's attempt to refute Caspar's interpretation fails to convince, cf. idem, *Die Gallienpolitik*, 131–32 and 152.

50 *Epistolae Arelatenses* 39 (October 18, 543: JK 912), 40 (May 22, 545: JK 914), and 42 (May 22, 545: JK 915).

51 *Epistola Arelatensis* 44 (August 23, 546: JK 918): Gundlach, MGH Epp. 3, p. 66 (an alternative manuscript reading is: *gratiae inactae federa*). On this letter, see also Langgärtner, *Die Gallienpolitik*, 153.

52 Cf. *Epistola Arelatensis* 43 (August 23, 546: JK 919): Gundlach, MGH Epp. 3, p. 63.

53 Cyril of Alexandria was the most prominent opponent of Nestorius of Constantinople and his theology.

54 *Epistola Arelatensis* 45: "sed et ea, quę in eiusdem sanctę fidei iniuriam verbo dicta vel reperiuntur scripta, anathematizanda exsecrandaque iudicavimus [...], simili pena plectentes etiam eos, qui fidem beati Cyrilli [...] execranda superbia impiam vocaverunt." (Gundlach, MGH Epp. 3, p. 67).

55 It should be noted that it is not fully clear to which of the Merovingian kingdoms Arles belonged in 549/550; see Rudolf Buchner, *Die Provence in merowingischer Zeit: Verfassung, Wirtschaft, Kultur* (Stuttgart: Kohlhammer, 1933), 7–10. As argued by Buchner on the basis of *Epistolae Arelatenses* 43 and 44, Arles still belonged to the realm of Childebert I (511–558) in 546. From the letter of Aurelianus of Arles to King Theudebert I (*EA* 10, 106), where the bishop presents himself as a subject to the Austrasian king (*exigua portio obsequii vestri*), Buchner has concluded that Arles had fallen to Theudebert I shortly afterwards: "So wäre die Besetzung von Arles [by Theudebert] ein Druckmittel gegenüber Childebert und eine Repressalie gegenüber Aurelian gewesen, der als Vermittler zwischen Byzanz, Rom und seinem König eine wichtige Rolle gespielt zu haben scheint. Sie hätte zugleich dazu dienen sollen, die Verbindung zwischen dem Kaiser und Childebert für die Zukunft unmöglich zu machen." (See Buchner, *Die Provence*, 9; his hypotheses were supported later by numismatic research, cf. Malaspina, *Il Liber epistolarum*, 247–248 nn. 295 and 297.) As in *Epistola Arelatensis* 45 Aurelianus is seen to negotiate between Childebert and the pope, Buchner presumes Arles to have been under Austrasian sway again in 550, the year the letter was written.

56 *Epistolae aevi merowingici collectae* 4: Gundlach, MGH Epistolae III, 438–44; I cite the edition from: Schwartz, *Vigiliusbriefe*, 18–25. As the codex had been kept at Saint-Rémi-de-Reims until the seventeenth century, Valentin Rose, *Verzeichniß der lateinischen Handschriften der königlichen Bibliothek zu Berlin*. Vol. 1 (Berlin: A. Asher & Co., 1893), 171–79 presumed its composition at Reims. According to Hubert Mordek, *Kirchenrecht und Reform im Frankenreich* (Berlin: De Gruyter, 1975), 10 n. 38 (following Bernhard Bischoff, "Panorama der Handschriftenüberlieferung aus der Zeit Karls des Großen," in idem, *Mittelalterliche Studien: Ausgewählte Aufsätze zur Schriftkunde und Literaturgeschichte*. Vol. 3 (Stuttgart: Hiersemann, 1981) 17–18 n. 57) the manuscript should rather be localized to the territory around Bourges, as it displays notable similarities to other manuscripts originating from that area, whereas there seems to be no paleographical connection to Reims. On this manuscript, see also Hubert Mordek, *Bibliotheca capitularium regum Francorum manuscripta* (München: Monumenta Germaniae Historica, 1995), 56–7.

57 On the manuscript tradition of the *Epistolae Arelatenses*, see Wilhelm Gundlach, *Der Streit der Bisthümer Arles und Vienne um den Primatus Galliarum: Ein philologisch-diplomatischer-historischer Beitrag zum Kirchenrecht* (Hannover: Hahnsche Buchhandlung, 1890), 27–92, to be supplemented by the recent

observations of Rainer Jakobi, "Die Überlieferung der *Epistulae Arelatenses*," *Deutsches Archiv für Erforschung des Mittelalters* 71 (2015): 175–8.

58 According to Ewig, *Die Merowinger*, 22 and Schwartz, *Vigiliusbriefe*, 28 with n. 2, the letter addressed the Austrasian embassy of Leudardus, traveling to Constantinople to negotiate with Justinian on territories recently occupied by Theudebert (the embassy is mentioned by Procopius, *Bell. Goth.* IV.24, p. 622). Being subject to constant quarrel between Reims and Constantinople, Byzantium managed to regain these territories only after Theudebald's death, cf. Marius of Avenches, ad a. 556, Favrod, *La chronique*, 78. On this, see Roger Collins, "Theudebert I, Rex Magnus Francorum," in *Ideal and Reality in Frankish and Anglo-Saxon Society: Studies Presented to J. M. Wallace-Hadrill*, ed. Patrick Wormald (Oxford: Blackwell, 1983), 7–8.

59 See Richard Price, *The Acts of the Council of Constantinople of 553 with Related Texts on the Three Chapters Controversy*. Vol. 1 (Liverpool: University Press, 2009), 165 n. 12: "This undated letter was clearly composed before Vigilius' flight to St Euphemia's on 23 December 551 or, rather, before news of this reached to Milan." Schwartz, *Vigiliusbriefe*, 28 thus suggests that "jene Berichterstatter [whose information the Milanese letter is based upon] im Herbst 551 Konstantinopel verließen und gegen Ende des Jahres in Oberitalien ankamen." The author also did not know of the death of Bishop Datius of Milan, having occurred on February 5, 552.

60 *Epistola legatariis*: Schwartz, *Vigiliusbriefe*, p. 19.

61 *Epistola legatariis*: Schwartz, *Vigiliusbriefe*, pp. 23–4; the quoted translation is taken from Price, *The Acts*, 169.

62 *Epistola Arelatensis* 45: MGH Epp. 3,1, pp. 67–8.

63 *Epistola legatariis*: Schwartz, *Vigiliusbriefe*, p. 24.

64 This aspect is emphasized by Wood, *The Franks*, 234–5.

65 On their connection, see Bruno Dumézil, "Gogo et ses amis: Écriture, échanges et ambitions dans un réseau aristocratique de la fin du VIe siècle," *Revue historique* 643 (2007): 564, 577–78. Paolo Radiciotti, "Note su Floriano abate di Romeno e la cultura intellettuale in Italia alla metà del VI secolo," *Rivista di Filologia e di Istruzione Classica* 126, no. 2 (1998): 183–88, localizes Florianus' monastery Romenum in the Val di Non (South Tyrol).

66 See Dumézil, *Gogo et ses amis*, 578: "Nizier est donc invité à prier pour Datius, mais peut-être aussi à agir de façon un peu plus pratique pour sa libération, en faisant intervenir les Mérovingiens. Au même moment, les clercs de Milan envoient une lettre au roi franc Théodebald pour lui raconter les souffrances de Datius et pour lui demander son aide. On peut ici clairement affirmer que la lettre privée de Florentius à Nizier sert à renforcer la procédure officielle du clergé milanais."

67 *EA* 5.4, p. 76. See also Wood, *The Franks*, 232–4. In another letter (*EA* 6, pp. 78–81), Florianus hoped that Nicetius would exert his influence on King Theudebald, when

asking him to secure the king's support for a monastery situated on an island in Lake Como.

68 While our sources shed some light on the political preferences of Childebert and the Austrasian kings, we do not have equally illuminating evidence regarding Chlothar I (d. 561), whose fragmented realm included the Touraine and the Poitou as well as the area around the Meuse and the Scheldt. It seems quite possible that due to the geographical position of his *regnum*, he did not entertain any widespread interests regarding foreign policy at the time, as suggested by Zöllner, *Geschichte der Franken*, 97.

69 The next comparable assembly took place at Paris in 614, after all three Frankish realms had been unified under the sway of the Neustrian king Chlothar II.

70 Heike Grahn-Hoek, "*Quia Dei potentia cunctorum regnorum terminus singulari dominatione concludit*. Kirchlicher Einheitsgedanke und weltliche Grenzen im Spiegel der reichsfränkischen Konzilien des 6. Jahrhunderts," in *Religiöse Bewegungen im Mittelalter. Festschrift für Matthias Werner zum 65. Geburtstag* eds. Enno Bünz, Stefan Tebruck, and Helmut G. Walther (Cologne: Böhlau, 2007), 48. Furthermore, Grahn-Hoek (ibid., 41–42 and 50) convincingly argues that the period following the death of Chlothar I saw the development of differing expectations towards regional church councils (*Teilreichskonzilien*) within the single Merovingian kingdoms.

71 On the authoritative role usually played by kings in convoking regional Church councils, see Gregory I. Halfond, *The Archaeology of Frankish Church Councils: AD 511–768* (Leiden: Brill Publishers, 2010), 57–66 and Yitzhak Hen, "The Church in Sixth-Century Gaul," in *A Companion to Gregory of Tours* ed. Alexander Callander Murray, (Leiden: Brill 2016), 232–55.

9 Reconciling Disturbed Sacred Space: The Ordo for "Reconciling an Altar Where a Murder Has Been Committed" in the *Sacramentary of Gellone* in its Cultural Context

1 The text literally reads: "it does not have ours"; parallel texts read "terminum," where the Gellone sacramentary reads "tamen nostrum." The reading in the Gellone text seems to be the result of some miscopying.

2 The text literally reads "boasting" (*iactantiam*), but it seems unlikely that God should erect the boasting; probably it this should read "iacentia" here.

3 *Sacramentary of Gellone*, nrs. 352, ed. A. Dumas, Liber Sacramentorum Gellonensis, CC SL159 (Turnhout: Brepols 1981), pp. 351–2. I thank Els Rose for assistance with translating these complicated prayers.

4 The manuscript was included in the exhibition in Paris (2016–2017) devoted to the Merovingian period, but in the section on the transition to Carolingian rule and

culture, see, Isabelle Bardiès-Fronty, Charlotte Denoël and Inès Villela-Petit, *Les Temps Mérovingiens. Trois siècles d'art et de culture* (Musée de Cluny – Musée National de Moyen Âge 26 octobre 2016 – 13 février 2017) (Paris, 2016), 256.

5 Ms. Paris, BnF, lat. 12048.

6 See the discussion of these works in Yitzhak Hen, *The Royal Patronage of Liturgy in Frankish Gaul. To the Death of Charles the Bald (877)*, Henry Bradshaw Society, Subsidia 3 (London: Boydell Press, 2001), 57–6.

7 Sacramentary of Angoulême, 2027 and 2028, ed. Patrick Saint-Roch, *Liber Sacramentorum Engolismensis. Manuscrit B.N. Lat. 816. Le Sacramentaire Gélasien d'Angoulême*, CCSL 159C (Turnhout: Brepols, 1987), pp. 304–5 and the Sacramentary of Autun, nr. 1447 and 1448, in *Liber Sacramentorum Augustodunensis*, ed. Odilo Heiming, CCSL 159 B (Turnhout: Brepols, 1984), pp. 165–6.

8 Hen, *Royal Patronage*, 57–61; Cyrille Vogel, *Medieval Liturgy. An Introduction to the Sources*, translated by William G. Storey and Niels K. Rasmussen (Washington: The Pastoral Press, 1986), 70–78; Bernard Moreton, *The Eighth-Century Gelasian Sacramentary. A Study in Tradition* (Oxford: Oxford University Press, 1976).

9 Vogel, *Introduction*, 74; Hen, *Royal Patronage*, 60.

10 Council of Agde, c. 14, in *Conciliae Galliae A. 314 – A. 506*, ed. Charles Munier, CCSL 148 (Turnhout: Brepols, 1963), 200.

11 Council of Orleans, c. 10, in *Concilia Galliae A. 511 – A. 695*, ed. Charles De Clercq, CCSL 148A (Turnhout: Brepols, 1963) pp. 7–8; Council of Epaone, c. 33, ibid, 33.

12 Caesarius, *Sermo*, 228: "quia quamvis sancta sint templa, quae videmus de lignis et lapidibus fabricari, tamen plus apud deum pretiosa sunt templa cordis et corporis nostri," Caesarius of Arles, *Sermones*, ed. G. Morin, *Sancti Caesarii episcopi Arelatensis opera omnia nunc primum in unum collecta*, CC 104 (Turnhout: Brepols, 1953), 901; see the discussion in Miriam Czock, *Gottes Haus. Untersuchungen zur Kirche als heiligem Raum von der Spätantike bis ins Frühmittelalter* (Berlin: De Gruyter, 2012), 82–86. The same basic idea is ventilated by Bede, see Conor O'Brien, "The cleansing of the temple in early medieval Northumbria," *Anglo-Saxon England* 44 (2015), 201–20, at 211.

13 Ms. Vatican, BAV, Reg. lat. 316 + Paris, BnF, lat.7193; *Liber Sacramentorum Romanae ecclesiae ordinis anni circuli (Sacramentarium Gelasianum)*, eds. Leo C. Mohlberg, Leo Eizenhöfer, Petrus Siffrin (2nd rev. edition Rome 1968); see discussion in Vogel, *Introduction*, 64–70; Yitzhak Hen, *Culture and Religion in Merovingian Gaul A.D. 481–751* (Leiden, New York, Cologne: Brill, 1995), 44–5; Czock, *Gottes Haus*, 150–1.

14 *Sacramentarium Gelasianum*, 88, Orationes in dedicatione basilicae novae, ed. Leo C. Mohlberg, pp. 107–10; the *Missale Francorum* 12 from the early eighth century contains in essence the same material, see *Missale Francorum*, ed. L. Mohlberg (Rome: Herder, 1957), pp. 17–19.

15 Sacramentary of Gellone nrs. 358-360, ed. Dumas, pp. 364-5.
16 Sacramentary of Gellone, nr. 356, ed. Dumas, pp. 360-4.
17 Sacramentary of Angoulême, 2020, ed. Patrick Saint-Roch, *Liber Sacramentorum Engolismensis*, p. 302.
18 Autun Sacramentary 347, ed. Odilo Heiming, *Liber Sacramentorum Augustodunensis*, pp. 166-8.
19 Czock, *Gottes Haus*.
20 *Concilia Africae*, ed. C. Munier, CCSL 149 (Turnhout: Brepols, 1974), p. 359: "Item placuit ut de altaribus quae passim per agros aut uias tanquam memoriae martyrum constituuntur, in quibus nullus corpus aut reliquiae martyrum conditae probantur, ab episcopis qui iisdem locis praesunt, si fieri potest, euertantur."
21 *GC* 20, pp. 309-10; see Czock, *Gottes Haus*, 61-62; also Robert Bartlett, *Why the Dead can do Such Great Things?: Saints and Worshippers from the Martyrs to the Reformation* (Princeton: Princeton University Press, 2013), 445.
22 See Harald Siems, "Zur Entwicklung des Kirchenasyls zwischen Spätantike und Mittelalter," in *Libertas. Grundrechtliche und rechtsstaatliche Gewährungen in Antike und Gegenwart. Symposion aus Anlaß des 80. Geburtstages von Franz Wieacker*, eds. Malte Diesselhorst, Okko Behrends (Ebelsbach: Gremer, 1991), 139-86; Anne Ducloux, *Ad Ecclesiam Confugere. Naissance du droit d'asile dans les églises (IVe - milieu du Ve s.)* (Paris: De Boccard, 1994).
23 For example, *Hist*. VII, 21-2 and 29, pp. 339-43 and 346-9, I discussed this case in some detail in Rob Meens, "The sanctity of the basilica of St. Martin. Gregory of Tours and the practice of sanctuary in the Merovingian period," in *Texts and Identities in the early Middle Ages*, eds. Richard Corradini, Rob Meens, Christina Pössel, Philip Shaw (Vienna: Verlag der Österreichischen Akademie der Wissenschaften, 2006), 277-87.
24 See Meens, "The sanctity of the basilica"; for a Carolingian example in Tours, see Rob Meens "Sanctuary, penance and dispute settlement under Charlemagne. The conflict between Alcuin and Theodulf of Orléans over a sinful cleric," *Speculum* 82 (2007), 277-300.
25 For Theodore and the different versions of Theodore's penitential, see Rob Meens, *Penance in Medieval Europe, 600-1200* (Cambridge: Cambridge University Press, 2014) 89-96. Paenitentiale Theodori, Discipulus Umbrensium(=U) I,4,6, in *Die Canones Theodori Cantuariensis und ihre Überlieferungsformen*, ed. Paul W. Finsterwalder, Untersuchungen zu den Bußbüchern des 7., 8. und 9. Jahrhunderts, 1 (Weimar: Hermann Böhlaus Nachfolger, 1929), 294; compare Canones Cottoniani (=Co) 134, ibid 280; Canones Gregorii (=G) 110, ed. ibid 263 and Canones Basilienses (=B) 45, ed. Franz B. Asbach, "Das Poenitentiale Remense und der sogen. Excarpsus Cummeani: Überlieferung, Quellen und Entwicklung zweier

kontinentaler Bußbücher aus der 1. Hälfte des 8. Jahrhunderts" (Diss., Universität Regensburg, Regensburg, 1975), Anhang, 84.

26 P. Theodori U I,14, ed. Finsterwalder, 306 ; compare Capitula Dacheriana (= D) 34, Finsterwalder, 242 ; G 62, Finsterwalder, 259 ; Co 78, Finsterwalder, 276; B 34b, ed. Asbach, Anhang, 83; for the association between weddings and sex in this context, see James A. Brundage, *Law, Sex, and Christian Society in Medieval Europe* (Chicago, London: University of Chicago Press , 1987), 159 and Pierre J. Payer, *Sex and the Penitentials. The Development of a Sexual Code, 550–1150* (Toronto: University of Toronto Press, 1984), 118–19.

27 P. Theodori U II,12,30, ed. Finsterwalder, *Canones Theodori*, 330; G 182, ibid, 269.

28 P. Theodori U I,8,8, ibid, 301.

29 P. Theodori U I,14,17, ibid, 308; D 42, ibid, 243 ; G 125, ibid, 265; Co 105, ibid, 278; B 43a, ed. Asbach, "Poenitentiale Remense," Anhang, 83.

30 P. Theodori U, I,14,18, ed. Finsterwalder, *Canones Theodori*, 309; D 42, ibid, 243 ; G 126, ibid, 265; Co 106, , ibidem, 278; B 43a, ed. Asbach, "Poententiale Remense," Anhang, 83.

31 See Rob Meens, "A Background to Augustine's Mission to Anglo-Saxon England," *Anglo-Saxon England* 23 (1994), 5–17; on the continuing coexistence of different attitudes in this matter, see Rob Meens, "Ritual purity and the influence of Gregory the Great in the early Middle Ages," in *Unity and diversity in the Church*, ed. R. Swanson, Studies in Church History 32 (Oxford: Blackwell, 1995), 31–43; Michael D. Elliot, "Boniface, incest, and the earliest extant version of Pope Gregory I's Libellus responsionum (JE 1843)," *Zeitschrift der Savigny-Stiftung für Rechtsgeschichte, Kanonistische Abteilung* 113 (2014), 62–111. The Libellus has recently been edited as *Rescriptum Beati Gregorii Papae ad Augustinum Episcopum quem Saxoniam in praedicatione direxerat (seu Libellus responsionum)*, ed. Valeria Mattaloni, Edizione Nazionale dei Testi Mediolatini d'Italia, 43 (Florence: Edizioni del Galluzzo, 2017).

32 For this collection, see the fundamental study of Hubert Mordek, *Kirchenrecht und Reform im Frankenreich. Die Collectio Vetus Gallica, die älteste systematische Kanonessammlung des fränkischen Gallien. Studien und Edition*. Beiträge zur Geschichte und Quellenkunde des Mittelalters, 1 (Berlin and New York: de Gruyter, 1975); for its use of Theodore's penitential, ibidem, 52 and 86.

33 *Paenitentiale Parisiense simplex*, 45: "Qui facit furnica<ti>onem in aecclesia, penetencia eius omnibus diebus uitae suae praebeat obsequium domui dei." ed. Raymund Kottje, *Paenitentialia minora Franciae et Italiae saeculi VIII–IX*, CCSL 156 (Turnhout: Brepols, 1994), 78.

34 That this is a theme that we find mostly discussed in texts dating from around the year 1000 and later, is demonstrated by Dyan Elliott, "Sex in holy places. An exploration of a medieval anxiety," *Journal of Women's History* 6, no. 3 (1994), 6–34 [repr. in idem, *Fallen Bodies. Pollution, Sexuality, and Demonology in the Middle Ages* (Philadelphia: University of Pennsylvania Press, 1999), 61–80]. For the Paenitentiale Vindobonense

C, c. 6, see Rob Meens, "'Aliud Benitenciale': The ninth-century *Paenitentiale Vindobonense C*," *Mediaeval Studies* 66 (2004), 1–26, at 22 with comment on 7–9.
35 Sacramentary of Gellone nr. 349, ed. Dumas, 350. For dietary taboos in penitential books, see Rob Meens, "Pollution in the early Middle Ages: The case of the food regulations in penitentials," *Early Medieval Europe* 4 (1995), 3–19.
36 Sacramentary of Gellone nr. 354: Oratio super hominem christianum qui a demonio vexatur, ed. Dumas, 352; cf.P. Theodore U II, 10: De vexatis a demonio, ed. Finsterwalder, *Canones Theodori*, 324.
37 Sacramentary of Gellone nr. 464: Exercissimum aque super fontes ubi aliqua negligentia contingit, ed. Dumas, p. 451. For the impurity of wells in penitentials, see Meens, "Pollution in the Early Middle Ages," 10.
38 Elliot, "Sex in Holy Places," 9, remarks on the same prayer as it was included in the so-called Pontificale Romano-Germanicum that the prayer was "fraught with the language of defilement and purgation."
39 *Paenitentiale Cummeani*, c. (XI) XII, De questionibus sacrificii, ed. Ludwig Bieler, *The Irish Penitentials*, with an appendix by Daniel A. Binchy, Scriptores Latini Hiberniae 5, (Dublin: Dublin Institute for Advanced Studies, 1963), pp. 130–2; see Hubertus Lutterbach, "The Mass and holy communion in the medieval penitentials (600-1200). Liturgical and religio-historical perspectives," in *Bread of Heaven. Customs and Practices Surrounding Holy Communion. Essays in the History of Liturgy and Culture*, eds. Charles Caspers, Gerard M. Lukken, Gerard Rouwhorst (Kampen: Kok Pharos, 1995), 61–82.
40 For bishops as judges, see Laurent Jégou, *L'évêque, juge de paix. L'autorité épiscopale et le règlement des conflits (VIIIe-XIe siècle)* (Turnhout: Brepols, 2011).
41 See for example the council of Mâcon in 585, c. 8 complaining about powerful people behaving violently against someone who had sought refuge in a church, ed. De Clercq, Concilia, 242–3. This complaint may be related to the Eberulf affair in the church of Tours as I suggested in Meens, "Sanctity," 286, see *Hist*. VII.21–22, 29, pp. 339–43, 346–9.

10 Imitation and Rejection of Eastern Practices in Merovingian Gaul: Gregory of Tours and Vulfilaic the Stylite of Trier

1 *Hist*. VIII.15, pp. 381–2.
2 *Hist*. VIII.15–16, pp. 380–4.
3 *Hist*. VIII.15, pp. 380–1.
4 *Hist*. VIII.15, p. 381.

5   *Hist.* VIII.15, p. 382.
6   *Hist.* VIII.15, p. 382.
7   *Hist.* VIII.15, pp. 382–3.
8   *Hist.* VIII.15, p. 383.
9   Hubert Collin, "Grégoire de Tours, saint Walfroy le Stylite et la dea Arduinna. Un épisode de la christianisation des confins des diocèses de Reims et de Trèves au VIe siècle," in *La piété populaire au Moyen Âge, Actes du 99e congrès des sociétés savantes, Besançon, 1974, Section de philosophie et d'histoire jusqu'à 1610*, (Paris: Bibliothèque nationale, 1977), 387–400.
10 Walter Goffart, "Foreigners in the *Histories* of Gregory of Tours," *Florilegium* 4 (1982): 80–99 at 91–2.
11 Yitzhak Hen, *Culture and Religion in Merovingian Gaul, A.D. 481–751* (Leiden: Brill, 1995), 174.
12 Hen, *Culture and Religion*, 174.
13 Conrad Leyser, "'Divine Power Flowed from this book': Ascetic Language and Episcopal Authority in Gregory of Tours' *Life of the Fathers*," in *The World of Gregory of Tours*, eds. Kathleen Mitchell and Ian Wood (Leiden, Boston and Köln: Brill, 2002), 281–94.
14 For further reading on Simeon Stylites and his cult, see Susan Ashbrook Harvey, "The Sense of a Stylite: Perspectives on Simeon the Elder," *Vigiliae Christianae* 42, no. 4 (1988): 376–94; idem, "The Stylite's Liturgy: Ritual and Religious Identity in Late Antiquity," *Journal of Early Christian Studies* 6, no. 3 (1998): 523–39; idem and Robert Doran, *The Lives of Simeon Stylites* (Kalamazoo: Cistercian Publications, 1992); Antony Eastmond, "Body vs. Column: The Cults of St. Symeon Stylites," in *Desire and Denial in Byzantium*, ed. Liz James (Aldershot: Ashgate, 1999), 87–100.
15 *GC* 26, p. 314.
16 *GC* 26, p. 314.
17 Contemporary Gallic sources hardly mention Simeon Stylites. May Vieillard-Troiekouroff, in her extensive study of shrines in Merovingian Gaul, says nothing about Simeon, which leads to the conclusion that in the early Merovingian period Simeon was not venerated as a saint in Gaul. See *Les monuments religieux de la Gaule d'après les œuvres de Grégoire de Tours* (Paris: Librairie Honoré Champion, 1976).
18 *GM* 85, 94–102, pp. 95–6, 100–7.
19 There is some evidence of cults in honor of a few eastern saints in Gaul, for instance, in *GM* 85 Gregory refers to celebrations of Saint Polycarp of Smyrna in Riom and in *GM* 100 he relates miracles that took place in Gaul in the presence of the relics the holy martyr George. In his *Histories*, Gregory also records the presence of other relics of Syrian martyrs in Gaul, see *Hist.* VII.31 and X.31 for the relics of Saint Sergius and *Hist.* X.31 for the relics of Saints Cosmas and Damian

(all three saints are also included in the *GM* Sergius in *GM* 96 and Cosmas and Damian in *GM* 97). Some of these relics and traditions may have reached Gaul through Syrians living in Gaul. For general discussion on Syrian presence in Merovingian Gaul see Ingrid Heidrich, "Syrische Kirchengemeinden im Frankenreich des 6. Jahrhunderts," in *Aus Archiven und Bibliotheken. Festschrift für Raymund Kottje zum 65. Geburtstag*, ed. Hubert Mordek (Frankfurt am Main: Peter Lang, 1992), 21–32. It is also worth mentioning saint Polyeuctus of Constantinople who is mentioned in *GM* 102 in a Byzantine context and in *Hist.* VII.6 in a Merovingian context. For further discussion of his popularity in Gaul see Stefan Esders, "Avenger of all perjury" in Constantinople and Metz: Saint Polyeuctus, Sigibert I, and the Division of Charibert's Kingdom in 568," in *Western Perspectives on the Mediterranean: Cultural Transfer in Late Antiquity and the Early Middle Ages, 400–800 AD*, eds. Andreas Fischer and Ian Wood (London: Bloomsbury, 2014), 23–76. I give a detailed discussion of the veneration of the eastern saints in Merovingian Gaul in my PhD dissertation, see Tamar Rotman, "Miraculous History between East and West: Hagiography, Historiography and Identity in Sixth-Century Gaul" (PhD diss., Ben Gurion University of the Negev, Be'er Sheva, 2018).

20 For further discussions of eastern saints in the hagiographical collections of Gregory of Tours see Rotman, "Miraculous History" and Pia Lucas, "Heilige in Ost und West bei Gregor von Tours" (PhD diss., Freie Universität Berlin, Berlin, forthcoming).

21 Peter Brown, "The Rise and Function of the Holy Man in Late Antiquity," *Journal of Roman Studies* 61 (1971): 80-101; Brown later revised his theory, see "Arbiters of the Holy: The Christian Holy Man in Late Antiquity," in idem, *Authority and the Sacred: Aspects of the Christianisation of the Roman World* (Cambridge: Cambridge University Press, 1995), 57–78. Other scholars also revised and continued Brown's theory. See for instance the various contributions in the collected volume edited by James Howard-Johnston and Paul Antony Hayward, *The Cult of Saints in Late Antiquity and the Early Middle Ages. Essays on the Contribution of Peter Brown* (Oxford: Oxford University Press, 1999).

22 Brown, "Rise and Function," 91–3.

23 Brown, "Rise and Function," 97–101.

24 Martin Heinzelmann, "L'aristocratie et les évêchés entre Loire et Rhin, jusqu'à la fin du VIIe siècle," *Revue d'histoire de l'Église de France* 62, no.168 (1976): 75–90; idem, *Bischofsherrschaft in Gallien. Zur Kontinuität römischer Fuhrungsschichten vom 4. bis zum 7. Jahrhundert: soziale, prosopographische und bildungsgeschichtliche Aspekte* (Munich: Artemis Verlag, 1976), 61–183; Patrick Geary, *Before France and Germany: The Creation and Transformation of the Merovingian World* (New York and Oxford: Oxford University Press, 1988), 123–35; Allen E. Jones, *Social Mobility in Late Antique Gaul: Strategies and Opportunities for the non-Elite* (Cambridge: Cambridge University Press, 2009), 52–4; Hen, *Culture and Religion*, 16; Idem, "The

Church in Sixth Century Gaul," *A Companion to Gregory of Tours*, ed. Alexander Callander Murray (Leiden and Boston: Brill, 2015), 238–44; Ian Wood, *The Merovingian Kingdoms 450–751* (London and New York: Longman, 1994), 71–3.
25 Hen, "The Church in Sixth Century Gaul," 242–4.
26 Ian Wood, *Gregory of Tours* (Oxford: Headstart History, 1994), 10–13; Helmut Reimitz, *History, Frankish Identity and the Framing of Western Ethnicity* (Cambridge: Cambridge University Press, 2015), 32–4; For further reading about the delicate geo-political circumstances of Tours see Stefan Esders, "Gallic Politics in the Sixth Century," in *A Companion to Gregory of Tours*, ed. Alexander Callander Murray (Leiden and Boston: Brill, 2015), 433–9.
27 *Hist.* V.49, p. 262.
28 This is also apparent in Gregory's writings in which he tends to write more about the history of the Auvergne and Lyons rather than that of Tours and its area. See Raymond Van Dam, *Saints and their Miracles in Late Antique Gaul* (Princeton: Princeton University Press, 1993), 50–62.
29 The sole evidence for Gregory's ordination ceremony is a poem written by one of his good friends, the poet and bishop Venantius Fortunatus. See: Venantius Fortunatus, "Ad ciues turonicos de Gregorio episcopo," in *Venance Fortunat, Poèmes*, ed. and trans. M. Reydellet, 3 vols (Paris: Les Belles Lettres, 2003), 3:17.
30 "Conc. Aurelianense A. 541, c. 5," in *Concilia Galliae A. 511 – A. 695*, ed. Charles de Clercq, CCSL 148A (Turnhout: Brepols, 1963), 133.
31 The most prominent example of the opposition against Gregory is given in *Hist.* V.47–49 in which Gregory described Leudast's conspiracy against him. See also Wood, *Merovingian Kingdoms*, 86–7.
32 *VSM*; Gregory also mentions Martin, his church and relics numerous times in his hagiographical collections. See for instance *GM* 10, 14, 46, pp. 45, 48, 69; *GC* 4–10, 20, 45, 58, 79, 102, pp. 301–4, 309–10, 324–5, 331–2, 346–8; and *VP* VIII.1, IX.2, XV.1, XVI.1, XIX.2, XX.2, pp. 241–2. 253–4, 271–2, 274–5, 287–8, 292.
33 *VSM* I.33–34, 36, II.1, 2, 22, 60, III.1, 17, 60, IV.1–2, pp. 154–5, 159–60, 166, 179–80, 182, 186–7, 199–200.
34 *VSJ*.
35 For the martyrdom of Julian see *VSJ* 1, pp. 113–14; for miracles that Gregory and his relatives had experienced see *VSJ* 23–25, pp. 124–5.
36 *VSJ* 34, p. 128.
37 Ibid, trans. by Giselle de Nie in: Gregory of Tours, "The Miracles of the Martyr Julian," in idem, *Lives and Miracles* (Cambridge Mass: Harvard University Press, 2015), 387.
38 Peter Brown, "Relics and Social Status in the Age of Gregory of Tours," in idem, *Society and the Holy in Late Antiquity* (London and New York: Faber and Faber, 1982), 237–8. e. g. *GM* 14, 68, 76–77, 89, 101, 103–4, pp. 48, 84, 89–90, 97–8, 105,

107–10; *GC* 3, 9, 21, 32, 48, 58, 102, pp. 300, 304, 310–11, 318, 327, 331–2, 363; *VP* II.1, VII.2, VIII.4, 8, IX.2–3, XIV.2, XVI.3, 4, XVII.2, 4, XVIII.1, 3, XIX.3–4, pp. 219, 237–8, 244, 248–9, 253–5, 268–9, 276, 279–80, 281–2, 284, 285, 288–91.

39 *Hist.* VIII.15, p. 380.
40 *Hist.* VIII.15, 380–1.
41 *Hist.* VIII.16, pp. 383–4.
42 It is worth mentioning that Gregory knew Aredius in person. Several miracle stories about Julian of Brioude and Martin of Tours that Gregory recorded in his works were told to him by Aredius. See: *VSM* II.39, III.24, IV.6, pp. 173, 188–9, 200–1; *VSJ* 40, 44, pp. 130, 131; *GM* 36, 41, pp. 61, 65–6; *GC* 9, 10, 102, pp. 303–4, 363. Moreover, in his *Vita Nicetii* Gregory quotes Aredius and admits that they had met several times. See: *VP* XVII.preaf., pp. 277–8 Thus, it is clear that Gregory trusted Aredius and his stories, and, therefore, there is no wonder that he also trusted Aredius' disciple, Vulfilaic.
43 See for example Pia Lucas' contribution to this volume.

11 *Magnus et Verus Christianus*: The Portrayal of Emperor Tiberius II in Gregory of Tours

1 This article is based on a paper held in 2014 at a workshop of the project "East and West in the Early Middle Ages – The Merovingian Kingdoms in Mediterranean Perspective." Since then, two articles have been published that also regard the depiction of Tiberius: Simon Loseby, "Gregory of Tours, Italy, and the Empire," in *A Companion to Gregory of Tours*, ed. Murray, Alexander C. (Leiden, Boston: Brill, 2016), 462–97; Robert Winn, "Gregory of Tours, the Eastern Emperor, and Merovingian Gaul," *Northwestern Review* 2, no. 1 (2017): 1–36.
2 The translation is my own, following Krusch's edition in the MGH, pp. 171–2, 225, 235, 298.
3 Justin only reigned for 13 years.
4 Cf. *Hist.* III.32, p. 128; IV.8–9, p. 140; IV.40, p. 171.
5 For example *Hist.* VI.30, p. 298–9; X.2, p. 482–3; X.4, p. 486–7.
6 This goes only for *Hist.*, in *GM* 5, p. 41, as part of a completely different narrative, he is depicted more neutrally.
7 Henri Pirenne, *Mahomet et Charlemagne* (1937. Reprinted. Paris: Les Presses universitaires de France, 1992).
8 Michael McCormick: *The Origins of the European Economy: Communications and Commerce A. D. 300-900* (Cambridge: Cambridge University Press, 2002), e. g. 81, 106–7.

9   Syrian merchants: *Hist.* VII.31, p. 350; X.26, p. 519; wine: *Hist.* III.19, p. 121; VII.29, p. 348; *GC* 64, p. 336; saffron: *Hist.* V.4, p. 199; papyrus: *Hist.* V.5, p. 200.
10 McCormick, *Origins*, part III.
11 McCormick, *Origins*, 292–301. See also Yitzhak Hen, "Les authentiques des reliques de la Terre Sainte en Gaule franque" *Le Moyen Âge* 105 (1999): 71–90.
12 Deacons e. g. *Hist.* X.1, pp. 477, 481; *GM* 1, p. 38; *GM* 82, pp. 93–4; *GM* 87, p. 97. For possible sources of information on the Holy Land in particular, see also Yitzhak Hen, "Gregory of Tours and the Holy Land," *Orientalia Christiana Periodica* 61 (1995): 47–64.
13 Pilgrims e. g. *GM* 5, pp. 41–2; *GM* 18, pp. 49–50; *GM* 31, p. 57; Bishop Simon: *Hist.* IV.40, pp. 171–3; X.24, pp. 515–6.
14 See the detailed account of the embassy to Constantinople under Gripo, *Hist.* X.2, pp. 482–3; Spanish embassies: *Hist.* V.43, p. 249; VI.18, p. 287; VI.40, p. 310. For an overview concerning relations between Merovingian Gaul and Constantinople, see Eugen Ewig, *Die Merowinger und das Imperium* (Opladen: Westdeutscher Verlag, 1983); Jörg Drauschke, "Diplomatie und Wahrnehmung im 6. und 7. Jahrhundert: Konstantinopel und die merowingischen Könige," in *Byzanz in Europa: Europas Östliches Erbe*, ed. Michael Atripp (Turnhout: Brepols, 2011), 246–58. For Maurice's reign, see Paul Goubert, *Byzance avant l'Islam, t. 2: Byzance et l'occident sous les successeurs de Justinien vol. I: Byzance et les Francs* (Paris: Éditions A. et J. Picard et Cie, 1955), 105–72.
15 *Hist.* VIII.13, p. 379; IX.20, p. 434.
16 For the importance of oral channels of transfer, see Claudia Rapp, "Hagiography and monastic literature between Greek East and Latin West in Late Antiquity," in *Cristianità d'Occidente e cristianità d'Oriente: (secoli VI – XI), t. 2* (Spoleto: Presso la sede della Fondazione, 2004), 1251–66.
17 Peter Schreiner, "Gregor von Tours und Byzanz," in *Päpste, Privilegien, Provinzen: Beiträge zur Kirchen-, Rechts- und Landesgeschichte. Festschrift für Werner Maleczek zum 65. Geburtstag*, ed. Johannes Gießauf (Vienna: Böhlau, 2010), 403–18; Averil Cameron, "The Byzantine Sources of Gregory of Tours," *The journal of theological studies* 26 (1975): 421–6.
18 Schreiner, "Gregor," 407–8, 412; Cameron, "Sources," 424–6.
19 Cameron, "Sources," 422–4.
20 Evagrius *HE* V.1, pp. 195–6; V.13, pp. 208–9; Joh. Eph. *Eccl.* III.3.4, p. 92; III.3.11, pp. 100–1.
21 *GM* 95, p. 102, see also *Passio sanctorum Septem dormientium apud Ephesum*, MGH SS rer Merov. II, ed. Bruno Krusch, pp. 396–403.
22 *Hist.* I.18–43, pp. 16–28.
23 *Hist.* I.36, pp. 26–7; I.42–3, p. 28. For a theory concerning the absence of Arianism in book I, consider Loseby, "Italy," 472–3.

24 *Hist.* X.24, pp. 515–16; IV.40, pp. 172–3. On the outbreak of the Persian war: Ernst Stein, *Studien zur Geschichte des byzantinischen Reiches vornehmlich unter den Kaisern Justinus II u. Tiberius Constantinus* (Stuttgart: J. M. Metzlersche Verlagsbuchhandlung, 1919), 4–25.

25 *Hist.* II.34, pp. 82–3. For the Three Chapters controversy and references, see Till Stüber's article in this volume.

26 *Hist.* IV.40, p. 172.

27 Averil Cameron, "The Early Religious Policies of Justin II," *Studies in Church History* 13 (1976): 53, 62–7. Schreiner, "Gregor," 406, suggests to take the heresy as a reference not to Pelagius, the fifth-century heretic, but to Pope Pelagius I, who was regarded skeptically in Gaul, and therefore to the Three Chapters controversy.

28 *Hist.* V.30, p. 236.

29 Ewig, *Imperium*, 12–14. Walter Goffart, "Byzantine policy in the West under Tiberius II and Maurice: The Pretenders Hermenegild and Gundovald (579–858)," *Traditio* 13 (1957): 74–7. Drauschke, "Diplomatie," 249–51, 254, 261; Stein, *Geschichte des byzantinischen Reiches*, 107; Fritz Beisel, *Studien zu den fränkisch-römischen Beziehungen. Von ihren Anfängen bis zum Ausgang des 6. Jahrhunderts* (Idstein: Schulz-Kirchner Verlag, 1987), 99–111.

30 Drauschke, "Diplomatie," 263–5; Ewig, *Imperium*, 19–20, 61; but see Hans-Werner Goetz, "Byzanz in der Wahrnehmung fränkischer Geschichtsschreiber des 6. und 7. Jahrhunderts," in *Osten und Westen 400-600 n. Chr. Kommunikation, Kooperation und Konflikt*, eds. Carola Föller and Fabian Schulz (Stuttgart: Franz Steiner Verlag, 2016), 84.

31 Beisel, *Fränkisch-römische Beziehungen*, 85–6; Drauschke, "Diplomatie," 250, 266–9.

32 E. g. *Hist.* VI.30, p. 298; X.2, p. 483.

33 *Hist.* III.32, p. 128. He even omits that Theudebert had agreed to an alliance: Ewig, *Imperium*, 12. Winn's argument of Gregory respecting Italy as imperial possession remains unconvincing and disregards the wider context of the *Histories*: Winn, "Eastern Emperor," 9–11.

34 *Hist.* IV.9, pp. 140–1, cf. Loseby, "Italy," 480.

35 *Hist.* III.32, p. 128; IV.9, pp. 140–1. See Loseby, "Italy," 482, 497; cf. Ewig, *Imperium*, 58.

36 "quas male pervaserant," *Hist.* IV.8, p. 140.

37 Drauschke, "Diplomatie," 265. However, sometimes Gregory calls them Gr(a)eci (*Hist.* V.38, p. 245; VI.40, p. 310; VI.43, p. 316), a pejorative term in Procopius *Bell. Goth.*; I.18.40 [V.18.40], pp. 95–6. Remarkably, this term is only used when Gregory relates the events in Spain around Hermenegild (unless it concerns the Greek language, *Hist.* V.44, p. 254), so this might be either connected to his source or to the fact that "Roman" serves to describe those of Catholic faith, cf. Loseby, "Italy," 471.

38 Goetz, "Byzanz," 82–3; Loseby, "Italy," 470, 483.

39 Ewig, *Imperium*, 30; Loseby, "Italy," 493. See also the article by Yaniv Fox in this volume.

40 Mischa Meier, "Die Translatio des Christusbildes von Kamulianai und der Kreuzreliquie von Apameia nach Konstantinopel unter Justin II: Ein übersehenes Datierungsproblem," *Zeitschrift für antikes Christentum* 7 (2003): *passim*, esp. 245.

41 Moreira seems to think Gregory meant Jerusalem: Isabel Moreira, "Provisatrix optima: St. Radegund of Poitiers' relic petitions to the East," *Journal of Medieval History* 19 (1993): 296–7, but see *Hist.* IX.40, p. 464 and *GM* 5, p. 40, "in partibus Orientis" and "Hierusolymis ac per totam Orientis plagam," which theoretically includes Constantinople. For the bestowal of the relic, see Cameron, "Religious Policies," 55–62.

42 Sigibert was Radegund's stepson, a son of her husband Chlothar I by another wife. *Hist.* IX.40, p. 464 , cf. Martin Heinzelmann, *"Zehn Bücher Geschichte": Historiographie und Gesellschaftskonzept im 6. Jahrhundert* (Darmstadt: Wissenschaftliche Buchgesellschaft, 1994), 30.

43 *GC* 104, pp. 364–6, cf. Moreira, "Provisatrix," 287.

44 *Venanti Honori Clementiani Fortunati presbyteri Italici Opera poetica*, App. Carm. 2 (Ad Justinum et Sophiam Augustos), ed. Friedrich Leo, MGH AA 4,1, pp. 275–8. Cf. Cameron, "Religious Policies," 58.

45 *Hist.* IX.40, p. 464.

46 *Hist.* IV.40, p. 172.

47 This dating has first been argued for by Stefan Esders, "'Avenger of all Perjury' in Constantinople, Ravenna and Metz: Saint Polyeuctus, Sigibert I, and the Division of Charibert's Kingdom in 568," in *Western Perspectives on the Mediterranean: Cultural Transfer in Late Antiquity and the Early Middle Ages, 400–800 AD*, eds. Andreas Fischer and Ian N. Wood, (London: Bloomsbury, 2014), 33–5.

48 Goffart, "Byzantine Policy" 77–80; Drauschke, "Diplomatie," 252–3; but see Goubert, *Byzance*, 17 and Stein, *Geschichte des byzantinischen Reiches*, 16, n.18.

49 Cameron, "Religious Policies," 59–61; Esders, "Polyeuctus," 34–5.

50 Ewig, *Imperium*, 29–30; Goffart, "Byzantine Policy," 80–2.

51 See Anna Gehler-Rachůnek's contribution to this volume for details and further references.

52 For example: Goffart, "Byzantine Policy"; Goubert, "Byzance," 29–68; Constantin Zuckerman, "Qui a rappelé en Gaule le Ballomer Gondovald?" *Francia* 25 (1998), 1–18; Bernard S. Bachrach: *The Anatomy of a Little War: A Diplomatic and Military History of the Gundovald Affair (568–586)*, (Boulder: Westview Press, 1994).

53 Hermenegild: *Hist.* V.38, pp. 243–5; VI.18, pp. 287–8; VI.40, p. 310; VI.43, pp. 314–6; Gundovald: *Hist.* VI.24, pp. 291–2; VI.26, pp. 293–4; VII.10, p. 332; VII.32–VII.36, pp. 352–8.

54 *Hist.* VI.24, p. 292; VII.35, p. 355; Goffart, "Byzantine policy," 100–2; Ewig, *Imperium*, 33–6; Goubert, "Byzance," 34.
55 *Hist.* VI.24 and VI.26, pp. 291–4. Note that some translations insert the name of an emperor for clarity despite Gregory's omission.
56 Goubert, "Byzance," 32–4.
57 *Hist.* VI.21, p. 289; VI.24, VI.25, pp. 291–3. Due to the time required for travel and negotiations, I agree with Goffart's reconstruction, "Byzantine policy," 101–3. Irrespective of this, note that Gregory reports Tiberius' death in the context of 583 instead of 582, *Hist.* VI.30, pp. 298–9.
58 *Hist.* V.38, p. 245; VI.18, p. 287; VI.43, pp. 314–6.
59 Averil Cameron, "Early Byzantine *Kaiserkritik*: Two Case Histories," *Byzantine and Modern Greek Studies* 3 (1977): 9. See also Loseby, "Italy," 483, 487–8.
60 Schreiner, "Gregor," 406; Cameron, "Religious Policies," *passim*; Loseby, "Italy," 482.
61 Joh. Eph. *Eccl.* III.3.1–4, pp. 88–92; Evagrius *HE* V.10–11, pp. 206–8.
62 Winn, "Eastern Emperor," 11–22, has Gregory pair Guntram and Justin and Tiberius and Chilperic, but the relationship is more complex and works several ways.
63 *Hist.* VI.46, pp. 320–1.
64 "Defuncto igitur Chilperico inventamque, quam diu quaesierat, mortem [...]," *Hist.* VII.2, p. 327.
65 Guy Halsall, "Nero and Herod? The death of Chilperic and Gregory's writing of history," in *The World of Gregory of Tours*, eds. Kathleen Anne Mitchell and Ian Wood (Leiden: Brill, 2002), 342–4, 349; to some extent also Ian Wood, "The secret histories of Gregory of Tours," *Revue belge de philologie et d'Histoire* 71, no. 2 (1993): 254–6. Like Justin, Chilperic is treated more neutrally in the Miracle Books.
66 *Hist.* IV.28, pp. 160–1.
67 *Hist.* V.18, pp. 216–5; V.28, p. 234. Gregory has to defend himself in front of the king in V.49, pp. 258–63, but he did not put the blame on Chilperic.
68 *Hist.* IV.47, pp. 183–4; IV.50, p. 187; V.4, pp. 198–200; V.14, p. 213; VI.12, pp. 282–3; VI.31, pp. 299–301.
69 *Hist.* V.4, pp. 198–200; V.14, p. 213.
70 *Hist.* V.28, pp. 233–4; VI.45, p. 318.
71 *Hist.* V.34, pp. 238–41.
72 *Hist.* VI.23, p. 290; VI.31, pp. 299–302; VI.41, p. 313.
73 *Hist.* V.14, pp. 210–11; V.50, p. 263.
74 Compare Heinzelmann, *Zehn Bücher*, 48, 197 n. 33.
75 *Hist.* VI.30, p. 298, against VI.46, p. 321, "nullum umquam pure dilexit, a nullo dilectus est." Cf. Loseby, "Italy," 484.
76 Drauschke, "Diplomatie," 267; Loseby, "Italy," 483–4.
77 *Hist.* V.44, pp. 252–4; VI.46, p. 320.

78　*Hist.* V.43, p. 252; V.44, p. 253. Both the Arian and Chilperic frustratedly gnash their teeth, Winn, "Byzantine Emperor," 17.
79　*Hist.* VI.5, pp. 268–72; VI.17, pp. 286–7.
80　*Hist.* V.17, p. 216; VI.2, p. 266–7.
81　Cf. *Hist.* V.19, pp. 225–7; similarly interpreted by Loseby, "Italy," 484.
82　See source excerpt, *Hist.* V.19; Joh. Eph. *Eccl.* III.3.14, p. 103.
83　Cf. Heinzelmann, *Zehn Bücher*, 125, 240 n. 81.
84　*Hist.* IV.48, pp. 184–5; V.preface, pp. 193–4.
85　*Hist.* V.34, pp. 238–41.
86　*Hist.* VIII.30, p. 395.
87　*Hist.* II.37, pp. 85–6.
88　*Hist.* III.25, p. 123. Yet he chose a bad wife, and he tricked his uncle, III.26, pp. 123–4, and III.31, p. 128.
89　These qualities are also praised in Queen Chlothild, *dux* Chrodinus, Queen Ingoberga and others: *Hist.* III.18, p. 120; VI.20, pp. 288–9; IX.26, p. 445.
90　Heinzelmann, *Zehn Bücher*, 157.
91　Winn, "Byzantine Emperor," 13–5; to a lesser extent Heinzelmann, who is aware of the more negative passages but does not discuss them, *Zehn Bücher*, 49–69, 128; 158; 196–7 n. 32.
92　John M. Wallace-Hadrill, "Gregory of Tours and Bede: their views on the personal qualities of kings" *Frühmittelalterliche Studien* 2 (1968): 36; see also Halsall, "Nero and Herod," 340, 343, 347.
93　Wives: *Hist.* IV.25, pp. 156–7; V.35, pp. 241–2; sins: V.17, p. 216 (Chilperic: VI.3, p. 267); churches: VII.29, pp. 346–9; IX.10, p. 425; but respect: IX.3, p. 416; bishops: VI.24, pp. 291–2; VIII.12, pp. 378–9; mistrust: IX.20, p. 434; IX.28, pp. 446–7; IX.32, p. 451.
94　*Hist.* VIII.20, pp. 386–7; VIII.30, pp. 395–6.
95　Chilperic: *Hist.* V.14, pp. 208–9; V.18, pp. 219–23; V.44, pp. 252–3; Guntram: VIII.5, p. 374; IX.20, pp. 439–41.
96　*Hist.* V.30, p. 235.
97　Two of them were related to Gregory. *Hist.* VI.46, p. 320; VIII.5, p. 374., cf. Heinzelmann, *Zehn Bücher*, 58. On these visions and their political message, see also Yitzhak Hen, "Visions of the Afterlife in the Early Medieval West," in *Visions of the Afterlife*, eds. Richard M. Pollard (Cambridge: Cambridge University Press, forthcoming). I thank Yitzhak Hen for letting me consult the pre-print version of this article.
98　*Hist.* IX.21, pp. 441–2, "acsi bonus sacerdus." This and other aspects of Gregory's image of the ideal Christian ruler can also be found in older Gallic traditions, see Bruno Dumézil, "Le modèle royal à l'époque mérovingienne," in *L'empreinte*

chrétienne en Gaule du IVè au IXè siècle, ed. Michèle Gaillard (Turnhout: Brepols, 2014), 135–6.
99 *Hist.* VIII.30, p. 395. Before this, his army plunders, as well: *Hist.* VII.12–13, pp. 333–4; VII.24, p. 344, etc.
100 *Hist.* VII.7, p. 330; VII.40, p. 363; VIII.3, p. 373; VIII.30, pp. 395–6; IX.21, p. 441.
101 *Hist.* I.43, p. 28; VI.31, pp. 300–2; V.30, p. 236.
102 *Hist.* IV.22, pp. 154–5; esp. VI.41, p. 313.
103 Tiberius: *Hist.* V.19, pp. 225–7; V.30, p. 236; Guntram: VII.40, p. 363; VIII.3, p. 373.
104 *Hist.* VII.18, p. 338; VIII.44, pp. 410–11; IX.3, pp. 415–16. Childebert II is also saved when he goes to pray, X.18, p. 509.
105 *Hist.* V.17, p. 216; V.30, p. 235; VI.46, p. 319; compare Heinzelmann, *Zehn Bücher*, 196 n. 25.
106 *Hist.* V.19, pp. 225–7; IX.21, pp. 441–2.
107 For a theory, see Heinzelmann, *Zehn Bücher*, 202 n. 67.

12 When Contemporary History Is Caught Up by the Immediate Present: Fredegar's Proleptic Depiction of Emperor Constans II

1 Fredegar *Chron.* IV.81, p. 162; my translation. The translation given in *The Fourth Book of the Chronicle of Fredegar with its Continuations*. Translation from the Latin with Introduction and Notes by John Michael Wallace-Hadrill (Oxford: Oxford University Press, 1960), 67 and 69, is less precise.
2 See Robert G. Hoyland, *Seeing Islam as Others Saw It. A Survey and Evaluation of Christian, Jewish and Zoroastrian Writings on Early Islam* (Princeton: Darwin Press, 1998), 216–19.
3 See on this Andreas Fischer, "Rewriting History: Fredegar's Perspectives on the Mediterranean," in *Western Perspectives on the Mediterranean. Cultural Transfer in Late Antiquity and the Early Middle Ages, 400–800 AD*, eds. Idem and Ian Wood (London: Bloomsbury, 2014), 55–75 and 135–43.
4 Fredegar *Chron.* IV.82, p. 162–3; on this passage see Stefan Esders, "Chindasvinth, the 'Gothic disease', and the Monothelite crisis," *Millenium-Jahrbuch* (in press).
5 Roger Collins, *Die Fredegar-Chroniken* (München: MGH, 2007), 26.
6 See Fischer, "Rewriting history," 60–9.
7 The much-debated question of the identity of "Fredegar" and of multiple authorship that may have had a hand in the process of writing and redacting the chronicle (on which see Collins, *Die Fredegar-Chroniken*, 8–25) can be skipped over here, as the chapter under investigation clearly was written by one author, who put his personal stamp on the narrative, apparently not before 658/9.

8   On Fredegar's sources see Collins, *Die Fredegar-Chroniken*, 46–65; Fischer, "Rewriting history," 58–9, suggesting written and orally transmitted information as a source for Fredegar in his depiction of contemporary events.
9   Fredegar *Chron.* IV.62–6, pp. 151–4.
10 In what follows I am recounting some results of my earlier research on Fredegar. See Stefan Esders, "Herakleios, Dagobert und die «beschnittenen Völker». Die Umwälzungen des Mittelmeerraums im 7. Jahrhundert in der fränkischen Chronik des sog. Fredegar," in *Jenseits der Grenzen. Studien zur spätantiken und frühmittelalterlichen Geschichtsschreibung*, eds. Andreas Goltz, Hartmut Leppin and Heinrich Schlange-Schöningen (Berlin and New York: De Gruyter, 2009), 239–311.
11 See Stefan Esders, "The prophesied rule of a 'circumcised people'. A traveling tradition from the seventh-century Mediterranean," in *Barbarians and Jews. Jews and Judaism in the Early Medieval West*, eds. Yitzhak Hen and Thomas F. X. Noble (Turnhout: Brepols, 2018), 119–54.
12 Fischer, "Rewriting history," 65–6.
13 Wolfram Brandes, "'Juristische' Krisenbewältigung im 7. Jahrhundert? Der Prozess gegen Papst Martin I. und Maximus Homologetes," in *Fontes Minores X*, ed. Ludwig Burgmann (Frankfurt a. M.: Klostermann, 1998), 141–212.
14 See Esders, "Chindasvinth" (above, n. 4); Idem, "Die gallische Kirche des 7. Jahrhunderts zwischen *imperium* und *regna*. Der Brief des merowingischen Königs Sigibert III. an Bischof Desiderius von Cahors (650) und die fränkische Rezeption des Monotheletismus-Streites," in *Gallien zwischen* imperium *und* regna. *Die Darstellung von Kontingenz und ihrer Bewältigung*, eds. Matthias Becher and Hendrik Hess (in press).
15 Ekkehart Rotter, *Abendland und Sarazenen. Das okzidentale Araberbild und seine Entstehung im Frühmittelalter* (Berlin and New York, De Gruyter, 1986), 149–58; Walter E. Kaegi, *Byzantium and the Early Islamic Conquests* (Cambridge: Cambridge University Press, 1992), 98.
16 See Rotter, *Abendland und Sarazenen*, 173.
17 Alfred J. Butler, *The Arab Conquest of Egypt and the Last Thirty Years of Roman Dominion*, 2nd edition (Oxford: Oxford University Press, 1978), 465–83; Alexander Daniel Beihammer, *Quellenkritische Untersuchungen zu den ägyptischen Kapitulationsverträgen der Jahre 640–646* (Vienna: Verlag der Österreichischen Akademie der Wissenschaften, 2000).
18 See Michael F. Hendy, *Studies in the Byzantine Monetary Economy, c. 300–1450* (Cambridge: Cambridge University Press, 1985), 168–75; Jairus Banaji, *Agrarian Change in Late Antiquity. Gold, Labour, and Aristocratic Dominance* (Oxford: Oxford University Press, 2001), 65; Constantin Zuckerman, "Learning from the Enemy and More: Studies in 'Dark Centuries' Byzantium," *Millennium-Jahrbuch* 2

(2005): 79–135, at 102–6. On the religious issues see e.g. Friedhelm Winkelmann, "Ägypten und Byzanz vor der arabischen Eroberung," *Byzantinoslavica* 40 (1979): 161–82.

19 Esders, "Herakleios," 289–91.

20 Stefan Esders, "'Getaufte Juden' im westgotischen Spanien. Die antijüdische Politik König Chintilas zum Jahreswechsel 637/638 und ihre Hintergründe," in *Jüdische Lebenswelten. Von der Antike bis zur Gegenwart*, eds. Ernst Baltrusch and Uwe Puschner (Frankfurt a. M.: P. Lang, 2016), 53–96, at 82–9.

21 James T. Palmer, *The Apocalypse in the Early Middle Ages* (Cambridge: Cambridge University Press, 2014), 11–22 and 79–106.

22 Walter E. Kaegi, "Initial Byzantine Reactions to the Arab Conquest," *Church History* 38 (1969): 139–49; Sebastian Brock, "Syriac Views of Emergent Islam," in *Studies on the First Century of Islamic Society*, ed. Gautier Herald A. Juynboll (Carbondale u. Edwardsville/Ill: Southern Illinois University Press, 1982), 9–21 and 199–203; Harald Suermann, *Die geschichtstheologische Reaktion auf die einfallenden Muslime in der edessenischen Apokalyptik des 7. Jahrhunderts*, (Frankfurt a. M.: P. Lang, 1985); Daniel J. Sahas, "The Seventh Century in Byzantine-Muslim Relations: Characteristics and Forces," *Islam and Christian-Muslim Relations* 2 (1991): 3–22; Gerrit J. Reinink, "From Apocalyptics to Apologetics: Early Syriac Reactions to Islam," in *Endzeiten. Eschatologie in den monotheistischen Weltreligionen*, eds. Wolfram Brandes and Felicitas Schmieder (Berlin and New York: De Gruyter, 2008), 75–87; Palmer, *The Apocalypse*, 107–19.

23 Vassilios Christides, *Byzantine Libya and the March of the Arabs towards the West of Africa* (Oxford: British Archaeological Reports, 2000), 37–43; Walter E. Kaegi, *Muslim Expansion and Byzantine Collapse in North Africa* (Cambridge: Cambridge University Press, 2010), 92–115 and 174–6.

24 Walter E. Kaegi, "Byzantine Sardinia and Africa Face the Muslims: Seventh-Century Evidence," *Bizantinistica* 3 (2001): 1–24, at 4.

25 On Gregory's revolt see Yves Modéran, "Le dossier des sources non musulmanes sur l'exarque Grégoire et l'expedition Arabe en Ifrîkiyya en 647/648," in *Del Nilo al Ebro. Estudios sobre les fuentes de la conquista islámica* (Alcalá de Henares: Universidad de Alcalá, Servicio de Publicaciones, 2009), 141–78.

26 Kaegi, *Muslim Expansion*, 69–91.

27 Phil Booth, *Crisis of Empire: Doctrine and Dissent at the End of Late Antiquity* (Berkeley: University of California Press, 2013), 285–58.

28 Kaegi, *Muslim Expansion*, 116–44.

29 In modern translations this is usually misrepresented, for instance by Wallace-Hadrill, *The Fourth Book of Fredegar*, 69, who translates *paululum* with "quickly."

30 As is illustrated by the "Futūh Misr" of Ibn 'Abd el-Hakem: "So 'Abd Allah set out for Africa. Now the seat of rule in Africa at that time was a city called Quartājenna

[Carthage], where was reigning a king whose name was Jurjir [Gregorios]. He had originally been appointed vice-regent there by [the Byzantine emperor] Heraclius, but had revolted and coined dīnārs in his own name. His domain extended from Itrābulus to Tanja [Tanger]. So when ʿAbd Allah approached, Jurjir met him, and a battle was fought, in which the latter was killed and his army put to flight. [...] When the chieftains of the country saw this, they began to treat with ʿAbd Allah, offering to give him a sum of money if he would go forth from their land. He agreed, and took the money and returned to Egypt, without appointing any Muslim governor over them or establishing any military station in their land." Charles Cutler Torrey, "The Mohammedan Conquest of Egypt and North Africa in the Years 643 to 705 A.D." Translated from the Original Arabic of Ibn "Abd el-Hakem," in *Biblical and Semitic Studies. Critical and Historical Essays by the Members of the Semitic and Biblical Faculty of Yale University* (New York: Charles Scribner's Sons, 1901), 277–330, at 301–2; on the legalistic bias of this report see Robert Brunschvig, "Ibn ʿAbdalhʾakam et la conquête de l'Afrique du Nord par les Arabes: Étude critique," *Annales de l'Institut des études orientales* (Algiers) 6 (1942–47): 108–55.

31 Guido Bausenhart, *"In allem uns gleich außer der Sünde," Studien zum Beitrag Maximos' des Bekenners zur altkirchlichen Christologie* (Tübingen: Grünewald, 1990), 196–317; Booth, *Crisis of Empire*, 282–9.

32 Luis Agostín García Moreno, "Una desconicida embajada de Quindasvinto al África bizantina," *Boletín de la Real Academia de la Historia* 206 (2009): 445–64.

33 Hugh Kennedy, *The Great Arab Conquests. How the Spread of Islam changed the World we live in* (Philadelphia: W&N, 2007), 324–43.

34 Andreas N. Stratos, "The Naval Engagement at Phoenix," in *Charanis Studies. Essays in Honor of Peter Charanis*, ed. Angeliki E. Laiou-Thomadakis (New Brunswick: Rutgers University Press, 1980), 229–47, at p. 231; Salvatore Cosentino, "Constans II and the Byzantine Navy," *Byzantinische Zeitschrift* 100 (2007): 577–603, here: 583.

35 Clive Foss, "Egypt under Muʿāwiya, Pt. I: Flavius Papas and Upper Egypt," *Bulletin of the School of Oriental and African Studies* 72 (2009): 1–24.

36 Cosentino, "Constans II," 592. The famous inscription from Soloi (649/650): Dénis Feissel, "Inscriptions chrétiennes et byzantines," *Revue des études grecques* 100 (1987): 380–1.

37 *Regesten der Kaiserurkunden des Oströmischen Reiches von 565–1453*, vol. I, 1: *Regesten 565–867*, 2nd edition, eds. Johannes Preiser-Kapeller, Alexander Riehle and Andreas E. Müller (Munich: C.H. Beck, 2009), no. 226, p. 102 (not mentioning Fredegar).

38 Theophanes, *Chronographia* A. M. 6146, ed. Karl de Boor (Leipzig: Teubner, 1883), I, pp. 345–6; translation *The Chronicle of Theophanes Confessor. Byzantine and Near*

Eastern history A.D. 284–813, eds. Cyril Mango and Roger Scott (Oxford: Clarendon Press, 1997), p. 482; similar Dionysios of Tel-Mahrē in: *The Seventh Century in West-Syrian Chronicles*. Introduced, translated and annotated by Andrew Palmer, with added Annotation and an historical Introduction by Robert Hoyland (Liverpool: Liverpool University Press, 1993), § 101, pp. 179–80. Stratos, "The Naval Engagement at Phoenix," 231–2.

39 Ps.-Sebeos, Armenian History, cc. 48–50: *The Armenian History attributed to Sebeos*. Translated by R. W. Thomson. Historical Commentary by James Howard-Johnston (Liverpool: Liverpool University Press, 1999), Vol. I, pp. 135, 143–6. See Shaun O'Sullivan, "Sebeos' Account of an Arab Attack on Constantinople in 654," *Byzantine and Modern Greek Studies* 28 (2004): 67–88; Robert Hoyland, "Sebeos, the Jews and the Rise of Islam," in *Medieval and Modern Perspectives on Muslim-Jewish Relations*, ed. Ronald Nettler (Luxemburg: Harwood Academic Publishers, 1995), 89–102; Zuckerman, "Learning from the Enemy," 115. On this chronicle see also James Howard-Johnston, *Witnesses to a World Crisis: Historians and Histories of the Middle East in the Seventh Century* (Oxford: Oxford University Press, 2010), 70–102.

40 Ps.-Sebeos, cc. 48–50, pp. 135, 143–6.

41 Kenneth M. Setton, "The Emperor Constans II and the Capture of Corinth by the Onogur Bulgars," *Speculum* 27 (1952): 351–62.

42 Zuckerman, "Learning from the Enemy," 79.

43 On the background see e.g. Martin Hinds, "The Murder of the Caliph Uthman," *International Journal of Middle East Studies* 3 (1972): 450–69.

44 Theophanes, *Chronographia* A.M. 6150: "Τούτῳ τῷ ἔτει ἐστοιχήθη μεταξὺ Ῥωμαίων καὶ Ἀράβων, τοῦ Μαυΐου πρεσβεύσαντος διὰ τὴν ἀνταρσίαν, ἵνα τελῶσι τοῖς Ῥωμαίοις οἱ Ἄραβες καθ' ἡμέραν νομίσματα χίλια καὶ ἵππον καὶ δοῦλον" (ed. De Boor, I, p. 347); see Alexander Daniel Beihammer, *Nachrichten zum byzantinischen Urkundenwesen in arabischen Quellen (565–811)* (Bonn: Dr. Rudolf Habelt, 2000), 303; *Regesten der Kaiserurkunden*, no. 228b, pp. 104–5 suggesting a date of 657/658.

45 Andreas Kaplony, *Konstantinopel und Damaskus. Gesandtschaften und Verträge zwischen Kaisern und Kalifen 639–750. Untersuchungen zum Gewohnheits-Völkerrecht und zur interkulturellen Diplomatie* (Berlin: Klaus Schwarz Verlag, 1996), 23–32 (omitting evidence provided by Fredegar).

46 See Kaplony, *Konstantinopel und Damaskus*, 99–113 with references; Ralph-Johannes Lilie, *Die byzantinische Reaktion auf die Ausbreitung der Araber. Studien zur Strukturwandlung des byzantinischen Staates im 7. und 8. Jahrhundert* (München: Institut für Byzantinistik und Neugriechische Philologie der Universität, 1976), 60–83 and 99–111.

47 Matthias Hardt, *Gold und Herrschaft. Die Schätze europäischer Könige und Fürsten im ersten Jahrtausend* (Berlin: Akademie-Verlag, 2004), 63–4.

48 Fredegar *Chron.* IV.45, p. 143.
49 Michael Hendy, "From Public to Private: The Western Barbarian Coinages as a Mirror of the Disintegration of Late Roman State Structures," *Viator* 19 (1988): 29–78, at 62–5; idem, "East and West: The Transformation of Late Roman Financial Structures," in *Roma fra Oriente e Occidente* (Spoleto: Centro Italiano di Studi sull'alto medioevo, 2002), vol. 2, 1307–70, at 1338.
50 Alan M. Stahl, "Coinage (Origins of the European Economy: A Debate with Michael McCormick)," *Early Medieval Europe* 12 (2003): 293–9.
51 Helmut Reimitz, *History, Frankish identity and the Framing of Western Ethnicity, 550-850* (Cambridge: Cambridge University Press, 2015), 44–73.
52 Fischer, "Rewriting History," 63–9.
53 See also Ian N. Wood "Fredegar's Fables," in *Historiographie im frühen Mittelalter*, eds. Anton Scharer and Georg Scheibelreiter (Munich: Oldenbourg, 1994), 359–66; Esders, "Herakleios"; Fischer, "Rewriting History."

13 Byzantium, the Merovingians, and the Hog: A Passage of Theophanes' *Chronicle* Revisited

1 My special thanks go to Marco Stoffella and Stefan Esders for discussion of the Carolingian sources and advice. Yitzhak Hen significantly improved the manuscript's readability. Mistakes are mine.
2 *The Chronicle of Theophanes Confessor: Byzantine and Near Eastern History AD 284–813*, transl., introd., and comm. Cyril Mango and Roger Scott (Oxford: Oxford University Press, 1997), 556–7, with Mango's commentary. By permission of Oxford University Press. The Italic is mine and identifies a line not translated by Anastasius, on whom see below, note 7. Greek text in *Theophanis chronographia*, ed. Carl de Boor, vol. 1 (Leipzig: Teubner, 1883, repr. Hildesheim, New York: Georg Olms 1980), 402–3.
3 See the contributions in *Studies in Theophanes*, eds. Federico Montinaro and Marek Jankowiak, Travaux et mémoires 19 (Paris: Association des Amis du Centre d'Histoire et Civilisation de Byzance, 2015). On the attribution to the famous confessor, see below, note 32.
4 A general outline of Theophanes' sources can be found in *The Chronicle of Theophanes*, lxxiv–xcv.
5 See the contributions in *Der Dynastiewechsel von 751. Vorgeschichte, Legitimationsstrategien und Erinnerung*, eds. Matthias Becher and Jörg Jarnut (Münster: Scriptorium, 2004).
6 *Theophanis chronographia*, vol. 1, 402; *The Chronicle of Theophanes*, 557.
7 *Theophanis chronographia*, ed. Carl de Boor, vol. 2 (Leipzig: Teubner 1885, repr. Hildesheim, New York: Georg Olms, 1980), 272–3.

8 A meaningless sequence of characters also pops up in the manuscripts close to the passage. De Boor interpreted it as a possible misunderstanding of the Greek word for "scholion" originally found in the margin.
9 *Le Liber pontificalis*, ed. Louis Duchesne, vol. 1 (Paris: Thorin, 1886), XCIV, Ch. 21–23, p. 446.
10 *Einhardi Vita Karoli Magni*, ed. Georg Waitz, MGH Scriptores rerum Germanicarum 25 (Hannover, Leipzig: Hahn, 1911), Ch. 1–2, pp. 2–4. On the composition, see Rosamond McKitterick, *History and Memory in the Carolingian world* (Cambridge: Cambridge University Press, 2004), 29–30, arguing for an early date, and Steffen Patzold, "Einhards erste Leser: Zu Kontext und Darstellungsabsicht der 'Vita karoli'," *Viator Multilingual* 42 (2011), 33–56, for a recent defense of a dating in the winter of 828/829.
11 *Einhardi Vita Karoli Magni*, Ch. 1–2, pp. 2–5.
12 For a useful summary of this debate, see Ilse Rochow, *Byzanz im 8. Jahrhundert in der Sicht des Theophanes*, Berliner byzantinische Arbeiten 57 (Berlin: Akademie Verlag, 1991), 108–10.
13 *Einhardi Vita Karoli Magni*, Ch. 2, pp. 4–5.
14 *Les gestes des évêques d'Auxerre*, ed. Marcel Sot, Les classiques de l'histoire de France au Moyen Âge (Paris: Les Belles Lettres, ²2006), 129. The translation is mine.
15 See Michel Rouche, "Les Aquitains ont-ils trahi avant la bataille de Poitiers? Un éclairage événementiel sur les mentalités," *Le Moyen Âge* 74 (1968), 5–26.
16 *Chronicon Moissiacense*, ed. Georg H. Pertz, MGH SS 1 (Hannover: Hahn, 1826), 291. This piece of information is clearly visible, in spite of the lamentable state of the manuscript in the relevant section.
17 *Theophanis chronographia*, vol. 1, 472–3; *The Chronicle of Theophanes*, 649.
18 See Federico Montinaro, "The *Chronicle* of Theophanes in the indirect tradition," in *Studies in Theophanes*, 177–205, at 204. A stricter translation of the *Chronicle*'s Greek would be "those of Rome [genitive], relatives of the blessed pope Adrian." *Romae* is instead, appropriately, a *genitivus loci* in Anastasius' translation and may have been so in the chronicler's own Latin source.
19 See the contributions in *Am Vorabend der Kaiserkrönung*, eds. Peter Godman, Jörg Jarnut, and Peter Johanek (Berlin: Akademie Verlag, 2002).
20 *Theophanis chronographia*, vol. 1, 471.
21 See, for example, the *Annales Laureshamenses*, ed. Georg H. Pertz, MGH SS 1, (Hannover: Hahn, 1826), 38, s. a. 801. These were a contemporary source, composed c. 803, as illustrated by Roger Collins, "Charlemagne's imperial coronation and the Annals of Lorsch," in *Charlemagne: empire and society*, ed. Joanna Story (Manchester, New York: Manchester University Press, 2005), 52–70.
22 See for example *Aëtii Amideni libri medicinales I–IV*, ed. Alexander Olivieri, Corpus medicorum Graecorum 8 (1) (Leipzig: Teubner, 1935), I, Ch. 38, p. 40, sixth century,

describing whole-body anointment with chamomile oil "from head to foot" against fever.

23 *Le Liber pontificalis*, ed. Louis Duchesne, vol. 2 (Paris: Thorin 1892), XCVIII, Ch. 23–24, p. 7; p. 38, notes 34–5.

24 *Thegan, Die Taten Kaiser Ludwigs. Astronomus. Das Leben Kaiser Ludwigs*, MGH, Scriptores rerum Germanicarum 64 (Hannover: Hahn, 1995), Ch. 1 and 17, pp. 176 and 198. On Thegan's work and its date, see now *Charlemagne and Louis the Pious. The Lives by Einhard, Notker, Ermoldus, Thegan, and the Astronomer*, transl., introd., and comm. Thomas F.X. Noble (University Park, PA: Penn State Press, 2009), 187–94.

25 See the older review in Peter Classen, *Karl der Große, das Papsttum und Byzanz* (Düsseldorf: Schwann, 1968), 48–9, in favor of historicity. For a similar position, see also the following note. Rosamond McKitterick, *Charlemagne. The Formation of European Identity* (Cambridge: Cambridge University Press, 2008), makes no mention of the ritual.

26 Robert-Henri Bautier, "Sacres et couronnements sous les Carolingiens et les premiers Capétiens: recherches sur la genèse du sacre royal français," *Annuaire-Bulletin de la Société de l'histoire de France* (1987–8), 7–56, repr. Id., *Recherches sur l'histoire de la France médiévale* (Aldershot: Variorum, 1991), n° II. On the *Annals*, see above, note 21.

27 For the context, see Mayke de Jong, *The Penitential State* (Cambridge: Cambridge University Press, 2009).

28 See Thomas Pratsch, *Theodoros Studites (759–826). Zwischen Dogma und Pragma*, Berliner byzantinische Studien 4 (Frankfurt am Main: Peter Lang, 1998), 231–34, and Id., "Nikephoros I.," in *Die Patriarchen der ikonoklastischen Zeit. Germanos I.-Methodios I. (715 847)*, ed. Ralph-Johannes Lilie, Berliner byzantinische Studien 5 (Frankfurt am Main: Peter Lang, 1999), 109–47, at 131–42.

29 See Mango's introduction to *The Chronicle of Theophanes*, lxxii.

30 *Le liber pontificalis*, vol. 2, XCVIII, Ch. 20 and 26, pp. 6 and 8 (the exile is mistakenly mentioned twice); XCIX, Ch. 2, p. 49 (the return of the exiles). On the similar practice concerning hostages, see Adam J. Kosto, "Hostages in the Carolingian world (714–840)," *Early Medieval Europe* 11, no. 2 (2002), 123–47.

31 Godefroid Kurth, "Une source byzantine d'Eginhard," *Bulletin de l'Académie royale de Belgique, Classe des Lettres*, 3rd series, 30, no. 1 (1895), 580–90.

32 See, however, the powerful argument against the attribution of the *Chronicle* to Theophanes the Confessor brought forward by Constantin Zuckerman, "Theophanes the Confessor and Theophanes the Chronicler," in *Studies in Theophanes*, 31–52.

33 See the references in Rochow, *Byzanz* and Mango's commentary.

34 *La Chanson de Roland*, ed. Cesare Segre, transl. Madeleine Tyssens, 2nd edn, Textes littéraires français (Geneva: Droz, 2003), 254, laisse 233, v. 3218–3223. On this catalogue of peoples, see Gustav A. Beckmann, *Onomastik des Rolandsliedes*, Beihefte zur Zeitschrift für romanische Philologie 411 (Berlin, Boston: De Gruyter 2017), 3–173.

35 Transl. Gerald J. Brault, *The Song of Roland. An Analytical Edition* (University Park, PA, London: Penn University Press, 1978), 197, as laisse 232.
36 Henri Grégoire, "La Chanson de Roland de l'an 1085," *Bulletin de l'Académie royale de Belgique, Classe des Lettres* 25 (1939), 211–73, at 241–2; Id. and Raoul de Keyser, "La Chanson de Roland et Byzance," *Byzantion* 14 (1939), 265–319, at 283–6.
37 See, for example, Michelina Di Cesare, *The pseudo-historical image of the prophet Muḥammad in Medieval Latin literature*, Studien zur Geschichte und Kultur des islamischen Orients 26, (Berlin, New York, Boston: De Gruyter, 2012), 71–3, 84–9, and 165–7.
38 Cf. Beckmann, *Onomastik*, 23–4.

Conclusion

1 Henri Pirenne, *Mahomet et Charlemagne*, eds. Jacques Pirenne and Fernand Vercauteren (Paris, 1937); English trans. *Mohammed and Charlemagne* (London: George Allen, 1939; rev. 1954), 189.
2 The amount of literature on Pirenne's thesis and its influence is enormous and cannot be listed here. For some discussion and further references, see the introduction to *East and West in the Early Middle Ages: The Merovingian Kingdoms in Mediterranean Perspective*, eds. Stefan Esders, Yaniv Fox, Yitzhak Hen and Laury Sarti (Cambridge: Cambridge University Press, 2019). See also Bonnie Effros, "The enduring attraction of the Pirenne thesis," *Speculum* 92 (2017): 184–208.
3 Pirenne, *Mohammed and Charlemagne*, 164.
4 For a recent and most eloquent expression of these views, see Chris Wickham, *Medieval Europe* (New Haven and London: Yale University Press, 2016), 22–42.
5 On this concept, see the various papers in *Kingdoms of the Empire: The Integration of Barbarians in Late Antiquity*, ed. Walter Pohl (Leiden, New York and Köln: Brill, 1997); and *Regna and Gentes: The Relationship Between Late Antique and Early Medieval Peoples and Kingdoms in the Transformation of the Roman World*, ed. Hans-Werner Goetz, Jörg Jarnut and Walter Pohl (Leiden and Boston: Brill, 2003). See also Herwig Wolfram, *The Roman Empire and Its Germanic Peoples*, trans. Thomas Dunlap (Berkeley, Los Angeles and London: University of California Press, 1997).
6 See, for example, the *Histories* of Gregory of Tours. For some discussion, see Helmut Reimitz, *History, Frankish Identity and the Framing of Western Ethnicity, 550–850* (Cambridge: Cambridge University Press, 2015).
7 See, for example, Jamie Kreiner, *The Social Life of Hagiography in the Merovingian Kingdom* (Cambridge: Cambridge University Press, 2014). See also some of the papers in *East and West in the Early Middle Ages*, eds. Esders, Fox, Hen and Sarti (2019).
8 See, for example, Patrick J. Geary, *The Myths of Nations: The Medieval Origins of Europe* (Princeton and Oxford: Princeton University Press, 2002).

Bibliography

Primary sources

The Acts of the Council of Constantinople of 553 with Related Texts on the Three Chapters Controversy, translated by Richard Price. Liverpool: Liverpool University Press, 2009.

Aëtii Amideni libri medicinales I–IV, edited by Alexander Olivieri. Corpus medicorum Graecorum 8 (1). Leipzig: Teubner, 1935.

Agathias. *The Histories*, edited by Hans-Georg Beck, Athanasios Kambylis and Rudolf Keydell. Corpus fontium historiae Byzantinae IIa. Berlin: De Gruyter, 1975.

Ammianus Marcellinus. *Res Gestae*, edited by John C. Rolfe, 3 vols. Cambridge, MA and London: Harvard University Press, 1935–1940.

Annales Laureshamenses, edited by Georg H. Pertz. MGH SS 1, 19–39. Hannover: Hahn, 1826.

Appian of Alexandria. *Roman History*, edited by Horace White, 4 vols. Cambridge, MA and London: Harvard University Press, 1912–1913.

Avitus of Vienna. *Lettres*, edited by Elena Malaspina and Marc Reydellet. Paris: Les Belles Lettres, 2016.

Sancti Caesarii Arelatensis Sermones nunc primum in unum collecti et ad leges artis criticae ex innumeris Mss. recogniti, edited by G. Morin, 2 vols. CCSL 103 and 104. Turnhout: Brepols, 1953.

Cassiodorus. *Orationum reliquiae*, edited by Ludwig Traube, MGH Auct. ant. 12. Berlin: Weidmann, 1894.

Cassiodorus. *Variae*, edited by Theodor Mommsen. MGH Auct. ant. 12. Berlin: Weidmann, 1894.

Cassiodorus. *Variae*, edited by Åke J. Fridh. CCSL 96. Turnhout: Brepols, 1973.

Cassiodorus. *Variae*, translated by Samuel J. B. Barnish. Liverpool: Liverpool University Press, 1992.

Charlemagne and Louis the Pious. The Lives by Einhard, Notker, Ermoldus, Thegan, and the Astronomer, translated by Thomas F. X. Noble. University Park, PA: Penn State Press, 2009.

Chronicon Moissiacense, edited by Georg H. Pertz. MGH SS 1, 280–313. Hannover: Hahn, 1826.

Codex Theodosianus, edited by Theodor Mommsen and Paul Meyer. Berlin: Weidmann, 1905.

Concilia Aevi Merovingici, edited by Friedrich Maassen. MGH Conc. 1. Hannover: Hahn, 1893.

Concilia Africae, edited by C. Munier. CCSL 149. Turnhout: Brepols, 1974.
Concilia Galliae A. 314 – A. 506, edited by C. Munier. CCSL 148. Turnhout: Brepols, 1963.
Concilia Galliae A. 511 – A. 695, edited by C. De Clercq. CCSL 148A. Turnhout: Brepols, 1963.
Concilios visigóticos e hispano-romanos, edited by José Vives. Barcelona: Instituto Enrique Flórez, 1963.
Concilium Matisconense, edited by Friedrich Massen. MGH Conc. 1, 163–73. Hannover: Hahn, 1894.
Corpus Inscriptionum Latinarum 13: Inscriptiones trium Galliarum et Germaniarum Latinae, edited by Otto Hirschfeld and Carl Zangemeister, 1899. Reprint, Berlin: De Gruyter, 1966.
Corpus Iuris Civilis, edited by Theodor Mommsen and Paul Krüger. Berlin: Weidmann, 1877.
Dionysios of Tel-Mahrē. *Chronicle of AD 1234*. In *The Seventh Century in West-Syrian Chronicles*, translated by Andrew Palmer, 111–221. Liverpool: Liverpool University Press, 1993.
Eberwin of St. Martin of Trier. *Vita Magnerici*. AASS, Iul. VI, 183–91.
Einhardi Vita Karoli Magni, edited by Georg Waitz. MGH SS rer. Germ. 25. Hannover, Leipzig: Hahn, 1911.
Ennode de Pavie. *Lettres*, edited by Stephane Gioanni. Paris: Les Belles Lettres, 2006.
Epistola legatariis. In *Vigiliusbriefe*, edited by Eduard Schwartz, 18–25. Munich: C. H. Beck, 1940.
Epistolae Arelatenses genuinae, edited by Wilhelm Gundlach. MGH Epp. 3, 1–83. Berlin: Weidmannsche Buchhandlung, 1892.
Epistolae Austrasicae, edited by Wilhelm Gundlach. MGH Epp. 3, 110–53. Berlin: Weidmann, 1892.
Epistolae Wisigothicae, edited by Johannes [Juan] Gil. Miscellanea Wisigothica, 2nd ed. Sevilla: Universidad de Sevilla, 1991.
The Ecclesiastical Works of Evagrius, edited by J. Bidez and L. Parmentier. London: Methuen&Co., 1898.
Expositio totius mundi et gentium, edited and translated by Jean Rougé. SC 124. Paris: Cerf, 1966.
Chronicarum quae dicuntur Fredegarii scholastici libri IV cum continuationibus, edited by Bruno Krusch. MGH SS rer. Merov. 2, 1–193. Hannover: Hahn, 1888.
The Fourth Book of the Chronicle of Fredegar with its Continuations, translated by John Michael Wallace-Hadrill. Oxford: Oxford University Press, 1960.
Gregor von Tours, *Zehn Bücher Geschichten*, translated by Wilhelm Giesebrecht, revised by Rudolf Buchner. 2 vols. 1955. Reprint, Darmstadt: Wissenschaftliche Buchgesellschaft, 2000.
Gregorius Turonensis. *Decem Libri Historiarum*, edited by Bruno Krusch and Wilhelm Levison. MGH SS rer. Merov. 1,1. Hannover, 1937.

Gregorius Turonensis. *Liber de Passione et Virtutibus Sancti Iuliani martyris*, edited by Bruno Krusch. MGH SS rer. Merov. 1,2, 112–33. Hannover: Hahn, 1885.
Gregorius Turonensis. *Liber in Gloria Confessorum*, edited by Bruno Krusch. MGH SS rer. Merov. 1,2, 284–370. Hannover: Hahn, 1885.
Gregorius Turonensis. *Liber in Gloria Martyrum*, edited by Bruno Krusch. MGH SS rer. Merov. 1,2, 34–111. Hannover: Hahn, 1885.
Gregorius Turonensis. *Liber Vitae Patrum*, edited by Bruno Krusch. MGH SS rer. Merov. 1,2, 211–83. Hannover: Hahn, 1885.
Gregorius Turonensis. *Libri I–IV de Virtutibus Sancti Martini Episcopi*, edited by Bruno Krusch. MGH SS rer. Merov. 1,2, 134–211. Hannover: Hahn, 1885.
Gregory of Tours. *History of the Franks*, translated by Lewis Thorpe. London: Penguin, 1974.
Gregory of Tours. *The History of the Franks*, translated by Ormonde M. Dalton. Oxford: Clarendon Press, 1927.
Gregory of Tours. *The Life of the Fathers*, translated by Edward James. 2nd ed. Liverpool: Liverpool University Press, 1991.
Gregory of Tours. *The Miracles of the Martyr Julian*, translated by Giselle de Nie. In Gregory of Tours. *Lives and Miracles*, 299–419. Cambridge, Mass.: Harvard University Press, 2015.
Gregory the Great. *Registrum epistolarum Libri I–VII*, edited by Paul Ewald and Ludwig Hartmann. MGH Epp. 1. Berlin: Weidmann, 1891.
Gregory the Great. *Registrum epistularum*, edited by Dag L. Norberg, CCSL 140–140A. Turnhout: Brepols, 1982.
Ibn 'Abd el-Hakem, *The Mohammedan Conquest of Egypt and North Africa in the Years 643 to 705 A.D. Translated from the Original Arabic of Ibn 'Abd el-Hakem*, translated by Charles Cutler Torrey. In *Biblical and Semitic Studies. Critical and Historical Essays by the Members of the Semitic and Biblical Faculty of Yale University*, 277–330. New York: Charles Scribner's Sons, 1901.
Il Liber epistolarum della cancelleria austrasica, edited by Elena Malaspina. Rome: Herder, 2001.
Iohannis Abbatis Biclarensis. *Chronica*, edited by Theodor Mommsen. MGH Auct. ant. 11, 163–220. Berlin: Weidmann, 1892.
Iohannis Ephesini Historiae ecclesiasticae pars tertia, edited by E. W. Brooks. CSCO 106. Leuvan: Peeters Publishers, 1936.
Isidore of Sevilla. *Geschichte der Goten, Vandalen und Sueven nebst Auszügen aus der Kirchengeschichte des Beda Venerabilis*, translated by David Coste, edited by Alexander Heine. Essen and Stuttgart: Phaidon, 1986.
Isidore of Seville. *Las historias de los Godos, Vandalos y Suevos de Isidoro de Sevilla*, edited and translated by C. Rogríguez Alonso. León: Centro de Estudios e Investigación "San Isidoro," 1975.
Isidori Iunioris episcopi Hispalensis. *Historia de regibus Gothorum, Vandalorum et Suevorum*, edited by Theodor Mommsen. MGH Auct. ant. 11, 241–303. Berlin, 1892.

John Chrysostom. *In Illud, Paulus Vocatus et de Mutatione Nomininum*, PG 51. Paris, 1862.

John of Biclaro. *Chronicle*. In *Conquerors and Chroniclers of Early Medieval Spain*, translated by Kenneth B. Wolf, 51–66. Liverpool: Liverpool University Press, 1999.

Jordanes. *De origine actibusque Getarum*, edited by Theodor Mommsen. MGH Auct. ant. 5,1, 53–138. Berlin: Weidmann, 1882.

Julius Caesar. *De bello Gallico*, edited by Otto Seel. Leipzig: Teubner, 1961.

La Chanson de Roland, edited by Cesare Segre, translated by Madeleine Tyssens, 2nd edn. Textes littéraires français. Geneva: Droz, 2003.

Laws of the Alamans and Bavarians, translated by Theodore John Rivers. Philadelphia, PA: University of Pennsylvania Press, 1977.

Laws of the Salian and Ripuarian Franks, translated by Theodore John Rivers. New York: AMS Press, 1986.

Le Liber Pontificalis. Texte, introduction et commentaire, edited by Louis Duchesne. Vol. 1. Paris: Ernest Thorin, 1886.

Le Liber Pontificalis. Texte, introduction et commentaire, edited by Louis Duchesne. Vol. 2. Paris: Ernest Thorin, 1892.

Leges Alamannorum, edited by Karl Lehmann, revised by Karl August Eckhardt. MGH LL nat. Germ. 5,1. 2nd edition. Hannover: Hahn, 1966.

Leges Burgundionum, edited by Rudolf von Salis. MGH LL nat. Germ. 2, 1. Hannover: Hahn, 1892.

Leges Visigothorum, edited by Karl Zeumer. MGH LL nat. Germ. 1. Hannover: Hahn, 1902.

Lex Baiuvariorum, edited by Ernst von Schwind. MGH LL nat. Germ. 5, 2. Hannover: Hahn, 1926.

Lex Ribuaria, edited by Franz Beyerle and Rudolf Buchner. MGH LL nat. Germ. 3, 2. Hannover: Hahn, 1954.

Pactus legis Salicae, edited by Karl August Eckhardt. MGH LL nat. Germ 4.1. Hannover: Hahn, 1962.

Lex Salica, edited by Karl August Eckhardt. MGH LL nat. Germ 4.2. Hannover: Hahn, 1969.

Liber Sacramentorum Augustodunensis, edited by O. Heiming. CCSL 159B. Turnhout: Brepols, 1984.

Liber Sacramentorum Engolismensis. Manuscrit B.N. Lat. 816. Le Sacramentaire Gélasien d'Angoulême, edited by P. Saint-Roch. CCSL 159C. Turnhout: Brepols, 1987.

Liber Sacramentorum Gellonensis, edited by A. Dumas. CCSL 159. Turnhout: Brepols, 1981.

Liber Sacramentorum Romanae ecclesiae ordinis anni circuli (Sacramentarium Gelasianum), edited by L. Mohlberg, L. Eizenhöfer, and P. Siffrin. 2nd rev. edition. Rome: Roma Herder, 1968.

The Lives of the Fathers of Merida. In *Lives of the Visigothic Fathers*, edited and translated by Andrew T. Fear, 45–106. Liverpool: Liverpool University Press, 1997.

Lupus of Ferrières. *Letters*, edited and translated by Graydon W. Regenos. The Hague: Martinus Nijhoff, 1966.

Marius of Avenches. *La chronique de Marius d'Avenches (455–581)*, edited and translated by Justin Favrod. Lausanne: Université de Lausanne, 1991.

Missale Francorum (Cod. Vat. Reg. lat. 257), edited by L. Mohlberg. Rerum Ecclesiasticarum Documenta. Ser. Maior. Fontes 2. Rome: Herder, 1957.

Orosius, *Historiarum adversum paganos libri VII*, edited by Karl Zangemeister. CSEL 5, 1882. Reprint, Hildesheim: Georg Olms Verlagsbuchhandlung, 1967.

Paenitentiale Cummeani. In *The Irish Penitentials*, edited by L. Bieler, with an appendix by D.A. Binchy. Scriptores Latini Hiberniae 5, 108–35. Dublin: Dublin Institute for Advanced Studies, 1963.

Paenitentiale Parisiense simplex, In *Paenitentialia minora Franciae et Italiae saeculi VIII–IX*, edited by R. Kottje. CCSL 156, 74–9. Turnhout: Brepols, 1994.

Paenitentiale Theodori, Canones Basilienses, edited by F. B. Asbach. In Asbach, F. B. "Das Poenitentiale Remense und der sogen. Excarpsus Cummeani: Überlieferung, Quellen und Entwicklung zweier kontinentaler Bußbücher aus der 1. Hälfte des 8. Jahrhunderts," 79–89. PhD diss. Universität Regensburg, 1975.

Paenitentiale Theodori, Canones Cottoniani. In *Die Canones Theodori Cantuariensis und ihre Überlieferungsformen, Untersuchungen zu den Bußbüchern des 7, 8. und 9. Jahrhunderts, 1*, edited by Paul W. Finsterwalder, 271–84. Weimar: H. Böhlaus Nachf, 1929.

Paenitentiale Theodori, Canones Gregorii. In *Die Canones Theodori Cantuariensis und ihre Überlieferungsformen, Untersuchungen zu den Bußbüchern des 7., 8. und 9. Jahrhunderts, 1*, edited by Paul W. Finsterwalder, 253–70. Weimar: H. Böhlaus Nachf, 1929.

Paenitentiale Theodori, Discipulus Umbrensium. In *Die Canones Theodori Cantuariensis und ihre Überlieferungsformen, Untersuchungen zu den Bußbüchern des 7., 8. und 9. Jahrhunderts, 1*, edited by Paul W. Finsterwalder, 285–334. Weimar: H. Böhlaus Nachf, 1929.

Paenitentiale Vindobonense C, edited by Rob Meens. In "'Aliud Benitenciale': The Ninth-Century Paenitentiale Vindobonense C," *Mediaeval Studies* 66 (2004): 1–26.

Passiones vitaeque sanctorum aevi Merovingici II, edited by Bruno Krusch. MGH SS rer. Merov. 4. Hannover: Hahnsche Buchhandlung, 1902.

Passiones vitaeque sanctorum aevi Merovingici IV, edited by Bruno Krusch. MGH SS rer. Merov. 6. Hannover: Hahnsche Buchhandlung, 1913.

Procopius. *De bello Gothorum*. In *Procopii Caesariensis opera omnia*, edited by Jakob Haury. Vol. 2: De bellis libri V–VIII. Leipzig: Teubner, 1963.

Ps.-Sebeos. *The Armenian History Attributed to Sebeos*, translated by R. W. Thomson. Liverpool: Liverpool University Press, 1999.

Ravennatis anonymi Cosmographia, edited by Joseph Schnetz. Rev. edn, Stuttgart: Teubner, 1990.

Regesten der Kaiserurkunden des Oströmischen Reiches von 565–1453, vol. I.1: Regesten 565–867, edited by Johannes Preiser-Kapeller, Alexander Riehle and Andreas E. Müller. 2nd edition, Munich: C.H. Beck, 2009.

Sallust. *De bello Iugurthino*, edited by Leighton D. Reynolds. Oxford: Clarendon Press, 1991.
The Song of Roland. An Analytical Edition, edited by Gerald J. Brault. University Park, PA, London: Penn University Press, 1978.
Tacitus, *De origine et situ Germanorum*, edited by Michael Winterbottom. Oxford: Clarendon Press, 1975.
The Visigothic Conversion to Catholicism: Third Council of Toledo, translated by David Nirenberg. In *Medieval Iberia. Readings from Christian, Muslim, and Jewish Sources*, edited by Olivia R. Constable, 12–20. Philadelphia, PA: University of Pennsylvania Press, 1997.
Thegan. *Gesta Hludowici imperatoris*. in *Die Taten Kaiser Ludwigs. Astronomus. Das Leben Kaiser Ludwigs*, edited by Ernst Tremp, 1–53. MGH, Scriptores rerum Germanicarum 64. Hannover: Hahn, 1995.
The Theodosian Code and Novels and Sirmondian Constitutions, translated by Clyde Pharr, 1952. Reprint, Union, NJ: The Lawbook Exchange, 2001.
Theophanes. *Chronographia*, edited by Carl de Boor. Leipzig: Teubner, 1883.
The Chronicle of Theophanes Confessor. Byzantine and Near Eastern History A.D. 284–813, edited by Cyril Mango and Roger Scott. Oxford: Clarendon Press, 1997.
The History of Theophylact Simocatta, translated by Michael Whitby and Mary Whitby. Oxford: Clarendon Press, 1986.
Venance Fortunat. *Poèmes*, edited by Marc Reydellet. Paris: Les Belles Lettres, 1994.
Vetus orbis descriptio, edited by Jacques Godefroy. Geneva: P. Chouet, 1628.
Vita S. Domitiani episcopi Traiectensis. AASS Mai II, 146–54.
Vitas sanctorum patrum Emeretensium, translated by Joseph N. Garvin. Washington (DC): The Catholic University of America Press, 1946.

Scholarship

Abellán, Salvador Iranzo. "La epistolografía hispana de época visigótica." In *Artes ad humanitatem*, II, edited by Esperança Borrel Vidal and Lambert Ferreres Pérez, 87–96. Barcelona: Secció Catalana de la SEEC, 2010.
Adams, J. N. *The Text and Language of a Vulgar Latin Chronicle (Anonymus Valesianus II)*. London: Institute of Classical Studies, 1976.
Althoff, Gerd. "*Ira regis*: A History of Royal Anger." In *Anger's Past: The Social Uses of Emotion in the Middle Ages*, edited by Barbara H. Rosenwein, 59–74. Ithaca and London: Cornell University Press, 1998.
Althoff, Gerd. *Family, Friends, and Followers: Political and Social Bonds in Early Medieval Europe*, translated by Christopher Carroll. Cambridge: Cambridge University Press, 2004.
Amory, Patrick. *People and Identity in Ostrogothic Italy, 489–554*. Cambridge: Cambridge University Press, 1997.

Anderson, W. J. "Vatic. Ottob. lat. 1210 and Vatican Palat. lat. 869 ff. 62–69." *Revue Bénédictine* 43 (1931): 104–5.

Arnold, Jonathan J. *Theoderic and the Roman Imperial Restoration*. Cambridge: Cambridge University Press, 2014.

Arnold, Jonathan J., Shane Bjornlie and Kristina Sessa (eds.). *A Companion to Ostrogothic Italy*. Leiden and Boston: Brill, 2016.

Ashbrook Harvey, Susan. "The Sense of a Stylite: Perspectives on Simeon the Elder." *Vigiliae Christianae* 42, no. 4 (1988): 376–94.

Ashbrook Harvey, Susan. "The Stylite's Liturgy: Ritual and Religious Identity in Late Antiquity." *Journal of Early Christian Studies* 6, no. 3 (1998): 523–39.

Ashbrook Harvey, Susan and Doran, Robert. *The Lives of Simeon Stylites*. Kalamazoo: Cistercian Publications, 1992.

Auerbach, Erich. *Mimesis. The Representation of Reality in Western Literature*, translated by Willard R. Trask. Princeton: Princeton University Press, 1968.

Bachrach, Bernard S. *The Anatomy of a Little War. A Diplomatic and Military History of the Gundovald Affair (568–586)*. Boulder: Westview Press, 1994.

Balzaretti, Ross. *Dark Age Liguria: Regional Identity and Local Power, c. 400–1020*. London and New York: Bloomsbury, 2013.

Banaji, Jairus. *Agrarian Change in Late Antiquity. Gold, Labour, and Aristocratic Dominance*. Oxford: Oxford University Press, 2001.

Bardiès-Fronty, Isabelle, Charlotte Denoël and Inès Villela-Petit. *Les Temps Mérovingiens. Trois siècles d'art et de culture* (Musée de Cluny—Musée National de Moyen Âge 26 Octobre 2016 – 13 Février 2017). Paris: Éditions de la Réunion des Musées Nationaux, 2016.

Barnwell, Paul. "War and Peace: Historiography and Seventh Century Embassies." *Early Medieval Europe* 6, no. 2 (1997): 127–39.

Barrett, Graham and George Woudhuysen. "Assembling the Austrasian Letters at Trier and Lorsch." *Early Medieval Europe* 24, no. 1 (2016): 3–57.

Barrett, Graham and Woudhuysen, George. "Remigius and the 'Important News' of Clovis Rewritten." *Antiquité Tardive* 24 (2016): 471–500.

Bartlett, Robert. *Why the Dead Can Do Such Great Things? Saints and Worshippers from the Martyrs to the Reformation*. Princeton: Princeton University Press, 2013.

Basdevant, Brigitte. *Les canons des conciles mérovingiens*. Paris: Cerf, 1989.

Bausenhart, Guido. *"In allem uns gleich außer der Sünde," Studien zum Beitrag Maximos' des Bekenners zur altkirchlichen Christologie*. Tübingen: Grünewald, 1990.

Bautier, Robert-Henri. "Sacres et couronnements sous les Carolingiens et les premiers Capétiens: recherches sur la genèse du sacre royal français." *Annuaire-Bulletin de la Société de l'histoire de France* (1987–8): 7–56. Reprint [...] in Robert-Henri Bautier. *Recherches sur l'histoire de la France médiévale*. Aldershot: Variorum, 1991.

Becher, Matthias and Jörg Jarnut (eds.). *Der Dynastiewechsel von 751. Vorgeschichte, Legitimationsstrategien und Erinnerung*. Münster: Scriptorium, 2004.

Beckmann, Gustav A. *Onomastik des Rolandsliedes*, Beihefte zur Zeitschrift für romanische Philologie 411. Berlin, Boston: De Gruyter 2017.

Beihammer, Alexander Daniel. *Nachrichten zum byzantinischen Urkundenwesen in arabischen Quellen (565–811)*. Bonn: Dr. Rudolf Habelt, 2000.

Beihammer, Alexander Daniel. *Quellenkritische Untersuchungen zu den ägyptischen Kapitulationsverträgen der Jahre 640–646*. Vienna: Verlag der Österreichischen Akademie der Wissenschaften, 2000.

Beisel, Fritz. *Studien zu den fränkisch-römischen Beziehungen. Von ihren Anfängen bis zum Ausgang des 6. Jahrhunderts*. Idstein: Schulz-Kirchner Verlag, 1987.

Berschin, Walter. "Dinamius Patricius von Marseille († nach 597)." In Walter Berschin, *Mittellateinische Studien*, 9–16. Heidelberg: Mattes, 2005.

Bischoff, Bernhard. "Panorama der Handschriftenüberlieferung aus der Zeit Karls des Großen." In Bernhard Bischoff, *Mittelalterliche Studien: Ausgewählte Aufsätze zur Schriftkunde und Literaturgeschichte*. Vol. 3, 5–38. Stuttgart: Hiersemann, 1981.

Bischoff, Bernhard. *Die Abtei Lorsch im Spiegel ihrer Handschriften*. Lorsch: Laurissa, 1989.

Bjornlie, Shane. "What Have Elephants to Do with Sixth-Century Politics? A Reappraisal of the 'Official' Governmental Dossier of Cassiodorus." *Journal of Late Antiquity* 2, no. 1 (2009): 143–71.

Bjornlie, Shane. *Politics and Tradition Between Rome, Ravenna and Constantinople: A Study of Cassiodorus and the* Variae, *527–554*. Cambridge: Cambridge University Press, 2013.

Bloch, Marc. "Comment et pourquoi finit l'esclavage antique." In Marc Bloch, *Melanges historiques*, vol. 1, 261–86. Paris: S.E.V.P.E.N, 1963. (Reprinted as "How and Why Ancient Slavery Came to an End." In Marc Bloch. *Slavery and Serfdom in the Middle Ages. Selected Essays*, translated by William R. Beer, Berkeley: University of California Press, 1975).

Booth, Phil. *Crisis of Empire: Doctrine and Dissent at the End of Late Antiquity*. Berkeley: University of California Press, 2013.

Bracht, Katharina. "Can Women be Called 'Man'? On the Background of a Discussion Led at the 2nd Council of Mâcon (585 AD)." *Acta patristica et byzantina* 17 (2006): 144–54.

Brandes, Wolfram. "'Juristische' Krisenbewältigung im 7. Jahrhundert? Der Prozess gegen Papst Martin I. und Maximus Homologetes." In *Fontes Minores X*, edited by Ludwig Burgmann, 141–212. Frankfurt a. M.: Klostermann, 1998.

Braun SJ, Joseph. *Die liturgische Gewandung im Occident und Orient: Nach Ursprung und Entwicklung, Verwendung und Symbolik*. Freiburg i. Brsg.: Herdersche Verlagsbuchhandlung, 1907.

Brennan, Brian. "St Radegund and the Early Development of Her Cult at Poitiers." *Journal of Religious History* 13, no. 4 (1985): 340–54.

Brock, Sebastian. "Syriac Views of Emergent Islam." In *Studies on the First Century of Islamic Society*, edited by Gautier Herald A. Juynboll, 9–21 and 199–203. Carbondale u. Edwardsville, IL: Southern Illinois University Press, 1982.

Brown, Peter. "The Rise and Function of the Holy Man in Late Antiquity," *Journal of Roman Studies* 61 (1971): 80–101.
Brown, Peter. "Relics and Social Status in the Age of Gregory of Tours," in idem, *Society and the Holy in Late Antiquity*, 222–50. London and New York: Faber and Faber, 1982.
Brown, Peter. *Society and the Holy in Late Antiquity*. Berkeley: University of California Press, 1982.
Brown, Peter. "Arbiters of the Holy: The Christian Holy Man in Late Antiquity," in idem, *Authority and the Sacred: Aspects of the Christianisation of the Roman World*, 57–78. Cambridge: Cambridge University Press, 1995.
Brown, Peter. "Gregory of Tours. Introduction." In *The World of Gregory of Tours*, edited by Ian N. Wood and Kathleen Mitchell, 1–28. Leiden, Boston and Cologne: Brill, 2002.
Brown, Peter. *The Rise of Western Christendom: Triumph and Diversity, A.D. 200–1000*, 3rd ed. Oxford: Blackwell, 2013.
Brown, Peter. *Through the Eye of a Needle*. Princeton: Princeton University Press, 2012.
Brunschvig, Robert. "Ibn 'Abdalh'akam et la conquête de l'Afrique du Nord par les Arabes: Étude critique." *Annales de l'Institut des études orientales* (Algiers) 6 (1942–47): 108–55.
Buc, Philippe. *Dangers of Ritual. Between Early Medieval Texts and Social Scientific Theory*. Princeton: Princeton University Press, 2001.
Buchner, Rudolf. *Die Provence in merowingischer Zeit: Verfassung, Wirtschaft, Kultur*. Stuttgart: Kohlhammer, 1933.
Bury, John Bagnell. *A History of the Later Roman Empire: From Arcadius to Irene (395 AD to 800 AD)*, 2 vols. London and New York: Macmillan and Co., 1889.
Butler, Alfred J. *The Arab Conquest of Egypt and the Last Thirty Years of Roman Dominion*. 2nd edition. Oxford: Oxford University Press, 1978.
Cain, Andrew. "Miracles, Martyrs, and Arians: Gregory of Tours Sources For His Account Of the Vandal Kingdom." *Vigiliae* 59, no. 5 (2005): 412–37.
Cameron, Averil. "Agathias on the Early Merovingians." *Annali della Scuola Normale Superiore di Pisa, Classe di Lettere e Filosofia* 2, no. 37 (1968): 95–140.
Cameron, Averil. "The Early Religious Policies of Justin II." *Studies in Church History* 13 (1976): 51–67.
Cameron, Averil. "Early Byzantine *Kaiserkritik*: Two Case Histories." *Byzantine and Modern Greek Studies* 3 (1977): 1–17.
Cameron, Averil. "On the Byzantine Sources of Gregory of Tours." *Journal of Theological Studies* 26, no. 2 (1975): 421–6. Reprinted in Averil Cameron. *Continuity and Change in Sixth-century Byzantium*. London: Variorum Reprints, 1981.
Cameron, Averil. "Defining the Holy Man." In *The Cult of Saints in Late Antiquity and the Middle Ages*, edited by Paul Antony Hayward and James Howard-Johnston, 27–44. Oxford: Oxford University Press, 1999.
Cameron, Averil. *Byzantine Matters*. Princeton: Princeton University Press, 2014.

Caries, Valerie A. "Evagrius Scholasticus and Gregory of Tours: A Literary Comparison." PhD diss., University of California, Berkeley, 1976.

Caspar, Erich. *Geschichte des Papsttums von den Anfängen bis zur Höhe der Weltherrschaft.* Vol. 2: Das Papsttum unter byzantinischer Herrschaft. Tübingen: J. C. B. Mohr, 1933.

Chadwick, Henry. *The Church in Ancient Society: From Galilee to Gregory the Great.* Oxford: Oxford University Press, 2001.

Christensen, Arne S. *Cassiodorus, Jordanes and the History of the Goths: Studies in a Migration Myth.* Copenhagen: Museum Tusculanum Press, 2002.

Christides, Vassilios. *Byzantine Libya and the March of the Arabs towards the West of Africa.* Oxford: British Archaeological Reports, 2000.

Classen, Peter. *Karl der Große, das Papsttum und Byzanz.* Düsseldorf: Schwann, 1968.

Claude, Dietrich. *Geschichte der Westgoten.* Stuttgart: Kohlhammer, 1970.

Claude, Dietrich. *Adel, Kirche und Königtum im Westgotenreich.* Sigmaringen: J. Thorbecke, 1971.

Claude, Dietrich. "Gentile und territoriale Staatsideen im Westgotenreich." *Frühmittelalterliche Studien* 6 (1972): 1–38.

Claude, Dietrich. *Der Handel im westlichen Mittelmeer während des Frühmittelalters. Bericht über ein Kolloquium der Kommission für die Altertumskunde Mittel- und Nordeuropas im Jahr 1980 (Untersuchungen zu Handel und Verkehr der vor- und frühgeschichtlichen Zeit in Mittel- und Nordeuropa, Teil II).* Göttingen: Vandenhoeck und Ruprecht, 1985.

Collin, Hubert. "Grégoire de Tours, saint Walfroy le Stylite et la dea Arduinna. Un épisode de la christianisation des confins des diocèses de Reims et de Trèves au VIe siècle." In *La piété populaire au Moyen Âge, Actes du 99e congrès des sociétés savantes, Besançon, 1974, Section de philosophie et d'histoire jusqu'à 1610,* 387–400. Paris: Bibliothèque nationale, 1977.

Collins, Roger. "Theodebert I, Rex Magnus Francorum." In *Ideal and Reality in Frankish and Anglo-Saxon Society: Studies Presented to J. M. Wallace-Hadrill,* edited by Patrick Wormald, 7–33. Oxford: Blackwell, 1983.

Collins, Roger. "King Leovigild and The Conversion of The Visigoths." In *Law, Culture and Regionalism in Early Medieval Spain,* edited by Roger Collins, 1–12. Aldershot: Variorum, 1992.

Collins, Roger. "Charlemagne's Imperial Coronation and The Annals of Lorsch." In *Charlemagne: Empire and Society,* edited by Joanna Story, 52–70. Manchester and New York: Manchester University Press, 2005.

Collins, Roger. *Die Fredegar-Chroniken.* Munich: Hahnsche Buchhandlung 2007.

Collins, Roger. "Gregory of Tours and Spain." In *A Companion to Gregory of Tours,* edited by Alexander C. Murray, 498–515. Brill: Leiden, 2015.

Cosentino, Salvatore. "Constans II and the Byzantine Navy." *Byzantinische Zeitschrift* 100 (2007): 577–603.

Croke, Brian. "Cassiodorus and the *Getica* of Jordanes." *Classical Philology* 82 (1987): 117–34.

Croke, Brian. "Late Antique Historiography, 250–650 CE." In *A Companion to Greek and Roman Historiography*, edited by John Marincola, 567–81. Oxford: Blackwell, 2007.

Croke, Brian. "Historiography." In *The Oxford Handbook of Late Antiquity*, edited by Scott F. Johnson, 405–36. Oxford: Oxford University Press, 2012.

Czock, Miriam. *Gottes Haus. Untersuchungen zur Kirche als heiligem Raum von der Spätantike bis ins Frühmittelalter*. Berlin: De Gruyter, 2012.

Dailey, Erin T. "Gregory of Tours, Fredegund, and the Paternity of Chlothar II: Strategies of Legitimation in the Merovingian Kingdoms." *Journal of Late Antiquity* 7, no. 1 (2014): 3–27.

Dailey, Erin T. *Queens, Consorts, Concubines: Gregory of Tours and Women of the Merovingian Elite*. Leiden and Boston: Brill, 2015.

de Jong, Mayke. *The Penitential State*. Cambridge: Cambridge University Press, 2009.

Delaplace, Christine. "L''affaire Gondovald' et le dispositif défensif de l'Aquitaine wisigothique et franque." *Aquitania: revue interrégionale d'archéologie* 25 (2009): 199–211.

Di Cesare, Michelina. *The Pseudo-Historical Image Of the Prophet Muḥammad in Medieval Latin Literature*, Studien zur Geschichte und Kultur des islamischen Orients 26. Berlin, New York, Boston: De Gruyter, 2012.

Diesenberger, Maximilian. "Hair, Sacrality and Symbolic Capital in the Frankish Kingdoms." In *The Construction of Communities in the Early Middle Ages: Texts, Resources and Artefacts*, edited by Richard Corradini, Maximilian Diesenberger, and Helmut Reimitz, 173–212. Leiden and Boston: Brill, 2003.

Drabek, Anna M. "Der Merowingervertrag von Andelot aus dem Jahr 587." *Mitteilungen des Instituts für Österreichische Geschichtsforschung* 78 (1970): 34–41.

Drauschke, Jörg. "Diplomatie und Wahrnehmung im 6. und 7. Jahrhundert: Konstantinopel und die merowingischen Könige." In *Byzanz in Europa: Europas Östliches Erbe*, edited by Michael Atripp, 244–75. Turnhout: Brepols, 2011.

Drews, Wolfram. "Hermenegild's Rebellion and Conversion—Merovingian and Byzantine Connections." In *East and West in the Early Middle Ages: The Merovingian Kingdoms in Mediterranean Perspective*, edited by Stefan Esders, Yaniv Fox, Yitzhak Hen, and Laury Sarti. Cambridge: Cambridge University Press, 2019.

Drexhage, Hans-Joachim. "Die *Expositio totius mundi et gentium*: Eine Handelsgeographie aus dem 4. Jh. n. Chr., eingeleitet, übersetzt und mit einführender Literatur (Kap. XXII–LXVII) versehen." *Münstersche Beiträge zur antiken Handelsgeschichte* 2 (1983): 3–41.

Ducloux, Anne. *Ad Ecclesiam Confugere. Naissance du droit d'asile dans les églises (IVe – milieu du Ve s.)*. Paris: De Boccard, 1994.

Dumézil, Bruno. "Gogo et ses amis: écriture, échanges et ambitions dans un réseau aristocratique de la fin du VIe siècle." *Revue Historique* 643 (2007): 553–93.

Dumézil, Bruno. "La différence confessionnelle dans les couples du haut moyen âge: facteur de stabilité ou motif de rupture? (Ve–VIIIe siècle)." In *Répudiation, séparation, divorce dans l'Occident médiéval*, edited by Emmanuelle Santinelli, 257–73. Valenciennes: Presses universitaires de Valenciennes, 2007.

Dumézil, Bruno. *La reine Brunehaut*. Paris: Fayard, 2008.

Dumézil, Bruno. "Le patrice Dynamius et son réseau: culture aristocratique et transformation des pouvoirs autour de Lérins dans la seconde moitié du VIe siècle." In *Lérins, une île sainte de l'Antiquité au Moyen Âge*, edited by Yann Codou and Michel Lauwers, 167–94. Turnhout: Brepols, 2009.

Dumézil, Bruno. "Les ambassadeurs occidentaux au VIe siècle: recrutement, usages et modes de distinction d'une élite de représentation à l'étranger." In *Théorie et pratiques des élites au Haut Moyen Age: Conception, perception et réalisation sociale*, edited by François Bougard, Hans-Werner Goetz, and Régine Le Jan, 243–60. Turnhout: Brepols, 2011.

Dumézil, Bruno. "Le modèle royal à l'époque mérovingienne." In *L'empreinte chrétienne en Gaule du IVè au IXè siècle*, edited by Michèle Gaillard, 131–50. Turnhout: Brepols, 2014.

Dumézil, Bruno. "Le meurtre du père: jugements contrastés sur la révolte d'Herménégild." In *Splendor Reginae. Passions, genre et famille. Mélanges en l'honneur de Régine Le Jan*, edited by Laurent Jégou, Sylvie Joye, Thomas Lienhard and Jens Schneider, 29–38. Turnhout: Brepols, 2015.

Dumézil, Bruno and Thomas Lienhard. "Les 'Lettres austrasiennes': Dire, cacher, transmettre les informations diplomatiques au haut Moyen Âge." In *Les relations diplomatiques au Moyen Âge. Formes et enjeux*, edited by Marie-Céline Isaia and Armand Jamme, 69–80. Paris: Publications de la Sorbonne, 2011.

Eastmond, Antony. "Body vs. Column: The Cults of St. Symeon Stylites." In *Desire and Denial in Byzantium*, edited by Liz James, 87–100. Aldershot: Ashgate, 1999.

Eco, Umberto. *Lector in fabula. Cooperazione interpretatativa nei testi narrative*. Milano: Bompiani, 1979. Translated in Eco, Umberto. *The Role Of the Reader: Explorations in the Semiotics Of texts*. Bloomington: Indiana University Press, 1984.

Effros, Bonnie. "The Enduring Attraction of the Pirenne Thesis." *Speculum* 92, no. 1 (2017): 184–208.

Effros, Bonnie and Isabel Moreira (eds.). *The Oxford Handbook of the Merovingian World*. Oxford: Oxford University Press, expected for 2019.

Eger, Christoph. "Zur Imperialisierung des westgotischen Königtums aus archäologischer Sicht." In *Spolien im Umkreis der Macht: Akten der Tagung in Toledo vom 21.-22.09.2006*, edited by Thomas G. Schattner and Fernando Valdés Fernández, 151–69. Mainz: Philipp von Zabern, 2009.

Ehrhardt, Arnold. "Rechtsvergleichende Studien zum antiken Sklavenrecht I: Wergeld und Schadenersatz." *Zeitschrift der Savigny-Stiftung für Rechtsgeschichte. Romanistische Abteilung* 68 (1951): 74–130.

Elliott, Dyan. "Sex in Holy Places: An Exploration Of a Medieval Anxiety." *Journal of Women's History* 6, no. 3 (1994): 6–34. Reprint [...] in Elliot, Dyan. *Fallen Bodies. Pollution, Sexuality, and Demonology in the Middle Ages*, 61–80. Philadelphia: University of Pennsylvania Press,1999.

Elliot, Michael D. "Boniface, Incest, and the Earliest Extant Version Of Pope Gregory I's Libellus responsionum (JE 1843)." *Zeitschrift der Savigny-Stiftung für Rechtsgeschichte, Kanonistische Abteilung* 113 (2014): 62–111.

Epp, Verena. *Amicitia: zur Geschichte personaler, sozialer, politischer und geistlicher Beziehungen im frühen Mittelalter*. Stuttgart: Anton Hiersemann, 1999.

Esders, Stefan. *Römische Rechtstradition und merowingisches Königtum. Zum Rechtscharakter politischer Herrschaft in Burgund im 6. und 7. Jahrhundert*. Göttingen: Vandenhoeck & Ruprecht, 1997.

Esders, Stefan. "Herakleios, Dagobert und die 'beschnittenen Völker'. Die Umwälzungen des Mittelmeerraums im 7. Jahrhundert in der fränkischen Chronik des sog. Fredegar." In *Jenseits der Grenzen. Studien zur spätantiken und frühmittelalterlichen Geschichtsschreibung*, edited by Andreas Goltz, Hartmut Leppin and Heinrich Schlange-Schöningen, 239–311. Berlin and New York: De Gruyter, 2009.

Esders, Stefan. "'Avenger Of All Perjury' in Constantinople and Metz: Saint Polyeuctus, Sigibert I, and the Division of Charibert's Kingdom in 568." In *Western Perspectives on the Mediterranean: Cultural Transfer in Late Antiquity and the Early Middle Ages, 400–800 AD*, edited by Andreas Fischer and Ian N. Wood, 17–40. London: Bloomsbury, 2014.

Esders, Stefan. "Gallic Politics in the Sixth Century." In *A Companion to Gregory of Tours*, edited by Alexander C. Murray, 429–61. Leiden and Boston: Brill, 2015.

Esders, Stefan. "Late Roman Military Law in the Bavarian Code." *Clio@themis. Revue électronique d'histoire du droit* 10 (accessed June 16, 2016).

Esders, Stefan. "'Getaufte Juden' im westgotischen Spanien. Die antijüdische Politik König Chintilas zum Jahreswechsel 637/638 und ihre Hintergründe." In *Jüdische Lebenswelten. Von der Antike bis zur Gegenwart*, edited by Ernst Baltrusch and Uwe Puschner, 53–96. Frankfurt a. M.: Peter Lang, 2016.

Esders, Stefan. "Roman Law as an Identity Marker in Post-Roman Gaul (5th–9th centuries)." In *Transformations of Romanness: Early Medieval Regions and Identities*, edited by Walter Pohl, Clemens Gantner, Cinzia Grifoni, Marianne Pollheimer-Mohaupt, 325–44. Berlin: De Gruyter 2018.

Esders, Stefan. "Chindasvinth, the 'Gothic disease', and the Monothelite crisis," *Millennium-Jahrbuch*, in press.

Esders, Stefan. "The Prophesied Rule of 'Circumcised People'. A Travelling Tradition from the Seventh-Century Mediterranean." In *Barbarians and Jews. Jews and Judaism in the Early Medieval West*, edited by Yitzhak Hen and Thomas F. X. Noble, 119–54. Turnhout: Brepols, 2018.

Esders, Stefan. "Die gallische Kirche des 7. Jahrhunderts zwischen *imperium* und *regna*. Der Brief des merowingischen Königs Sigibert III. an Bischof Desiderius von

Cahors (650) und die fränkische Rezeption des Monotheletismus-Streites." In *Gallien zwischen imperium und regna. Die Darstellung von Kontingenz und ihrer Bewältigung*, edited by Matthias Becher and Hendrik Hess. Göttingen: Vandenhoeck & Ruprecht, in press.

Esders, Stefan and Helmut Reimitz "After Gundovald, Before Pseudo-Isidore: Episcopal Jurisdiction, Clerical Privilege, and The Uses of Roman Law in The Frankish Kingdoms." *Early Medieval Europe*. Forthcoming.

Esders, Stefan, Yaniv Fox, Yitzhak Hen and Laury Sarti (eds.). *East and West in the Early Middle Ages: The Merovingian Kingdoms in Mediterranean Perspective*. Cambridge: Cambridge University Press, 2019.

Ewig, Eugen. *Die fränkischen Teilungen und Teilreiche (511–613)*. Wiesbaden: F. Steiner, 1953.

Ewig, Eugen. "Die fränkischen Teilungen und Teilreiche (511–613)." In Eugen Ewig, *Spätantikes und fränkisches Gallien: Gesammelte Schriften (1952–1973)*, vol. 1: 114–71. Munich: Artemis, 1979.

Ewig, Eugen. *Die Merowinger und das Imperium*. Opladen: Westdeutscher Verlag, 1983.

Ewig, Eugen. "Die Namengebung bei den ältesten Frankenkönigen." *Francia* 18 (1991): 21–69. (reprinted in his *Spätantikes und Fränkisches Gallien*. Vol. 3: Gesammelte Schriften (1974–2007), edited by Matthias Becher, Theo Kölzer, and Ulrich Nonn, 163–211. Ostfildern: Jan Thorbecke Verlag, 2009).

Fanning, Steven. "Langobard Arianism Reconsidered," *Speculum* 56 (1981): 241–58.

Fasiori, Ivo. "Storia della decima dall'editto di Milano (313) al secondo Concilio di Mâcon (585)." *Vetera Christianorum* 23 (1986): 39–61.

Fastrich-Sutty, Isabella. *Die Rezeption westgotischen Rechts in der Lex Baiuvariorum*. Cologne: Heymann, 2001.

Feissel, Dénis. "Inscriptions chrétiennes et byzantines." *Revue des études grecques* 100 (1987): 380–1.

Fischer, Andreas. "Rewriting History: Fredegar's Perspectives on the Mediterranean." In *Western Perspectives on the Mediterranean. Cultural Transfer in Late Antiquity and the Early Middle Ages, 400–800 AD*, edited by Andreas Fischer and Ian N. Wood, 55–75. London: Bloomsbury, 2014.

Fischer, Andreas. "Money for Nothing: Franks, Byzantines and Lombards in the Sixth and Seventh Centuries." In *East and West in the Early Middle Ages: The Merovingian Kingdoms in Mediterranean Perspective*, edited by Stefan Esders, Yaniv Fox, Yitzhak Hen and Laury Sarti. Cambridge: Cambridge University Press, 2019.

Fischer, Andreas and Ian N. Wood (eds.). *Western Perspectives on the Mediterranean: Cultural Transfer in Late Antiquity and the Early Middle Ages, 400–800 AD*. London: Bloomsbury, 2012.

Folz, Robert. "Sur l'inspirateur du pacte d'Andelot: Gontran roi de Bourgogne." *Les Cahiers haut-marnais* 175 (1988): 14–20.

Foss, Clive. "Egypt under Muʿāwiya, Pt. I: Flavius Papas and Upper Egypt." *Bulletin of the School of Oriental and African Studies* 72 (2009): 1–24.

Fox, Yaniv. "The Bishop and The Monk: Desiderius of Vienne and The Columbanian Movement." *Early Medieval Europe* 20, no. 2 (2012): 176–94.

Fox, Yaniv. *Power and Religion in Merovingian Gaul: Columbanian Monasticism and the Formation of the Frankish Aristocracy.* Cambridge: Cambridge University Press, 2014.

Fox, Yaniv. "New *honores* for a Region Transformed: The Patriciate in Post-Roman Gaul." *Revue Belge de Philologie et d'Histoire* 93 (2015): 249–86.

Frend, W. H. C. *The Rise of the Monophysite Movement.* Cambridge: Cambridge University Press, 1972.

Fritze, Wolfgang Hermann. "Die fränkische Schwurfreundschaft der Merowingerzeit." *Zeitschrift der Savigny-Stiftung für Rechtsgeschichte* 71 (1954): 74–125.

Galonnier, Alain. "*Anecdoton Holderi* ou *Ordo generis Cassiodororum*: Introduction, édition, traduction et commentaire." *Antiquité tardive* 4 (1996): 299–312.

Ganz, David. *Corbie in The Carolingian Renaissance.* Sigmaringen: Thorbecke, 1990.

Gaudemet, Jean and Basdevant, Brigitte. *Les canons des conciles mérovingiens (VIe–VIIe siècles).* Vol. 1. Paris: Éditions du Cerf, 1989.

Gauthier, Nancy. *L'évangélisation dans les pays de Moselle. La province romaine de Première Belgique entre Antiquité et Moyen-Age (IIIème-VIIIème siècles).* Paris: De Boccard, 1980.

Geary, Patrick J. *Before France and Germany: The Creation and Transformation of the Merovingian World.* New York and Oxford: Oxford University Press, 1988.

Geary, Patrick J. *The Myths of Nations: The Medieval Origins of Europe.* Princeton and Oxford: Princeton University Press, 2002.

George, Philippe. "Vies et miracles de Saint Domitien: Évêque de Tongres-Maastricht (535–549)." *Analecta Bollandiana* 103 (1985): 305–354 and 119 (2001): 5–32.

Gil, Juan. *Miscellanea Wisigothica.* Sevilla: Universidad de Sevilla, 1972.

Gillett, Andrew. *Envoys and Political Communication in the Late Antique West, 411–533.* Cambridge: Cambridge University Press, 2003.

Gillett, Andrew. "Love and Grief in Post-Imperial Diplomacy: The Letters of Brunhild." In *Power and Emotions in the Roman World and Late Antiquity*, edited by Denijel Dizno and Barbara Sidwell, 127–65. Piscataway, NJ: Gorgias Press, 2010.

Gillett, Andrew. "Ethnography and Imperium in the Sixth Century: Frankish and Byzantine Rhetoric in the *Epistolae Austrasicae*." In *Basileia: Essays on Imperium and Culture in Honour of E.M. and M.J. Jeffreys*, edited by Geoffrey Nathan and Linda Garland, 67–81. Brisbane: Australian Association for Byzantine Studies, 2011.

Glatthaar, Michael. "Der Edictus Chilperichs I. und die Reichsversammlung von Paris (577)." *Deutsches Archiv für Erforschung des Mittelalters* 73 (2017): 1–74.

Godman, Peter, Jörg Jarnut and Peter Johanek (eds.). *Am Vorabend der Kaiserkrönung.* Berlin: Akademie Verlag, 2002.

Goetz, Hans-Werner. "Byzanz in der Wahrnehmung fränkischer Geschichtsschreiber des 6. und 7. Jahrhunderts." In *Osten und Westen 400–600 n. Chr. Kommunikation, Kooperation und Konflikt*, edited by Carola Föller and Fabian Schulz, 77–98. Stuttgart: Franz Steiner Verlag, 2016.

Goetz, Hans-Werner, Jörg Jarnut and Walter Pohl (eds.). *Regna and Gentes: The Relationship Between Late Antique and Early Medieval Peoples and Kingdoms in the Transformation of the Roman World*. Leiden and Boston: Brill, 2003.

Goffart, Walter. "Byzantine Policy in the West under Tiberius II and Maurice: The Pretenders Hermenegild and Gundovald (578–585)." *Traditio* 13 (1957): 73–118.

Goffart, Walter. "Foreigners in the *Histories* of Gregory of Tours." *Florilegium* 4 (1982): 80–99.

Goffart, Walter. *Narrators of Barbarian History (AD 550–800). Jordanes, Gregory of Tours, Bede and Paul the Deacon*, 2nd edn. Princeton: Princeton University Press, 2005.

Goffart, Walter. "The Frankish Pretender Gundovald, 582–585: A Crisis of Merovingian Blood." *Francia* 39 (2012): 1–27.

Görres, Franz. "Rekared der Katholische (586–601). Neue kirchen- und culturgeschichtliche Forschungen auf dem Gebiete des Vormittelalters." *Zeitschrift für wissenschaftliche Theologie* 42 (1899): 270–322.

Goubert, Paul. "Byzance et l'Espagne wisigothique (554–711)." *Études byzantines* 2 (1944): 5–78.

Goubert, Paul. *Byzance avant l'Islam, tome seconde: Byzance et l'occident sous les successeurs de Justinien vol. I: Byzance et les Francs*. Paris: Éditions A. et J. Picard et Cie, 1956.

Gradowicz-Pancer, Nira. "De-Gendering Female Violence: Merovingian Female Honour as an 'Exchange of Violence'." *Early Medieval Europe* 11, no. 1 (2002): 1–18.

Gradowicz-Pancer, Nira. "Femmes royales et violences anti-épiscopales à l'époque mérovingienne: Frédégonde et le meurtre de l'évêque Prétextat." In *Bischofsmord im Mittelalter—Murder of Bishops*, edited by Natalie Fryde and Dirk Reitz, 37–50. Göttingen: Vandenhoeck & Ruprecht, 2003.

Grahn-Hoek, Heike. "Quia Dei potentia cunctorum regnorum terminus singulari dominatione concludit. Kirchlicher Einheitsgedanke und weltliche Grenzen im Spiegel der reichsfränkischen Konzilien des 6. Jahrhunderts." In *Religiöse Bewegungen im Mittelalter. Festschrift für Matthias Werner zum 65. Geburtstag*, edited by Enno Bünz, Stefan Tebruck, and Helmut G. Walther, 1–54. Cologne: Böhlau, 2007.

Graus, Frantisek. "Die Gewalt bei den Anfängen des Feudalismus." *Jahrbuch für Wirtschaftsgeschichte* 1 (1961): 61–156.

Greatrex, Geoffrey and Lieu, Samuel N. C. *The Roman Eastern Frontier and the Persian Wars AD 363–628*. London: Routledge, 2002.

Grégoire, Henri. "La Chanson de Roland de l'an 1085." *Bulletin de l'Académie royale de Belgique, Classe des Lettres* 25 (1939): 211–73.

Grégoire, Henri and de Keyser, Raoul. "La Chanson de Roland et Byzance." *Byzantion* 14 (1939): 265–319.

Grüll, Tibor. "*Expositio totius mundi et gentium*: a Peculiar Work on the Commerce of [the] Roman Empire from the Mid-fourth Century—compiled by a Syrian textile dealer?." In *Studies in Economic and Social History of the Ancient Near East in*

Memory of Péter Vargyas, edited by Zoltán Csbai, 629–42. Budapest: L'Harmattan, 2014.

Gundlach, Wilhelm. "Die Sammlung der Epistolae Austrasicae." *Neues Archiv der Gesellschaft für ältere deutsche Geschichtskunde* 13 (1888): 365–87.

Gundlach, Wilhelm. *Der Streit der Bisthümer Arles und Vienne um den Primatus Galliarum: Ein philologisch-diplomatischer-historischer Beitrag zum Kirchenrecht.* Hannover: Hahnsche Buchhandlung, 1890.

Halfond, Gregory I. *The Archaeology of Frankish Church Councils: AD 511–768.* Leiden: Brill, 2010.

Halsall, Guy. "Nero and Herod? The Death of Chilperic and Gregory of Tours' Writing of History." In *The World of Gregory of Tours*, edited by Kathleen Mitchell and Ian N. Wood, 337–50. Leiden, Boston and Cologne: Brill, 2002.

Halsall, Guy. *Barbarian Migrations and the Roman West, 376–568.* Cambridge: Cambridge University Press, 2007.

Hammer, Carl I. "Early Merovingian Bavaria: A Late Antique Italian Perspective." *Journal of Late Antiquity* 4, no. 2 (2011): 217–44.

Hammer, Carl I. "*De gestis Langobardorum*: Queen Theodelinda and Langobard Royal Tradition." *Frühmittelalterliche Studien* 48, no. 1 (2015): 237–60.

Hardt, Matthias. *Gold und Herrschaft. Die Schätze europäischer Könige und Fürsten im ersten Jahrtausend.* Berlin: Akademie-Verlag, 2004.

Harper, Kyle. *Slavery in the Late Roman World.* Cambridge: Cambridge University Press, 2011.

Harris, W. V. "Child Exposure in the Roman Empire." *Journal of Roman Studies* 84 (1994): 1–22.

Hartmann, Martina. *Die Königin im frühen Mittelalter.* Stuttgart: Kohlhammer, 2009.

Häse, Angelika (ed.). *Mittelalterliche Bücherverzeichnisse aus Kloster Lorsch.* Wiesbaden: Harrassowitz, 2002.

Heather, Peter J. *The Goths.* Oxford: Blackwell Publishing, 1996.

Heidrich, Ingrid. "Syrische Kirchengemeinden im Frankenreich des 6. Jahrhunderts." In *Aus Archiven und Bibliotheken. Festschrift für Raymund Kottje zum 65. Geburtstag*, edited by Hubert Mordek, 21–32. Frankfurt a. M.: Peter Lang, 1992.

Heinzelmann, Martin. "L'aristocratie et les évêchés entre Loire et Rhin, jusqu'à la fin du VIIe siècle." *Revue d'histoire de l'Église de France Année* 62, no. 168 (1976): 75–90.

Heinzelmann, Martin. *Bischofsherrschaft in Gallien: Zur Kontinuität römischer Führungsschichten vom 4. bis zum 7. Jahrhundert.* Zurich: Artemis Verlag, 1976.

Heinzelmann, Martin. *"Zehn Bücher Geschichte": Historiographie und Gesellschaftskonzept im 6. Jahrhundert.* Darmstadt: Wissenschaftliche Buchgesellschaft, 1994. Translated in Heinzelmann, Martin. *Gregory of Tours. History and Society in the Sixth Century*, translated by Chris Caroll. Cambridge: Cambridge University Press, 2001.

Hen, Yitzhak. *Culture and Religion in Merovingian Gaul A.D. 481–751.* Leiden, New York and Cologne: Brill, 1995.

Hen, Yitzhak. "Gregory of Tours and the Holy Land." *Orientalia Christiana Periodica* 61 (1995): 47–64.

Hen, Yitzhak. "Les authentiques des reliques de la Terre Sainte en Gaule franque." *Le Moyen Âge* 105 (1999): 71–90.

Hen, Yitzhak. *The Royal Patronage of Liturgy in Frankish Gaul to the Death of Charles the Bald (877)*. Henry Bradshaw Society, Subsidia 3. London: Boydell Press, 2001.

Hen, Yitzhak. *Roman Barbarians: The Royal Court and Culture in the Early Medieval West*. Basingstoke: Palgrave-Macmillan, 2007.

Hen, Yitzhak. "Changing Places: Marculf, Chrodobert and the Wife of Grimoald." *Revue belge de philologie et d'histoire* 90 (2012): 225–43.

Hen, Yitzhak. "The Church in Sixth-Century Gaul." In *A Companion to Gregory of Tours*, edited by Alexander C. Murray, 232–55. Leiden: Brill 2015.

Hen, Yitzhak. "Visions of the Afterlife in the Early Medieval West." In *Visions of the Afterlife*, edited by Richard M. Pollard. Cambridge: Cambridge University Press, forthcoming.

Hendy, Michael *Studies in the Byzantine Monetary Economy, c. 300–1450*. Cambridge: Cambridge University Press, 1985.

Hendy, Michael. "From Public to Private: The Western Barbarian Coinages as a Mirror of the Disintegration of Late Roman State Structures." *Viator* 19 (1988): 29–78.

Hendy, Michael. "East and West: The Transformation of Late Roman Financial Structures." In *Roma fra Oriente e Occidente*, vol. 2, 1307–70. Spoleto: Centro Italiano di Studi sull'alto medioevo, 2002.

Henning, Joachim. "Slavery or Freedom? The causes of early medieval Europe's economic advancement." *Early Medieval Europe* 12, no. 3 (2003): 269–77.

Hillner, Julia. *Prison, Punishment and Penance in Late Antiquity*. Cambridge: Cambridge University Press, 2015.

Hinds, Martin. "The Murder of the Caliph Uthman." *International Journal of Middle East Studies* 3 (1972): 450–69.

Hoffmann, Hartmut. "Kirche und Sklaverei im frühen Mittelalter." *Deutsches Archiv für Erforschung des Mittelalters* 42 (1986): 1–24.

Hofmann, Julia. "The Men Who Would be Kings. Challenges to Royal Authority in the Frankish Kingdoms, c. 500–700." PhD diss., Oxford University, 2008.

Howard-Johnston, James. *Witnesses to a World Crisis: Historians and Histories of the Middle East in the Seventh Century*. Oxford: Oxford University Press, 2010.

Howard-Johnston, James and Paul Anthony Hayward (eds.). *The Cult of Saints in Late Antiquity and the Early Middle Ages. Essays on the Contribution of Peter Brown*. Oxford: Oxford University Press, 1999.

Hoyland, Robert G. "Sebeos, the Jews and the Rise of Islam." In *Medieval and Modern Perspectives on Muslim-Jewish Relations*, edited by Ronald Nettler, 89–102. Luxemburg: Harwood Academic Publishers, 1995.

Hoyland, Robert G. *Seeing Islam as Others Saw It. A Survey and Evaluation of Christian, Jewish and Zoroastrian Writings on Early Islam*. Princeton: Darwin Press, 1998.

Inglebert, Hervé. *Interpretatio christiana: les mutations des savoirs (cosmographie, géographie, ethnographie, histooire) dans l'Antiquité chrétienne*. Paris: Institut d'études augustiniennes, 2001.

Innes, Matthew. "'He Never Even Allowed His White Teeth to be Bared in Laughter': The Politics of Humour in the Carolingian Renaissance." In *Humour, History and Politics in Late Antiquity and the Early Middle Ages*, edited by Guy Halsall, 131–56. Cambridge: Cambridge University Press, 2002.

Jakobi, Rainer. "Die Überlieferung der *Epistulae Arelatenses*." *Deutsches Archiv für Erforschung des Mittelalters* 71 (2015): 175–8.

James, Edward. "Gregory of Tours, the Visigoths and Spain." In *Cross, Crescent and Conversion: Studies on Medieval Spain and Christendom in Memory of Richard Fletcher*, edited by Simon Barton and Peter Linehan, 43–64. Leiden and Boston: Brill, 2008.

James, Edward. *Europe's Barbarians, AD 200–600*. Harlow: Pearson-Longman, 2009.

Jégou, Laurent. *L'évêque, juge de paix. L'autorité épiscopale et les règlements des conflits (VIIIe–XIe siècle)*. Turnhout: Brepols, 2011.

Jones, Allen E. *Social Mobility in Late Antique Gaul: Strategies and Opportunities for the non-Elite*. Cambridge: Cambridge University Press, 2009.

Jonkers, Engbert Jan. "Application of Roman Law by Councils in the Sixth Century." *Tijdschrift voor Rechtsgeschiedenis* 20 (1952): 340–3.

Judic, Bruno. "La production et la diffusion du Registre des lettres de Grégoire le Grand." In *Actes des congrès de la Société des historiens médiévistes de l'enseignement supérieur public, 32ᵉ congrès*. 71–87. Paris: Publications de la Sorbonne, 2002.

Jussen, Bernhard. *Patenschaft und Adoption im frühen Mittelalter*, Veröffentlichungen des Max-Planck Instituts für Geschichte 98. Göttingen: Vandenhoeck & Ruprecht, 1991.

Kaegi, Walter E. "Initial Byzantine Reactions to the Arab Conquest." *Church History* 38 (1969): 139–49.

Kaegi, Walter E. *Byzantium and the Early Islamic Conquests*. Cambridge: Cambridge University Press, 1992.

Kaegi, Walter E. "Byzantine Sardinia and Africa Face the Muslims: Seventh-Century Evidence." *Bizantinistica* 3 (2001): 1–24.

Kaegi, Walter E. *Muslim Expansion and Byzantine Collapse in North Africa*. Cambridge: Cambridge University Press, 2010.

Kaplony, Andreas. *Konstantinopel und Damaskus. Gesandtschaften und Verträge zwischen Kaisern und Kalifen 639–750. Untersuchungen zum Gewohnheits-Völkerrecht und zur interkulturellen Diplomatie*. Berlin: Klaus Schwarz Verlag, 1996.

Kennedy, Hugh. *The Great Arab Conquests. How the Spread of Islam Changed the World We Live In*. Philadelphia: W&N, 2007.

Kleinschmidt, Beda. "Das bischöfliche Rationale und der 6. Kanon der Synode von Macon." *Historisches Jahrbuch* 27 (1906): 799–803.

Klingshirn, William E. *Caesarius of Arles: The Making of a Christian Community in Late Antique Gaul*. Cambridge: Cambridge University Press, 1994.

Klotz, Alfred. "Über die *Expositio totius mundi et gentium*." *Philologus* 65 (1906): 97–127.

Koch, Manuel. *Ethnische Identität im Entstehungsprozess des spanischen Westgotenreiches*. Berlin: De Gruyter, 2012.

Koebner, R. *Venantius Fortunatus. Seine Persönlichkeit und seine Stellung in der geistigen Kultur des Merowinger-Reiches*. Leipzig and Berlin: Teubner, 1915.

Konstan, David. *Friendship in the Classical World*. Cambridge: Cambridge University Press, 1997.

Kosto, Adam J. "Hostages in the Carolingian world (714–840)." *Early Medieval Europe* 11, no. 2 (2002): 123–47.

Kötter, Jan-Markus. *Zwischen Kaisern und Aposteln: Das Akakianische Schisma (484–519) als kirchlicher Ordnungskonflikt der Spätantike*. Stuttgart: Franz Steiner Verlag, 2013.

Kötter, Jan-Markus. "Die Suche nach der kirchlichen Ordnung: Gedanken zu grundlegenden Funktionsweisen der spätantiken Reichskirche." *Historische Zeitschrift* 298, no. 1 (2014): 1–28.

Kreiner, Jamie. "About the Bishop: The Economy of Government in Post-Roman Gaul." *Speculum* 86 (2011): 321–60.

Kreiner, Jamie. *The Social Life of Hagiography in the Merovingian Kingdom*. Cambridge: Cambridge University Press, 2014.

Kurth, Godefroid. "Une source byzantine d'Eginhard." *Bulletin de l'Académie royale de Belgique, Classe des Lettres*, 3rd series, 30, no. 1 (1895): 580–90.

Kurth, Godefroid. "Le concile de Mâcon et l'âme des femmes." *Revue des questions historiques* 51 (1892): 556–60. Reprinted in Kurth, Godefroid. *Études franques*, vol. 1, 161–68. Paris: Honoré Champion, 1919.

Lafferty, Sean D. W. *Law and Society in the Age of Theoderic the Great: A Study of the Edictum Theoderici*. Cambridge: Cambridge University Press, 2013.

Langgärtner, Georg. *Die Gallienpolitik der Päpste im 5. und 6. Jahrhundert: Eine Studie über den apostolischen Vikariat von Arles*. Bonn: Hanstein, 1964.

Leyser, Conrad, "'Divine Power Flowed from this book': Ascetic Language and Episcopal Authority in Gregory of Tours' *Life of the Fathers*." In *The World of Gregory of Tours*, edited by Kathleen Mitchell and Ian N. Wood, 281–94. Leiden, Boston and Cologne: Brill, 2002.

Liebs, Detlef. *Römische Jurisprudenz in Gallien (2.–8. Jahrhundert)*. Freiburger Rechtsgeschichtliche Abhandlungen NF 38. Berlin: Duncker & Humblot, 2002.

Lilie, Ralph-Johannes. *Die byzantinische Reaktion auf die Ausbreitung der Araber. Studien zur Strukturwandlung des byzantinischen Staates im 7. und 8. Jahrhundert*. Munich: Institut für Byzantinistik und Neugriechische Philologie der Universität, 1976.

Limmer, Josef. *Konzilien und Synoden im spätantiken Gallien von 314–696 nach Christi Geburt*. Frankfurt a. M.: Peter Lang, 2004.

Linehan, Peter. *History and the Historians of Medieval Spain*. Oxford: Clarendon Press, 1993.

Loening, Edgar. *Geschichte des deutschen Kirchenrechts*. Strasbourg: Trübener, 1878.

Loseby, Simon. "Gregory of Tours, Italy, and the Empire." In *A Companion to Gregory of Tours*, edited by Alexander C. Murray, 462–97. Leiden, Boston: Brill, 2016.

Lozovsky, Natalia. *The Earth is Our Book: Geographical Knowledge in the Latin West ca. 400–1000*. Ann Arbor: University of Michigan Press, 2000.

Lucas, Pia. "Heilige in Ost und West bei Gregor von Tours." PhD diss., Freie Universität Berlin, Berlin, Forthcoming.

Lutterbach, H. "The Mass and Holy Communion in the Medieval Penitentials (600–1200). Liturgical and Religio-Historical Perspectives." In *Bread of Heaven. Customs and Practices Surrounding Holy Communion. Essays in the History of Liturgy and Culture*, edited by Charles Caspers, Gerard M. Lukken, Gerard Rouwhorst, 61–82. Kampen: Kok Pharos, 1995.

MacGeorge, Penny. *Late Roman Warlords*. Oxford: Oxford University Press, 2007.

MacMullen, Ramsay. *Christianizing the Roman Empire, A.D. 100–400*. New Haven and London: Yale University Press, 1984.

Marasco, Gabriele. "L'*Expositio totius mundi et gentium* e la politica religiosa di Constanzo II." *Ancient Society* 27 (1996): 183–203.

Marasco, Gabriele (ed.). *Greek and Roman Historiography in Late Antiquity*. Leiden: Brill, 2003.

Markus, Robert A. and Sotinel, Claire. "Epilogue." In *The Crisis of the Oikoumene: The Three Chapters and the Failed Quest for Unity in the Sixth-Century Mediterranean*, edited by Celia Chazelle and Catherine Cubitt, 265–78. Turnhout: Brepols, 2007.

Martelli, F. *Introduzione alla "Expositio totius mundi." Analisi etnografica e tematiche politiche in un'opera anonima del IV secolo*. Bologna: Giorgio Barghigiani, 1982.

Martindale, John R. *The Prosopography of the Later Roman Empire*. Vol. III: A.D. 527–641. Cambridge: Cambridge University Press, 1992.

Mathisen, Ralph W. *Ecclesiastical Factionalism and Religious Controversy in Fifth-Century Gaul*. Washington D. C.: Catholic University of America Press, 1989.

Mathisen, Ralph. "The First Franco-Visigothic War." In *The Battle of Vouillé, 507 CE: Where France Began*, edited by Ralph Mathisen and Danuta Shanzer, 3–9. Berlin: De Gruyter, 2012.

Matthews, John. *Western Aristocracies and Imperial Court*. Oxford: Clarendon Press, 1990.

McCormick, Michael. *Eternal Victory. Triumphal Rulership in Late Antiquity, Byzantium, and the Early Medieval West*. Cambridge: Cambridge University Press, 1986.

McCormick, Michael. "Epistolae Austrasicae." In *The Oxford Dictionary of Byzantium*, edited by Aleksandr Petrovich Kazhdan, vol. 1: 717–8. Oxford: Oxford University Press, 1991.

McCormick, Michael. "New Light on the Dark Ages: How the Slave Trade Fuelled the Carolingian Economy." *Past and Present* 177, no. 1 (2002): 17–54.

McCormick, Michael. *The Origins of the European Economy: Communications and Commerce, A. D. 300–900*. Cambridge: Cambridge University Press, 2002.

McKitterick, Rosamond. *History and Memory in the Carolingian World*. Cambridge: Cambridge University Press, 2004.

McKitterick, Rosamond. *Charlemagne. The Formation of European Identity*. Cambridge: Cambridge University Press, 2008.

Meens, Rob. "A Background to Augustine's Mission to Anglo-Saxon England." *Anglo-Saxon England* 23 (1994): 5–17.

Meens, Rob. "Pollution in the Early Middle Ages: The Case of the Food Regulations in Penitentials." *Early Medieval Europe* 4 (1995): 3–19.

Meens, Rob. "Ritual Purity and the Influence of Gregory the Great in the Early Middle Ages." In *Unity and diversity in the Church*, edited by R. Swanson, 31–43. Studies in Church History 32, Oxford: Blackwell, 1995.

Meens, Rob. "'Aliud Benitenciale': The Ninth-century *Paenitentiale Vindobonense C*." *Mediaeval Studies* 66 (2004): 1–26.

Meens, Rob. "The Sanctity of the Basilica of St. Martin. Gregory of Tours and the Practice of Sanctuary in the Merovingian Period." In *Texts and Identities in the early Middle Ages*, edited by Richard Corradini, Rob Meens, Christina Pössel, and Philip Shaw, 277–87. Vienna: Verlag der Österreichischen Akademie der Wissenschaften, 2006.

Meens, Rob. "Sanctuary, Penance and Dispute Settlement Under Charlemagne. The Conflict Between Alcuin and Theodulf of Orléans Over a Sinful Cleric." *Speculum* 82 (2007): 277–300.

Meens, Rob, *Penance in Medieval Europe, 600–1200*. Cambridge: Cambridge University Press, 2014.

Meier, Mischa. "Die Translatio des Christusbildes von Kamulianai und der Kreuzreliquie von Apameia nach Konstantinopel unter Justin II. Ein übersehenes Datierungsproblem." *Zeitschrift für antikes Christentum* 7 (2003): 237–50.

Merrills, Andrew D. *History and Geography in Late Antiquity*. Cambridge: Cambridge University Press, 2005.

Mittag, Peter. "Zu den Quellen der *Expositio totius mundi et gentium*. Ein neuer Periplus?." *Hermes* 134 (2006): 338–51.

Modéran, Yves. "Le dossier des sources non musulmanes sur l'exarque Grégoire et l'expedition Arabe en Ifrîkiyya en 647/648." In *Del Nilo al Ebro. Estudios sobre les fuentes de la conquista islámica*, edited by Luis A. Gracia Moreno and María Jesús Viguera Molins, 141–78. Alcalá de Henares: Universidad de Alcalá, Servicio de Publicaciones, 2009.

Momigliano, Arnaldo. "The Origins of Ecclesiastical Historiography." In Momigliano, Arnaldo. *The Classical Foundations of Modern Historiography*, Sather Classical Lectures 54, 132–56. Berkeley: University of California Press, 1992.

Mommsen, Theodor. *Römisches Strafrecht*. Leipzig: Duncker, 1899.

Montinaro, Federico. "The *Chronicle* of Theophanes in the Indirect Tradition." In *Studies in Theophanes*, edited by Federico Montinaro and Marek Jankowiak. 177–205. Travaux et mémoires 19. Paris: Association des Amis du Centre d'Histoire et Civilisation de Byzance, 2015.

Montinaro, Federico and Marek Jankowiak (eds.). *Studies in Theophanes*. Travaux et mémoires 19. Paris: Association des Amis du Centre d'Histoire et Civilisation de Byzance, 2015.

Mordek, Hubert. *Kirchenrecht und Reform im Frankenreich. Die Collectio Vetus Gallica, die älteste systematische Kanonessammlung des fränkischen Gallien. Studien und Edition*. Beiträge zur Geschichte und Quellenkunde des Mittelalters 1. New York: De Gruyter, 1975.

Mordek, Hubert. *Bibliotheca capitularium regum Francorum manuscripta*. Munich: Monumenta Germaniae Historica, 1995.

Moreira, Isabel. "Provisatrix optima: St. Radegund of Poitiers' relic petitions to the East." *Journal of Medieval History* 19 (1993): 285–305.

Moreno, Luis Agostín García. "Una desconicida embajada de Quindasvinto al África bizantina." *Boletín de la Real Academia de la Historia* 206 (2009): 445–64.

Mülke, Markus. "Romana religio oder catholica fides? Der Westgotenkönig Leovigild und das arianische Reichskonzil von 580 n. Chr. in Toledo." *Frühmittelalterliche Studien* 43 (2009): 53–69.

Müller, Gernot Michael. "Briefkultur im merowingischen Gallien. Zu Konzeption und Funktion der Epistulae Austrasicae." In *Zwischen Alltagskommunikation und literarischer Identitätsbildung. Studien zur lateinischen Epistolographie in Spätantike und Frühmittelalter*, edited by Gernot Michael Müller, 302–52. Stuttgart: Franz Steiner Verlag, 2018.

Mullett, Margaret. "The Language of Diplomacy." In *Byzantine Diplomacy*, edited by Jonathan Shepard and Simon Franklin, 203–16. Aldershot: Variorum Reprints, 1992.

Murray, Alexander C. *From Roman to Merovingian Gaul. A Reader*. Peterborough, Ontario: Broadview Press, 2000.

Murray, Alexander C. "Chronology and the Composition of the Histories of Gregory of Tours." *Journal of Late Antiquity* 1, no. 1 (2008): 157–96.

Nehlsen, Hermann. *Sklavenrecht zwischen Antike und Mittelalter: Germanisches und römisches Recht in den germanischen Rechtsaufzeichnungen I: Ostogoten, Westgoten, Franken, Langobarden*. Göttinger Studien zur Rechtsgeschichte 7. Göttingen, Frankfurt and Zurich: Muster-Schmidt, 1972.

Nelson, Janet L. "A propos des femmes royales dans les rapports entre le monde wisigothique et le monde franc à l'Époque de Reccared." In *Concilio III. de Toledo. XIV Centenario, 589–1989*, edited by Arzobispado de Toledo con la colaboracibon de Caja Toledo, 465–76. Toledo: Arzobispado de Toledo, 1991.

O'Brien, Conor. "The Cleansing of the Temple in Early Medieval Northumbria." *Anglo-Saxon England* 44 (2015): 201–20.

O'Donnell, James J. *Cassiodorus*. Berkeley: University of California Press, 1979.

Orlandis, José. "Baddo, gloriosa regina." In *De Tertullien aux Mozarabes: Antiquité tardive et christianisme ancien: mélanges offerts à Jacques Fontaine à l'occasion de son 70e anniversaire par ses élèves, amis et collègues*, edited by Louis Holtz and Jean-Claude Fredouille, 83–91. Paris: Institut d'études augustiniennes, 1992.

Österberg, Eva. *Friendship and Love, Ethics and Politics. Studies in Mediaeval and Early Modern History*. Budapest and New York: Central European University Press, 2010.

O'Sullivan, Shaun. "Sebeos' Account of an Arab Attack on Constantinople in 654." *Byzantine and Modern Greek Studies* 28 (2004): 67–88.

Palmer, James T. *The Apocalypse in the Early Middle Ages*. Cambridge: Cambridge University Press, 2014.

Patzold, Steffen. "Einhards erste Leser: Zu Kontext und Darstellungsabsicht der 'Vita Karoli'," *Viator Multilingual* 42 (2011): 33–56.

Paxton, Frederick S. "Vocabularies of Grief and Consolation in Ninth-Century Francia." *Annual Meeting of the Medieval Academy of America*. Chicago, 2009. Presentation.

Payer, Pierre. *Sex and the Penitentials. The Development of a Sexual Code, 550–1150*. Toronto: University of Toronto Press, 1984.

Perels, Ernst. *Die kirchlichen Zehnten im karolingischen Reiche*. Berlin: Weidmann, 1904.

Pietri, Charles and Luce Pietri (eds.). *Prosopographie chrétienne du Bas-Empire*. Vol. II: Italie (313–604). Rome: École française de Rome, 1999.

Pietri, Luce and Marc Heijmans (eds.) *Prosopographie chrétienne du Bas-Empire*. Vol. IV: Gaule (314–614). Paris: Association des amis du Centre d'histoire et civilisation de Byzance, 2013.

Pirenne, Henri. *Mahomet et Charlemagne*, edited by Jacques Pirenne and Fernand Vercauteren. Paris, 1937. Translated in Pirenne, Henri. *Mohammed and Charlemagne*, translated by Bernard Miall. London: George Allen, 1939; rev. edn. 1954.

Pohl, Walter (ed.). *Kingdoms of the Empire: The Integration of Barbarians in Late Antiquity*. Leiden, New York and Cologne: Brill, 1997.

Pohl, Walter. "The Empire and the Lombards: Treaties and Negotiations in the Sixth Century." In *Kingdoms of the Empire: The Integration of Barbarians in Late Antiquity*, edited by Walter Pohl, 75–134. Leiden, New York and Cologne: Brill, 1997.

Pohl, Walter. "Deliberate Ambiguity: The Langobards and Christianity." In *Christianizing Peoples and Converting Individuals*, edited by Guyda Armstrong and Ian N. Wood, 47–60. Turnhout: Brepols, 2000.

Pohlsander, Hans A. "A Call to Repentance. Bishop Nicetius of Trier to the Emperor Justinian." *Byzantion* 70 (2000): 457–73.

Pontal, Odette. *Die Synoden im Merowingerreich*. Paderborn: Ferdinand Schöningh, 1986.

Pratsch, Thomas. *Theodoros Studites (759–826). Zwischen Dogma und Pragma, Berliner byzantinische Studien 4*. Frankfurt a. M.: Peter Lang, 1998.

Pratsch, Thomas. "Nikephoros I." In *Die Patriarchen der ikonoklastischen Zeit. Germanos I.-Methodios I. (715–847)*, edited by Ralph-Johannes Lilie, 109–47. Berliner byzantinische Studien 5. Frankfurt a. M.: Peter Lang, 1999.

Price, Richard M. "The Three Chapters Controversy and the Council of Chalcedon." In *The Crisis of the Oikoumene: The Three Chapters and the Failed Quest for Unity in the Sixth-Century Mediterranean*, edited by Celia Chazelle and Catherine Cubitt, 17–37. Turnhout: Brepols, 2007.

Raaflaub, Kurt A. and Richard J. A. Talbert (eds.). *Geography and Ethnography: Perceptions of the World in pre-Modern Societies*. Chichester: Wiley-Blackwell, 2010.

Rapp, Claudia. "Hagiography and Monastic Literature Between Greek East and Latin West in Late Antiquity." In *Cristianità d'Occidente e cristianità d'Oriente (secoli VI–XI): t. 2*, 1221–1281. Spoleto: Presso la sede della Fondazione, 2004.

Reimitz, Helmut. *History, Frankish Identity and the Framing of Western Ethnicity, 550–850*. Cambridge: Cambridge University Press, 2015.

Reimitz, Helmut. "*Pax inter utramque gentem:* The Merovingians, Byzantium and the History of Frankish Identity in the Last Decades of the Sixth Century." In *East and West in the Early Middle Ages: The Merovingian Kingdoms in Mediterranean Perspective*, edited by Stefan Esders, Yaniv Fox, Yitzhak Hen, and Laury Sarti. Cambridge: Cambridge University Press, 2019.

Reimitz, Helmut. "The History of Historiography in the Merovingian Kingdoms." In *The Oxford Handbook of the Merovingian World*, edited by Bonnie Effros and Isabel Moreira. Oxford: Oxford University Press, forthcoming.

Reimitz, Helmut. "Historicizing Rome. Gregory of Tours and the Roman past." In *Transforming the Early Medieval World. Studies in Honor of Ian N. Wood*, edited by Kivilicim Yavuz. Kismet Press, forthcoming.

Reimitz, Helmut. "Genre and Identity in Merovingian Historiography." In *Historiography and identity*, vol. 2: Post-Roman multiplicity, edited by Gerda Heydemann and Helmut Reimitz. Turnhout: Brepols, forthcoming.

Reinink, Gerrit J. "From Apocalyptics to Apologetics: Early Syriac Reactions to Islam." In *Endzeiten. Eschatologie in den monotheistischen Weltreligionen*, edited by Wolfram Brandes and Felicitas Schmieder, 75–87. Berlin and New York: De Gruyter, 2008.

Richards, Jeffrey. *The Popes and the Papacy in the Early Middle Ages: 476–752*. London: Routledge, 1979.

Riché, Pierre. *Éducation et culture dans l'Occident barbare, vi^e–viie siècle*. Paris: Seuil, 1962.

Rio, Alice. *Legal Practice and the Written Word in the Early Middle Ages: Frankish Formulae, c. 500–1000*. Cambridge: Cambridge University Press, 2009.

Rio, Alice. *Slavery after Rome 500–1100*. Oxford: Oxford University Press, 2017.

Rochow, Ilse, *Byzanz im 8. Jahrhundert in der Sicht des Theophanes*. Berliner byzantinische Arbeiten 57. Berlin: Akademie Verlag, 1991.

Rohrbacher, David. *The Historians of Late Antiquity*. London and New York: Routledge, 2002.

Rose, Valentin. *Verzeichniß der lateinischen Handschriften der königlichen Bibliothek zu Berlin*. Vol. 1. Berlin: Asher, 1893.

Rosenwein, Barbara H. *Emotional Communities in the Early Middle Ages*. Ithaca and London: Cornell University Press, 2007.

Rotman, Tamar. "Miraculous History between East and West: Hagiography, Historiography and Identity in Sixth-Century Gaul." PhD diss., Ben Gurion University of the Negev, Beer Sheva, 2018.

Rotter, Ekkehart. *Abendland und Sarazenen. Das okzidentale Araberbild und seine Entstehung im Frühmittelalter*. Berlin and New York, De Gruyter, 1986.

Rouche, Michel. "Les Aquitains ont-ils trahi avant la bataille de Poitiers? Un éclairage événementiel sur les mentalités." *Le Moyen Âge* 74 (1968): 5–26.

Rouche, Michel. *L'Aquitaine des Wisigoths aux Arabes 418–781: Naissance d'une région*. Paris: Jean Touzot, 1979.

Rousseau, Philip. *The Early Christian Centuries*. London and New York: Longman, 2002.

Sahas, Daniel J. "The Seventh Century in Byzantine-Muslim Relations: Characteristics and Forces." *Islam and Christian-Muslim Relations* 2 (1991): 3–22.

Schäferdiek, Knut. *Die Kirche in den Reichen der Westgoten und Suewen bis zur Errichtung der westgotischen katholischen Staatskirche*. Berlin: De Gruyter, 1967.

Scheidel, Walter. "The Roman Slave Supply." In *Cambridge World History of Slavery, Vol. 1 The Ancient Mediterranean*, edited by Keith Bradley and Paul Cartledge, 287–310. Cambridge: Cambridge University Press, 2011.

Scholz, Sebastian. *Die Merowinger*. Stuttgart: Kohlhammer, 2015.

Schreiner, Peter. "Gregor von Tours und Byzanz," In *Päpste, Privilegien, Provinzen: Beiträge zur Kirchen-, Rechts- und Landesgeschichte. Festschrift für Werner Maleczek zum 65. Geburtstag*, edited by Johannes Gießauf, 403–18. Vienna: Böhlau, 2010.

Scorpo, Antonella Liuzzo. *Friendship in Medieval Iberia: Historical, Legal, and Literary Perspectives*. Burlington: Ashgate, 2014.

Selle-Hosbach, Karin. *Prosopographie der merowingischen Amsträger von 511–613*. Bonn, 1974.

Setton, Kenneth M. "The Emperor Constans II and the Capture of Corinth by the Onogur Bulgars." *Speculum* 27 (1952): 351–62.

Shanzer, Danuta. "Foreword." In *The Battle of Vouillé, 507 CE: Where France Began*, edited by Ralph Mathisen and Danuta Shanzer, ix–xxiv. Berlin: De Gruyter, 2012.

Siems, Harald. "Zur Entwicklung des Kirchenasyls zwischen Spätantike und Mittelalter." In *Libertas. Grundrechtliche und rechtsstaatliche Gewährungen in Antike und Gegenwart. Symposion aus Anlaß des 80. Geburtstages von Franz Wieacker*, edited by Malte Diesselhorst and Okko Behrends, 139–86. Ebelsbach: Gremer, 1991.

Siems, Harald. *Handel und Wucher im Spiegel frühmittelalterlicher Rechtsquellen*. MGH Schriften 35. Hannover: Hahn, 1992.

Sogno, Cristiana, Bradley K. Storin and Edward J. Watts (eds.). *Late Antique Letter Collections: A Critical Introduction and Reference Guide*. Oakland: University of California Press, 2017.

Sot, Marcel (ed.). *Les gestes des évêques d'Auxerre*. Les classiques de l'histoire de France au Moyen Âge. Paris: Les Belles Lettres, 2006.

Sotinel, Claire. "Autorité pontificale et pouvoir impérial sous le règne de Justinien: le pape Vigile." *Mélanges de l'Ecole française de Rome. Antiquité* 104, no. 1 (1992): 439–63.

Staab, Franz. "Ostrogothic Geographers at The Court of Theoderic The Great: A Study of Some Sources of the Anonymous Cosmographer of Ravenna." *Viator* 7 (1976): 27–64.

Stahl, Alan M. "Coinage (Origins of the European Economy: A Debate with Michael McCormick)." *Early Medieval Europe* 12 (2003): 293–9.

Stein, Ernst. *Studien zur Geschichte des byzantinischen Reiches vornehmlich unter den Kaisern Justinus II. u. Tiberius Constantinus.* Stuttgart: J. M. Metzlersche Verlagsbuchhandlung, 1919.

Stratos, Andreas N. "The Naval Engagement at Phoenix." In *Charanis Studies. Essays in Honor of Peter Charanis*, edited by Angeliki E. Laiou-Thomadakis, 229–47. New Brunswick: Rutgers University Press, 1980.

Stroheker, Karl F. *Germanentum und Spätantike.* Zürich: Artemis, 1965.

Stüber, Till. "Der inkriminierte Bischof. Verratsvorwürfe und politische Prozesse gegen Bischöfe im westgotischen und fränkischen Gallien (466–614)." PhD diss., Freie Universität Berlin, Berlin, 2017.

Suermann, Harald. *Die geschichtstheologische Reaktion auf die einfallenden Muslime in der edessenischen Apokalyptik des 7. Jahrhunderts*, Frankfurt a. M.: Peter Lang, 1985.

Suntrup, Aloys. *Studien zur politischen Theologie im frühmittelalterlichen Okzident: Die Aussage konziliarer Texte des gallischen und iberischen Raumes.* Münster: Aschendorff, 2001.

Taviani-Carozzi, Huguette. "Une histoire 'édifiante': L'hérésie d'Orléans en 1022." In *Faire l'évènement au Moyen Âge*, edited by Claude Carozzi and Huguette Taviani-Carozzi, 275–98. Aix-en-Provence: Publications de l'Université de Provence 2007.

Thompson, Edward A. "The Conversion of the Visigoths to Catholicism." *Nottingham Medieval Studies* 4 (1960): 4–35.

Traina, Giusto. "Mapping The New Empire: A Geographical Look at The Fourth Century." In *East and West in the Roman Empire of the Fourth Century: An End to Unity*, edited by Roald Dijkstra, Sanne van Poppel and Daniëlle Slootjes, 49–62. Leiden and Boston: Brill, 2015.

Tyrrell, Vida A. "Merovingian Letters and Letter Writers." PhD diss., Center for Medieval Studies, University of Toronto, Toronto 2012.

Ubl, Karl. *Inzestverbot und Gesetzgebung. Die Konstruktion eines Verbrechens (300–1100).* Berlin: De Gruyter, 2008.

Vallejo Girvés, Margarita. "Byzantine Spain and the African Exarchate. An Administrative Perspective." *Jahrbuch der Österreichischen Byzantinistik* 49 (1999): 13–23.

Vallejo Girvés, Margarita. *La Hispania y Bizancio. Una relación desconocida.* Madrid: Ediciones Akal, 2012.

Van Dam, Raymond. *Saints and their Miracles in Late Antique Gaul.* Princeton: Princeton University Press, 1993.

Van Nuffelen, Peter. *Orosius and the Rhetoric of History*. Oxford: Oxford University Press, 2012.

Vassiliev, Alexander. "*Expositio totius mundi*: an anonymous geographic treatise of the fourth century A.D." *Seminarium Kondakovianum* 8 (1936): 1–39.

Verboven, Koenraad. *The Economy of Friends: Economic Aspects of Amicitia and Patronage in the Late Republic*. Brussels: Latomus, 2002.

Verlinden, Charles. *L'esclavage dans l'Europe médiévale*. Bruges: De Tempel, 1977.

Verlinden, Charles. "Ist mittelalterliche Sklaverei ein bedeutsamer demographischer Faktor gewesen?" *Vierteljahrsschrift für Sozial- und Wirtschaftsgeschichte* 66 (1979): 153–73.

Vieillard-Troiekouroff, May. *Les monuments religieux de la Gaule d'après les œuvres de Grégoire de Tours*. Paris: Librairie Honoré Champion, 1976.

Vogel, Cyrille. *Medieval Liturgy. An Introduction to the Sources*. translated by W. G. Storey and N. K. Rasmussen. Washington D.C.: Pastoral Press, 1986.

von Hefele, Karl Joseph and Leclercq, Henri. *Histoire des conciles d'après les documents originaux*. Vol. 3.1. Paris: Letouzey et Ané, 1909.

Wallace-Hadrill, J. M. "Gregory of Tours and Bede: Their Views on the Personal Qualities of Kings." *Frühmittelalterliche Studien* 2 (1968): 31–44.

Walstra, Gerardus J. J. *Les cinq épîtres rimées dans l'appendice des Formules de Sens*. Leiden: Brill, 1962.

Wickham, Chris. *The Inheritance of Rome: A History of Europe from 400 to 1000*. London: Allen Lane, 2009.

Wickham, Chris. *Medieval Europe*. New Haven and London: Yale University Press, 2016.

Widdowson, Marc. "Gundovald, 'Ballomer' and the Politics of Identity." *Revue Belge de Philologie et d'histoire* 86 (2008): 607–22.

Widdowson, Mark. "Merovingian Partitions: A 'Genealogical Charter'?." *Early Medieval Europe* 17 (2009): 1–22.

Williard, Hope D. "Letter-Writing and Literary Culture in Merovingian Gaul." *European Review of History: Revue européenne d'histoire* 21, no. 5 (2014): 691–710.

Winkelmann, Friedhelm. "Ägypten und Byzanz vor der arabischen Eroberung." *Byzantinoslavica* 40 (1979): 161–82.

Winn, Robert. "Gregory of Tours, the Eastern Emperor, and Merovingian Gaul." *Northwestern Review* 2, no. 1 (2017): 1–36.

Wissemann, Michael. "Eine gesetzliche Beschränkung des Menschenhandels." *Münstersche Beiträge zur antiken Handelsgeschichte* 3 (1984): 88–90.

Wolfram, Herwig. *History of the Goths*, translated by Thomas J. Dunlop. Berkeley, Los Angeles and London: University of California Press, 1990.

Wolfram, Herwig. *The Roman Empire and Its Germanic Peoples*, translated by Thomas J. Dunlop. Berkeley, Los Angeles and London: University of California Press, 1997.

Wood, Ian N. *The Merovingian North Sea*. Occasional Papers on Medieval Topics 1. Alingsås: Viktoria bokförlag, 1983.

Wood, Ian N. "Disputes in Late-fifth and Sixth Century Gaul: Some Problems." In *The Settlement of Disputes in Early Medieval Europe*, edited by Wendy Davies and Paul Fouracre, 7–22. Cambridge: Cambridge University Press, 1986.

Wood, Ian N. "Frankish Hegemony in England." In *The Age of Sutton Hoo. The Seventh Century in North-Western Europe*, edited by Martin Carver, 235–41. Woodbrigde: Boydell Press, 1992.

Wood, Ian N. "Letters and Letter Collections from Antiquity to the Middle Ages: The Prose Works of Avitus of Vienne." In *The Culture of Christendom: Essays in Medieval History in Commemoration of Denis T. Bethell*, edited by Marc A. Meyer, 29–43. London: Bloomsbury, 1993.

Wood, Ian N. "The Code in Merovingian Gaul." In *The Theodosian Code. Studies in the Imperial Law of Late Antiquity*, edited by Jill D. Harries and Ian N. Wood, 161–77. London: Duckworth, 1993.

Wood, Ian N. *The Merovingian Kingdoms 450–751*. London and New York: Longman, 1993.

Wood, Ian N. "The Secret Histories of Gregory of Tours." *Revue Belge de philologie et d'Histoire* 71, no. 2 (1993): 253–70.

Wood, Ian N. "Fredegar's Fables." In *Historiographie im frühen Mittelalter*, edited by Anton Scharer and Georg Scheibelreiter, 359–66. Munich: Oldenbourg, 1994.

Wood, Ian N. *Gregory of Tours*. Oxford: Headstart History, 1994.

Wood, Ian N. "Roman Law in the Barbarian Kingdoms." In *Rome and the North*, edited by Alvar Ellegård and Gunilla Åkerström-Hougen, 5–14. Jonsered: Åström, 1996.

Wood, Ian N. "Gregory of Tours and Clovis." *Revue Belge de Philologie et d'Histoire* 63 (1985): 249–72, reprinted in *Debating the Middle Ages* edited by Lester K. Little and Barbara H. Rosenwein, 73–91. Oxford: Blackwell, 1998.

Wood, Ian N. "Topographies of Holy Power in Sixth-Century Gaul." In *Topographies of Power in the Early Middle Ages*, edited by Mayke de Jong, Frans Theuws and Carine van Rhijn, 137–54. Leiden: Brill, 2001.

Wood, Ian N. "Constructing Cults in Early Medieval France. Local Saints and Churches in Burgundy and The Auvergne 400–1000." In *Local Saints and Local Churches in the Early Medieval West*, edited by Richard Sharpe and Alan Thacker, 155–87. Oxford: Oxford University Press, 2002.

Wood, Ian N. "The individuality of Gregory of Tours." In *The World of Gregory of Tours*, edited by Kathleen Mitchell and Ian N. Wood, 29–46. Leiden, Boston and Cologne: Brill, 2002.

Wood, Ian N. "Deconstructing the Merovingian Family." In *The Construction of Communities in the Early Middle Ages: Texts, Resources, Artefacts*, edited by Richard Corradini, Maximilian Diesenberger and Helmut Reimitz, 149–72. Leiden and Boston: Brill, 2003.

Wood, Ian N. "The Franks and Papal Theology, 550–660." In *The Crisis of the Oikoumene: The Three Chapters and the Failed Quest for Unity in the Sixth-Century*

Mediterranean, edited by Celia Chazelle and Catherine Cubitt, 223–41. Turnhout: Brepols, 2007.

Wood, Jamie. "Defending Byzantine Spain: Frontiers and Diplomacy." In *Early Medieval Europe* 18, no. 3 (2010): 292–319.

Woodman, Jesse E. "The Expositio totius mundi et gentium: Its Geography and Its Language." PhD diss., Ohio State University, Columbus, 1964.

Woods, David. "Late Antique Historiography: a Brief History of Time." In *A Companion to Late Antiquity*, edited by Philip Rousseau, 357–71. Oxford: Wiley-Blackwell, 2007.

Wyatt, David. *Slaves and Warriors in Medieval Britain and Ireland, 800–1200*. Leiden: Brill, 2009.

Zöllner, Erich. *Geschichte der Franken bis zur Mitte des sechsten Jahrhunderts*. Munich: C. H. Beck, 1970.

Zuckerman, Constantin. "Qui a rappelé en Gaule le Ballomer Gundovald?." *Francia* 25 (1998): 1–18.

Zuckerman, Constantin. "Learning from the Enemy and More: Studies in 'Dark Centuries' Byzantium." *Millennium-Jahrbuch* 2 (2005): 79–135.

Zuckerman, Constantin. "Theophanes the Confessor and Theophanes the Chronicler," in *Studies in Theophanes*, edited by Federico Montinaro and Marek Jankowiak. Travaux et mémoires 19, 31–52. Paris: Association des Amis du Centre d'Histoire et Civilisation de Byzance, 2015.

Index

Aachen 157
Abderachman (also ʿAbd ar-Raḥman) 152, 154
Acacian Schism 17
Adrian I, pope 155
Africa 84, 94, 141, 145–6, 151
Agde, council (506) 105
Agila I, Visigothic king 35
Aistulf (Astulphos), Lombard king 151–3
Alamans 63, 88
Alaric I, Visigothic king 16, 84
Alaric II, Visigothic king 45–6
    Breviary 46–7
Alcuin 42
Alemannia 88–9
Alexandria 14, 141, 145
ʿAlī ibn Abī Ṭālib 147
Althoff, Gerd 44, 51–2
amicitia 4, 42–53, 99
Anastasia, Byzantine empress 68
Anastasius the Librarian 153, 158
Anastasius, papal legate 93–6, 101
Andelot, treaty 38, 42, 49, 51, 60
Aniane, monastery 104
Annales regni Francorum 156
Annals of Fulda 156
Annals of Lorsch 156
Annals of Moissac 154
Antidius of Agen 21
Antioch 14, 50, 129–30
Apamea 50, 129
Apennine peninsula, *see* Italy
Apollinaris, Sidonius 59
Apostles 1, 25
Appian 12
    Ῥωμαϊκά 12
Aquitaine 20, 36, 104, 154
Arabs 6, 85–6, 90, 141, 143–8, 151–3
Aredius of Limoges 114, 122
Arianism 31–3, 66, 70, 97, 100, 105, 132, 134–5
Arles 12, 37, 61, 94, 99–101

Armenia 49–50, 129, 131, 147
Asclepiodotus 83
Astulphos, *see* Aistulf
Athanagild I, Visigothic king 33, 35, 37
Athanagild II, Visigothic king 5, 36, 38, 67, 70–3, 75
Athanaric, courtier of Theoderic 15
Athanaric, Gothic king 46
Augustine of Canterbury 109
Aurelianus of Arles 5, 93–5, 99–100
Aurelius Victor
    Liber de caesaribus 12
Austrasia 20, 22–3, 32–3, 36–8, 52, 56, 60–1, 66, 69–70, 73–4, 83–5, 91, 98–9, 101–2, 120, 144
Austrasian Letters see Epistolae Austrasicae
Authari, Lombard king 38, 74
Autun 105
Auvergne (*see also* Clermont) 120
Auxanius of Arles 99
Avars 58, 131
Avitus of Vienne 60

Baddo, Visigothic queen 38
Baligant, Emir of Babylon 158
Balzaretti, Ross 70
Barrett, Graham 56–60, 67
Bautier, Robert-Henri 156
Bavarians 88–9
Bede 13
    Ecclesiastical History of the British People 17
Benedict of Aniane 104
Bertram of Bordeaux 19, 21–3
Bischoff, Bernhard 56
Boethius 16
Bohemia 83
Bordeaux 21
Britain 86, 161
Brown, Peter 2, 25, 27, 118
Brunhild, Frankish queen 20, 33–6, 38–9, 41, 48–9, 51–2, 59–60, 67–8, 72–3

Buccelenus, duke 132
Burgar of Septimania
    letter collection 57
Burgundy 17, 20, 36, 39, 66, 83, 129, 154
Bury, J. B. 71
Byzantium 2, 4–7, 17, 20, 32–3, 35–6, 38–9,
    44, 48–50, 55, 58–61, 65–71, 74–5,
    98–102, 115–16, 123, 129–34, 139,
    143, 145, 147, 151–2, 160

Caesarius of Arles 99, 105
    sermons 106
Caliphate 85–6, 90, 160
Cambrai 104
Cameron, Averil 2, 50, 130–1, 133
Campania 11
Candidus, priest 87
Carignan 113
Carolingians 2, 4, 56, 58–60, 62, 85, 87, 90,
    104–5, 154–6
Carthage 14, 67
Carthage, fifth council (401) 107
Cassiodorus 16–18
    Chronicle 17
    Gothic History 17
    Variae 57
Chalcedon, 147
Chalcedon, synod (451) 93–4, 101
Châlons, synod 89
Chalon-sur-Saône 51
Chanson de Roland 154, 158
Chararic, Frankish king 47
Charlemagne 154–7, 159
    coronation 7, 152, 155–6
Charles Martel 154
Childebert I, Frankish king 93–4, 97,
    99–102
Childebert II, Frankish king 5, 21, 23,
    31–2, 35–9, 41–2, 45, 47–8, 51–3,
    59–61, 63, 65–73, 74, 83, 129
Childeric III, Frankish king 153
Chilperic, Frankish king 19–22, 26–7,
    32–6, 38–9, 61, 120, 134–9
Chindasvinth, Visigothic king 142
Chintila, Visigothic king 142
Chloderic, Frankish king 46–7
Chlodosuintha, Frankish princess 37–9,
    41, 49, 52, 74
Chlothar I, Frankish king 20, 36, 47, 108, 133

Chlothar II, Frankish king 20–1, 35, 52, 83
Chlothild, Frankish queen 73
Chotro, chamberlain 63
Chramnesind, a Frank 44, 53
Claude, Dietrich 87–8
Claudius II, Roman Emperor 16
Clermont 49, 97, 121
Clichy, synod (626/7) 89
Clovis, Frankish king 43, 45–7, 50, 53, 67,
    108, 137
Clovis II, Frankish king 89, 149
Codex Remensis 100
Collectio Corbeiensis 61
Collin, Hubert 115
Cologne 47
Columbanus
    penitential 109
Comminges 21
Constans II, Byzantine emperor 6, 141–9
Constantine the Great 81, 84, 130, 141,
    155
Constantinople 5, 35–6, 38, 44, 64, 67, 71,
    81, 94–6, 99–101, 127, 131–3, 137,
    141–3, 146–8, 153, 155, 157–8
Constantinople, synod (448) 93
Constantius II, Roman emperor 14–15
Corbie, monastery 109
Cordoba 35
Cosmographer of Ravenna 15
Cyprus 147
Cyril, saint 100
Czock, Miriam 107

Dagobert I, Frankish king 83, 143
Danube 46, 147
Datius of Milan 101
Dax 19, 22
de Boor, Carl 153
Deeds of the Bishops of Auxerre 154
Descriptio totius mundi 15–16
Desiderius, dux 36
Diana, goddess 113–15, 117
Diocletian, Roman emperor 152
diplomacy 3–5, 32, 34–5, 37, 39, 42, 44–53,
    55–6, 58, 60–2, 63–7, 69–70, 75,
    98–9, 102, 132, 152
Domitianus of Tongres 97–8
Domitius Celsus 84
Drabek, Anna-Maria 51

Duchesne, Louis 156
Dynamius of Marseille 58, 60–1

Ebregisel, envoy 49
Effros, Bonnie 86
Egidius of Reims 60–1
Egypt 1, 141, 143–5, 147
Einhard 153–4, 156, 158
   Life of Charlemagne 153, 157
Eligius 87
   Vita Eligii 87
embassies and envoys 7, 31–4, 36–7, 41,
   45–6, 48–3, 64, 68–9, 94, 98–101,
   117, 129, 133, 135
England (*see also* Britain) 17, 81–2
Ennodius of Pavia 60, 102
   letter collection 57, 59
Epaone, council (517) 105
Ephesus, first synod (431) 93
Epistolae Austrasicae 4, 48, 55–62, 63,
   67–71, 74
Epp, Verena 42
Eridanos, river 152
Eufronius of Tours 107, 132
Eusebius of Caesarea 134
   Ecclesiastical History 13
Eutharic, Ostrogoth and consul 17
Eutropius
   Breviarium ab urbe condita 12
Eutyches 95–6
Evagrius Scholasticus 130, 134
   Ecclesiastical History 50
Expositio totius mundi et gentium 3, 14–16,
   18

Faustianus of Dax 21–3
Felix of Châlons-en-Champagne 41,
   51–2
Firminus, count of Clermont 49
Fischer, Andreas 2, 149
Flavigny, monastery 105
Florianus, abbot 101–2
Formulary of Sens 57
Fortunatus, *see* Venantius Fortunatus
Francia 58, 90, 106–9, 153, 155, 157
Franks 4–7, 32–4, 36–9, 45–8, 58, 63–4,
   66–75, 80–3, 86–90, 95, 98, 100–2,
   104–5, 109, 111, 129, 131–3, 136,
   139, 142, 148–9, 151–7, 159, 161

Fredegar 6, 83
   Chronicle 6, 17, 73, 83, 86, 141–9
Fredegund, Frankish queen 33–4, 36, 41,
   52, 65, 135–6
Fritze, Wolfgang 51
Frominius of Agde 34

Gallus of Clermont 97
Galsuinth, Visigothic princess 33–4
Gaul 1–3, 5–6, 12, 17, 20–1, 24, 26–8, 35–6,
   42, 47, 61–2, 64, 66–7, 73, 75, 82,
   86–7, 93–5, 99, 101, 107–9, 113–20,
   122, 128–9, 131–4, 139, 143, 148,
   153, 160–1
Gaza 129
Gellone, monastery 104
Genoa 70
George, Philippe 97–8
Gillett, Andrew 45, 71–3
Gioanni, Stephane 57
Godefroy, Jacques 14
Goffart, Walter 32, 36, 115
Gogo, Merovingian count 60–1
Goisuinth, Visigothic queen 33–4, 36,
   38–9
Goths (*see also* Visigoths and Ostrogoths)
   12, 15, 17–18, 74, 93
Goubert, Pierre 56
Greater Armenia 49–50
Grégoire, Henri 158
Gregory of Langres 44
Gregory of Tours 1–2, 4, 6, 17, 19–28,
   31–4, 36–9, 41–53, 58, 60, 64, 68–72,
   74, 87, 97, 107–9, 111–12, 113–23,
   127–39, 141, 145–6, 148
   Glory of the Confessors 116–17
   Glory of the Martyrs 116–17
   Histories 1–2, 4, 6, 17, 21–2, 24, 26–7,
      31–2, 34, 37, 41–5, 47, 49–51, 53, 58,
      64–5, 68, 70–1, 74, 113–16, 120, 122,
      127–30, 132, 134–5, 137–9
   Legend of the Seven Sleepers of Ephesus
      130
   Liber de Virtutibus Martini 120–1
   Liber Vitae Patrum 97
Gregory the Great 44, 53, 60, 87, 109
   Libellus Responsionum 109
Grüll, Tibor 15
Gundlach, Wilhelm 56, 58

Gundovald, Merovingian pretender 19–23, 25–6, 28, 35–6, 38–9, 49, 51, 133, 137, 160
Guntram, Frankish king 19–24, 26, 31–9, 48–9, 51–3, 66–7, 69, 72, 83, 129, 137–9

Haimo, king of Saragossa 154
Hainmar of Auxerre 154
Halsall, Guy 26
Harper, Kyle 81
Heldebald, courtier of Theoderic 15
Helena, Roman empress 130
Henschen, Godefroid 97
Heraclius, Byzantine emperor 6, 142–4, 146
heresy 34, 69–70, 74, 96–8, 105, 127, 131, 134–5, 143, 147
Hermenegild, Visigothic prince 32–9, 67, 72, 133–4
Herodotus 14
Hilary of Poitiers 122
Hildoard of Cambrai 104
Hishām b. ʿAbd al-Malik, caliph 153
Historia tripartita 158
Holy Land 129
Hospicius, recluse 1
Huns 45, 47

Iberian Peninsula 33, 35, 37
iconoclasm 152, 156–7
imitatio imperii 131, 135
Ingund, Visigothic queen 31, 33–4, 36–8, 41, 52, 67, 71–2
Irene, Byzantine empress 155
Isidore of Seville 13
    Chronicle 17
    History of the Goths, Vandals and Sueves 11, 17
    Laus Spaniae 18
Islam 158–9
Italy 4–5, 11, 15–16, 32, 35, 38, 42, 48, 52, 66–71, 74–5, 87, 94, 98–9, 131–3, 144, 161

Jerome
    Chronicle 13
Jerusalem 132, 141, 144–5
Jews 15, 87, 89, 135–6, 143

Jocundus, bishop 63
John of Biclaro
    Chronicle 17
John Chrysostom 81
John of Ephesus
    Ecclesiastical History 50, 130, 134, 136
John, patriarch of Constantinople 68
Jordanes 13, 16, 18
    De origine actibusque Getarum 13
Julian of Brioude 121
Julian "the Apostate" Roman emperor 15
Julius Caesar
    De bello Gallico 12
Juret, François 14
Justin I, Byzantine emperor 17
Justin II, Byzantine emperor 6, 49, 127–8, 130–6, 139
Justinian, Byzantine emperor 18, 35, 49, 67, 94–6, 98–101, 127–8, 131, 133

Kurth, Godefroid 157

Lampagia, daughter of Odo duke of Aquitaine 154
Lateran Synod (649) 143–4
Lawrence of Milan 70
Leclercq, Henri 97
legislation
    Burgundian law 83–4
    canon law 4, 21, 24, 62, 109
    Codex Theodosianus 82, 84, 91, 108
    Collectio Vetus Gallica 109
    ecclesiastical legislation 26, 107
    Lex Alamannorum 88–9
    Lex Baiuvariorum 89
    Lex Burgundionum 84
    Lex Fabia de plagiariis 81, 84–5, 89
    Lex Ribuaria 5, 80–5, 88
    Lex Romana Burgundionum 84
    Lex Salica 5, 79–85, 88, 91
    Lex Visigothorum 82
    Pauli sententiae 80
    Roman law 4–5, 24, 27, 80–5, 89, 91
Lent 1
Leo I the Great, pope 96
Leo III, pope 155–7
Leo V, Byzantine emperor 152, 156, 158
Leo, slave 44
Leovigild, Visigothic king 32–9, 133

Leudegisel, duke 19
Levant 85
Lex Dei 4, 27
Leyser, Conrad 115
Liber historiae Francorum 17
Liber pontificalis 94, 153, 156–7
liturgy 3, 5, 104–7, 109, 111–12
Liuva, Visigothic king 37
Lombards 1, 3–4, 32, 35, 38, 41, 45, 47–8, 52, 58, 61 65–6, 69–71, 74–5, 87, 113, 115, 131, 133, 148, 151, 153, 161
Lorsch, monastery of 56–7, 59, 61–2
Loseby, Simon 68, 74
Louis the Pious 156–7
Lupus of Champagne 61
Lycian coast 147
Lyon 19–20, 24–5, 95, 109, 120

Mâcon, second council (585) 3–4, 19–28
Magneric of Trier 55, 58, 60–2
Malaspina, Elena 56
Mango, Cyril 153, 156–7
Manthelan 44
Marcomir, courtier of Theoderic 15
Marculf's Formularies 57
Marcus of Orléans 97
Marius of Avenches 66
    Chronicle 17
Marseille 22, 37, 87, 129
Martin I, pope 144
Martin of Tours 23, 43, 107–8, 114, 120–2
Maurice, Byzantine emperor 35, 38, 44, 48, 63–5, 67–9, 71–3, 87, 128, 133
Maximus Confessor 144
McCormick, Michael 2, 85–7, 90, 129
Meaux 104
Mediterranean 1–7, 14–15, 18, 32, 35–7, 39, 82, 85–8, 90–1, 94, 102, 123, 129, 142, 148–9, 159–61
Mediterranean Sea 14, 18, 36, 85, 159–61
Megas the Curator 48
Menander of Ephesus 14
merchants 1, 15, 51, 86–7, 117, 129, 160
Merovech, son of Chilperic 20
Merovingians *passim*
Merovingian kingdoms *passim*
Merrills, Andy 13, 18
Metz 56, 58, 67, 70
Milan 100–1

Miro, Suevic king 34, 39
Mommsen, Theodor 81
Monophysites 96, 131, 134
Monothelitism 143–4, 146
Moravia 83
Moselle valley 60
Mu'āwiya 147
Muhammad 147
Muslims 3, 85

Narbonne 31, 37, 87
Nehlsen, Hermann 80
Nestorians 94, 100
Nestorius 95–6
Neustria 20, 33–4, 36, 120, 144
Nicaea, first council (325) 93
Nicaea, second council (787) 107
Nicasius of Angoulême 21
Nice 1
Nicetius of Lyon 24–5
Nicetius of Trier 55, 95–6, 98, 101
    letters 58, 98
Nikephoros, patriarch of Constantinople 157
Nisibis 14
North Africa 17, 85, 143–6
North Sea 82
Numidia 12

Odo, duke of Aquitaine 154
Old Gelasian Sacramentary 105–6, 109, 112
Old Testament 19
Orestes of Bazas 19, 22–3
Orléans 21
Orléans, fifth council (549) 93–102
Orléans, first council (511) 105, 108
Orléans, fourth council (541) 120
Orosius 13, 16, 18, 134
    Historiarum adversum paganos libri septem 13
Ostrogoths 15–17, 66, 98–9, 131

Paenitentiale Parisiense simplex 109
Paenitentiale Vindobonense C 109
Palestine 14, 143–4
Palladius of Saintes 19, 21–3
Pannonia 12
Paris 49, 99, 102, 104, 109

Pelagian heresy 127, 134
Pelagius II, pope 132
penitentials 107–10
  Irish penitential books 109
  penitential of Cummean 110
Persarmenians 50, 53
Persian war 130, 134, 147
Persians 14, 49–50, 129, 131, 138
Peter, apostle 96, 155
Phocas, Byzantine emperor 142
Phoenix Mountains 147
Picenum 11
pilgrims 1, 117–18, 129, 160
Pippin "the Short", Carolingian king 105, 152–4, 156
Pirenne, Henri 85–7, 90, 129, 159
plagium 81, 83–5, 89, 91
Poitiers 133, 158
Praetextatus of Rouen 19–20, 22–3, 25–7, 135
Priscus of Lyon 19–20, 24–5
Procopius of Caesarea 98–9, 152
Provence 37, 67, 83, 101

Radegund, Frankish queen 73, 132–3
Ravenna 15–16, 35, 58–9, 70, 153
Reccared, Visigothic king 31–4, 36–9, 41, 49, 52, 72, 74
Reccesvinth, Visigothic king 142
Reims 44, 61, 100, 120–1, 157
relics 7, 64, 106–7, 109, 116–17, 121–2, 129, 132–4
Remigius of Reims 61–2, 67
Rhône, river 37, 154
Rigunth, Frankish princess 34, 36, 38, 65
Roman Empire 2–3, 5, 12–14, 16, 18, 26, 42, 71, 99, 118, 131, 142, 144–5, 149, 155, 159–60
Romanus, Exarch of Ravenna 58, 68–9
Rome 1, 3, 11, 14, 16, 17, 44, 51, 62, 70, 93–4, 99, 133, 141–6, 151, 153, 155, 157–8
Romulf of Champagne 61
Rouche, Michel 154, 158
Rougé, Jean 15
Rufinus of Aquileia 13

Sacerdos of Lyon 95
Sacramentary of Angoulême 105–6
Sacramentary of Gellone 5, 103–7, 109–10, 112
Saint Sophia, church 157
Saint Denis, church 153
Saintes 21–3
Sallust
  De bello Iugurthino 12
Samo, Slavic king 83, 85–6, 91
sanctuary 107–8, 111–12, 135, 137
Saracens 141–6, 148, 154
Sebeos 147
  Armenian chronicle 147
Seneca 59
Sens, relic collection 129
Septimania 32, 34, 36–9, 57
Seville 33, 35
Sichar, a Frank 44, 53
Siems, Harald 81–2
Sigibert I, Frankish king 20–1, 33, 37, 45, 47, 49, 60, 66–7, 119–20, 132–3
Sigibert III, Frankish king 83
Simeon Stylites 6, 114–19, 123
Simon of Armenia 129
slavery 5, 43–4, 79, 81–91, 148
Smaragdus of Ravenna 70
Soissons, vase 65
Sophia, Byzantine empress 127, 132, 136
Sophronius, patriarch of Jerusalem 143
Spain 4–5, 17, 31, 33, 35–7, 39, 49, 74, 129, 131–3, 135, 142, 145–6, 151, 161
Stephen II, pope 151–4, 156
Stephen IV, pope 156–7
Stephen of Dora 143
Sufetula 146
Syagrius, Roman ruler of Gaul 47
Syria 6, 14, 87, 116–19, 129–30, 147–8, 152

Tacitus
  Germania 12
Thegan of Trier 156
Theodebert II, Frankish king 58, 62
Theoderic the Great, Ostrogothic king 15, 17
Theodore of Marseille 21
Theodore of Canterbury 108–10
Theodosius, Roman emperor 84, 130, 138
Theodotos of Constantinople 157
Theophanes the Confessor 7, 148
  Chronicle 151–8

Theudebald, Frankish king 98–101, 131–2
Theudebert I, Frankish king 67, 98–9, 131–2, 137
Theudebert II, Frankish king 72–3
Theuderic II, Frankish king 72–3
Thrace 141, 143, 146
Three Chapters controversy 5, 94–6, 98, 100–1, 131
Thucydides 14
Tiberius II, Byzantine emperor 6, 35, 38, 49–50, 53, 63–4, 127–39
Toledo 34
Toledo, third council (589) 32, 38–9
Totila, Ostrogothic king 93–4, 98–100
Toul 98
Toulouse 36, 46
Tours 23, 46, 51, 107–8, 114, 119–23
trade 1, 5, 15, 81, 85–91, 129
Trajan, Roman emperor 11
Trier 12, 55–60, 62, 95, 98, 101, 114–15, 156
True Cross 132, 134, 139
Tyrrhenian Sea 86

Umayyad Caliphate 147, 160
Ursicinus of Cahors 19, 22
'Uthmān, caliph 147

Valens, Roman emperor 46
Valentinian III, Roman emperor 82, 84–5
Vandals 63
Venantius Fortunatus 42, 55, 58, 60–1, 132–3
Venice 86–7
Vicar of Africa 84
Victor of Tununna
    Chronicle 17
Vigilius, pope 5, 93–5, 99–101
Vincentius of Saragossa 34
Visigothic Letters 57
Visigoths 3–5, 17, 31–9, 45–6, 49, 52, 57, 60, 66–7, 72–4, 80, 83–4, 91, 129, 131–3, 135, 142, 145–6, 149, 161
Vita Boniti 87
Vita Domitiani vetustissima 98
von Hefele, Karl Joseph 97
Vouillé, battle 46,
Vulfilaic of Trier 6, 113–23

Wickham, Chris 2
Wood, Ian 2, 33, 45, 73, 81–2, 95
Woudhuysen, George 56–60, 67

Yarmouk, battle 144, 146

Zachary, pope 153

www.ingramcontent.com/pod-product-compliance
Lightning Source LLC
Chambersburg PA
CBHW062125300426
44115CB00012BA/1812